THE HIDDEN HITLER

Lothar Machtan

TRANSLATED BY *John Brownjohn*

NOTES TRANSLATION BY *Susanne Ehlert*

BASIC
BOOKS

A Division of the Perseus Books Group

Originally published in German by Alexander Fest Verlag, Berlin

Copyright © 2001 by Lothar Machtan
Translation copyright © 2001 John Brownjohn

Published by Basic Books
A Member of the Perseus Books Group

Book design and composition by Mark McGarry,
Texas Type & Book Works, Inc.
Set in Sabon

ISBN 0-465-04308-9

A CIP catalog record for this book
is available from the Library of Congress

Contents

Acknowledgments   VII

Introduction   I

1   The Would-be Aesthete: Hitler, 1905–1914   27

2   Comrade Hitler: Blackmail with Fatal Consequences   65

3   Private Phases in a Public Career   105

4   Love's Labor's Lost   141

5   The Röhm Campaign   181

6   Posthumous Revelations:
    Erich Ebermayer and His Sources   231

7   Dangerous Machinations:
    Kurt Lüdecke and Ernst Hanfstaengl   265

Epilogue   313
Postscript   319
Notes   323
Bibliography   403
Index   419

Acknowledgments

This book would never have been written without the help of Malte Ritter, whose care, competence and efficiency have made the biggest contribution to its genesis. My thanks go also to Karsten Linne and Hans-Rudolf Wahl for performing spadework of various kinds, likewise to my friends Maja Lobinski-Demedts and René Ott for once more assisting me in the role of shrewd critics. Then there was another form of help no less valuable than the assistance I received from professional quarters: the "fireside chats" during which the main ideas underlying this study assumed definite shape. In this regard it was principally Anne Tietjen and Kristina Nanns-Eggers who supported or dissuaded me, inspired me or warned me of pitfalls. It was wonderful to be able to speak so frankly to two such listeners. No praise can be too high for my editor Gunnar Schmidt and his brilliant work, and, in particular, for the fair fight we waged over the structure of the text. A special thanks to my literary agent Agnes Krup. It is because of her exceptional commitment that this book is being published in eight languages simultaneously and can thus be discussed by an international readership. As representatives of the many helpers who have attended to my concerns in archives, libraries and other institutions, I should like to mention the following: Hauke Hirsinger, Edith Lienenlüke, Jayna Maleri, Jens Müller-Koppe and Michael Sohn. Thank you all.

THE HIDDEN HITLER

Introduction

ANYONE WRITING about Hitler takes on a great responsibility. But however daunting the task, historians must continue to tackle the subject for as long as mysteries remain. One would think that the existing literature on Hitler, which fills miles of bookshelves, would be a store of intellectual capital which historians could draw ad libitum, but I have found this a handicap to be mentally discarded before making progress of my own. Discovering something new about Hitler entails the courage to form one's own opinion. *What Hitler did* in history has been amply documented in the literature. *Who Hitler was*, however, is a question on which I hope to shed light.

A DEMON, A "CENTENNIAL MONSTER"?

Adolf Hitler. No other German politician is associated with such far-reaching historical changes and such monstrous crimes. His name alone is emblematic of world war and Holocaust. But what sort of person was this criminal? What drove him, and what personal contribution did he make to his unique rise in the world? The more time goes by, the harder it is to answer these questions. Hitler's personal traits do indeed seem already to have receded into "chimerical obscurity."[1]

Why is this so? Ian Kershaw cited what is reputed to be the most important reason in a recent interview: "Take away what is political about him, and there's little or nothing left."[2] In Kershaw's eyes Hitler was "a man without characteristics"[3] to whom the public domain was all-important and who had no private life. But is that really true? Was there really nothing personal, aside from banalities, that transcended the public figure and the image cultivated by himself and other people? If so, that would indeed be a unique historical phenomenon: a strongman who seduced the masses and shook the world, but who was himself a complete vacuum. In other words, a genuine—again in Kershaw's words—"monstrosity of filth"[4] that owed its political advancement solely to an unfortunate combination of specific circumstances: the erosion of social structures after World War I and the dire effects of a dark period in which "monstrosities" were catapulted into positions of power. Or is this a monster impossible to judge by human criteria? Is that the essence of the vast mountain of research literature that has accumulated in recent decades? If so, then the approximately 120,000 publications[5] have far from fulfilled their promise. John Lukacs, who has tried to instill some sort of order into the chaotic jumble of Hitler literature, comes to the following significant conclusion: "We are not yet finished with Hitler . . ."[6] This is a remarkable admission when one reflects that few historical figures have attracted such immense and—even after half a century—undiminished scholarly interest.

We have naturally learned a great deal in that time about the history of National Socialism, World War II and political developments in the Third Reich. The same applies to the landslidelike changes in the party-political and electoral landscape around 1930; to the long underestimated intrigues of the power brokers in the entourage of elderly Reich President Hindenburg, to whom Hitler owed his nomination as Reich Chancellor; and to the morally and intellectually shameful way in which the traditional elites ingratiated themselves with Germany's self-appointed savior. We know something about the workings of the Führer dictatorship, about Hitler's ideology and the cultural history of German nationalism from which it derived. Numerous research institutes and commemorative establishments devote themselves to the crimes of the National Socialist tyranny, as does the autonomous academic field known as "Holocaust studies." It has also claimed the attention of a journalist as shrewd and critical as Ron Rosenbaum, author of what is probably the most lucid overview to date of (non-German) attempts to "explain Hitler."[7] But his book is expressly defined as "a search for the origin of evil." Like many other publications of similar provenance, it stresses the *inexplicability* of Hitler[8] and refrains from reexamining the actual circumstances of his life.

Where reputable publications are concerned, anyone desiring information about Hitler's personality, character and private life is left with a handful of standard biographical works, an even smaller number of detailed studies, and the writings of a few outsiders who approach the subject from a psychological, medical or journalistic angle. There are also many books on Hitler that do not deal with Hitler himself but with the images people have formed, and are still forming, of him. Based mainly on widespread stereotypes and seldom on historically attested knowledge, these Hitler images say much about the society that has produced them but little about the actual circumstances of the man in question.

"MACHIAVELLIAN TYRANT"
OR "ANTIBOURGEOIS PLEBEIAN"?

When the dead of World War II had been buried, most of its resulting debris cleared away, and at least some of the authors of the catastrophe tried and punished, it was only natural for people to begin to ask how all of this had come about and to debate the nature of the man who bore political responsibility for it. These were pressing questions, and two young authors in the field of modern history and political science dedicated themselves to finding, or at least attempting to find, the answers.

The first milestone in Hitler research was laid by the British historian Alan Bullock, whose *Hitler: A Study in Tyranny* was published in 1952 and continues to stand the test of time.[9] Building on the great tradition of Anglo-Saxon historiography, which focuses its attention on the actors on the political stage, Bullock had the additional advantage of being an adviser at the Nuremberg Trials, giving him access to the extensive documentary sources that had been assembled there. His book portrays Hitler as a Machiavellian of the worst kind, a man concerned solely with his personal abundance of power and prepared to destroy Germany to retain it, not impelled by any kind of dogma but desirous of power for naked power's sake—in short, a tyrant for the sake of tyranny. Hitler, we are told, was a man devoid of scruples and inhibitions, a rootless individual without a home or family—someone for whom there were no human ties, no traditions, no respect for God or humankind, someone fundamentally indifferent to all intellectual achievements, someone whose own intellect never transcended social Darwinism of the crudest sort. He owed his power to two outstanding qualities: rhetorical skill and histrionic talent. Hitler manipulated the emotions of others by talking incessantly. This loquacity was logically complemented by his profound dislike of engaging in argument, his insuperable distrust of intellectuals and his tendency to shout opponents down. Bullock further states that Hitler also possessed the ability to become completely wrapped up in his role of the moment, and to believe in the truth of what he happened to be saying at the time. This "self-dramatization"[10] helped him to convince others and successfully concealed his brutal thirst for power. Hitler built up a myth around his person, cultivated it with care and employed it for his own ends. As long as he did this, he scored brilliant successes. It was only when he developed a genuine faith in the myth that his intuition failed him.

But politically important characteristics are only one aspect of Bullock's multifaceted sketch of Hitler's personality. He also speaks of Hitler's most intimate side, his sexuality. Bullock tells us that Hitler felt thoroughly in his element with women, but was probably syphilitic and impotent. More than that, we are introduced to the minutiae of Hitler's everyday life: what dishes he favored (vegetarian) and disliked (cooked); his susceptibility to insomnia and indigestion; his daily routine at the Berghof, near Berchtesgaden; his predilections and favorite pastimes (Wagner, big fast cars, cream cakes, pretty but stupid women, flowers, dogs, vapid movies, studying architect's plans, listening to flattery); his dislikes (being contradicted, going to bed, alcohol, regular and concentrated work, cigarette smoke, modern art). These human aspects, which could equally have been found in other people, demythologized Hitler. By devoting himself to the everyday world of this politician's existence, and not just its irrational core, Bullock rendered Hitler palpable.

But how convincing is Bullock's picture of Hitler from *today's* standpoint? As he himself remarks: "No man can sit down to write about the history of his own times—or perhaps of any time—without bringing to the task the preconceptions which spring out of his own character and experience."[11] Bullock modified some of these "preconceptions" in later years. In *Hitler and Stalin*, the double biography published in 1991, he construes National Socialism as an ideology comparable to communism; Hitler's *Mein Kampf* is now a political program[12] and its author far more than a mere tyrant for tyranny's sake who hauled himself into power with little more than a talent for oratory and histrionics.[13] This changed interpretation proved necessary because research had since adduced plausible evidence that Hitler must have had at least some genuine convictions, and that his band of adherents had also been motivated by them, not merely seduced by skillful demagogy. Bullock adopted this view without revising his portrayal of Hitler's character. In a recent conversation with Ron Rosenbaum, he interpreted Hitler's ideology as "the ideology *is* central. I think it's what armors Hitler against remorse, guilt, anything."[14] For Bullock, an unscrupulous striving for power remains Hitler's most salient trait. He continues to see him as "an intellectually and emotionally primitive tyrant,"[15] albeit one that has now been certified as suffering from a specific form of ideological self-delusion.

By 1973, twenty-one years after Bullock's milestone, Joachim Fest again made Hitler the subject of a large-scale biography. The political situation and the spirit of the times had changed considerably. World War II lay almost half a generation in the past, the Cold War was giving way to a policy of relaxation, and the 'sixty-eighters were radically diverging from accepted beliefs and patterns of justification. Political controversy centered largely on the older generation's role in the Third Reich, on guilt and responsibility. The German middle classes, in particular, were hauled into the moral dock and—in the jargon of the time—"ideologicocritically" questioned about their past. People had lost faith in the immediately postwar notion that the Third Reich was a monolithic, totalitarian state that served as the willing tool of an omnipotent dictator. At the same time, biography as a historiographic genre was exposed to charges of exculpation—indeed, there were demands that it be wholly excluded from the historian's repertory—and social history staked a claim to primacy in its place. Under these auspices, Fest's book, which took the form of a classical biography and leaned heavily on psychological (not psychoanalytical) patterns of interpretation, was a decidedly conservative venture. It was fiercely censured from the start, one need hardly add (especially as Fest was an influential journalist, not a professional historian). His ambitious study was more than a historical work in the academic sense. It was also a political attempt to salvage the reputation of the German bourgeoisie and, with it, of those humanitarian and democratic ideals that lie at the heart of bourgeois culture.

Fest painted Hitler as an unbourgeois representative of revolutionary, right-wing radicalism, leaving out the medial abilities that enabled him to absorb public moods and thereby lead a party like the NSDAP to its predestined success. Hitler subsisted on the resentment of life's failures, of those threatened with social degradation by the crises of the Weimar Republic, and he was able to do this because he himself was inflamed by their dark emotions—because he had personal experience of hostels for the homeless and all forms of social abasement. He and the party he created were vulgar, uncouth and brutal. Although his histrionic talent enabled him to disguise this brutality for some time, it reemerged in all its stark crudity during the latter years of World War II. Hitler, a plebeian who never really succeeded in making bourgeois culture and humanity his own, nursed violently antibourgeois emotions for that very reason. The term Fest coined for him, "unperson,"[16] was universally adopted thereafter.

As Fest saw him, Hitler the plebeian was motivated by extreme radicalism and always came to the most extreme conclusions. His "excessive character"[17] made the German version of right-wing-extremist totalitarianism particularly dangerous. At the same time, and in spite of everything, he also cherished an "admiration for the bourgeois world"[18] and a marked "desire to belong"[19] to it. He feigned an interest in Wagner, Nietzsche and architecture, for example, although he never really understood the first thing about them. In other respects, while sharing Bullock's belief that playacting and rhetoric were Adolf Hitler's two great personal strengths, Fest lays far more stress on them. Hitler's public appearances were characterized by a well-developed sense of theater; he had an intuitive grasp of his audience's state of mind, expectations and emotional needs, and nearly always struck the right note.

But Fest also credits Hitler with a politician's classical qualities. He was a gifted tactician who could recognize situations and detect underlying interests, discover other people's weaknesses and engineer temporary coalitions of use to him. He was cold-blooded, cunning and always prepared to take extreme risks. Like all German nationalists after the October Revolution of 1917, he was mortally afraid of the Red Terror and profoundly skeptical of a universal process of modernization; unlike all his rivals, however, he was able to develop his fear into a program. The campaign against Jewry and the conquest of living space were the central objectives of a policy he consistently pursued, all tactical swerves notwithstanding, as soon as he acquired the power to enforce it.

Hitler's private life, says Fest, was overshadowed by chronic loneliness and sexual frustration. We are shown someone whose friendships were never more than brief and casual during his early years in Austria, then a reclusive front-line soldier, then a professional politician more harried than surrounded by a servile, power-hungry camarilla, and finally a prematurely aged man in the closing years of his life—lonely, ill, melancholic and ever more inclined to take refuge in his bunker. According to Fest, the ecstatic public appearances of his "great days" in the 1920s and 1930s resembled substitutes for sex, and only his relationship with his niece, Geli Raubal, developed into something resembling an intimate human bond: "She was, oddly inappropriate though the phrase sounds, his great love, a tabooed love of Tristan moods and tragic sentimentality."[20] Fest does not, however, discuss this subject in greater detail.

Where Hitler's private life is concerned, the main reason for Fest's restraint is probably that it yields too little material conducive to his central purpose. Adolf Hitler the man interests Fest only insofar as his psychology and politics supply aids to understanding the spirit of the times, the so-called epochal nostalgia. He consequently focuses his account on the years 1929–41—against his better judgment, one might say, for no Hitler expert has emphasized more strongly than Fest that Hitler's character and beliefs were formed at an early stage and scarcely changed after the mid-1920s.

To avoid any misunderstanding, I must stress that we owe Alan Bullock and Joachim Fest nearly all we now know, or think we know, about Hitler. They are the best Hitler biographies we have so far, and I say that well aware of Ian Kershaw's recent and important contributions, which I will discuss shortly. Like Bullock, whose double biography, *Hitler and Stalin*, reentered the debate in 1991, Fest is fully aware of his enduring importance as a Hitler biographer. The fact that he felt justified in bringing out a new and unrevised edition of his study in 1995 clearly bears this out: although Hitler's enduring topicality has led to "a continuously rising tide of writings and investigations," many of them "wrest little additional knowledge"[21] from his image. This is probably true. No better documented or more comprehensive biographical studies than Bullock's and Fest's have so far been written. They are the Nestors on whose shoulders Hitler research still stands to this day. Their portraits of Hitler are our image of him. That, we say, is more or less what he must have been like. But even they, as I shall show, saw "only" the dictator, not the whole man.

INTENTIONALISTS AND FUNCTIONALISTS

During the 1970s the market was positively inundated with books about Hitler—"the Hitler deluge," as people soon began to call it. Intense public interest in the National Socialist period inspired authors of the most diverse provenance, and there is no doubt that the phenomenon of Adolf Hitler and his origins has never been more heatedly discussed than at that time. By 1980, when two academic schools began to develop a monopoly on interpretation, this lively debate and passionate controversy subsided. Prior to that, however, a wide range of theories had been submitted to very serious consideration. Here is a brief overview of the most important of them: Hitler was a thoroughly normal, middle-class individual (Werner Maser); Hitler was a "mystery" defying rational explanation (John Toland); Hitler was an outstanding military leader whom the British totally misjudged and drove to suicide (David Irving); Hitler was a psychopath (Robert G. L. Waite); Hitler was the victim of an unhappy childhood (Alice Miller and Erich Fromm); Hitler suffered from a life-long obsession with avenging his mother, who had been wrongly treated by a Jewish doctor (Rudolph Binion).

With the last-named interpretations of Hitler, the so-called psychohistorians—strict Freudians for the most part—entered the arena. In the United States their influence on public debate was far from small, and they are still, to some extent, in vogue there today.[22] For a while they also influenced discussions in Germany, although they never attained a comparable measure of authority. Subjecting Hitler's case to the explanatory force of Freudian doctrine presents an eternal problem, namely, that its "long-range diagnosis" cannot be confirmed or rebutted by valid sources. Those who pursue a purely psychoanalytical approach argue not only unhistorically but in an extremely reductionist manner, irrespective of whether Hitler was a "psychoneurotic of the obsessive and hysterical sort"[23] or a "narcissistic pervert."[24] They confine themselves largely to attributions for which the psychoanalyst can produce sound reasons unsupported by historical sources. Lack of biographical information about Hitler permitted the long-range analysts to delude themselves about the limits of our knowledge and to derive conjectures from pure conjectures. Thus, historians found it only too easy to reject their explanatory models as serious hypotheses. Historians, for their part, showed themselves to be impressed by something else: ideological criticism and sociostructural analysis. The "intentionalists" and "functionalists" entered the arena.

The intentionalists took Hitler's worldview seriously—so seriously that they made it the exclusive focus of their attention. According to them, National Socialism was a relatively compact ideological edifice constructed by Hitler out of various traditional components and subsequently promoted to the status of a political program. Viewed in this light, the Third Reich was simply a more or less consistent implementation of National Socialism, although controversy still surrounded the extent to which this attempt at implementation was modified or even fundamentally called into question by the vicissitudes of contemporary politics, and how Hitler's program should be classified in relation to other contemporary programs. As important as it may be to clarify these issues, and important as it is to place them on the scholarly agenda, since they are primarily concerned with the history of ideas, they ultimately remain divorced from the circumstances of their fanatical protagonist's life. Indeed, we do not even know how authentic Hitler's avowed worldview really was, and whether he "took his ideas as seriously as the ideological school does."[25]

This is the point at which the functionalists level their criticism. To them, what matters above all is the actual wielding of social power under National Socialism, not programs of any kind. Employing current catch phrases such as a "weak dictator" in the midst of a "polycratic system" and "cumulative radicalization," they point out that the National Socialists played havoc with the government machine after 1933, and that their swiftly proliferating bureaucracies served as power bases for various senior Nazi functionaries who devoted much of their time and energy to waging furious power struggles, sometimes even resorting to downright violence. Matters escalated, leading to the excesses of war and genocide, but also, in the end, to the "crash" of a system that was structurally unviable and doomed to self-destruction.

One could thoroughly concur with the functionalist position thus far, but for the existence of a problem: the utterly ungovernable figure of Adolf Hitler, whose supremacy defied all the structural defects in his system of government and remained intact to the bitter end. Hitler is disruptive of this model theory, so what can be done to render him compatible with it?[26]

The doyen of the functionalist school, Hans Mommsen, lays primary stress on the personality cult, which originally emanated from the Munich branch of the NSDAP, was systematically developed by Goebbels, and eventually became the true foundation of Hitler's position of power. Moreover, says Mommsen, Hitler had himself shielded from the rest of the Nazi leaders by a small circle of blindly devoted followers, and was thus enabled to maintain a special aura even among his intimates. His own conception of politics was purely propagandistic in nature, however, which was why—according to Mommsen—he was ultimately responsible for his regime's administrative chaos and initiated the process of cumulative radicalization that destroyed it. In short, Hitler was a "political counterfeiter"[27] who subsisted on the fact that others habitually overrated him.

What is doubtful, however, is whether such an effective myth about a "weak dictator" could so easily have been manufactured from without. Adolf Hitler may have been a "political counterfeiter," but counterfeiting is an art, if not a particularly respectable one. It has seldom been successful, and even its shrewdest practitioners are usually convicted in short order. That this did not apply in Hitler's case, against all the odds, testifies to his exceptional ability. Power without ability remains impotent or swiftly declines. But Hitler's power was a factor with which politics had to reckon more than with any other—until 1945. There is no doubting Mommsen's wish to render the part played by Hitler's personality smaller than it was in historical fact, but "Hitler the counterfeiter" is not the way to do this. The Hitler phenomenon cannot be comprehended with the aid of vague concepts that obscure more than they clarify. Rather, they reveal the limitations of a conception of history in which there is no room, by definition, for powerful individuals. Or, to put it another way: What is left of a person who has, from the outset, forfeited any claim to individual characteristics?

CHARISMA OR PERSONALITY?

Ian Kershaw has to some extent inherited Mommsen's mantle and made it his task to reconcile the intentionalists and functionalists. He has published some important—indeed, trailblazing—studies on public opinion in the Third Reich and the Hitler myth, and his big two-volume book on Hitler[28] is a masterly collation of almost everything historians have published in the course of half a century about the political, economic and social history of the Weimar Republic and the early Nazi years. But Kershaw is at his best when analyzing the exercise of power—more precisely, of personalized power. He is clearly fascinated by the "mystique of power," one of whose greatest historical triumphs was, without doubt, Hitler's dictatorship. To Kershaw it was principally a product of German society, of the hopes and fears vested in Hitler by his supporters. That is why he perceives Hitler merely as a projection screen for the expectations reposed in him. His biographical approach takes a questionable turn, however, when he comes to speak of the "charismatic nature" of Hitler's power, for Kershaw's Hitler is far from charismatic: he lacked all the prerequisites for turning his personality into something like charisma. According to Kershaw, Hitler was totally devoid of personality. Not only was it a fact that "outside politics Hitler's life was largely a void," but he had "as good as no personal life outside that of the political events in which he is involved."[29] Kershaw goes on to state that the biographer has consequently "to focus not upon the personality of Hitler, but . . . upon the character of his power."[30]

If a historian categorically emphasizes that Adolf Hitler's person was an "empty husk," a poor creature, indeed, a "black hole,"[31] he does so for a reason. It is a truism that the best stylistic method of firmly dissociating oneself has always been the use of strong, apodictic language. But why should a historian as brilliant as Kershaw have need of that? What prompted him to make a precipitate assertion that cannot be justified by sources and is no more than a subjective statement of opinion? This, perhaps: he was too fixated from the first on a Hitler whose existence was entirely under the spell of the forces he conjured into being and then unleashed. In other words, Kershaw is not really interested in investigating Hitler's personal life story. He prefers to divest himself of Hitler the private individual because, after ten years' concentrated study, he finds him "even more abhorrent than before."[32] This is precisely why the genuinely biographical passages in his book are rather uninteresting. Whenever he does come to speak of Hitler the man, he is quick to trot out moralizing verdicts and clichés. Strange that his study should be greeted as a new Hitler *biography*, for it is nothing of the kind. Kershaw's biographical comments are all secondhand, just as his interpretations of Hitler's personal destiny are more or less products of his sociohistorical analysis. To this extent, Klaus Hildebrand is quite correct in saying that Kershaw has "nothing new" to say about Hitler.[33]

Kershaw has since incurred criticism from another quarter for failing to blend in the private and public aspects of what he describes as Hitler's charismatic quality.[34] Such a sweeping political success on the part of a private "unperson" would be explicable only if one assumed extremely pathological motives, not only in Hitler himself but in the collective psyche of the Germans of his day. It remains open to debate, however, whether Hitler's rise to power was, for that reason, a "lunatic career."[35] Ludolf Herbst, who likewise dissociates himself from Kershaw, argues more convincingly when he points to Hitler's "*non-charismatic personality*" and states that his success was due to an effective interplay of "stage management and charisma politics."[36] But he, too, refrains from questioning "the emptiness of the private person"[37] imputed to the dictator's private person by Kershaw.

HITLER'S "POSTHUMOUS BIOGRAPHY"

Judging by the reaction to Ian Kershaw's book, the Hitler debate has maneuvered itself into an impasse. On the one hand, we find rapturous praise for a work alleged to have finally presented us with an exhaustive and possibly definitive portrait of Hitler; on the other, access to Hitler continues to be obstructed (at least in the German press) by paradoxical or nonsensical phrases like the following: "The charisma of an unperson without an inner core" (*Frankfurter Rundschau*),[38] "Unperson without characteristics" (*Welt am Sonntag*),[39] "The dragon that was a worm" (*Frankfurter Allgemeine Zeitung*).[40] We also encounter downright relief at Hitler's marginalization: "Ian Kershaw drives out devils" (*Die Welt*).[41] At the same time, however, it is quite impossible to ignore the fact that opinion formers continue to be oppressed by the "Führer's" traumatic presence. Can he really be "minimized,"[42] contrary to all the historical evidence, by making a "worm" out of a fabulous beast stylized as a "dragon"?

The widespread view that Hitler the unperson has now been thoroughly dissected, that no nook or cranny of his dark soul has been left unexplored and no detail of his life story unilluminated, turns out to be as naive as it is unfounded. We do not know too much about him even now. A number of mysteries remain. Historical research has done little to tackle Hitler's *persona ingratissima* from any angle save that of ideology and politics. This phenomenon, which can only be termed Hitler's "posthumous biography," explains why he has haunted not only his contemporaries but also posterity in so fateful a manner. If only because of the barbarity for which he was responsible, the person

of Adolf Hitler has become an anxiety neurosis, a vision of horror.
And that is why he remains for later generations what he was to many
of his contemporaries: an incomprehensible mystery.

Why, therefore, should we continue to believe that this remarkable
character "lacked substance"? Solving the puzzle entails delving
deeper into Hitler's past, and we would be well advised to start with
the thirty years—the greater part of his lifetime, incidentally—during
which he was *not*, or not yet, a politician. If we are to look for the
archetypal behavior patterns and traits of personality that have given
Hitler's life its unmistakable profile, this is where we are most likely to
find them. By the time Hitler decided to seek his salvation in politics,
he had already acquired some experience of life, and therein may lie
the secret of his success.

In order to reconstruct these formative experiences, we must begin
by examining his environment and his emotional life. Where and how
did Hitler seek—and possibly find—what everyone craves: happiness,
love, recognition, confirmation that one is worthy to be loved? In his
case, none of these things can be detected in his relations with women,
in marriage and a family. Something prior to (and additional to) politics must have given his life a leitmotif, an emotional orientation.

HITLER'S HOMOSEXUALITY

Hitler's murderous acts defy all justification, yet it is wrong to see
him merely as a rabid beast. The man had human qualities that were
far from irrelevant to his actions, and we must not distort his image
still further by divesting him of them. Rather, we must consistently
reduce him to human dimensions, particularly with regard to his
emotional life. So far, our ideas about Hitler's emotional life derive
more from the traumatic impact of his reign of terror than from any
definite knowledge. The caricatures associated with them make the

dictator appear even more monstrous and incomprehensible than he actually was.

There has been a failure—one might even say, unwillingness—to explore the connection between Hitler's entry into politics and the possibility of his homosexuality. During this period in his life there was an extraordinary variety of events, encounters and connections so striking that they make sense only when looked at in a homosocial context. The closer one looks, the more compelling this observation becomes. This is the component of Hitler's life that I wish to explore, not in a sensational way, but as objectively as possible. I will be using some surprising and long-overlooked sources, but not without submitting them to critical evaluation.

Finding one's way around the Hitler of Auschwitz and getting to the man, to his life story, seems nearly impossible, as I have said, particularly when dealing with the period during which he seemingly rose from nothing and before he became the charismatic Führer. Because of the paucity of documents, these years seem barred to us. For the biographer, who is primarily expected to produce an explanation for the Holocaust, for the evil embodied in and perpetrated by Hitler, the barrier to these years is often impenetrable. Because of what he wrought, nothing is considered more important to a historicocritical analysis of Hitler than complete dissociation—the opposite of getting close to him, in other words. For the historian, this dissociation is something quite exceptional, given that he must dispense with a methodological step that is normally one of the essentials of his craft: an assimilation of the actual circumstances of those who are rightly regarded as representatives of history. True, Hitler is not a historical phenomenon whom one can simply describe, render vivid and leave it at that. But there is no reason why one should not "historicize" him consistently, for once, and get to the bottom of his carefully guarded secrets and desires.

This undertaking harbors a number of difficulties, however. Foremost among them is the charge that one may be exculpating Hitler, or at least humanizing him in some way, by citing problems in his sex life. This is a predictable, defensive reaction. In view of this, it is not easy to take a purely scientific interest in the question of how much biographical and political weight to attach to his private life. Those who strive to understand this nexus, if you will, between the political and the private in Hitler's life are often suspected of concocting an apologia. Yet the biographer's most important task has always been to investigate and interpret *all* the relevant facts. It is also the historian's duty to cast aside feelings of embarrassment, especially when dealing with people whose public life cannot be adequately understood without knowledge of their private life. To suppress such awkward facts and avenues of inquiry for reasons unrelated to scholarship is to abandon important sources of information. By exploring Hitler's sexuality I am not, therefore, attempting to "relativize" his guilt in any way: on the contrary, in seeking information about the links between his personal and political history, I am searching for understanding.

What must the historian do in order to form a really well-founded assessment of the significance of Hitler's homosexuality? Of primary importance, naturally, is proof that he had erotically based relations with men, and/or any information about his sexual dealings with those men. Psychohistorically obtained evidence is insufficient here,[43] and such interpretations must not be confused with historical facts. The indications and allusions to which psychological, long-range diagnoses attach themselves are far too vague to be regarded as genuine evidence. Hitler's poses, his gestures and body language in photographs and films, his accessories (mustache, whip, etc.), his effeminate cast of feature, his taste for muscular, monumental art, the marked pleasure he derived from contemplating the male physique—none of this can ever provide us with cogent information about his homosexuality, or even "latent" homosexuality. To assert the contrary is to enlist dubious "evidence" in the service of dubious psychology, and any such patterns of interpretation must remain pure conjecture. Relatively reliable information must be sought on a different investigative plane: we need statements by credible witnesses recorded in writing, facts that supply information about Hitler's homosexual and homo-erotic relations, and about the men he was in love with. Only when such a well-documented procedure has been completed will it be possible to speak of conclusive historical proof. One must realize from the outset, however, that we cannot expect the impossible of documentary sources. There are gaps that cannot be filled—gaps that exist and will doubtless continue to do so.

Given that homosexuality was until recently one of the unmentionables in the history of the West,[44] we need not be surprised by the dearth of primary source material. Hitler is no exception in this respect. Homosexuals tended to discuss their sexual orientation only with a handful of initiates[45] and to entrust only a small part of their true emotional life to paper, if they did so at all. Even such fragmentary evidence was often destroyed by the persons it "incriminated" for fear of stigmatization. We must always bear in mind that well into the 20th century homosexuals were widely regarded as morally depraved and that homosexual love was unacceptable. Homosexuals were subjected to constant mental strain by the ever present threat of disgrace.

So the main difficulty besetting any reconstruction of Hitler's private life has as much to do with the man himself as it does with the historical taboo on homosexuality. We are confronted by a seemingly impenetrable jungle of distortion, hypocrisy and camouflage. The self-revelations of Thomas and Klaus Mann are proverbial exceptions to the rule. Classical primary sources that might furnish comparable information about Hitler's homosexuality—photographs, love letters or diaries—do not exist, as everyone knows.[46] In his constant anxiety that incriminating evidence might come to light, he eschewed correspondence of a private nature.[47]

In all that related to his private life, Hitler showed himself a true master of secrecy. His erstwhile friend Ernst Hanfstaengl was not the only one to sense "his ever wary mistrust as soon as one deliberately or unconsciously sought to explore his past, his character, his private life. Then he would promptly shut up like an oyster or enshroud the subject in a verbal smokescreen."[48] He was absolutely brilliant at falsifying the facts, and few could equal him when it came to suppressing certain matters. He was so much at pains to obscure any facts that concerned him, even when conversing with his immediate circle, that one could almost speak of a concealment neurosis. To some extent this probably had its origins in his personal history. Deception and the twisting of facts become second nature to someone who has always struggled through life under false colors. This is what makes it so hard to interpret Hitler's semiofficial pronouncements on sex, women, and marriage. They often served as deliberate disinformation and were a major constituent of the camouflage net he wove behind the scenes.

No sworn statements about Hitler's homosexuality, made in the course of criminal proceedings or police interrogations, have come down to us in the original, although documents of this kind relating to Hitler's early years (1910–23) did at one time exist and may still be buried in personal files and archives not accessible to scholars. For instance, the personal papers of General Lossow, which may be relevant to the years under discussion, have never been released for purposes of research. We owe our knowledge of at least some items that may be in this archive to Eugen Dollmann, about whom more later. There may also be documents locked away in Swiss strong rooms that would shed light on these years. We may never know. It is relatively safe to assume that there is no evidence of any similar documents bearing upon Hitler's later "years of struggle." If they ever existed, they would undoubtedly have been destroyed by him and his henchmen. Seen in this light, even such lacunae can become circumstantial evidence of a person's strategic need to cover his tracks.

Hitler's determination to destroy anything that might have provided an insight into his private life is well documented. He got rid of anything he could, and his arm was long, even before 1933. Those privy to his secrets were bribed, sworn to secrecy, blackmailed or killed. Such conduct makes it clear that Hitler was anxious to avoid being compromised at any price, that the real threat to his reputation—as he must have perceived it—lay in revelations about his private life. It is unlikely that he was afraid of being thought a "loser" because of the adverse circumstances surrounding the first half of his life. Despite his questionable past and his rantingly demagogic manner, from the mid-1920s on he was regarded as a semirespectable professional politician who was well known to have come from a humble background. Hitler's great secret, I will argue, was his homosexuality and his homoerotic relationships. This was the stigma from his past that threatened at any time to rear its head as he rose politically. Hitler had to live a lie in order to conceal his proclivity, and he defended that secret by all available means. This was his Achilles' heel, and it was a permanent feature of his political existence, not only in the struggle for power and its preservation, but in safeguarding his posthumous reputation. Hitler himself tore the crucial pages out of his life story. In this he was no different from other prominent homosexuals. What was peculiar to his conduct was simply the ultramethodical and unscrupulous way in which he eliminated every threat of exposure.[49]

What happened to the people who shared Hitler's secrets and might have divulged them? For a start, those who really knew something were never more than a very, very small circle, and most were dead by 1945 or 1946. Some of them Hitler ordered to be killed (Ernst Röhm and his cronies, Captain Karl Mayr, his wartime comrade Hans Mend, the journalist Fritz Gehrlich, the police chiefs August Schneidhuber and Count Helldorf); others committed suicide (Geli Raubal, Eva Braun, Walter Hewel, Philipp Bouhler, Martin Bormann, Heinrich Himmler, Hermann Göring); and others were executed (Julius Streicher, Hans Frank).

The few initiates who survived Hitler kept faith with their

"Führer" despite the collapse of the Nazi regime. Even when it was all over, they remained under the spell of his mania for secrecy. Many, of whom Winifred Wagner is the best example, destroyed revealing documents and kept their mouths shut. Others did their utmost to lend Adolf Hitler's private life a posthumous gloss in their memoirs. Worthy of special note here are Albert Speer, Baldur von Schirach, Heinrich Hoffmann, Fritz Wiedemann and Heinz Linge. They often omitted or added individual aspects, but falsifications and omissions of this kind can sometimes be more effective historical misrepresentations than downright lies. These former satraps wrote and sold their memoirs for the same motive that had once prompted them to serve Hitler: self-interest—coupled, of course, with an overpowering urge for self-justification, because these intimates had attached themselves predominantly to the *private* Hitler and thus bore a personal responsibility. They undoubtedly knew things about him, but were neither willing nor able to divulge their knowledge completely. Perhaps, too, it was simply that the spell cast over them by Hitler remained intact. In any event, the concealment of Hitler's true life story cannot be laid at his door alone.

No one in Hitler's former entourage ever dared to associate him with homosexual tendencies. Not only would that have been an outrageous breach of taboo, but "outing" him would have would have resulted, if not in death, then in total ostracism on the part of erstwhile "comrades." That doubtless explains why prominent intimates such as Hitler's senior aide Wilhelm Brückner preserved as stubborn a silence as less prominent ones such as Julius Schaub, Emil Maurice and Ernst Schmidt.

There remains a small number of contemporaries, however, whose evidence can be taken seriously, and who were pretty explicit on the subject of Hitler's sex life. These include August Kubizek, Kurt Luedecke, Ernst Hanfstaengl, Rudolf Diels, Erich Ebermayer, Eugen

Dollmann, Christa Schröder and Hans Severus Ziegler. They are unanimous in stating, quite positively, that Hitler did not have sex with women. Some of them expressly say that Hitler was homosexual; others convey the same thing obliquely. Only a critical examination of sources, a procedure that must here be carried out with special rigor, can determine the credibility of such witnesses. Which documents are genuine? Did their authors know what they were talking about? Why do such documents exist? How are they to be construed? How can we lend them a voice? Finally, what conclusions do they warrant?

Questions like the above are central to my endeavor here, which is, to some extent, a record of the process of stripping away the camouflage surrounding our sources. We must objectively sift and interpret any source that may supply clues to Hitler's sexual orientation. Not only must each piece of testimony be submitted to thorough "external" scrutiny; its content must also be submitted to a plausibility test. The purpose of this analysis is to combine those sources that genuinely withstand strict evaluation into a chain of evidence. For all his attempts to disavow and disguise it, we shall see that Hitler was unable to conceal his homosexuality entirely, because there were people in his life who at some stage, for honest as well as dishonest reasons, were prompted to confide in others.

Another important aid to buttressing my theory is a detailed examination of Hitler's more intimate friendships. He continually sought the proximity of men with whom he formed long-lasting personal ties and whom he trusted to an exceptional extent. Most of these men were homosexual, or at least had pronounced homoerotic tendencies, and it is noteworthy that Hitler abruptly terminated some of these relationships under very peculiar circumstances. Many of these friendships with men are known, of course, to historians and biographers, but I will argue that, contrary to previous assumptions, they were fundamentally homoerotic in nature, whatever else they might have been politically. To gain information about these partners and friends—about their traits and social background—is to gain information about the person of Adolf Hitler himself.

From the very outset of his political career, Hitler made himself at home in his entourage's male environment. He clearly felt so at ease there that he cultivated this group existence to the end of his life. His entourage was absolutely devoted to him. That Hitler nonetheless encouraged many of them to marry should not be surprising: every conspiracy requires camouflage. The Mafia-like structure of his inner circle not only guaranteed its cohesion but warded off the threat of denunciation or blackmail. It was a community bound together for good or ill. All of its members had something to hide—some their sexual proclivities, others their shady business transactions—and Hitler was able to use this to forge ever stronger links between his closest henchmen and his political destiny. Thus developed ". . . the resolutely small-time conniver who was forever enmeshed in petty blackmail schemes, devious subterfuges: Hitler as sleazy con-man, small-time crook,"[50] but one who succeeded in defying all these adversities and saving his neck. The self-assurance he radiated at a later stage is partly attributable to the incredible way in which he evaded the dangers of his early career as a politician. It is well-nigh miraculous that no one could seriously question his integrity during the years 1930–34. This he translated into "providence"—indeed, into the "destiny" of an entire nation.

Hitler's political vocation was largely a product of his personal experiences, said Albert Speer in 1945, and he based his optimism on the fact "that he had, in the course of his life, encountered many difficult situations which had always turned out favorably for him."[51] And indeed, few politicians of his generation could have gone to a harder school than Adolf Hitler. Like his adaptability, his toughness and the iron nerves on which he liked to pride himself were attributable largely to that fight for survival. So there is material for a more accurate picture of Hitler's private life. We must merely reexamine and analyze the available material in a sober and objective manner.

———

Before drawing any further conclusions, however, we must examine our sources. Hitler's homosexual tendencies can be demonstrated, as the following chapters will show. Beyond that, however, it is important to recognize his sexual orientation as a *historical* fact. While such recognition does not supply *the* key to his career, it will, I hope, put us on the path to a new perception of the "Hitler phenomenon." Therein lies the challenge of this book.

CHAPTER ONE

The Would-be Aesthete: Hitler, 1905–1914

IN HIS YOUTH Hitler imagined himself destined for higher things: he aspired to be an artist, not a civil servant or clerk. Despite this firm resolve, however, he drifted along aimlessly between his sixteenth and twenty-fifth years (between 1905 and 1914) and could at best be described as a pseudobohemian. Our knowledge of this period in his life is sketchy. Although it is possible to reconstruct certain contexts and events, Hitler's early life remains singularly obscure.[1]

Here is what we do know.[2] In June 1905 Hitler's mother, who had been a widow since 1903, sold the family home in Leonding. Together with her two children, Adolf and Paula, and her sister Johanna Pölzl, nicknamed "Hanitante," she moved to 31 Humboldtstrasse in nearby Linz. At this time, sixteen-year-old Adolf was still attending the junior high school in Steyr, some fifty miles away, where he lodged during the week. Armed only with a poor report card for the year 1904/5 and no diploma, he quit school and returned to his family. It was at Linz's

Landestheater in the latter part of 1905, when he was living in the town full-time, that he met an apprentice decorator named August Kubizek, who was then seventeen. The two youngsters became close friends.

In May 1906 Hitler paid his first visit to Vienna, where he stayed for at least two weeks. A year later the family moved from Linz to Urfahr on the other side of the Danube. Early in September 1907 Hitler paid Vienna another visit to sit for a place at the Academy of Fine Arts. Although he passed the first part of the examination, he failed the drawing test at the beginning of October. Deeply disappointed, he returned to his mother, who was terminally ill with cancer and already bedridden. She died just before Christmas. In February 1908, having settled her estate, he moved to Vienna for good. At eighteen, he had an inheritance of around 1000 crowns and an orphan's monthly pension of twenty-five crowns.

He was followed not long afterward by his friend August Kubizek, who was now studying music, and they both moved into a room let to them by a Frau Zakreys at 31 Stumpergasse, where Hitler had stayed during his second trip to Vienna. They lived together for some four months. Then, at the end of the academic year, Kubizek rejoined his parents in Linz, where he spent the summer. He received several postcards and letters from Hitler, the last of them at the end of August, when the latter was staying in Waldviertel with "Hanitante." Back in Vienna in September, Hitler made another attempt to get into the Academy of Fine Arts, but was this time denied admission even to the drawing test. On November 18 he quit the room in Stumpergasse and moved, describing himself as a "student," to nearby Felberstrasse, where he lived for nine months until August 20, 1909. Two days thereafter, this time registered as a "writer," he moved into new lodgings at 56 Sechshauser Strasse, which was also in the vicinity of the Westbahnhof. Less than four weeks later, on September 16, 1909, he moved from there to "address unknown."

There is no official record of Hitler's whereabouts during the next five months. He clearly had no fixed abode before moving into the Meldemannstrasse men's hostel in the Brigittenau district on February 9, 1910, but it is likely that he spent some time at the hostel for the homeless in Meidling. It was there, too, that he probably made the acquaintance of Reinhold Hanisch, five years his senior, with whom he maintained close contact in the ensuing months. The two of them developed a kind of business partnership: Hitler painted postcards and pictures, and his friend Hanisch endeavored to sell them. Before long, however, Hanisch acquired a competitor in the shape of a secondhand dealer named Josef Neumann. Hitler and Hanisch fell out because the latter had allegedly embezzled some of their joint proceeds, an offense that found its way into police records and earned him a spell in prison.

In the spring of 1911 Hitler's financial situation changed for the worse: his orphan's pension had been reassigned to his now widowed half sister, Angela Raubal. He was now entirely dependent on his own earnings and remained so for a good two years. In May 1913, by which time he had turned twenty-four, he came into 820 crowns from his late father's estate. He thereupon left Vienna accompanied by Rudolf Häusler, who was nearly five years younger, and moved to Munich, where they rented a room at 34 Schleissheimer Strasse from a tailor named Popp. Hitler had failed to do his military service in Austria, but the authorities tracked him down in Munich, and in January 1914 he was interviewed by the police. After sundry bureaucratic arguments he was obliged to report for duty at Salzburg early in February, but was found to be "too frail"[3] for military service, was pronounced unfit and was permitted to return to Munich.[4] On February 15, 1914, Häusler moved out of their shared room but continued to live in Hitler's neighborhood until he returned to Vienna at the beginning of August.[5] At the same time, Hitler volunteered for war service in Munich.[6]

Of course, none of these particulars, registration forms or court records tell us much about Hitler himself and his private life, nor do the sparse documents relating to him and his friends convey a meaningful picture of them. We are dependent on the oral accounts and memoirs of a few contemporaries, for instance those of August Kubizek dating from 1953, a series of articles by Reinhold Hanisch published after his death in 1939, and an interview given by Frau Popp in 1934. But even these meager forms of testimony are questionable. Closer examination of the circumstances under which they originated soon discloses that none of the above-named was able, willing or at liberty to tell all that he or she knew. We should not capitulate in the face of this problem, however, for the said witnesses definitely had something to impart. They wanted to say something—even if it sometimes conflicted diametrically with the historical truth. This, clearly, is the task facing us: we must extract a coherent picture from our sources, despite their remarkably obfuscatory and/or revelatory nature. The best way to achieve this, I think, is to interpret them with reference to the world of experience one might presume Hitler to have been living in at this period: the homosexual milieu, which then bore a social stigma.[7] I say "one might presume" because of what we do know about the world he inhabited shortly thereafter. If we do adopt this procedure, the blurred outlines of his early years come more into focus.

"GUSTL AND ADI"

Who Was August Kubizek?

"The personality of my boyhood friend is like a thread that runs throughout my life."[8] By saying this in 1949, August Kubizek was expressing what his relationship with Hitler meant to him. Four years later he devoted an entire book to the subject.

August Kubizek was born in Linz on August 3, 1888.[9] After leaving school he embarked on a decorator's apprenticeship in his father's firm, but his real love was music. His friendship with Hitler reinforced this enthusiasm to such an extent that in February 1908, with his parents' consent, he moved to Vienna and became a music student. Having graduated in the fall of 1911,[10] he worked as a conductor at various theaters. In Vienna on September 1, 1914, shortly after the outbreak of war, he married a violinist named Anna Funke, with whom he later had three sons.[11] His career was abruptly cut short by conscription into the army, and in 1918, when he tried to resume his former profession, few satisfactory openings were available. Thus an advertisement for a municipal official's job in the small town of Eferding, near Linz, where Kubizek's mother was now living, could not have been more timely. He obtained the post, although he had no administrative experience, because the authorities were seeking "someone qualified to act as artistic director of the musical society and to attend to cultural matters,"[12] so Kubizek was the ideal applicant. In 1926 he became municipal secretary and was three years later promoted to municipal director, a post he retained until 1945. He always felt more of a musician than a public servant, however, and even found it "understandable that, being an *artist*, I may sometimes be rather liberal in my management of municipal affairs, because, as a musician, I am subject to moods."[13]

In 1923, fifteen years after they had last seen one another, Kubizek's attention was drawn to his former friend and companion by the front page of the *Münchner Illustrierte*. Hitler had already attained a certain notoriety, and Kubizek was promptly reminded of the postcards, letters and drawings that bore witness to his former friendship with the party leader. But the time was not yet ripe to hawk them around; for the moment, Kubizek confined himself to following Hitler's career from afar.[14] He did not attempt to get in touch with him for another ten years, when in 1933 he sent him a letter of congratulations. Hitler seemed to be informed about Kubizek's career and current circumstances, because his rather offhand reply sent regards to Kubizek's mother but did not mention his father. Could he have been aware that the latter had died? "I should very much like—when the worst of my struggles is over—to reminisce in person about those happiest years of my life."[15] However, it is doubtful if any such meeting took place.

But then, in the spring and summer of 1938, Hitler's interest in his old friend suddenly revived. In March, shortly after the annexation of Austria, three SS men from Berlin appeared at Kubizek's door with the intention of relieving him of his Hitler documents. He managed to get rid of them.[16] What Kubizek does not tell us is that he was in trouble in 1938, having been charged with a criminal and disciplinary offense.[17] This may have filtered through to Berlin. In any event, Hitler found time while visiting Linz to meet with him and, no doubt, to discuss his current problems. Kubizek needed assistance, and Hitler did not withhold it. His memoirs merely state that Hitler lectured him on his reconstruction plans for Linz, as he used to in the old days, questioned him about his present circumstances and undertook to finance his sons' music studies at Linz Conservatory.[18] Hitler was clearly anxious to help his former friend. In April 1938 he invited him to the Obersalzburg, and a private visit to Eferding was also planned.[19] We do not know whether these meetings actually took place, but it is certain that Kubizek had a conversation at Linz with Rudolf Hess, Hitler's lieutenant. "I sensed at once that his cordiality was genuine and truly heartfelt."[20] Kubizek had suddenly become of interest to Hitler again, as we can see, and it seems logical to surmise that this sudden interest was connected with the charges pending against him.

But what were those charges? It transpires from the files of the Upper Austrian provincial government that in May 1938 a subordinate of Kubizek named Franz Neuburger, town clerk of Eferding, had publicly accused his superior in an inn. Neuburger was an avowed National Socialist who had since March 1938 been district treasurer of the NSDAP.[21] He obviously felt powerful enough to pick a fight with Kubizek, who had no party-political affiliations, doubtless in the hope that it would further his own career. But Kubizek defended himself—successfully: in October 1938 Neuburger issued a formal apology retracting his charges. The relevant documents have survived, but certain passages in the one that details Neuburger's original accusations were obliterated: "I hereby declare, quite publicly, that Kubizek has stolen and embezzled money. Kubizek tried to incite me to commit theft. Kubizek is a [word deleted] incompetent official [sentence deleted]. I have already seen to it that Kubizek can no longer gain access to the Führer." Neuburger's surprising retraction states that he had "no grounds of any kind for laying serious accusations and charges against Herr Amtsleiter Kubizek. My remarks to that effect were attributable to a mistaken view of his management of the municipal finances, which was perfectly unobjectionable in terms of criminal law, and partly to incitement."[22] What can account for such a retreat? Had some powerful friend protected Kubizek in the nick of time? The criminal charges were dropped, at all events, and in the spring of 1939 Neuburger applied for a transfer.[23]

Was there far more to this affair than a charge of embezzlement? Why would passages in Neuburger's statement have been subsequently deleted? Some aspect of his remarks must have been too delicate to remain on file. In July 1938 the deputy mayor of Eferding, Hugo Wanivenhaus, made a statement which suggests that blackmail formed the background to the whole affair: "Kubizek always exerted himself on behalf of his fierce antagonist, and Neuburger actually owed him his whole livelihood." He also stated that Neuburger had told him (Wanivenhaus): "I am going to destroy Kubicek . . . , professionally, socially, and in every respect." Neuburger could not have expressed himself so strongly without having something up his sleeve.

Wanivenhaus referred to "circumstances that are known and spoken of among the general population," but which he did not wish to go into "here" in greater detail.[24] Kubizek had been harassed by Neuburger for two years.

All of this has the trappings of a classic case of sexual denunciation, one that might—although Neuburger would never have dreamed it— have cast a shadow over Hitler's past. This certainly would more readily account for Hitler's renewed interest in Kubizek than a charge of having embezzled public money. It is also noteworthy that Hitler invited his boyhood friend to attend the Bayreuth Festival with him in the summer of 1939, not long after the whole affair. Kubizek thanked him in fulsome terms: "My Führer! You alone can appreciate that you have, by your noble generosity, made possible the fulfillment of my life's dearest dream. . . . With what overwhelming grandeur and glory you have fulfilled the vocation of which you were already fully aware thirty-five years ago. I bow before my Führer's unfathomable greatness! . . . I greet you, my Führer, with a profoundly stirred and most grateful heart."[25]

It is, of course, understandable that a musician and admirer of Wagner should be delighted by the prospect of finally attending the world-famous festival, but even so, this was laying it on with a trowel. Grateful as he must have been for attending Bayreuth, perhaps he was also thanking Hitler for a "generous" rescue operation that had delivered him from an extremely awkward predicament. In 1940 they met at Bayreuth once more and spent some hours together for the last time—another stirring experience from Kubizek's point of view.[26] They never again met face to face, but Hitler kept an eye on his old friend thereafter.

Kubizek, who had now become quite widely known as "the Führer's boyhood friend," was still in possession of the documents that attested to their friendship. Various Party authorities solicited those mementos, but Kubizek withstood their urgings and refused to surrender his treasure—or at least, not all of it. In April 1940 he joined the NSDAP[27] and was appointed "head of propaganda, cultural director and district administrator" in "Strength through Joy," the Party's recreational organization.[28] In 1943 he produced the first version of his Hitler memoirs at the Party's behest. The same year, probably in return for this, he was promoted by special authority to a higher salary grade.[29] He also received direct subventions from Hitler's privy purse: a single payment of RM 6000 and a regular monthly grant of RM 500[30]—a substantial amount of money in those days.

As soon as the war ended Kubizek was removed from office by the U.S. authorities and detained for sixteen months.[31] A denazification tribunal classified him as "incriminated," and it was only thanks to the efforts of Franz Jetzinger, a onetime Social Democrat politician[32] who was investigating Hitler's early years in Austria and had come across Kubizek in December 1948, that he managed to secure "less incriminated" status. This led to his reinstatement, followed immediately thereafter by his retirement.[33] So Kubizek had indirectly benefited once again from his former friendship with Hitler. Jetzinger's help should be regarded as a form of recompense for the information Kubizek had given him for his projected book about Hitler's youth. In the fall of 1953, three years before his death, Kubizek published a book of his own: *Adolf Hitler. Mein Jugendfreund.*

Kubizek's Hitler

What did Kubizek have in mind when he resolved to write a book about his relations with Hitler? It certainly seems to be conceived as more a novella or novel than as a sober factual account. Perhaps he believed that only such an approach could fittingly portray the destiny of his friend, "this unique human being."[34] He did, in fact, have a very definite exemplar in mind: *Schwammerl. Ein Schubertroman* (1910) by the German-Austrian regional author Rudolf Hans Bartsch.[35] This book tells of the composer Franz Schubert; of the tribulations to which his superabundance of talent gave rise; of his hectic, extravagant lifestyle; of his rapturous and despairing love for women; and, last but not least, of the intimacy of the friendships with his own sex in which "Schwammerl" continually sought refuge and consolation. There is, for instance, a long scene in which Franz Schubert the musician and Moritz von Schwind the painter dream of a relationship akin to marriage.[36] The novel is written in a cloyingly sentimental style, and the allusions in its erotic passages are discreet but unmistakable.

Another reason why Kubizek followed Bartsch's example was that he wanted to show Hitler in a different light and divest him of his "mask."[37] His old friend was once more to be perceived as a human being and "a unique phenomenon in the history of the German people." As he emphasized to Jetzinger: "After all, Napoleon also ended his days in exile even though he was one of his nation's greatest men. The truth rendered perception triumphant. One day it will be the same with Adolf Hitler."[38] Despite the crimes for which Hitler was responsible, therefore, Kubizek's faith in him remained unshaken and his love for him intact. He had something on his mind—something he wished to tell posterity about the friend of his youth. It is this desire on Kubizek's part that should govern our perception of him as a contemporary source and prompt us to take him seriously.

"From the outset, my friendship with Adolf Hitler bore the hallmark of the unusual,"[39] writes Kubizek, who adds that it was positively "singular"[40] in character. And indeed, his book describes a relationship far from typical of adolescents from a lower-middle-class background. We encounter two young men who are united by their fervid enthusiasm for Richard Wagner's music, who go to the theater together, roam the streets of their hometown and undertake long excursions into its charming rural environs. But they are very different in spite of their common interests. Hitler assumes the role of a didactic soliloquist, whereas Kubizek, fascinated by his friend's high-strung personality, contents himself with the role of a patient listener. He regards Hitler as an imaginative, intelligent, inquisitive person, but one who also has an erratic, impulsive, irascible side—a picture that fully accords with the notion of an artistic nature transcending bourgeois conventions. Kubizek portrays himself as Hitler's intellectual inferior, a somewhat meek youth utterly subservient to his admired companion. Many have pointed to this imbalance in their relationship and concluded that it was not a true friendship. According to them, naive Kubizek served only as a receptacle for egocentric Hitler's ceaseless flow of words.[41] It was Kubizek himself who supplied this interpretation with an apt catchword by referring to the "instrumental" nature of their friendship.

Looking more closely, however, we discover something that has hitherto been blithely ignored: an emotionally charged and thoroughly reciprocal relationship. In spite of their dissimilarity the two youths persistently sought each other's company—and found the "intimacy" and "profundity" to which Kubizek expressly refers. He speaks of true affection, mutual understanding and great empathy. Although his usually egocentric and dominant friend "clung doggedly to his own point of view," he could also "be so considerate that he often made me feel ashamed." Kubizek even concludes: "By God, no one on this earth, not even my mother, who loved me so dearly and knew me best of all, could express my secret desires as unexpectedly as my friend." The erstwhile "theater acquaintanceship" had swiftly "become transformed into a profound, romantically transfigured friendship."

Hitler watched jealously over Kubizek "because I cannot endure it when you consort and converse with other young people." He could never bear the idea that Kubizek "was interested in other people beside my friendship with him." What always mattered to him in this respect was "absolute exclusivity." Such language would do justice to a love affair. In February 1908, when Hitler traveled to Vienna a few days before Kubizek, he urged his friend to join him as soon as possible: "Am already eagerly awaiting news of your arrival. Write soon and definitely, so that I can make all the arrangements for your ceremonial reception. All Vienna is waiting. So come soon. Will naturally meet you." Kubizek's verdict on this postcard was that Hitler had felt terribly lonely in Vienna without him: "The 'eagerly' in the opening sentence is surely meant in earnest. The fact that he repeats the 'Come soon' in the form 'Again, please come soon!' proves how much he was looking forward to my arrival."

When Hitler penned those lines he could hardly wait for the dream he and Kubizek had cherished for so long to come true: a life of fulfillment as a pair of artists living in the Austrian capital. In Linz they used to long for a lottery win to make their dream of such a twosome possible. They pictured themselves setting up house together, and Hitler had already furnished the apartment in his mind's eye. He himself wanted to become an artist draughtsman, whereas Kubizek would at last be able to pursue his musical bent. They planned long trips in the summer, their primary objective—of course—being Bayreuth. They wanted to be a couple, outwardly as well: so that everyone would think they were "brothers"[42] they proposed to wear the same clothes on the street.

In Vienna in 1908, Kubizek and Hitler did to some extent try to make this daydream a reality. They demonstrated their partnership by wearing the same winter overcoats and "broad-brimmed black hats." Kubizek writes: "In those days we must have been taken for brothers, which was what we wanted."[43] Their long walks in the neighborhood of Linz or Vienna enabled them to be alone and undisturbed. In their Linz days they liked to spend time at a spot above the Danube "which no one else discovered,"[44] and in the summer they made excursions to a stream in which they could swim together. Many of their longer hikes took them to more distant places, where they would stay overnight.[45] But Kubizek and Hitler sensed that they were spiritually at one, not only in the countryside, but most definitely during their many visits to the opera, their chief object of veneration being the magical strains of Richard Wagner's music. They also attended Sunday performances by the Vienna Boys' Choir at the Burgkapelle, because "Adolf was particularly fond of that celebrated boys' choir."[46]

Kubizek's account coincides in many respects with contemporary descriptions of homosexual friendship. The sexologist Magnus Hirschfeld, for example, reports that lovers particularly liked and deliberately sought the seclusion of the countryside and the rapturous atmosphere prevailing in darkened opera houses.[47] We also know from contemporary literature that many of them admired Richard Wagner and his music,[48] and that Bayreuth was a notorious international rendezvous for prominent homosexuals.[49] The same, of course, could be said about many heterosexuals as well, but as with the opera singer Maria Callas today there was a cultlike quality to Wagner's following among homosexuals at the time. Although we do not know how far Kubizek and Hitler were aware of all of this, there is no doubt that their enthusiasm for Wagner formed an extremely important element in their relationship. According to Kubizek, the Wagnerian music dramas presented at the Vienna Hofoper were among the highlights of their friendship: "Having forged our youthful bond in the solemn atmosphere of the theater at Linz, we continually reinforced it in Europe's leading opera house."

Kubizek relates that Hitler found other people "physically repulsive." His friend was "constantly afraid" of "coming into physical contact with someone; he seldom shook hands, and then with only a few people!" With Kubizek, however, whenever Hitler felt particularly affectionate, Hitler would seize his companion's hand. Kubizek characterizes such contacts as "intimate."[50] One of them occurred during their happy reunion at Vienna's Westbahnhof in February 1908, which Kubizek described as follows in an early version of his memoirs: "My friend, who was already awaiting me on the platform, greeted me in joyful excitement with a kiss and took me straight to his lodgings, where I myself was to spend the first night."[51] This passage was deliberately toned down for publication: "Clearly delighted by my arrival, he greeted me warmly and, in accordance with contemporary custom, kissed me lightly on the cheek."[52] But another passage in Kubizek's volume of memoirs is more explicit. While roaming through the mountains the two friends were overtaken by a violent rainstorm. They took refuge in an isolated barn and decided to spend the night there.

Meantime, in the upper reaches of the barn, I had come across some big, square sheets of coarse linen which the peasants used for carrying hay down from the steep alpine meadows. I felt sorry for Adolf as he stood in the doorway in his sodden underclothes, shivering with cold and wringing out the sleeves of his jacket. Being susceptible to colds of every kind, he could easily have developed pneumonia. So I took one of the big cloths, spread it out on the hay, and told Adolf to remove his wet shirt and underpants and wrap himself in the dry cloth. This he did.

He lay down naked on the cloth. I folded the ends together and wrapped him up tightly in it. Then I fetched another cloth and draped it over the top. After that I wrung out our clothes and underclothes and hung them up in the hut, wrapped myself in one of the cloths, and lay down. To prevent us from getting cold during the night, I threw some hay over the bundle containing Adolf and another bale over myself.

We had no wristwatches, so we had no idea what the time was, but in our situation it was quite sufficient to know that it was pitch dark outside the hut, and that the rain was incessantly drumming on the roof. A dog barked somewhere in the distance, so we were not too far from some human habitation—a thought which greatly reassured me, but which, when I mentioned it to Adolf, left him completely indifferent. In this situation, people were quite superfluous to him. He was highly amused by the whole venture, whose romantic conclusion pleased him greatly. Besides, we were nice and warm by now. . . .

I still remember what a job it was to wake Adolf. He extricated his feet from the covers and, with the hay cloth around his waist, went to the door to see what the weather was like. His slim, lanky figure, swathed in the white cloth with one end thrown over his shoulder, toga fashion, resembled that of an Indian ascetic.[53]

This effusive passage reflects something of what, for Kubizek, constituted the special quality of his friendship with Hitler: tender concern for each other's welfare, physical proximity, erotic attraction and the desire for secluded togetherness *à deux*. Unconsciously, Kubizek drew the picture of a romantic love affair that continued to move him decades later. We do not know, of course, how far the two of them carried their inclinations, but one can readily detect from this hay barn episode that they found close physical contact desirable.

Where the two young men's acquaintanceships with women were concerned, on the other hand, Kubizek has nothing to report. Once during their time in Vienna, when one of his music pupils paid him a brief visit, "our worthy old landlady saw the pretty young girl" and "raised her eyebrows in surprise." Afterward, Hitler promptly made a jealous scene and flew into a rage. Their room was too small for a rendezvous with that "musical hussy," he said, and he refused to calm down even when Kubizek protested that the girl had not come because she was "lovesick."[54]

Although Hitler was extremely attractive to women,[55] wrote Kubizek, women held absolutely no sexual attraction for him. "It was understandable, therefore, that Adolf did not engage in love affairs or flirtations, and that he always rejected the coquettish advances of girls or women. Women and girls took an interest in him in Linz as well as Vienna, but he always evaded their endeavors." He even held up this indifference toward the opposite sex as an ideal to his dying day: "Subsequent conversations with the Führer proved this to me."[56]

The only women permitted to play a part in Hitler's and Kubizek's private life were their mothers. They were their most important spiritual reference points aside from each other—a phenomenon often observed in homosexuals by Magnus Hirschfeld.[57] Kubizek tells of Hitler's "boundless love for his mother" and says that a "unique spiritual harmony" reigned between them, most of all during the difficult months preceding Klara Hitler's death. Kubizek, whose love was wholly focused on his mother, enjoyed a similarly intimate relationship with her. It is even possible that the two mothers recognized, understood and approved of the special nature of their sons' friendship. This is at least implied in the scene in which Kubizek bids farewell to Klara Hitler on her deathbed: "'Gustl,' she said—she usually called me plain 'Herr Kubizek,' but at that juncture she used Adolf's name for me—'continue to be a good friend to my son, even when I am no more. He has no one else.' I promised with tears in my eyes."[58]

Jetzinger tells us that Kubizek "vigorously and angrily denied"[59] that Hitler had homosexual tendencies. This wholly accords with the tenor of his book, which is positively larded with passages designed to disabuse the reader of the (inescapable) suspicion that his relationship with Hitler was more than a normal friendship between two men. No, Kubizek is quite definite on this point: he can "fully and completely confirm that Adolf was absolutely normal, both physically and sexually. His exceptional quality lay not in the erotic or sexual domain, but in other areas of his character."[60] But no one knew better than Kubizek that Hitler was *not* sexually "normal." All his remarks on this subject are a covert allusion to the fact, and he obviously realized—or had it pointed out to him—that his descriptions required a very strong counterweight if they were not to leave the reader with an undesirable impression.

These attempts at concealment are most evident when Kubizek tells the story of Hitler and Stefanie, a girl around his own age and the daughter of a civil servant from Linz. Stefanie, who definitely existed,[61] was a boon to Kubizek because she enabled him to portray a Hitler who seemed capable of loving a woman, and thus to relativize their own relationship. He recounts this "romance" with Stefanie in great detail, and with good reason, but his very long-windedness robs it of credibility. She was everything to Hitler, the great love of his life, "the only person on God's earth extraneous to abominable humanity, a creature who, transfigured by radiant love, had imparted meaning and content to his tormented existence."[62] One quickly gets the impression that this is a mere projection, nothing more. In fact, Hitler made no effort to get together with his "beloved." Kubizek's intention is obvious: he was "heterosexualizing" Hitler in retrospect.

Another of Kubizek's contentions—that Hitler lived like a monk in self-imposed sexual abstinence and, not least for fear of venereal diseases, firmly withstood the manifold sexual temptations of the Austrian capital[63]—is likewise too overdone to be credible. One example of this is a remarkable scene that occurred during a joint search for lodgings for Kubizek immediately after his arrival in Vienna. While they were talking with one potential landlady, "an overly hasty movement loosened the cord that held her dressing gown together. 'Oh, sorry, gentlemen!' the lady promptly exclaimed, pulling it together again. But that moment had been sufficient to show us that all she wore under her silk dressing gown was a little pair of panties. Adolf turned puce, grabbed my arm, and said, 'Come, Gustl!'"[64]

Kubizek's purpose in recounting this incident was not simply to illustrate Hitler's moral integrity; he also wanted to justify the fact that the two young men eventually shared a small, cramped room. They had to endure more such peculiar experiences before Hitler could at last say, "'it would be best if we moved in together.' This solution suited us both, for one thing because we would finally move into a room, for another because we could be together permanently, and thirdly because we would complement one another in that way."[65] Why didn't they simply move into one room straight away? It would have been natural enough for them to do so, given the prevailing shortage of lodgings in Vienna, and besides, they had dreamed of living under the same roof ever since Linz. No, Kubizek insisted on including in his account a story that would invalidate any suspicion that his relationship with Hitler was a sexual one.

It was clearly with just such an intention that he added another very instructive occurrence that showed Hitler taking exception to the phenomenon of homosexuality:

One evening, at the intersection of Mariahilfer Strasse and Neubaugasse, we were accosted by a well-dressed man of very middle-class appearance who asked us what we did. When we told him we were students—"My friend is studying music," said Adolf, "and I'm studying architecture."—he invited us to dine at the Hotel Kummer. He let us order whatever we wanted. For once, Adolf could at last eat his fill of pastries and gâteaux. The man told us that he was a factory owner from Vöcklabruck, and that he was averse to forming friendships with women because they were only after money. I particularly liked what he said about amateur music-making, to which he was very partial. We thanked him—he even accompanied us out onto the street—and then we went home.

Back in our room Adolf asked me how I had liked this gentleman. "Very much indeed," I replied. "A very cultured man with strong artistic leanings."

"And what else?" demanded Adolf, with a look on his face that puzzled me.

"What else should there be?" I asked in surprise.

"Since you don't seem to grasp what this is all about, Gustl, take a look at this little card."

"What card?"

Without my noticing it, the man had actually slipped Adolf a visiting card bearing an invitation to visit him at the Hotel Kummer.

"He's a homosexual," Adolf said matter-of-factly.

I was startled. I hadn't even heard the word before, still less did I have any clear idea of what it meant, so Adolf enlightened me on the phenomenon. For him, of course, it had long been a problem he wished to see combated by all available means, being an unnatural phenomenon, just as he himself kept such people at arm's length in a positively anxious and conscientious manner. The visiting card of the splendid factory owner from Vöcklabruck vanished into our iron stove.[66]

This anecdote does, of course, achieve the exact opposite of what the author intended. Why did the man accost Kubizek and Hitler, of all people? His choice was not so wide of the mark, after all: Kubizek, in his innocent naivety, liked him "very much indeed." And why did Hitler, of all people, have to fend off such people "in a positively anxious and conscientious manner"? How did Kubizek know this? Was Hitler often accosted in this way? Whatever the truth, Kubizek's account is far too labored and spurious to fulfill its purpose.

Kubizek and Hitler spent only four months together in Vienna before going their separate ways. The precise reason remains obscure because conclusive explanations are lacking. Kubizek's own version is not particularly convincing. According to this, he did his military service after

spending the summer in Linz with his parents, and did not return to
Vienna until November 1908. Hitler, who was no longer living in their
shared room by then, had disappeared without a trace. However, Jetzinger plausibly states that Kubizek's age group was not liable to be
drafted until a year later, and that he probably did his military service
in 1909, not 1908.[67] It is also strange that he claims not to have heard
anything from Hitler after the end of August. How could such close
friends have remained without news of one another for so long? It
seems very probable that Kubizek was back in Vienna by September,
and that their parting of the ways—whatever form it took—occurred
at that time. But why the secrecy? Was there an unpleasant ending that
would have been inconsistent with Kubizek's stylized portrayal of the
male friendship he described as a "youthful bond"?

What really happened? Kubizek supplies a few hidden clues, for
instance, when he speaks of awkward moments in their relationship.
Apparently, he and his friend often differed over how to spend their
day. Kubizek went to the Conservatory in the mornings, whereas
Hitler slept until noon and then felt disturbed when Kubizek started
practicing—his "eternal tinkling,"[68] as he called it. In addition to this,
Hitler's interest in politics had grown considerably in Vienna, whereas
Kubizek himself was quite indifferent to the subject. "There is no
doubt," Kubizek emphasizes, "that this contrary development, which
rendered me less and less of a suitable interlocutor for Adolf, was one
of the reasons that prompted him to go his own way."[69] Kubizek
applied himself to his music studies with great earnestness and diligence, whereas Hitler roamed the city and even spent several nights
away from home. "God knows where he wandered off to, where he
slept, and how hungry he got."[70] Kubizek did not know exactly what
his friend was up to. Their relationship steadily disintegrated.

Hitler's situation deteriorated financially, too, after he split up with
Kubizek. Although "Hanitante" lent him enough money in 1908 to
keep him afloat for a few months, he remained sorely dependent on

additional sources of income, especially as the rent for his new lodgings in Felberstrasse was "certainly higher than at Frau Zakreys'."[71] In September 1909, after leaving his second lodgings in Vienna, Hitler disappears from any records. Was he genuinely homeless, as Reinhold Hanisch suggests,[72] or did an acquaintance put him up? It is also conceivable that he was not in Vienna at all during the months in question, but had gone off to try his luck elsewhere. We do not know.

Schools of Homosexuality — Vienna

Homosexuality was a constant topic of conversation during the years 1906–09 because of the charges laid against Philipp, Prinz zu Eulenburg, a friend of the German emperor. Writing in the political weekly *Die Zukunft*, the journalist Maximilian Harden had accused Eulenburg of moral misdemeanors, likewise of exerting a baneful influence on Wilhelm II. This affair, in which sexual denunciation was deliberately employed as a weapon against a political opponent, was centered on the profoundly irrational notion that homosexual tendencies made a man unfit for public office. Harden claimed, for example, that the political influence of those with "abnormal proclivities" disastrously conflicted with Germany's national interests. But this was not the only point at issue. Harden was a Jew, a circumstance that fomented prejudices of quite another kind: staunch nationalists ascribed the affair to a "Jewish muckraking campaign" designed, as they saw it, to besmirch not only the emperor's reputation but that of Germany as a whole.

Since more and more distasteful details about Eulenburg's years in Vienna, where he had served as German ambassador between 1894 and 1902, became public in the course of various hearings,[73] the scandal caused a great sensation in the Austrian press. "Our neighbor's roof is on fire,"[74] wrote the *Oesterreichische Kriminal-Zeitung*.

Alerted by these developments, the Austrians took a closer look at their own country and discovered the existence in Vienna—as in many other European capitals—of a substantial homosexual subculture. Anonymity functioned as a shield. Homosexuals from the provinces sometimes came to spend a few incognito days in the city and take advantage of its homosexual infrastructure (restaurants, coffeehouses, hotels, public baths, male prostitutes).[75] Kubizek, too, reported this. In turn-of-the-century Vienna, he wrote, "the obtrusively erotic prevailing atmosphere could be sensed at every turn."[76] Or, to quote Stefan Zweig: the city was conspicuous for an "unwholesomely sultry air laden with perfumed sensuality."[77] No wonder prostitution flourished in this singular blend of puritanical inhibition and sensual provocation.

The homosexual milieu was situated on the outer margin of Vienna's subcultural spectrum. Its denizens had developed an elaborate system of silence and concealment that presented blackmailers with a remunerative field of activity. Moreover, the sudden growth of public interest was such that the so-called *Kriminalzeitungen* made it their mission to shed a harsh light on this suspect environment. These newspapers published reports on homosexual rendezvous such as cafés or hotels and enlightened their curious readers on homosexual practices. They indignantly referred to the "pederastic mischief"[78] and "outrageous state of affairs" that had transformed the beautiful imperial city into "a pigsty, the Eldorado of unpardonable libertines and extortioners."[79] Some readers' letters opposed this denunciatory campaign and urged that its victims be treated fairly. The homosexual emancipation movement, too, strove for an enlightened approach.[80] At all events, public debate began to break down the barriers enclosing this hermetically sealed milieu, a process which those affected found extremely distressing and threatening.

Being an avid newspaper reader, Adolf Hitler was also gripped by the universal agitation aroused by the Eulenburg scandal. He later stated in *Mein Kampf* that he had followed events in Germany with the greatest interest. "I did not approve of the campaign conducted at this time against Wilhelm II." He had even been incensed that the Viennese press "gave expression to its misgivings about the German emperor with an air of apparent concern, but, so it seemed to me, with ill-concealed malice. . . . And now this finger was probing around in the wound to its heart's content. The blood shot to my head in such cases." Hitler referred approvingly to the "antisemitic *Deutsche Volksblatt*," which had behaved "more decently in connection with such an affair"[81] than the majority of the Viennese press. It had pointedly ranged itself on the German emperor's side and defended him against Harden. "Maximilian Harden, alias Isidor Witowski"—snarled the *Volksblatt*—was the "pigherd" of the Jewish Viennese press, which was now causing an uproar similar to that made by pigs in a sty when fodder is tipped into their trough.[82]

Where Hitler was concerned, strong language of this kind must have fallen on fertile ground, because he would already have discerned some connection between his own proclivities and the Jew Harden's public attacks on the German emperor's homosexual adviser. He must have felt personally assailed by Harden's revelations. And he detested not only Harden but the sexologist Magnus Hirschfeld as well: "What that swinish old Jew hawks around," he fumed in later years, "constitutes the filthiest slur on our nation."[83] Until well into the 1920s Hitler attacked those sections of the public who had morally condemned Eulenburg in his day but were now on Hirschfeld's side: "Once upon a time they couldn't have been more morally indignant about Eulenburg; today, the same liars extol a man like Magnus Hirschfeld as a pioneer of morality."[84]

Under the pressure of the spectacular Eulenburg affair, Hitler had clearly worked himself up into something that ultimately led to his furious antisemitic onslaughts. His profound loathing for Harden and Hirschfeld may have provided the foundation, poisoned by personal resentment, of his subsequent conspiracy theory relating to "international Jewry." We can only speculate whether a direct connection exists between his subsequent, lethal antisemitism and the hostile image of the Jews he formed during his years in Vienna, but he had undoubtedly internalized a prejudice that was reinforced by reading trashy racist literature.[85] "I myself," he rather casually remarked in a newspaper article in 1919, "had recognized the Jewish peril since I was eighteen"—and he had been eighteen in 1907, when the Eulenburg scandal was at its height."[86]

From now on, hatred of the Jews became an additional means of combating his fear of exposure. The provocative subject of homosexuality was the starting and reference point that governed the development on his views in this sphere. It was only because of the self-constructed connection between his problems in society and the Jews' public activities that Hitler came across the antisemitic pamphlets that supplied him with welcome slogans. His blind hatred was intensified still further when he saw how the Eulenburg scandal was being turned against the Germans as a whole, for instance, by Italian students in Vienna campaigning for equal opportunities, who mocked their German classmates with insinuations of sexual perversion and effeminacy,[87] or by the Pariser Kabarett, which was broadcasting obscene jokes about "*la vice allemande.*" "Those who wax indignant at this," declared *Der Sturm*, the Viennese art journal, "can be primarily grateful to Maximilian Harden. Not because he has given the Germans an unmeritedly bad name, but because he has trumpeted an abuse that actually exists in our midst."[88]

These sexually based animosities went hand in hand with the escalating hatred of other nations that was already being preached in turn-of-the-century Vienna by obscure utopians and race and conspiracy theorists. Thus developed the crudely prejudiced atmosphere that also molded the young Hitler.[89] He must have been fully aware how threatening and explosive the subject of homosexuality was. This background must be borne in mind when we come to examine the environment in which Hitler lived from the end of 1909 on, when he realized that he would not succeed as an artist.

The Men's Hostel, Hitler's Adoptive Family

It was an open secret at the beginning of the 20th century that municipal hostels for homeless males were hubs of homosexual activity as well as catchment centers for stray individuals. According to Hirschfeld, "homosexual occurrences formed a favorite and far from only theoretical topic of conversation"[90] in these emergency accommodations. For many of their occupants, homosexual intercourse was a substitute for lack of contact with women; others kept themselves afloat by engaging in prostitution. Hitler spent over three years in this environment. The hostel on Meldemannstrasse, a relatively modern and comfortable establishment by contemporary standards, was an exclusively male preserve.[91] Some 70 percent of its occupants were under thirty-five, and its low turnover bears witness to a fairly stable social structure. Reinhold Hanisch, whom Hitler first met at the hostel, records that he was anything but a loner; on the contrary, he had a remarkable capacity for developing contacts with his fellow occupants and building up something akin to a circle of friends.

With whom did Hitler have particularly close ties? First, with Reinhold Hanisch himself, who is our most important witness for this phase of Hitler's life. And who was Hanisch? The following picture emerges from the sparse biographical particulars on record. Hanisch was twenty-five when he came to Vienna in the fall of 1909. He had earlier worked as a manservant in Berlin, where he served two terms of imprisonment for theft. We cannot be certain whether he lived at the Meldemannstrasse hostel during the first half of 1910, as he himself stated, or elsewhere, as shown in the residents' register,[92] but he certainly spent some time in the hostel environment and got to know

Hitler there during the winter of 1909/10. They became friendly, but soon fell out and severed relations. It is probable that Hanisch often turned up at the hostel under a false name,[93] but several changes of abode are also recorded in Vienna's residents' register under his right name.[94] In August 1913 Hanisch returned to his hometown, Gablonz in Bohemia.[95] Thereafter, from 1914 to 1917, he served in the Austrian army. He got engaged and returned in July 1918 to Vienna, where he married the same month (the apparently childless marriage was dissolved ten years later). In 1923 Hanisch was again sent to prison for theft.

In the early 1930s, after the rapid rise to prominence of the NSDAP and its leader, he tried to make capital out of his former friendship with Hitler. He did not succeed; on the contrary, he put himself at risk. Having forged some pictures, he tried to market them as valuable early works by Hitler. He was twice arrested for that reason, once in 1932 and again in 1933. An Austrian National Socialist named Feiler was instructed by the Party to obtain, via Hanisch, some originals and forgeries of pictures by the Führer. Feiler, who was temporarily in touch with Hitler, denounced Hanisch for fraud, and he was sent to prison yet again. But Hanisch attracted the wrath of the powerful dictator not only because of his fraudulent activities, but also because he had collaborated with biographers critical of Hitler such as Konrad Heiden and Rudolf Olden, whose attention had been drawn to Hanisch in 1933, when his trial was reported in the press. In November 1936 Hanisch was arrested once more, allegedly for continuing to trade in fake Hitlers. What was doubtless more serious was the discovery at his home of two manuscripts—no longer extant, unfortunately—in which he described the time he had spent with Hitler. On February 4, 1937, only a few weeks after his arrest, Hanisch died at the age of fifty-three. The cause of death was officially certified as heart failure.[96]

Hanisch had been dead for two years when a three-part series of articles entitled "I Was Hitler's Buddy" was published by *The New*

Republic magazine in the United States in April 1939. We do not know how the manuscript got to America, nor on what original text the publication was based. Hanisch tells how he made Hitler's acquaintance at the hostel for the homeless (he describes him as completely down and out); how he helped him to get by there; and how, when various odd jobs failed to bring in enough money, they founded their own "firm." He also writes of Hitler's personal philosophy, his political role models and his attitude toward women. Hanisch's portrait is of a young man whom he found extremely eccentric and unreliable, but who was—at least for a while—a good friend of his.

How are we to classify and evaluate all this information? Let us assume that, when he met Hitler at the end of 1909, Hanisch was already at home in a homosexual environment. His circumstances in Berlin had been as questionable as those in Vienna, and as a "manservant" he pursued a positively classical form of homosexual occupation.[97] Hanisch asserts that Hitler and he had been "close friends" and "knew everything about each other."[98] This was confirmed by a former fellow inmate of the men's hostel, Karl Leidenroth, who worked with Hanisch during the 1930s. Hanisch and Hitler had been "on very close terms," and their relationship could certainly be "described as friendly."[99] Hanisch must therefore have been very hurt when, in the summer of 1910, a competitor appeared on the scene in the person of Josef Neumann, who evidently outbid him in the picture-selling stakes and also became a rival on the personal plane.

Neumann, thirty-one years old and unmarried, a casual laborer and secondhand dealer, was registered at Meldemannstrasse from the end of January until mid-July 1910.[100] According to Hanisch, "Neumann was a businessman by profession and didn't shrink from any work."[101] Neumann was a kindhearted man whose liking for Hitler was thoroughly reciprocated—indeed, Hanisch describes him as "a real friend" of Hitler.[102] In June 1910 Hitler checked out of the men's hostel for nearly a week,[103] during which time he apparently went off with Neumann and earnings of 20 crowns in his pocket—much to the chagrin of Hanisch, who "couldn't find him for a week. He was sightseeing Vienna with Neumann and spent much of the time in the Museum."[104] These few days are the only period on record during which Hitler was not living at the hostel. It is scarcely credible, however, that he and his companion absented themselves from their lodgings for a whole week purely for cultural edification's sake. It looks, on the contrary, as if Neumann's relations with Hitler amounted to something more than a "normal friendship."[105]

It also seems possible that the dispute between Hitler and Hanisch, which found its way into police records, was not really to do with embezzlement and forgery at all, but stemmed from rivalry, jealousy and revenge. For Hitler, this rift continued to have unpleasant consequences for years. Hanisch remained a danger until he died. His contacts with the foreign press presented a threat of disclosures, and Hitler could never be sure how far this troublesome man who knew too much would go.

Hanisch's death suited the "Führer" very well.[106] But why, one wonders, was Hanisch not more explicit in his statements? Why did he avoid the subject of homosexuality? Even though he had ventured a very long way down that path, he could not speak freely without endangering himself. With a past like his, he was extremely vulnerable. He could have been socially destroyed at any time; not only must he have sensed that, but it must have been intimated to him by interested parties. Probably for reasons of self-protection, therefore, he resisted the temptation to denounce Hitler sexually. Instead, he raised the subject of "Hitler and Women."[107] Precautionary compliance or a broad hint? Both, perhaps, but we do not know for sure.

Prostitution

According to Magnus Hirschfeld, overnight shelters and men's hostels were "hotbeds of male prostitution."[108] Those who landed up there were often obsessed with the idea of making easy money. Many occupants of Hitler's hostel on Meldemannstrasse, too, were sorely in need of some extra income[109]—not least Hitler himself.

From the spring of 1911 on, he is alleged to have earned a living solely from the sale of his postcards, drawings and watercolors. This seems unlikely, however. There are two conflicting accounts of his financial situation at the time. It emerges from an eyewitness account by the "Brünner Anonymus" [anonymous inhabitant of Brünn], whose text was published in Czech in 1935,[110] that in 1912 Hitler was earning between 20 and 40 crowns a month. That corresponds to an annual income of between 240 and 480 crowns, a sum on which no one could have survived.[111] Yet Karl Honisch, a fellow inmate of the hostel, stated that Hitler was in no kind of financial straits. Honisch's notes were commissioned by the NSDAP's central archive in 1939, so it is hardly surprising that their author testified to his former fellow inmate's "extremely respectable lifestyle."[112] Hitler had been very hardworking, Honisch stressed, and turned out one picture a day. This enabled him not only to support himself but to put something by "for his travel fund for Munich."[113] It is nonetheless worth noting that the young Hitler, as unanimously described by Kubizek and Hanisch, did not seem like the kind of person who would be either willing or able to engage in such concentrated work, so Honisch's "official" statements should be taken with a pinch of salt. That said, however, if there is a degree of truth to Honisch's observation that, comparatively speaking, Hitler seemed better off financially than other fellows at the hostel, he must have had other sources of income. If so, what were the possible sources available to him?

Given what we now know about the characteristics of this particular hostel in Vienna, it would be irresponsible to rule out the possibility that Hitler may have made approaches to wealthy men. His collaboration with Hanisch on the production and sale of pictures, a business in which artistic ambition was hardly the prime consideration, certainly opened up new avenues in this respect. We will never know, of course. However, this admittedly bold interpretative possibility gains plausibility not only from the specific conditions of the environment in which Hitler lived, but also from the rumors that always circulated about his past. For instance, Ernst Hanfstaengl, of whom we shall have more to say elsewhere, confided to the U.S. Secret Service in 1942 that the hostel Hitler occupied in Vienna was reputed to be "a place where elderly men went in search of young men for homosexual pleasures. It is probable that these types of old roués and young gigolos became familiar to the young Adolf at this time."[114] The Austrian chancellor, Engelbert Dollfuss, had some years later given instructions that incriminating material be compiled relating primarily to Hitler's time in Vienna. He is reported to have brought this file to the attention of his Italian friend and ally Mussolini in June 1934.[115] A few days after Dollfuss's assassination in July 1934, the Duce's press attacked the Nazi leaders as "murderers and homosexuals."[116]

Rudolf Häusler

"And so I began increasingly to lead a double life. Reason and reality bade me endure some hard but beneficial times in Austria; only my heart was elsewhere."[117] We know little more of Hitler's life in 1911 and 1912 than is conveyed by these sibylline words from *Mein Kampf*. It is only with the advent of Rudolf Häusler, who became a close friend of Hitler after moving into the men's hostel in February 1913, when he was nineteen years old, that we regain some understanding of Hitler's circumstances.

Häusler led a checkered, indeed, mysterious existence. In 1914, after spending a considerable time in Munich with Hitler, he went back to Vienna. He served in the army in Italy and Romania until 1918. In 1917 he got married, and his wife gave birth to a daughter a year later. After the war Häusler lived with his family in Vienna, where he worked during the 1920s as a businessman and bank clerk.

He never remarried after his wife's death in 1929. From 1933 to 1938 he was resident in Czechoslovakia, where he managed a hotel and briefly worked in a sugar refinery. In the spring of 1938 he moved back to Vienna and obtained a full-time job with the German Labor Front (DAF). There are conflicting accounts of when he joined the NSDAP, but he had probably been a member since 1929. It is fairly certain, however, that he was expelled from the Party in 1944. Something that merited expulsion had evidently occurred during his time in Czechoslovakia, but the precise background and circumstances are obscure.[118]

It took a long time to unearth any information about Häusler, who died in 1973. Although his name was mentioned in the *Neue Revue* in 1952, more than forty years elapsed before the historian Brigitte Hamann obtained further details from his daughter, Marianne Koppler—for instance, that her father had spent six weeks in Berlin in 1933 and sought an interview with Hitler. Unlike Kubizek at a later stage, however, he was denied access to his former companion.[119] For some unknown reason, Häusler had become persona non grata. Not only must his erstwhile Munich landords, Herr and Frau Popp, have received strict instructions to keep mum about Hitler's onetime roommate, but Häusler himself was peculiarly reticent on the subject. In 1939, in a DAF personnel questionnaire, he stated: "In 1911 I made the acquaintance of Adolf Hitler, who took me under his wing, politically enlightened me, and thus laid the foundations of my political and general education. In 1912 he took me with him to Munich, where we lodged together and did casual work."[120]

According to Marianne Koppler, Rudolf Häusler came from a middle-class family of Viennese civil servants. His father was strict and dominant, his mother kind and affectionate. Rudolf was regarded as the "black sheep" of the family. He was expelled from school "because of some uncouth boyish prank."[121] Subsequently, on his eighteenth birthday in December 1911, his father showed him the door. Häusler, who had started to train as a clerk, was out on the street.

It was probably around this time that Häusler and Hitler got to know each other. We do not know what form their relationship took in the ensuing months, but it is certain that Häusler joined Hitler in the Meldemannstrasse hostel in February 1913. "Adi" and "Rudi," as they called each other, went to the opera together, and it was not long before Häusler came to share Hitler's passion for Wagner. He had never severed relations with his mother, who continued to look after her outcast son, did his laundry and helped out with food. Häusler introduced his new friend, and Hitler—shades of Kubizek—managed to persuade Frau Häusler that it would be advantageous for the two of them to move to Munich. It was an opportune time for a change: Häusler had completed his training in the spring of 1913, and Hitler, having received a payment from his father's estate in May of that year, was once more in possession of a sum of money. The two friends were thus able to make a fresh start in Munich. They shared a room for almost nine months, after which Häusler, growing tired of Hitler's loquacity, irascibility and know-it-all attitude, looked for lodgings of his own.[122]

When interviewing Marianne Koppler, Brigitte Hamann asked the obvious question: Did her father and Hitler have a homosexual relationship? Hamann writes that, in conversation with his daughter, Häusler "made absolutely no allusions to anything more than a friendly relationship." And again: "Häusler's daughter 'simply cannot conceive of' this in relation to her father, who was far from being a spurner of women. She knows, on the other hand, that he would never have told her such a thing."[123] So the question remains unanswered.

There are, however, unmistakable echoes of Hitler's relationship with Kubizek: Häusler's middle-class background, his understanding mother, their jointly forged plans for the future, their fresh start in another city, and, last but not least, their inability to live together indefinitely. "Rudi's" malleable character presented "Adi" with another chance to try what had so miserably failed with Kubizek five years earlier. Hence his attempt to escape with Häusler, this time to Munich, an artistic metropolis whose inhabitants were reputed to be far less priggish than the bigoted Viennese.

The Pseudobohemian of Schwabing

"In the spring of 1912 I at last went to Munich. The city itself was as familiar to me as if I had dwelt within its walls for years."[124] Such was Hitler's description of his arrival in Germany when writing *Mein Kampf* in 1924. He had also given 1912 as the year of his move to Munich in an autobiographical statement made in 1921.[125] What accounted for this suppression of his last year in Vienna? Retrospectively, of course, the Führer's curriculum vitae looked better if he curtailed his time in Vienna, that hated "racial Babylon," and prolonged his sojourn in a purely "German" city. But it is also quite possible that Hitler really had been in Munich in 1912, at least for a while. His familiarity with the Bavarian metropolis may have derived less from books than from studying the milieu itself. Hitler had probably taken a look at the city before leaving Austria, like he had done with Vienna in 1906.

But Hitler had another major reason for leaving Vienna: the looming threat of military service. He had reacted to Kubizek's draft papers with "boundless fury" and had urged his friend to ignore them, simulate physical unfitness, or—in a pinch—to "secretly cross the frontier." He himself was firmly resolved to evade military service.

Aside from that, Munich was—to cite a contemporary observer—"a regular Eldorado for homosexuals."[126] Hitler and Häusler promptly settled in Schwabing, an urban district more representative of the bohemian lifestyle than any other. Schwabing was colored by the countless immigrants who hoped to find happiness there. The motley population that "made the Schwabing the urban district into Schwabing the cultural concept," as Erich Mühsam has so graphically put it, comprised the most diverse types: "Painters, sculptors, writers, models, loafers, philosophers, religious founders, revolutionaries, reformers, sexual moralists, psychoanalysts, musicians, architects, craftswomen, runaway girls of good family, eternal students, the industrious and the idle, those with a lust for life and those who were world-weary, those who wore their hair unkempt and those who parted it neatly."[127] This "mass settlement of oddballs"[128] had developed a kind of counterworld to Wilhelminism, an alternative society composed of self-styled avant-gardists who cultivated their antibourgeois sentiments and stylized their artistic way of life. Homosexuality was less disapproved of here than elsewhere, especially if its representatives assumed the guise of an Oscar Wilde impressionist or the pose of a Stefan George disciple.[129] There were also numerous highly regarded circles of intellectuals and artists that congregated in the relevant cafés and beer cellars of the Schwabing scene.[130] One can readily imagine how much "resplendent Munich" must have enthralled Adolf Hitler in 1912/13.

But, just as he had previously done in Vienna, he failed to establish himself as an artist. Success eluded him, the sole difference being that he was once more, five years after his relationship with Kubizek, living with a friend. The statements made by his landlady, Anna Popp, are totally implausible. She testified—under instructions, one presumes—that her "gentlemen lodgers" had led a thoroughly respectable life. Hitler was a reclusive, industrious student who read and worked from early in the morning until late at night, and earned his living by selling the pictures he painted.[131] It is highly improbable, however, that Hitler could have lived on his modest talent, considering that far more gifted fellow artists in contemporary Munich found it almost impossible to do so.[132] Unless he was lying to the municipal authorities at Linz, he had in any case devoted only "a fraction" of his time to earning a living "as a self-employed painter." This being so, it is a mystery how he managed to generate an annual income of 1200 reichsmarks in competition with over 3000 other Munich painters.[133]

Statements made by witnesses who acquired pictures from Hitler in Munich in 1913/14 may perhaps dispel a little of the obscurity surrounding this question.[134] We are told that the young artist favored shops and beer gardens as potential outlets for his work. Dr. Hans Schirmer of Munich, then in his mid-forties, recalled that, while sitting "over a mug of beer" in the garden of the Hofbräuhaus, he noticed a "very shabby-looking man" threading his way among the tables and offering customers a picture for sale: "It must have been around ten o'clock at night when I noticed him again, and saw that he still hadn't sold his picture. When he passed near me soon afterward, I asked him, being touched by his predicament from a purely human standpoint, whether he would be willing to sell the picture." They soon agreed on a price. Schirmer did not have quite enough money on him, however, so they arranged that Hitler should call at his home the next day. They got into conversation again, and Hitler offered to produce some more pictures. "Although my own financial situation wasn't easy at the time," Schirmer agreed. Hitler delivered the promised works within a week—once more to the doctor's home. Schirmer: "I again sensed that he was having a hard time of it, but that he was also too proud to accept charity. On the other hand, he seemed to have realized that I wasn't a wealthy man, and I think that was why he never called again."[135]

Young Hitler had better luck with Dr. Schnell, a Munich soap manufacturer and perfumery owner. One day, Schnell recalled, his shop was visited by a young painter "who had probably been told by someone that I occasionally assisted impoverished painters." Hitler sold him a picture and received further commissions. In Schnell's case, it is interesting that years later when Hitler was head of state he invited Schnell—"long after he came to power"—to the Hotel Vier Jahreszeiten. "There, Hitler asked how I was faring, inquired after the pictures, and offered to do me a favor if ever I wanted anything."[136] Why should the Reich Chancellor have taken such an interest in a Munich soap merchant who had bought pictures from him over twenty years before? One clue to this could be that Schnell had introduced Hitler to Ernst Hepp, then a judicial assessor and later a justice of the Reich Financial Court. And in Hepp, who was then thirty-six years old, Hitler evidently found the Munich friend and patron he had long been seeking.

An associate of the NSDAP central records office, who questioned Hepp and his sister Martha about the Führer's watercolors in 1939, was told that "the young artist" had often been invited to meals at the family home. Assessor Hepp, who had taken to Hitler, was "amazed at the young man's knowledge. He enjoyed conversing with him and often advised him on his problems."[137] Hitler was even invited to the Hepps' country house at Wolfratshausen. Hepp commissioned Hitler to paint more pictures, recommended his protégé's work to friends and acquaintances,[138] and several times gave him tickets for operas and concerts.[139] Of particular importance, finally, is the fact that Hepp assisted Hitler in his well-nigh desperate but ultimately successful attempts to join the Bavarian army.[140] After Hitler had been sent to the front, Martha Hepp supplied her brother's favorite with "socks, underclothes, and necessities."[141] Hitler expressed his gratitude in field postcards and in a twelve-page letter to Hepp.[142] The two men must have been close. Once again, however, the extent of their relationship can only be guessed at.

———

During his time in Munich before the war, Hitler was as far from pursuing any definite career plans as he had been in Vienna. He frequented the "Grössenwahn," a Schwabing café where he may have wished to observe the higher echelon of the bohemian lifestyle whose representatives remained beyond his reach.[143] The one possible exception was the mythologist Alfred Schuler, but he had by then become a marginal figure.[144] Schuler, a self-styled "erotic advocate" of the swastika and mother cult,[145] is reported while seeking homosexual contacts in Schwabing to have come across "a young man . . . named 'Adolf.'" Although this information comes from Karl Wolfskehl,[146] a lionized professor of literature and key figure in Schwabing's bohemian circles before the war, there is no reason to distrust his testimony. On the contrary: through Schuler, an antisemitic esotericist who was eloquently proclaiming the advent of a new era, Hitler could have gained direct access to the abstruse doctrines of the racist utopians among whom he had, on occasion, sought his ideological salvation in Vienna.[147]

Hitler was, as we have said, profoundly impressed by the Schwabing scene. It was an environment in which something resembling an aesthetically refined form of existence seemed palpable, and in which a life of sexual "otherness" could be pursued without personal detriment. The only question was when and with whom Hitler would find the route to that existence. The outbreak of World War I, however, offered him a new escape route, and with it a chance to continue to keep his options open. He could allow himself to be swept along for a while by the euphoria and excitement with which the Germans took the field against their "host of enemies." His personal problems temporarily receded into the background.

CHAPTER TWO

Comrade Hitler:
Blackmail with Fatal Consequences

The "Mend Protocol"

In September 1948 the German diplomat Werner Otto von Hentig received a registered letter from London. It contained a "Hitler document" that did not come into the possession of Munich's Institute of Contemporary History, together with other papers from Hentig's estate, until four decades later.[1] The cover letter from a certain Helge Knudsen has not survived, nor do we have any other clue to the document's provenance, perhaps because of its explosive nature.

Werner Otto von Hentig may have been one of the "German diplomats" who years later assured the historian Werner Maser that the "Mend Protocol" played "an important role" in the German resistance movement against Hitler, but "who do not wish to be named."[2] Does this make sense? Yes. The document exists elsewhere in the form of a copy made during the 1950s by General Karl Kriebel of Bavaria. Acquired by the Bavarian State Records Office in 1986, the document is accompanied by the following note: "On August 13, 1951, Herr

Professor Schmid-Noerr/Percha brought the accompanying transcript to my attention by way of a loan. He stated that he had known Hans Mend very well. . . . He, Schmid Noerr, had made the transcript on the instructions of the Abwehr [German military intelligence headed by Admiral Canaris], and had ensured by means of persistent cross-questioning that it contained nothing but definite particulars and was all aboveboard. He said that he alone possessed the transcript. It had at the time been brought to the attention of Canaris and General Beck [the figurehead of the German resistance movement], as well as one or two foreign diplomats."[3]

Friedrich Alfred Schmid Noerr, a philosopher and author, was active in the resistance movement and had in 1937/38 been commissioned by Beck to draft a new German constitution.[4] When he published this "resistance document" in 1961 he referred to his conversations shortly before the war with diplomats such as Hentig and other "resistance circles ready to act."[5] This brings us back to our starting point. We now know that the historical and political status of the "Mend Protocol" is not to be underestimated. Persons of high rank and reputation had a definite interest in assuming its contents to be credible and circulating them for that reason. It was probably one of the files the Abwehr opposition group placed in its "conspiratorial file depository"[6] for use in trying Hitler if he were arrested. Helmuth Groscurth, who played a central role in the November 1939 plans for a coup d'état, envisioned that "Hitler would be taken alive and examined by a medical board of inquiry. The result—a foregone conclusion—would then be published."[7] When Schmid Noerr pumped Mend in December 1939 he must also have been at pains to unearth incriminating evidence against Hitler.

We now come to the most important items of information Schmid Noerr elicited during his exhaustive interrogation of Mend and placed on file for posterity. They relate mainly to the years 1914-19, when Mend, a dispatch rider on the staff of the List Regiment, was serving with Hitler and had an opportunity to get to know him extremely well.[8] In particular, they concern Hitler's friends, his personal characteristics and his homosexuality. The following series of verbatim quotations may also be construed as an introduction to the witness himself:

Because he was an Austrian and physically unfit, Hitler had been rejected when he volunteered for service in August 1914. He was unemployed in Munich at the time, and his intention had simply been to get into the army so as to have a square meal again. . . . After being rejected by the medical board, he stationed himself outside the Wittelsbacher Palace in Munich at a time when he knew King Ludwig usually left the building. He managed to waylay the king as he emerged with his adjutant general, von Leonrod. Hitler barred Leonrod's path and accosted him: he was an Austrian, he said, but did not wish to serve in Austria. He had volunteered for wartime service in Munich, but had been turned down, so please would His Majesty endorse his request. Leonrod made a note of his name, and that, according to Hitler, was how he came to join the List Regiment.

Hitler never had anything to do with guns from the time he joined us at the front as a regimental orderly. He was never anything other than a runner based behind the lines at regimental headquarters. Every two or three days he would have to deliver a message; the rest of the time he spent "in back," painting, talking politics, and having altercations. He was very soon nicknamed "crazy Adolf" by all the men he came into contact with. He struck me as a psychopath from the start. He often flew into a rage when contradicted, throwing himself on the ground and frothing at the mouth. Private [Ernst] Schmid[t] (now a master builder at Garching, near Munich), with whom Hitler had been friendly earlier on, because he had sometimes worked on building sites with him, was his special pal. The others he was friendliest with were Privates Tiefenböck (now the owner of a coal merchant's in Munich) and Wimmer (now working as a Munich streetcar employee). All three were runners at regimental headquarters. The only one who had volunteered for combat duty was the Jew Lippert (a commercial traveler by profession; he later became a clerk at the Braunes Haus [Nazi Party headquarters], where he worked from 1934 on—and still does, so far as I know, not being subject to the Jewish laws). The List Regiment's battalion adjutant was Lieutenant Gutmann, a Jewish typewriter manufacturer from Nuremberg (now emigrated), whom Hitler made up to whenever he wanted preferential treatment of some kind. It was also Lieutenant Gutmann who got him his Iron Cross 2nd Class at Christmas 1914. That was at Bezaillère . . . near Ypres. Colonel Engelhardt of the List Regiment was wounded in this engagement. When he was carried to the rear, Hitler and Bachmann tended him behind the lines. Hitler contrived to make a big fuss about this exploit of his, so he managed to gain Lieutenant Gutmann's backing in the aforesaid manner.

Meantime, we had gotten to know Hitler better. We noticed that he never looked at a woman. We suspected him of homosexuality right away, because he was known to be abnormal in any case. He was extremely eccentric and displayed womanish characteristics which tended in that direction. He never had a firm objective, nor any kind of firm beliefs. In 1915 we were billeted in the Le Fèbre brewery at Fournes. We slept in the hay. Hitler was bedded down at night with "Schmidl," his male whore. We heard a rustling in the hay. Then someone switched on his electric flashlight and growled, "Take a look at those two nancy boys." I myself took no further interest in the matter.

Hitler could never forbear to deliver inflammatory political speeches to his comrades. He always described himself as a representative of the "class-conscious proletariat." Whenever he thought he was safe, he referred to his superiors as an "arrogant bunch of officers" and called them "robber knights," "highwaymen of the nobility," or "a clique of bourgeois exploiters." His oft repeated tirades included remarks like the following: "Those swine lie on horsehair mattresses, whereas we eat horseflesh soup." . . .

I met Adolf Hitler again at the end of 1918. I bumped into him on the Marienplatz in Munich, where he was standing with his friend "Schmidl." He greeted me as follows: "Well, Ghost Rider, where did you spring from? Thank God the kings have toppled off their perch. Now, we proletarians also have a say." Hitler was then living in a hostel for the homeless at 29 Lothstrasse, Munich. Soon afterward, having camped at my apartment for several days, he took refuge at Traunstein barracks because he was hungry. He managed to get by, as he often did in the future, with the help of his Iron Cross 1st Class and his gift of the gab. He laid less stress on the fact that in 1915, when the List Regiment was terribly mauled, he had been promoted to lance corporal [private first class] like every last one of the other survivors. It was striking, after all, that a man who had served throughout the World War from October 1914 to the very end should not have received any further promotion. In January 1919 I again ran into Hitler at the newsstand on Marienplatz. I couldn't help feeling ashamed for "Red Hitler," he looked so down at heel. . . . Then, one evening, while I was sitting in the Rathaus Café with a girl, "Adi" and his friend Ernst Schmid[t] came in. "Hello, Ghost Rider," Hitler said to me, "do you know of some lodgings for the two of us?" I offered to put him up for the night out of charity. Afterward my girl told me, "If you're friendly with people like that, I'm not going out with you anymore."

Next I heard that Hitler was appearing as a public speaker. The first time, so as not to run into him, I listened to him in secret at Geislgasteig. That was early in 1920. Later on I heard him speak at the Circus Krone and in various beer cellars. Aha, I said to myself,

Hitler's singing a very different song these days. Adi the Red has changed color!

Then, one day in January 1920, Hitler came to my apartment on Schleissheimer Strasse and complained that he couldn't go home. When I asked why, he didn't answer. I didn't care in any case. "All right," I told him, "you can sleep here." . . . He stayed at my place for a day or two. . . . But Hitler couldn't make out in Munich. He went to see Jakob Weiss at Abens in the Holledau . . ., who took him to his parents' house and fed him. It was this erratic roaming around that finally brought Adolf Hitler into contact with General Epp. . . .

My impression of Adolf Hitler in those early postwar days in Munich thoroughly confirmed my countless experiences with him in the field. Hitler struck me as a book with a thousand pages. He had always been two-faced. He was hypocrisy personified. One of his faces was that of the self-important busybody he impersonated to his superiors, and, if need be, to his comrades. When Hitler was off duty behind the lines or at headquarters and he heard that some success had been gained at the front, it was quite usual for him to burst in on the other men waving his arms and shouting, "We've won! We've given the French (or British) another bloody nose!" But with his superiors he always played the ingratiating telltale as soon as he saw it might benefit him in some way. That's why his comrades were wary of him. . . . Hitler's other face was that of a secret, sinister criminal. His whole attitude was that of a ruthless person who knows how to wrap himself in a halo. He has always, ever since I've known him, been . . . a great actor. Not a word he uttered could be trusted. He lied whenever he opened his mouth, always did the opposite of what he said. . . .

When Hitler returned to Munich in the winter of 1918 he made persistent attempts to obtain a senior position with the Communists, but he couldn't get into the Munich directorate of the Communist Party although he posed as an ultraradical. Since he promptly requested a senior Party post that would have exempted him from the need to work—his perpetual aim—the Communists distrusted him despite his mortal hatred of all property owners. They stalled him, and he may have thought they were spying on him from a certain stage onward. At all events, he took his revenge by joining the Freikorps Epp [a right-wing paramilitary organization] and gained Epp's confidence because of his Iron Cross 1st Class. Epp made it Hitler's first job to boost the troops' morale and paid him for it. He was soon able to call himself an "officer instructor." In that capacity he visited all kinds of hostelries at night and came across Anton Drexler. . . . Hitler thereupon joined Drexler's party and was assigned Party Membership No. 1512. But he promptly set about splitting the party by accusing Drexler's secretary, a man named Harrer, of complete incompetence and thrusting him aside. Drexler, who hated disputes of any kind, gave way to Hitler out of weakness. Hitler immediately made use of the burglar's tactic he later employed with such success, which entailed sticking his foot in the door and refusing to yield until he was on the inside. That was how he managed to smash Drexler's party. And then he opened his own shop with seven men.

Although Mend's portrait of Hitler could hardly be blunter or more direct, let us summarize the most important points he seems intent to convey. Between the ages of twenty-five and thirty Hitler had success-fully contrived to ingratiate himself with the Bavarian military; he performed his military service without any front-line ambitions and killed time in the rear echelon; and his favorite companions were Tiefenböck, Wimmer and Schmidt, the last of whom was on intimate terms with him. When the war ended Hitler and Schmidt looked for lodgings together. Hitler did not set foot in the extreme right-wing camp until he had been rejected by left-wing groups. This was where, with characteristic cunning and bombast, but also with the aid of "burglar's tactics," he finally made it as party leader.

If we wish to gauge the historical truth of Mend's statement, we must naturally check the "facts" presented by it. But first, who exactly was Hans Mend and what prompted him to settle accounts with Hitler?

HANS MEND

Schmid Noerr described Mend as a "wholesome son of the soil" who had during World War I been "a notoriously plucky, almost daredevil dispatch rider" nicknamed "Ghost Rider" by his comrades.[9] But this covers only a small part of his otherwise far from uncomplicated life.[10] Born into a smallholder's numerous family near Rothenburg ob der Tauber on March 16, 1888, Johannes Mend became inured to unremittingly hard work at an early age. He had to support himself as soon as he left school, and worked as an errand boy and stableboy for distinguished families. From 1908 to 1911 he served in the 2nd Bavarian Lancers, thereafter joining the Waldfried stud, near Frankfurt, as a so-called preparer, or trainer. On mobilization he reported to the army as a reservist, and from October 1914 to August 1916 he served as a dispatch rider in the List Regiment. It is an officially attested fact that he got to know the runner Adolf Hitler and was in close personal contact with him during this period. Mend was assigned to other units until his demobilization in December 1918. After returning to civilian life he tried to earn a living as a horse trader, but failed miserably. In August 1919 he received a five-month prison sentence at Munich for theft and false pretenses, although the sentence appears to have been suspended. In the same year, by then the father of an illegitimate son, Mend was expelled from the Bavarian capital. His whereabouts in the ensuing period are unknown, but it is on record that he committed some offenses against property in Nuremberg in 1920/21. In August 1921 the provincial court at Ansbach sentenced him to two years' imprisonment, and he was confined in the Liebtenau detention center until May 1923.

Mend was then presented with an undreamed-of opportunity by the spectacular rise of his wartime comrade Adolf Hitler to prominence among Bavaria's right-wing nationalists. He gambled on the assumption that his knowledge of their wartime years together would not be a matter of indifference to such an ambitious politician. Immediately after his release, therefore, he tried to dog the party leader's footsteps. Our only knowledge of his approach to Hitler stems from a letter, not extant in the original, which the latter wrote to Mend on June 28, 1923.[11] This letter and another communication sent to Mend's Stuttgart address on July 5, 1923, are recorded in the mail book kept by Fritz Lauboeck, Hitler's current secretary, which also contains another important clue: Mend was sent sums of money amounting to RM 100 and RM 300 respectively.[12] One can only speculate about the purpose of these payments. Were they meant to dissuade his wartime comrade from doing something stupid?

Thereafter Mend worked abroad as a jockey for several years, first in Amsterdam and later in Brussels. We are ignorant of the background to this fresh start in life, but it is conceivable that Hitler had something to do with it. The next thing we know about Mend is that he spent four months in a Würzburg hospital. Discharged early in 1930, he went to Stuttgart for six months and eventually, in November 1930, took up residence in Munich once more. He received another conviction during this period, this time for forging documents in an attempt to obtain a veteran's disability pension. But he soon bethought himself of a more lucrative field of activity. By 1930 his former comrade Hitler was a focus of public interest and on the brink of assuming political power in the German Reich. At any rate, we can readily imagine what this simple but enterprising man must have felt when he compared his own lot with that of the former regimental runner: Why should Hitler, who had done no more than himself during the war, be enjoying such a meteoric rise in the world? What could be more unfair! In any case we know that Mend succeeded in gaining access to Hitler's entourage at the end of 1930. The atmosphere was "frenzied," he later recalled. "Every thought and wish in Hitler's immediate circle was focused exclusively on self-interest."[13]

Astonishingly enough, Mend actually managed to gain access to the "Führer" himself. We know this from a reliable source: "He was a supporter of the NSDAP before it came to power," says a Gestapo file. "At that time, Mend consorted with senior figures in the NSDAP and with the Führer."[14] He was soon to be seen among the faithful followers whom Hitler used to gather around him at his regular haunt, the Café Heck. "I formed the impression," says Mend, "that Hitler was trying to get me on his side."[15] For what reason? The answer is embodied in *Adolf Hitler im Felde 1914–1918*, which Huber Verlag published under Hans Mend's name in the fall of 1931.[16] In Mend's own words, it was Hitler's "inner circle [that] urged me"[17] to write this book—a task for which he lacked the most elementary prerequisites. He couldn't string a sentence together properly, let alone a whole book. It would appear that something else was involved here. Was Hitler trying to purchase Mend's silence? This possibility is indicated not least by the political context in which Mend's literary project must be viewed. In 1931 the Social Democratic *Münchener Post* had begun to take a close look at Hitler's war record, and had promptly unearthed material that reflected badly on him.[18] What was now required was some well-directed counterpropaganda that would lend credence to the combat veteran myth publicized by Hitler in *Mein Kampf*. But the personal aspect was quite as important. The publication of Mend's war memoirs by a firm devoid of formal party-political ties (although known since the 1920s as a publisher of nationalistic literature)[19] was not only intended to present Hitler's irksome comrade with a source of income; above all, he was to be rendered harmless by getting him to present a favorable account of his wartime experiences with Hitler.[20] It was a successful coup, a precautionary device that generated useful "Führer" propaganda and drew Mend into the fold at the same time. He took the bait and was trapped from then on.

We do not know who concocted a semireadable book out of the wartime anecdotes and incidents Mend could still recall in 1930/31, but *Adolf Hitler im Felde* was published and, thanks not least to the NSDAP's media machine, widely read. It was promptly dismissed on the left as a "semiofficial Party publication"—indeed, Egon Erwin Kisch described it as "the military supplement" to Hitler's own book.[21] Its tendentious contents can be quickly summarized; the foreword and introduction say it all. According to the publisher, the book was directed at the numerous skeptics who wanted to know "where the new Führer . . . Adolf Hitler was during the World War and what he did there." Now, "a living witness and wartime comrade" had been found "who fought and suffered side by side with Adolf Hitler." The memoirs of this "simple soldier" would bring the German people "minor episodes from the unknown years" during which his comrade Adolf Hitler fought "for the German Fatherland." Mend: "In this book, I want to give the German people true and unvarnished information about 'Adolf Hitler as a front-line soldier.' As a comrade I had many opportunities to hear his pronouncements on the war, witness his bravery, and become acquainted with his brilliant traits of character. . . . I aim to prove that he was just the same in the field as he is today: courageous, fearless, outstanding." The quintessence runs as follows: "Everyone who knew him in the field had to admit that he was a model front-line soldier" who "as a combat orderly in static warfare performed superhuman feats in a dangerous and responsible position."

As if that were not enough, Hitler had also distinguished himself politically during the Great War. His "sound ideology" had even then amounted to a fusion of nationalism and socialism and, of course, to "delivering the Germanic race from Jewish parasites and sending those racial corruptors and exploiters of the nation to Palestine." Mend had prophesied as early as 1916 "that we will hear much more of him. We have only to wait until his time comes." Even under the impact of military defeat in November 1918 "he did not lose faith in the German people. He assured us that he was ready to risk his life and would throw his whole self into avenging the betrayal of the German nation and its dead. His sentiments never wavered, even during the revolution, and he remained just as we knew him for years in the field." The conclusion: "If every German had thought and acted in as German a way and done his soldierly duty in the war as well as Adolf Hitler did, . . . we should have been spared this shameful peace."

But Mend and his ghostwriter did not keep strictly to their unofficial agreement with those who were employing them. For one thing, they laid on their hagiographic colors a little too thickly, even for the gullible reader, and sometimes failed to present their hero in the best possible light. For another, they did something which then verged almost on sacrilege: they made fairly outspoken references to Hitler's shabby appearance, his quirks and poses, and it is in these unintentionally comical passages that their portrayal of him seems most authentic. Mend justified the disclosure of these details by saying that, after all, he and Hitler were bound by "a comradeship known only to the genuine front-line soldier." They were "as used to one another as brothers."

Here are a few samples of this approach: "I caught up to Adolf Hitler and Runner Schmidt behind the houses in Lavarie. They were surprised that I wasn't riding my gray and poked fun at me. Hitler, in his humorous way, bowed to me like a master of ceremonies bowing to his king. To cut his kidding short, I spurred my chestnut on, with the result that it lashed out and would have struck Hitler with its forefeet if he hadn't vaulted the trench as nimbly as a greyhound. . . .

Hitler and Schmidt . . . promptly continued on their way to the trench. Hitler doffed his helmet as he passed by and called, 'Au revoir, Herr Rittmeister [Captain of Cavalry]!' I called after him, 'Push off, or I'll throw a shovelful of muck at you!'" Or again: "There were innumerable rats in the room where we slept. Hitler passed the time by putting them to flight with his bayonet when they kept him awake during the night. He was lying beside me, and he trod so hard on my feet whenever he jumped up abruptly, I could have yelled. I was so angry, I hurled a riding boot at his head. Things like that didn't annoy him, though—he persisted in his rat hunt regardless. He didn't react to a variety of military nicknames, either. In the end I simply let him carry on hunting." Hitler as a humorist and nuisance: that was one side of him as recounted by Mend. The other was the bohemian attitude he preserved even in the war. "On quiet days, when there was little to do, everyone passed the time as he pleased. . . . Adolf Hitler occupied himself mainly with literature and painting. He used to caricature Viennese Jewish types with great skill." He could also expatiate "like a professor" on German art history, his "favorite subject." It is noticeable that Mend continually reverts to Hitler's inseparable friendship with Ernst Schmidt. The last scene in his book tells how he met them together on Munich's Rathausplatz in January 1919: "Hitler was in working clothes and looking for lodgings." When we reflect that Mend characterizes Hitler elsewhere as a thoroughgoing "misogynist," this was more than a jibe.[22]

By divulging all these piquant details, Mend was well on the way to making the "Führer" look ridiculous, and one wonders what inspired him: sly calculation, effrontery or mere stupidity? Hitler is said to have been extremely annoyed by the book, as we know from Mend himself and from Max Amann, Hitler's close friend.[23] It is all the more remarkable, therefore, that he made no attempt to disown Mend. This would clearly have been too risky. Hitler knew only too well that his private life and his past would be publicly debated, now that he possessed political clout, and that Mend's knowledge of him could easily become an object of public curiosity—in other words, dangerous to him. As long as hostile organs of the press regarded the book simply as a panegyric designed to present him "as a war hero"[24] for political purposes, he could live with it. In any event, the *Völkischer Beobachter* staunchly recommended Mend's volume of memoirs as "the finest Christmas gift for any supporter of Hitler."[25]

So Hitler had perforce to limit himself to cold-shouldering "Ghost Rider." This only provoked more trouble, however. Mend's self-importance had been boosted by his debut as an "author," so he could not have failed to take umbrage at this sudden rebuff from the man in whose company he had so recently preened himself. He had doubtless regarded his public testimony as the springboard to a new career, and now this!

But Mend, we must keep in mind, was a parasitical hanger-on (who had fallen into disfavor), not an astute tactician. He was itching for a fight, and the inevitable happened on October 8, 1932. Feeling thoroughly hard done by, he confronted Hitler in his usual hangout, the Café Heck, and made a scene. "Listen, Adolf," he is said to have shouted, "why are you ignoring me? Have you forgotten your benefactor? To whose credit is it that you're here at all? We'll talk about that later, you half-man, you jumped-up knife grinder. You're going to get it in the neck from me tomorrow, in writing. I'm warning you, Adolf, don't tempt me!"[26] And sure enough, instead of leaving it at this theatrical threat, Mend triggered a regular scandal. The very next day, Fritz Gerlich, Hitler's fiercest journalistic opponent,[27] published an open letter from Mend to Hitler in his periodical, *Der Gerade Weg*. With this, the whole affair took on the features of a classic blackmail maneuver. "If my book had cited all the details of what I deliberately suppressed," Mend wrote bluntly, "Hitler would certainly not have emerged as a great hero. I advise him not to venture too far into higher spheres. It would be far better for him and his party if he remembered what he used to be."[28] As he recalled some months later, Mend "wrote that letter in the language I had been accustomed to use to Hitler in the old days."[29] A language that may possibly have been acceptable between them hitherto. By going public now, however, Mend had broken one of the demimonde's elementary rules. That meant war—a war Mend could never win.

For one thing, it was unlikely that a sexual denunciation—the real crux of Mend's threat—would have led at that stage to Hitler's political downfall. It could easily have been dismissed as a "muckraking campaign by ignoble enemies of the Fatherland"—a point I shall discuss in greater detail in connection with the Röhm affair. For another, Mend was too insignificant and his credibility too vulnerable. Proof of his own "misdemeanors" could easily have been produced. Finally, by dissociating himself from his own war memoirs, which were on sale in every Nazi bookstore, he was bound to harm himself most of all. He had ventured too far—and overreached himself. The great response his open letter evoked in the anti-Nazi press may have confirmed that realization. Although his attacks on Hitler were registered with satisfaction, no effort was made to welcome or court him as an ally. And Hitler, the target of his blackmail, kept him in suspense by displaying strong nerves and simply biding his time.

At the end of November 1932, in view of this situation, Mend went to the defensive; that is the only possible conclusion to be drawn from his press release dated December 1, 1932.[30] Although a trace of muscle-flexing is still detectable in his assertion that the publisher had "substantially altered and abridged" the "original draft" of his Hitler memoirs in the Party's favor, or that Hitler had done no more, as a runner, "than duty strictly demanded," Mend's general tone has suddenly become quite muted. He conveys the impression that he went public "only out of resentment at Hitler's uncomradely behavior"— indeed, because "Adolf Hitler's entourage contrived to keep me from him although he had assured me of his friendship by letter." He did not deserve this curt rebuff because he had "selflessly supported and defended Adolf Hitler, my former wartime comrade, and his party, even at the risk of my own life." Such was the basic tenor of his extremely confused apologia, which made no further reference to any "deliberately suppressed" details relating to Hitler's past history.

The budding dictator could breathe freely again, but that did not prevent him from subjecting his challenger to immense pressure. "I felt I was under constant observation after that," Mend recorded in 1939, and pointed to the anonymous threatening letters and other attempts at intimidation with which he was suddenly confronted after New Year's 1933. However, worse was to come when Hitler assumed power. To cite Mend's own account of what happened: "I was fast asleep on the night of March 9, 1933 (the day the [Munich] Rathaus was stormed) when the door burst open and, on awakening, I saw two revolvers leveled at me. 'What do you want, you bandits?' I called from my bed. Answer: 'Say another word, and you'll get a bullet in the head.' I: 'I wouldn't put it past you.' In the darkness I made out two men in Party uniform. Then a third man in civilian clothes came in and said, in a quieter voice: 'Ghost Rider, you're coming with us.' I got dressed, the two men in SA uniform covering me with their cocked revolvers all the time. One of them was Kugler, later of the Reichstag directorate, and the other Groll, central office director. They took me down to the car. 'Braunes Haus?' I asked. "No,' replied the civilian, 'police headquarters.' I was greeted when I got there by Counselor Beck, later of the Gestapo. He ordered me into solitary confinement, his parting words being: 'Keep quiet.' Hitler learned of my arrest by chance (?). I was released at Whitsun on his personal orders, so I was told. I had been in strict solitary confinement throughout that time."[31]

We know that nothing was done in Mend's case without Hitler's express orders. He was "taken into protective custody on the instructions of Obergruppenführer Brückner, the Führer's personal aide."[32] What is striking and interesting here is this: the persecution of the would-be blackmailer did not yet extend to his physical annihilation, but was initially meant to place him under a renewed obligation with the aid of intimidation and subsequent clemency. Mend was intended to realize that Hitler alone could save him from perdition, but that the "Führer's" intervention entailed his absolute loyalty—indeed, his submission. Mend got the message at once, as witness his remorseful letter to NSDAP treasurer Schwarz, in which he requested readmission to the Party a few days after his release. All at once, it was "slanders and calumnies" that had disrupted his relations with Hitler and led to "the rift in our mutual friendship and comradeship." He "disclaimed all reponsibility in this matter" but was "ready at any time to issue a retraction [of his open letter]." Despite his three months in solitary, he was "in accordance with my personal impulses, totally and completely behind my wartime comrade Adolf Hitler and his work, and I am the last person to fail to support him in his onerous responsibilities in behalf of the German people."[33] Moreover, Mend had "at that time burned a great deal of incriminating evidence"[34]—doubtless at the behest of higher authority.

But readmission to the Party was as much out of the question as a personal audience with Hitler or his aides. Mend was merely tolerated and placed under surveillance. "It was outrageous for me simply to be expelled from the Party at the eleventh hour," he had written to Schwarz in July 1933. "All I want," he added fervently, "is my rights!" But his faux pas ruled this out. Mend made several attempts to see Hitler again and requested his aide "to submit [his letter] to the Führer in person," being "convinced that Adolf Hitler will grant me, his closest wartime comrade, an interview." He wanted to use this to make it clear, once for all, that he had been "only the victim of certain informers who wanted to make money out of my experiences with Adolf Hitler."[35] But the illusion that he might be officially rehabilitated, possibly by Hitler in person, was finally dispelled in March 1935, when Hitler's aide, Fritz Wiedemann, formally acquainted him with the fact that his presence would not be welcomed.[36] This had been preceded by an internal memo from Amann "not to admit Dispatch Rider Mend" because the Führer "[has] refused to speak with Mend." He added: "I consider Mend to be an unmitigated rogue."[37]

Although it might be supposed that Mend was finished after this brush-off, 1934 and 1935 appear to have been the most stable time of his life. Having changed his Munich address eight times between 1930 and 1933, he now, for the first time, moved into a decent apartment on Nymphenburger Strasse, where he lived for several years.[38] We are told that he also had lodgings in Berg on the Starnbergersee, where he helped to run the Elsholz estate. The parish clerk later recalled that he was "always neatly dressed but didn't work, and I often wondered what he lived on."[39] We know the answer: for a start, there was his book about Hitler, of which the Nazi Eherverlag brought out a new edition in 1934, despite the Führer's reprimand, and which must have earned him some royalties. A shorthand edition came out the same year. "By order of the Reich government," Mend wrote proudly to his brother, it was introduced as a textbook into "all the junior and senior high schools in Germany."[40] This must have constituted a substantial source of income. Mend's recollections of Hitler were also quoted on the radio, and there was even talk of filming them.[41] In addition, Mend was now operating as an art dealer; more precisely, he dealt in paintings and charcoal and pencil drawings by Hitler, which are known to have been much sought after in the mid-1930s. His customers included Baldur von Schirach, Otto Dietrich, Julius Schreck, and other prominent Nazis. In November 1935 he tried to interest Hitler in his pictorial treasures, but the latter let it be known that he had no wish to acquire any.[42] Mend's approach must have reawakened the dictator's mistrust of Mend, for he could hardly have welcomed the fact that his wartime paintings were being marketed by such an unreliable customer. Mend simply knew too much.

But there was something else: Mend possessed numerous original photographs of Hitler, and there was no doubt that he would now, in his art dealer's capacity, be hawking them around, mainly for publicity purposes. According to subsequent depositions, they depicted Hitler in poses that were not only highly unflattering but may also have attested to his suspiciously intimate relationship with many a fellow soldier.[43] For the purposes of Mend's business, however, they were a form of self-recommendation that showed he had been a close wartime friend of the "Führer." A woman who had seen these photographs stated in February 1958: "Mend said that the Gestapo were after him, and that Hitler wanted to get hold of the pictures at all costs."[44] This may have been why Hitler's henchmen targeted Mend yet again. After a two-year respite, trouble loomed once more.

To quote Mend's own account: "In the summer of 1936, I, too, was destined to get it in the neck. I was taken to court on a trivial, trumped-up charge. District Judge Welz, a holder of the Blood Order, presided. According to Kriminalrat [Detective Superintendent] Weiss of the Gestapo (formerly in the Bavarian People's Party and a good friend of mine), Welz had gone to the Gestapo and said, referring to me: 'Let's destroy him.' State Attorney Seiler led for the prosecution. As he himself told me later: 'It left a nasty taste in my mouth.'"[45]

What had happened? We do not know, exactly, because the police and court records of the case have disappeared—possibly an indication of how potentially explosive it was. Mend alleges that he was arrested without warning while being interviewed by the police. This enabled the Gestapo to take advantage of his absence to carry out exhaustive house searches in Munich and Berg, where they appropriated certain documents. Two years later, when Mend had long since been sentenced to a prison term and learned of this search from his attorney, he pressed his landlady for more details: Had the charcoal drawings and "other things by the Führer" in his possession also been taken away? He was thinking mainly of Hitler's "letters, which must not under any circumstances get into unauthorized hands." Had those "to me, irreplaceable documents been confiscated too?"[46] They had, and Mend would never see them again. The same applied to "my watch, which the Führer had given me." When Mend's attorney tried to get these articles returned, the Munich Gestapo informed him that "the photographs, etc., [had been] confiscated on orders from higher authority at Gestapo headquarters in Berlin. There was no longer any question of returning them."[47] At around the same time, Mend's book was also "withdrawn and destroyed on instructions from Gestapo headquarters in Berlin and by agreement with the Führer's Chancellery."[48]

We may assume that in 1936 Mend fell victim to an operation planned at long range and ordained by Hitler himself. He was to be finished off with the aid of a criminal charge that would not only consign him to prison but ruin his reputation. That charge—"sexual offenses against children"—earned him two and a half years' hard labor and three years' loss of civil rights. Mend denied it to his dying day, and he may well have been in the right, especially as we now know how unscrupulously the Nazi regime threatened or instituted trials for sexual offenses in order to damage awkward opponents' reputations and make them "see reason."[49] Criminal proceedings of this kind appeared to be quite legal, but their outcome was really dictated by Hitler. This applied to Hans Mend's trial, in which even the public prosecutor asked for no more than a term of imprisonment.[50] He was to be made a particularly brutal object lesson. A few weeks after being convicted he was taken to see District Forensic Physician Dr. Vogel, who happily confirmed to his superiors on December 16, 1936, that Mend was a "psychopath with a tendency to obey his sexual urges."[51] Mend had to spend six months in Straubing Penitentiary, Lower Bavaria, and was then sent "for observation" to the psychiatric wing of Munich's Stadelheim Penitentiary. "Expert" evidence was to be adduced "that Mend undoubtedly poses a grave danger to the public because of his criminal urges" and, thus, that the police should be authorized to take him into protective custody at any time. Such a decree was, in fact, issued on December 14, 1937.[52] Mend was taken first to Brual Rhede concentration camp and then to Esterwegen camp. His tribulations did not end, at least temporarily, until December 24, 1938, or exactly two years after he was detained. He was released, placed on probation until December 24, 1942, and permitted to return to Munich.

But what had the Nazis made of this man? Branded as a loathsome sex offender, Mend had lost his reputation and his moral integrity; he was a dangerous criminal who could be rearrested for the slightest misdemeanor. Why this policy of wholesale repression, these drastic methods of intimidation? Just to teach an insignificant braggart a lesson? One would think not. Despite the transparency of Mend's self-important behavior, he did possess a power Hitler was clearly afraid of: the power to divulge his insurmountable past. That past lived on within the unpredictable "Ghost Rider," and Hitler must have felt haunted by it. Yet his former comrade was playing with fire. Because Hitler regarded Mend as a constant source of danger, he embarked on a preemptive strike: the confiscation of Mend's letters, photographs and pictures, which was intended to banish the dictator's fear that his wartime comrade might ever embarrass him again. Furthermore, Mend's stigmatization as a "sex offender" had robbed him of all credibility.

It is possible that Mend had failed to realize all this when he returned to Berg in January 1939 and resumed work as an estate manager. He certainly did not go around in sackcloth and ashes, and in the fall of 1939 he had to be "admonished by the Gestapo for making subversive remarks."[53] In December 1939, as we recounted at the beginning of this chapter, he went so far as to divulge his secret information to an opponent of the regime. What can have prompted him to take such a suicidal step? His hatred of Hitler, certainly, and the powers of persuasion wielded by Schmid Noerr, who may perhaps have convinced him that Hitler would soon be overthrown. Or was it the despairing courage of a man who had nothing more to lose and took the plunge in consequence? Whatever his primary motive, Mend's statement acquires considerable credibility when set against the background described above. By making it, Mend risked more than he could ever hope to gain—indeed, he was gambling with his life. "I'm letting fate take its course," he told his landlady not long before he was released. "I've faced death so often, after all. I've become hardened."[54]

Persecution by the Nazi legal system seems to have made Mend more outspoken on the subject of Hitler's homosexual proclivities than ever before. "What he told me, he told a lot of people," the Starnberg theologian and art historian Dr. Herbert Paulus said later, and added: "It all strengthened me in my opposition to the National Socialist system, because he never exaggerated."[55] But in 1940 there were many more supporters than opponents of the National Socialist system, notably those who had been instructed to keep a close watch on the "psychopath." One of them, undoubtedly, was Karl Laux, mayor of Berg and local Nazi boss, who knew perfectly well that his Party members were only waiting to find some "valid reason" and suitable opportunity to get Mend back into "some form of protective custody."[56] It is hardly surprising, therefore, that Laux reported Mend in September 1940 for having "grossly slandered the Führer." The witness, Eva König, had laid this accusation "through an older Party member of her acquaintance in Munich."[57] The trap closed once more: Mend was arrested, retrospectively charged with various sexual offenses (this time against women) and sentenced by Munich's special court to two years' imprisonment.[58] On February 14, 1942, Zwickau Penitentiary tersely informed the public prosecutor's office in Munich that Mend had died.[59] He may have guessed his fate while on remand two years earlier, when he wrote to his girlfriend: "I can foresee my end. I've simply been in the world too long."[60]

As for the transcript of these last criminal proceedings, the prosecuting authorities were instructed to "submit [it] to the Reich Minister of Justice" without delay.[61] This underlines Hitler's continuing interest in the Mend affair—a well-founded interest, since the recent trial involved the question of "why the Führer doesn't get married." We shall never know whether Mend raised the subject himself, as the informer alleged, or whether, as Mend claimed, she deliberately provoked him into doing so. What matters more is Mend's answer to the question.[62] He said he knew it perfectly well, because no one knew the Führer better than he did. He had often seen him naked, and could not detect any malformation of the genitals. But the Führer was uninterested in women; he shared the same proclivities as Röhm. How did he know? Because during the war he had occupied the bunk beneath Hitler's. The court was in no doubt that Mend's remarks had imputed "homosexual love" to the Führer; "in particular, he did not shrink, as a former wartime comrade of the Führer's, from attacking him in the most shameless manner."[63] In 1958 Eva König disclosed that Mend had said something else: "When they had baths [thus Mend on the subject of Hitler's behavior during the war] they always ran around naked. Then Hitler did all kinds of things with them and went around with them in the night."[64] At around the same time, Mend is alleged to have told parish clerk Schneider: "In the billet . . . he [Mend] and other men had smeared Hitler's 'prick' with boot polish while he was asleep."[65] A peculiarly coarse way of shaming homosexual comrades, but evidently quite common in the extreme living conditions of the front line.

A familiarity with the relevant "customs" prevailing during World War I makes it easy to place Mend's outspoken account of these incidents in a historical context.[66] The communal existence of soldiers in wartime always embodied libidinous aspects as a matter of course. One must not overlook the "consciously erotic nature" of wartime comradeship, which Magnus Hirschfeld claims was "not exactly rare" during World War I.[67] Homosocial life at the front was perfectly suited to concealing homosexual relationships. These were seldom severely punished even when reported—indeed, there were male communities that shared this proclivity or at least accepted it. So why, provided he could be sure of his comrades' discretion, should Lance Corporal Hitler have refrained from following such inclinations?

This raises the question of what we actually know about Hitler in World War I.[68] Although he probably enjoyed being a soldier, he showed no interest in pursuing a military career. He performed his duties as a runner and orderly at regimental headquarters to his superiors' satisfaction, but repeatedly turned down offers of promotion. He clearly regarded the regiment as his home—indeed, the family from which he was reluctant to be parted under any circumstances. Being exempted from combat duties "up front," he came through the war without sustaining any serious wounds. In the rear echelon he spent his time making drawings—mostly of the billet and his comrades—or writing poetry. He wrote few letters, on the other hand, because there was little he cared for outside his life in the army. It is readily understandable, from the psychological aspect, that he seems to have been thoroughly content with army life: he felt accepted, just as he had in the men's hostel; more than that, he felt he belonged. Another reason for his almost conspicuous sense of well-being in a wartime environment may have been his friendship with Ernst Schmidt, which merits closer examination.

ERNST SCHMIDT

For five years, from the summer of 1914 to the summer of 1919, Adolf Hitler and Ernst Schmidt were inseparable. Hitler never had a closer or more enduring friendship. In particular, no one witnessed Hitler's transformation from a would-be artist without party-political affiliations into an extreme right-wing politician at closer quarters than Schmidt, his wartime comrade, who did not die until 1985. We would know considerably more about Schmidt if historians had taken a greater interest in him, publishers had encouraged him to write his memoirs or archivists had examined the papers he left behind. None of this happened, unfortunately. No trace of his personal papers can be found even at Garching, where he was mayor for years. We do, however, know this much about him:[69]

Born in Wurzbach, Thuringia, on December 16, 1889, Ernst Schmidt was one of a flour miller's numerous children. Apprenticed to a decorator after attending school (1896–1904), he qualified in 1907. On his own submission, he spent his journeyman's time working "in various parts of Germany until 1912, in Switzerland in 1913, in France, and, from the spring of 1914 until the outbreak of war, in Bolzano."[70] Although liable for the draft, he had done no military service prior to 1914. One reason for this may be his sojourns abroad, which were fairly exceptional for the period.

We do not know when and where Schmidt first made Hitler's acquaintance. The journeyman decorator may have been a Munich neighbor of his at 34 Schleissheimer Strasse,[71] but this cannot be ascertained beyond doubt. The only certainty is that Schmidt joined the Bavarian army on the same day as Hitler—August 6, 1914—and was assigned to the List Regiment on September 7. Schmidt and Hitler were together from the first day in barracks, and they both served on the Western Front from October 1914 on. Employed as regimental runners, they jointly delivered one message with such efficiency—or so we are told—that from November 1914 on they were permanently assigned to regimental headquarters as so-called combat orderlie. As such, they had more freedom within the military hierarchy than other enlisted men. They were "always together,"[72] in Schmidt's own words, and shared the same quarters. They were invariably to be seen as a couple, not only when jointly delivering regimental orders to brigade or battalion, but off duty behind the lines.

Although regimental runners were on quite close terms in any case,

Ernst Schmidt told a journalist in 1933 that "three of us in particular seemed to hang together: Hitler, Bachmann, and I. Personally, I was very much drawn to Hitler."[73] The runners' section at Fromelles and Fournes, where Hitler spent most time during the war, must have been a particularly close community. Balthasar Brandmayer refers, in a far from pejorative way, to the "runners' bunch" of which his friend "Adi" was a permanent feature.[74] To his dying day, Hitler never forgot what it had meant to him to have comrades such as Jacob Weiss, Franz Wimmer, Max Mund, Josef Inkofer and Brandmayer himself. The same went for his two most important superiors, senior orderly Karl Lippert and, above all, regimental clerk Max Amann. Thanks to them, Hitler successfully adapted to the military service he had so firmly rejected until 1914. Although his precipitate attempt to volunteer for the Bavarian army early in August 1914 may only have been a way of evading deportation to Austria, the more he realized that the exceptional conditions prevailing in wartime would enable him to shake off the burdensome constraints of bourgeois society, the more he must have found that the transition to a military existence improved his quality of life. For it was here that he discovered what he would later call "the glorious meaning of a male community"[75]—the community in which he could survive.

Hitler's dependence on these special circumstances became apparent on October 5, 1916, when he, Bachmann and Schmidt were wounded by a direct hit on the runners' dugout. Hitler and Bachmann were taken to the field hospital at Beelitz, Schmidt to Brandenburg. After being discharged they met up in Munich with two other runners, Max Mund and Franz Wimmer. They celebrated Christmas 1916 in the barracks, anxiously wondering whether they would be allowed to rejoin their regiment at the front. Hitler did his utmost to avoid a transfer. Immediately after being wounded in October 1916 he had almost tearfully implored the adjutant, Fritz Wiedemann, for permission to remain with the regiment. Writing from Munich in January

1917, he reiterated his request for reassignment "to the 16th Reserve Infantry Regiment" because it was his "most urgent wish" to rejoin his "former comrades."[76] Hitler also bombarded Sergeant Amann with similar requests. He could not have conveyed more clearly how vitally important to him this soldierly community was. The same thing is evident from his correspondence with his "dear partner" Brandmayer, of whom he thought "so often" that he wrote him three postcards in the space of a single week: "Hoping to see you again soon, your comrade and partner."[77] Hitler eventually attained his objective: in March 1917 he was reassigned to his regiment, his "elective family."

Therein probably lies the key to a still unanswered question: Why did Hitler remain a lance corporal throughout the war? His toadying to higher authority, if not his efficiency, should have earned him promotion. We are told that he was offered it[78] but refused. It would probably be more correct to say that he could not bring himself to accept. As a noncom he would sooner or later have been obliged to give up what had hitherto enabled him to tolerate war service so well: Ernst Schmidt, his other faithful partners, a relatively safe existence in the rear echelon, and, possibly also, a toleration of the homosexual tendencies he could not have pursued as a noncommissioned officer. Hitler would doubtless have been faced with an existential crisis, hence the positive "horror" with which he reacted to his sergeant's attempts to promote him.

Egon Erwin Kisch—himself a runner in World War I—asserted in 1933 that something had to be amiss with Hitler's military career: "He was a lance corporal for four years. Every old soldier knows that the (somewhat derided) rank of lance corporal is only brief and temporary, only a preliminary to (more senior) noncommissioned rank. Hundreds of thousands of men can be infantrymen and never make lance corporal, but a lance corporal who never makes sergeant in four years' 'front-line' service must be a very suspect type. Either he shirks commanding a squad, or he is incompetent to do so. . . . The nonpromotion of this eternally unpromoted lance corporal would seem still more grotesque if he had really been awarded the Iron Cross 1st Class, no evidence of which was found in his paybook aside from a scribbled entry; neither the recommendation nor the citation. Hitler . . . never breathes a word about the feat of arms for which he won the order."[79]

Such is the case, and we do not know to this day why Hitler really won the Iron Cross 1st Class in 1918. The most credible version was advanced by Eugen Tanhäuser in 1961. According to this, a Jewish staff officer named Sigmund Gutmann promised Hitler the decoration if he delivered a message in peculiarly dangerous circumstances, but later, when Hitler had accomplished his mission, found it hard to keep that promise. Gutmann told Tanhäuser that he had had to badger the divisional commander for two months or more[80]—indeed, it was stated in 1933 that Hitler had waited to be invested with the order for almost three years.[81] The probable reason for this delay was not that Gutmann's superiors considered his recommendation unjustified, but that it was unthinkable to confer so high a decoration on a lance corporal without simultaneously promoting him[82]—and Hitler would not be promoted. There must surely have been an informative exchange of letters on the subject, but Hitler saw to it that this military correspondence was later destroyed or manipulated.[83] It was a curious business notwithstanding, and Nazi propagandists during the years 1930–33 found it difficult to present the historical facts to the public in a reasonably convincing manner.[84]

But to revert to Hitler and Schmidt. The two men went on furlough together from September 30 to October 17, 1917. They made a sightseeing tour of Brussels, Cologne, Leipzig and Dresden, after which Hitler traveled on to Berlin, where he spent his time visiting museums, and Schmidt went home to Wurzbach.[85] Dating from this period is the only item of correspondence from Hitler to Schmidt whose contents are public knowledge: a postcard signed "Best regards. Yours, A.

Hitler"[86]—singularly colorless testimony to such a long and intimate friendship.

Hitler told Schmidt a great deal about his favorite subjects, art and architecture, during the war. He gave him a number of drawings and watercolors and probably made portraits of him as well, just as he did of other fellow soldiers. Schmidt was receptive to such things, being impressed by Hitler's "artistic nature." When Hitler kept talking about his professional future, Schmidt encouraged him to take advantage of his artistic talents and systematically develop them after the war.[87] Another of Hitler's comrades, Ignaz Westenkirchner, later recalled that he planned to become an artist. "In order to survive until the examination," he is said to have told Westenkirchner, "I shall sell my pictures again. Or perhaps I'll join those loudmouthed politicians."[88] Schmidt confirmed to the historian Werner Maser that Hitler had not known, up to the end of the war, whether to become a painter or a politician.[89] If a politician, one is bound to ask, of what color? Schmidt himself belonged to a free trade union, so it is unlikely that he was averse to Marxism and social reform. Thus the prime factor in his relationship with Hitler was probably less political than aesthetic.

On November 7, 1918, as the war was drawing to a close, Schmidt went to Munich. There, two weeks later, he met Hitler, who had come to Bavaria in a mood of deep concern[90] after a spell in a hospital at Pasewalk, Pomerania. The two homeless, unemployed men "cemented" their "old friendship," as Schmidt put it, and resolved to make their way through these troubled times together.[91] From the end of January 1919, after serving briefly in Traunstein POW camp, they scraped by, making a living as casual laborers with a Munich demobilization company. They nonetheless earned enough for visits to the opera: "We only bought the cheapest seats, but that didn't matter. Hitler was lost in the music to the very last note; blind and deaf to all else around him."[92] This statement is important because it says something about Hitler's continuing obsessions. Operatic music retained its enchantment for him, its intoxicating, escapist quality, even in those critical days of revolution and counterrevolution. Hitler also made contact with well-known Munich painters such as Max Zaeper, to whom he gave several of his works for expert appraisal. He had still not abandoned his artistic dreams, even in the revolutionary year 1919. All his options were open: he remained irresolute, both politically and professionally.[93]

For the most part, however, Hitler continued to cling during 1919 to the authority whose 40 marks' army pay could at least enable him to keep his head above water: the military. He soon received some extra income from the same source. On March 7, 1919, he made the acquaintance of Captain Ernst Röhm—"in a cellar," as Hitler himself claimed later, "where we racked our brains for ways of combating the revolutionary movement."[94] In all probability, this form of words was a euphemism for Hitler's employment as an informer by Röhm, who was then chief of staff to Epp, the Freikorps commander. Röhm had recently begun to recruit Bavarian mercenaries with the aid of a leaflet campaign.[95] Hitler's activities as an informer are attested by another source, which states that he had originally been hired by the intelligence service of that counterrevolutionary organization, and had there received his instructions from Röhm.[96] Hitler is reputed to have been particularly close to Munich's revolutionary "soldiers' councils" in the spring of 1919,[97] but only two months later he joined the 2nd Infantry's "discharge and fact-finding board," a body set up immediately after the counterrevolutionaries had triumphed. This job, which he would scarcely have obtained without Röhm's recommendation, entailed checking on the political convictions of comrades due for discharge.

Before long, Hitler was working for the intelligence department of Reichswehrgruppenkommando [military district headquarters] IV under Captain Karl Mayr, once again as an informer. Mayr, who had quickly discerned Hitler's special ability in this sphere, employed him to systematically denounce politically unreliable officers and enlisted men.[98] If Mayr's description of his "snitch" is correct, Hitler was very relieved to be offered a new "home,"[99] and he must have reacted in an extremely conformist and submissive manner. No book on Hitler has ever raised the question of what he really had to offer Mayr for the latter to protect him in this way. Nothing we know about that ambitious staff officer's life suggests that altruism could have been involved. In 1928 he coldly described Hitler as "an individual, paid by the month, from whom regular information could be expected."[100] Mayr was an unscrupulous, go-getting secret service chief who, once the imperial regime had collapsed, wanted to help the counterrevolution to triumph at all costs.[101] Thus there are only two possibilities: either he had personal reasons for making a protégé of Hitler, or he must have thought Hitler had a natural talent for spying and denunciation. The same goes for Röhm: already a devotee of the homoerotic aspects of militaristic nationalism,[102] he sponsored Hitler in a quite exceptional manner.

———

And so, while Hitler was gambling on continued employment in the army, Ernst Schmidt the journeyman decorator was looking for work in Munich. Discharged from the army on April 12, 1919, he rented a room on Implerstrasse on April 28 but lived there for only a month or so. In June 1919 he moved to 43 Schleissheimer Strasse, the very house in which Hitler's young friend Rudolf Häusler had lived in 1913/14.[103] Schmidt and Hitler saw each other every day, shared their meals and spent the evenings together. Hitler used the barracks only as a refuge and place to stay from time to time; it is doubtful if he had a circle of friends there.[104]

In the fall of 1919 Hitler decided to stake everything on a career in politics. For the moment, however, he left his best friend in the dark about this change of direction.[105] Hitler's attempt to take refuge in an aesthetic existence had failed; his escape into a political existence now began—and that would mean, ultimately, loosening his ties with Schmidt.

On March 1, 1920, or shortly after Hitler had acquired a decisive influence within its leadership, Schmidt obediently followed him onto the political terrain and joined the Deutsche Arbeiter Partei. They still met in private, although less often at Hitler's new abode on Thierschstrasse than in the Party's favorite hostelry, the legendary "Sterneckerbräu." Schmidt was also present at Hitler's thirty-first birthday party on April 20, 1920, but in the summer of 1922 he moved to Garching an der Alz, over sixty miles from Munich. Their relationship had ended, but not their mutual affection. Schmidt never lost touch. He visited Hitler often, notably in May 1924, when the latter was imprisoned in the fortress at Landsberg. Politically, too, he remained his friend's loyal henchman. He quit the Social Democratic trade union and, in the spring of 1924, founded a local branch of the Völkischer Block, which was later absorbed into the NSDAP. Hitler expressed his thanks to Schmidt for joining the Party on May 1, 1925, by presenting his "dear and faithful wartime comrade" with a gilt-edged copy of *Mein Kampf*.[106] It even contained a personal dedication, although Hitler misspelled his friend's name "Schmiedt."

Schmidt became Garching's local Party boss in 1926. In 1931 he joined the SA [Brownshirts] as a Scharführer [roughly: staff sergeant] and rose to the rank of Sturmführer [roughly: captain]. In 1932, when the "heroic legend" surrounding Hitler's time at the front became the subject of fierce public controversy and various lawsuits, Schmidt swore affidavits in his harassed friend's defense.[107] He probably returned to Munich often in this period. A photograph taken by Eva Braun in 1932 shows him at Hitler's side in the "Osteria Bavaria," the "Führer's" favorite restaurant. As Reich Chancellor, Hitler was able to reward Schmidt generously for his loyalty and discretion, making him relatively prosperous and highly respected.

Schmidt obtained his master decorator's diploma in 1928, when he was almost forty, but it was three years before he could set up in business on his own at Garching. At first he barely earned enough to support himself, but after 1933 his financial circumstances swiftly changed for the better. By 1934 he had seven employees and was able to build a house of his own. He also acquired an automobile, which was *the* symbol of social advancement in the 1930s. Evidence actually exists that Schmidt owed all this to the protection of his newly powerful friend.[108] In 1933 he became deputy mayor of Garching, which guaranteed him further advantages, and not only in the material sphere. He was privileged to join Hitler at the Braunes Haus after the commemorative march to the Feldherrnhalle on November 9, 1933, and in 1934, when he was awarded the Party's gold badge, he was photographed with Hitler beside the Chiemsee. He often visited the Reich Chancellery in the years that followed. The dictator's consideration for his wartime comrade should be ascribed not merely to a heartfelt wish; cold calculation came into it as well. Hitler wanted to secure his old friend's absolute loyalty and feel entirely sure of his discretion. That was why he included Schmidt in his public self-dramatizations—for instance, in 1937, when the *Illustrierter Beobachter* devoted a long article to "Adolf Hitler and his front-line comrade" and quoted the latter as saying: "If the Führer ever summoned me to perform some special task, I should abandon my job and everything else, and follow him."[109]

But the call came only once: in June 1940, shortly before the armistice was signed with France, Hitler took Schmidt and Max Amann on a visit to their former theater of operations.[110] Schmidt must have construed the elaborate Nazi propaganda devoted to this spectacle as his greatest ever token of public recognition—which was just what Hitler meant it to be. Compared to that, his appointment as mayor of Garching the following year and his promotion to district head of the NSDAP in 1942 were hardly worth mentioning.

Mayor Schmidt was detained by the Americans on May 28, 1945. Consigned a week later to the labor and internment camp at Dachau, he was not released for three years. His support for Hitler remained steadfast, however, even after the downfall of the Third Reich. When interrogated by the American military authorities in 1945, he claimed to have recognized Hitler's "genius" back in 1914, adding that he was a great man in private as well.[111] Good friends of Schmidt state that, even in later years, he took care never "to say anything about Hitler that might have harmed his reputation."[112]

———

Schmidt's friendship with Hitler endured for over thirty years. If we look back on it, and especially on the period 1914-19, everything seems to favor Hans Mend's contention that this male bond was an affair of the heart, the more so since there is no indication that either Schmidt or Hitler had any relationships with women while in the army. Schmidt displayed just as little interest in women after the war, and he remained a bachelor until 1935, when he was almost forty-seven. Then, probably at the insistence of Hitler, who could not have approved of this state of affairs, he married Elisabeth Obermüller, a woman more than twenty years younger than himself. Their marriage, which remained childless, was very possibly camouflage, in any case, because Schmidt evidently had to watch his step in Garching. This is at least implicit in a statement with which he sought to defend himself at his denazification hearing in 1948. He referred to a man named Philipp Oberbuchner—"a tattler, not to be taken seriously"—who had written him "anonymous letters of malicious content." Schmidt had nonetheless "refrained from preferring charges"[113]—and he knew why.

Schmidt's personality must have closely resembled that of August Kubizek, Hitler's early love. This seems likely, at any rate, from a characteristic attributed to him by an NSDAP assessment form dated 1934: "Tends to underestimate his own abilities."[114] It was this self-effacement that made Schmidt, like Kubizek before him, so receptive to Hitler's proprietorial tactics. But Schmidt was probably receptive to art and literature as well, as his well-stocked bookcase demonstrated in 1933, when a British journalist was surprised to note that it contained works by Goethe, Schiller, Shakespeare and many other classical authors[115]—rather unusual reading matter for a house painter from a humble background. Schmidt could also express himself eloquently, to judge by his few interviews and written statements. Unless appearances are deceptive, therefore, Schmidt and Hitler were two ambitious autodidacts whose mutual attraction was based on something more than their homosexual disposition. Hitler was the guiding light, of course, but in Schmidt he had found a receptive companion who must have reawakened his old dream of an artistic existence and an intimate symbiosis with a kindred spirit. That, after all, was just what Hitler had hoped for from Kubizek and Häusler before deleting them from his life. Schmidt represented his third attempt to fulfill that dream, except that this time its nonfulfillment coincided, for Hitler, with a promising fresh start. Moreover, he and Schmidt continued to preserve their bond. The homoerotic, possibly homosexual, part of their relationship, lasted a few years; their friendship, until Hitler's death. Schmidt never "outed" himself or, consequently, Hitler.

It was Hans Mend who refused to let Hitler's "Schmidl" take the secret of his grand passion to the grave with him. Mend's revelations were prompted by a strange mixture of stupidity and cunning, envy and disappointment, recklessness and indignation. Hitler's other wartime comrades were reluctant to speak out, if only because most of them had greatly benefited from his promotion to the status of Führer and Reich Chancellor. Nearly all those who had known him

well in the army were "remembered' in one way or another after
1933—in fact, it might be rewarding to make a closer study of those
whom Hitler pledged to silence by means of preferential treatment.[116]
They were recompensed because, despite their inside information,
they made no trouble for the dictator and would never have done so.
Mend, by contrast, did not feel pledged to silence.

It remains to be added that documents containing further details of
Hitler's sex life in the army are said to have turned up in the former
records of Himmler's Sicherheitsdienst [SD, Security Service], and that
a British writer claims to have seen them at the home of an erstwhile
SD associate. In France in 1916/17, according to the said documents,
Hitler posed in the nude for a homosexual officer named Lammers—
a Berlin artist in civilian life—and subsequently went to bed with him.
When questioned in 1936, Lammers intimated that the lance corporal
had enjoyed it quite as much as he himself had, and that the drawings
were still in existence.[117] Neither the transcript of this interrogation
nor the sketches have ever found their way into a reputable archive, so
this information cannot be verified and can easily be dismissed as gossip. Whatever the truth, however, it is a consistent with the general
picture as Hermann Rauschning's statement to U.S. intelligence that
Lance Corporal Hitler and an officer had been charged with engaging
in sexual relations.[118] Being equally conceivable, this is regarded as
inadmissible speculation only by those who have a priori concluded
otherwise.

FROM MILITARY SERVICE TO POLITICAL SERVICE

To summarize: Hitler's "August 1914 experience" was less a political
awakening than a personal one. He must suddenly have felt that he
had a promising future, not just an unsatisfactory past—a chance to
escape the constraints of bourgeois morality, convention and the labor

market. That was why he so ardently craved "the struggle of 1914," as he himself put it, and why it provided a "relief from the irksome emotions of youth."[119] His choice of words is revealing. It was not the international conflict that attracted him, but a longed-for personal catharsis, the prospect of a crucial turning point in his life, and—of course—money and companionship.

Germany's defeat deprived him of his "elective home" and threw him back on his own resources. What should he do? The transformation and radicalization of public life presented him with a new escape route: politics. Hitherto, Hitler had never evolved anything resembling a political creed; what he had brought with him from Vienna amounted to little more than a motley collection of personal grudges. He conceived of himself as an ally of "ordinary folk" and may possibly, until early 1919, have been a kind of sentimental socialist. But this was not a permanent stance; on the contrary, his sociorevolutionary tendencies proved to be merely a pose, not a product of intellectual discernment. Consequently, he began by seeking his personal advantage *between* the two camps. When Hitler resolved to become a professional politician on the *völkisch* right wing, he had no idea what he was talking about. Politics, as he saw it, was just a very welcome means of self-advancement. To attain his goal he resorted to any available weapon, from antisemitic tirades to counterrevolutionary terminology culled from the arsenal of extreme nationalism.

In 1920, when Hitler at last drew mass applause—indeed, aroused wild enthusiasm with his high-flown language—he instinctively exploited that newfound ability. Ambition is the last refuge of the failure, as Oscar Wilde so aptly put it. Hitler's rhetorical gifts proved to be the talent that gained him his first real success in life. He now applied himself to his task "heart and soul."[120] He perceived that his powers of persuasion were increasingly distinguishing him from the anonymous masses, indeed, making him the repository of their hopes. He was also fortunate in appealing to the "right" men—Röhm and

Mayr, for example, who not only made use of him but somehow, despite his eccentricities, liked him and fostered his politicization. Hitler, for his part, displayed plenty of initiative. He mobilized his talent for playacting and lying in order to fulfill, and if possible surpass, the expectations associated with him. He had already—of necessity—developed that talent. Humiliation and stigmatization must have taught Hitler a great deal that may at the time have seemed a terrible lesson, but he could now take advantage of some of these behavior patterns and character traits. And there was something else that strongly motivated him. He went into politics because the chaotic world of the Weimar Republic had suddenly brought him within reach of what he had probably always craved: social esteem, a reputation for being a "real man," and, beyond that, something in the nature of reparation or rehabilitation.

Hitler believed that he could attain all these things without the need for any drastic break with his existing way of life or abandonment of his homosocial orientation. What best exemplifies this is his liaison with Ernst Röhm. He sensed that he must stake his future on Röhm, not on Mayr—in other words, on someone whose talent for organization and military skill could bring him genuine power and combat-effective mercenaries: soldiers, not party-political militants. Was it coincidental that Hitler opted for Röhm, a homosexual, and that the latter fell under Hitler's spell? It seems unlikely. To a certain extent, the sexual baggage with which Hitler entered politics determined the direction of his subsequent career.

The same is true of one particular characteristic to which Hitler largely owed his swift success in politics: the knack of lying brilliantly. He was probably the finest con man ever to have set foot on the political stage. This should not be construed in a purely pejorative sense, because Hitler lied for survival's sake—lied in order to create a second, alternative life for himself and overcome his own self-doubt. This talent was allied with two other characteristics: extreme mistrust and a pronounced capacity for dissimulation. At the beginning of the 20th century, all homosexuals *had* to develop these characteristics for fear of criminal prosecution and social ruin. This has nothing to do with timelessly valid character traits, of course. What would now be rightly condemned as discriminatory disparagement of a minority was then still regarded as a criminological fact: that homosexuals make exceptionally skillful liars.[121] The intolerance and illiberality of contemporary society left them no choice but to strive for mastery in the art of dissimulation. The same applied to Adolf Hitler, except that he must have sensed in 1919/20 that the characteristics he had been compelled to develop could be put to good use in public life.

So the personal qualities he brought with him were ideally suited to his new field of activity. In political agitation he had found a medium through which he could give vent to his pent-up emotions and accumulated prejudices; in his audiences a sounding board of which most politicians could only dream. In the view of one contemporary observer, Hitler owed his success to "his ability to transmit stirrings of emotion" and strike "a note of emotional conviction."[122] But there was yet another reason for his incredible success: absolute self-identification with Germany's political destiny, which Hitler personified better than anyone else. What he could empathize with most was the humiliation inflicted on the disgraced and impotent German Empire in 1918/19. It shocked him to the core, because he suddenly saw the fundamental dilemma besetting his personal destiny reproduced on a higher, political plane. Self-identification enabled him to express his "steadfast love" of Germany as credibly as his contempt for the "betrayers of the Fatherland." This unique combination of outrage and empathy enabled him to reach out to the many Germans who had failed to come to terms with their country's defeat. Hitler promised to restore the nation's honor and subject its "violators" to condign punishment. This struck a chord, and the fanatical champion of "Deutschland über alles" sentiments steadily gained in self-assurance.

Little by little, Hitler became certain of his ability to get his own back on those who had never taken him seriously. He succeeded because he devoted himself heart and soul to politics, the last remaining refuge from his personal dilemma. He balked at nothing. Germany's "stroke of fate" in 1918/19 was a godsend to him, and the fight for its reversal became a fight for his personal future. He took the nation hostage, as it were, in order to escape his own stigma for good. His salvation lay in a policy of extreme nationalism; that was why he did his utmost to become its leading advocate. An outsider like him would never get a second chance, and he knew it.

That Hitler had by 1921 acquired a thorough understanding of how to gain influence by employing genuinely political methods of agitation and propaganda, and that he soon became adept at such techniques, does not conflict with the findings outlined above. It was a product of his burning ambition to become, if not in art, at least in politics, a great practitioner—possibly the greatest of all time. And he quickly grasped that this would require ideological objectives, organizational structures, specific rituals and, last but not least, official and unofficial means of enforcement.

CHAPTER THREE

Private Phases in a Public Career

WHEN HITLER JOINED the Deutsche Arbeiter Partei [DAP; German Labor Party] in September 1919, he was still, politically speaking, an unknown quantity. Only three years later he was regarded as *the* repository of the *deutsch-völkisch* [roughly: German ultranationalist] movement's hopes and exerted a considerable influence on the politics of the Bavarian Free State. By November 1923 he was able to venture an out-and-out coup d'état against the Reich government that was far less doomed to fail than it may appear in retrospect. The reasons for his meteoric rise were not only structural; without the patronage of certain men who helped to promote him in the right circles at the right time, it would have been quite impossible. Who were these patrons, and what motivated them?

ERNST RÖHM

Captain Ernst Röhm played an active part in Adolf Hitler's life from March 1919 on. He was present in October of that year, when Hitler delivered his first public speech as a "politician" at a DAP rally in Munich's Hofbräukeller.[1] Röhm was so impressed by the young agitator's performance that he not only encouraged him in his political ambitions but soon joined the splinter party himself. He defended him against all comers, and as early as the spring of 1920 Hitler was attending clandestine meetings of an extreme right-wing circle of conspirators code-named the "Iron Fist," which were usually held by Röhm "in the home of Captain Beppo Römer"[2] in Munich. This brought about a swift and substantial widening of Hitler's horizons. Röhm regularly consorted with senior representatives both of the official military and of the paramilitary Freikorps,[3] and it is doubtful if anyone in Munich was in closer touch with those circles or could offer more effective backing. From Hitler's point of view, therefore, it was a definite stroke of luck that this particular man should be making such an effort to further his career. He spotted his chance and made the most of it. The officers' mess atmosphere prevailing among Röhm's conspiratorial associates was well suited to Hitler's talent for self-promotion, and it was not long before he made a very favorable impression on the men who mattered. But his greatest asset was Röhm's liking for him.

Ernst Röhm, a career staff officer during World War I, had become adjutant to Ritter von Epp, the Freikorps commander, when the German Empire collapsed.[4] In company with Epp's troops he helped to bring down Munich's revolutionary "Councils Republic" in April–May 1919, and he remained bitterly opposed to the youthful Weimar democracy. Epp had been entrusted with command of the infantry stationed in Bavaria, so Röhm himself acquired a military key position. In 1921, however, their extremely cordial relationship turned sour because Röhm was made subordinate to Otto von Lossow, commander of the Reichswehr [new republican army] in Bavaria. "General von Epp found my collaboration with the new authorities awkward," Röhm wrote later. "Probably under the impression that I meant to detach myself from his influence by degrees, he turned cooler toward me." Thus their "loyal cooperation in the most difficult situations" culminated in "an estrangement from which I cannot, admittedly, exonerate myself."[5]

There are many indications that the relationship between Röhm and Epp was homoerotic,[6] and Hitler once let slip in later years that Röhm's homosexuality first became known around 1920.[7] At the end of 1920 their relationship was still so close that the then Reichswehr commander gave the then party leader contributions for party use from his secret fund—"a purely personal matter," as he termed it later.[8] Thus the Röhm–Epp axis was of immense benefit to Hitler, not only personally but politically. The two soldiers had resources at their disposal that greatly augmented the influence of Hitler the "politician," whose assets had hitherto been limited to his charisma as an orator and actor.[9]

Hitler would have been foolish not to recognize the opportunities Röhm so readily offered him at the time. Through Röhm he got to know potential party members and militants, and there were no more promising recruits to be found than in the Freikorps battalions. In Hitler's own words, they were "all vigorous young men, accustomed to discipline and reared during their military service in the principle that absolutely nothing is impossible, and that you can achieve anything if you want."[10] Hitler managed to commend himself to this nationalistic military milieu as a like-minded repository of political hopes. Röhm must have helped in this respect, so the remark made later by Gerhard Rossbach, the notorious Freikorps commander, may well have been apt: "Röhm helped this intelligent and weak but obsessive man into his boots and got him moving."[11] But for his ability to adopt a warlike, martial pose—perfectly modeled on Röhm's own— Hitler would never, as he himself wrote later, have managed to induce "loyal comrades" to join the Party by means of "verbal persuasion."[12] Nor would the leaders of the Deutscher Kampfbund [German Combat League] of 1923, an alliance of so-called Vaterländische Kampfverbände [Patriotic Combat Formations], ever have subordinated themselves to the authority of a thirty-four-year-old ex-lance corporal if Hitler had not been promoted and wholeheartedly supported by Röhm.

Hitler was profoundly impressed by Röhm's soldierly manner, which was a habitual blend of the staff officer and the trooper. Here was someone roughly his own age who staunchly went his own way and later publicly proclaimed that he saw the world from a "deliberately one-sided," exclusively "soldierly" standpoint. Someone, moreover, who uncompromisingly championed his political aim, which was "to gain the German combat veteran his due share in running the country, and to see to it that the ideal and real spirit of the combat veteran prevails in politics as well." Such a credo naturally entailed ostentatious contempt for everything effeminate and unsoldierly: "Windbags must shut up and men alone make decisions. Political deserters and hysterical women of both sexes must be unloaded; they hamper and harm you when there's fighting to be done."[13]

For someone of this mentality, the "Wandervogel" movement played a particularly important role—at any rate, if we are to believe Hans Blüher, who was probably that youth movement's leading theorist. In 1912 Blüher published three highly controversial pamphlets that soon aroused widespread interest.[14] The third of them was provocatively entitled "The German Wandervogel Movement as an Erotic Phenomenon." It discussed the cultural role of friendship in the form in which it had grown up primarily in male-bonded communities. They alone brought forth "heroic" males capable of exercising strong leadership and gaining the loyalty of militant followers by virtue of their personal, erotically based charisma. The programmatic article "Friendship or Homosexuality,"[15] published in 1925 by Dr. Karl-Günther Heimsoth, a close friend and Freikorps comrade of Röhm, betrays how popular Blüher's ideas were in *völkisch* circles—

and how readily the martial stylization of "male homosexual eroticism" could be racially charged and employed against the "inferiority of feminism and Semitism." "The evil counterpart of the male hero is the effeminate," who is represented as a product of "homosexual feminism" and, thus, of the movement that disgracefully reduces "homosexuality" to "the question of satisfying the sexual needs of individuals." This ideologizing of homosexual tendencies into "the German eros" not only drew a clear "dividing line" under Magnus Hirschfeld, the "Pope of homosexuality," who had long been an object of hatred in the *völkisch* camp, but paid tribute to homoeroticism for political purposes, so to speak: namely, as a contribution to the establishment of a male-structured *völkisch* state.

Blüher later posited a direct correlation between his theory and Hitler: "Hitler, who had read 'The Role of Eroticism,' also recognized that something of the kind [homoerotic male heroism] must exist."[16] Again: "Hitler was very well acquainted with my books, of course, and he knew that his movement was a male movement founded on the same basic forces as the Wandervogel."[17] Although this may be going a bit far, Ernst Röhm and his Freikorps socialization make it clear that such links actually existed, and that they had a major influence on the militant orientation of the National Socialist movement. It was no coincidence, either, that a man like Heimsoth was in close contact with several future Nazi bigwigs.[18] In short, ideologically charged homosexual eroticism and sexuality were cornerstones of the fascist male-bonding culture prior to 1933.

Such was the world in which Röhm lived—the one whose ideals he upheld and sought to impose on postrevolutionary German society, primarily by means of an unscrupulous, indeed, brutal assault on the values and representatives of a democratic political culture. Röhm's militant virility fantasies are in contrast to his aesthetic side. His memoirs, published in 1928, show him to have been an excellent wordsmith. He was probably a good public speaker, and he also loved music. One contemporary observer later described his recollections of Röhm at a big country house in Wolmirstedt, Thuringia, in 1924. During this "peaceful interlude" Röhm "played the piano nearly every night. We had a magnificent grand piano in the music room, and being a great Wagnerian he mostly played extracts from Wagner's operas, from *Siegfried* and later from *Die Meistersinger*. At any rate, Wagner was his forte. He was a fan of Bayreuth."[19] Or, to quote Röhm himself: "In line with my special predilection and object of veneration, I was privileged to be a frequent guest at Haus Wahnfried in Bayreuth, where I was able to let the overpowering musical creations of our most German of masters affect me in [an atmosphere of] consummate solemnity and beauty."[20] So uncouth in other respects, Röhm could also express himself very tenderly in private, for instance, when writing to his protégé and "sweetheart," the art student Martin Schätzl.[21]

Perhaps the best pointer to the way in which Röhm dealt with his homosexual proclivities is supplied by an article published in 1932, "National Socialism and Inversion," which, if not written by him, must at least have been instigated by him.[22] It was a tribute to homo-eroticism rooted in Blüher's world of ideas, and its anonymous author went so far as to make the—never disavowed—assertion that he was expressing "not just a personal view, but the opinion [that prevails all the way] up to the Führer." He began by making it clear that the "essential content of a loving homosexual relationship" was not "coitus *per anum, per os,* or *inter femora.*" Next, however, stress was laid on the importance of the private sphere, which was no one else's business. "We love creative eroticism; we do not campaign in behalf of coital eroticism, not that we despise it for that reason. Because we regard the sex drive as fundamental, we believe that a part of its force can safely be sublimated. That is why we are far from being suppressive. On the contrary, our interest in what goes on in a bivouac is not so great that we have to shout it from the rooftops." The gist of the article was that what really mattered was to do one's duty as a soldier and a comrade. Anyone who did that should be allowed a free hand in private—provided he concealed his activities from the public gaze. If that was the moral aspect of the matter, so to speak, what of the personal aspect?

"I fancy I'm homosexual," Röhm confided to his friend Heimsoth in 1929, "but I didn't really 'discover' it until 1924. I can recall a series of homosexual feelings and acts extending back into my childhood, but I've also had relations with plenty of women. Never with any great pleasure, though. I also caught three doses of the clap, which I later saw as nature's punishment for unnatural intercourse. I now detest all women, especially those who pursue me with their love—and there are quite a number of them, more's the pity. On the other hand, I'm absolutely devoted to my mother and my sister."[23]

Röhm is reputed to have had a fiancée before the war, but the liaison was evidently of brief duration.[24] He then entered the exclusively male society of the trenches and the Freikorps, in which he had no need to disguise his homoerotic preferences. We do not know with whom Röhm "really discovered" his homosexuality "in 1924," and the date may also be wrong. There are indications that he had a longish sexual relationship at the beginning of the 1920s, namely, with Edmund Heines, another of his "sweethearts."[25] Other sources state that he first became fully aware of his proclivity while in Stadelheim Prison in 1923/24.[26] Whatever the truth, Röhm accepted himself as he was, and in 1929 he confided to those who cared to listen that he was "far from unhappy" about his homosexuality—indeed, that he was "perhaps even inwardly proud" of it.[27] He seems in general to have been quite unabashed about such matters. It later transpired, for instance, that he had not only patronized male prostitutes in the mid-1920s but openly advocated the repeal of Paragraph 175 [the law against homosexuality].[28]

Röhm's antibourgeois impetus was another conspicuous trait of his. He had a particular fondness for flirting with the boogeyman of the middle classes: "Being an immature and evil person, I am more in favor of war and disorder than of well-behaved bourgeois order." He was always inveighing against the double standards of the middle classes: "Nothing is more mendacious than society's so-called morality; it lends itself to more dirty tricks than any other concept. I declare from the outset that I am not one of the 'well-behaved' and have no ambition to be one of their number. But I certainly have no desire to be numbered among the 'moral,' because in my experience the 'morality' of the 'moral' seldom amounts to much. . . . In the field I judged a soldier not by whether he fulfilled the moral requirements of bourgeois society, but by whether or not he was a real man."[29]

When Röhm and Hitler first met, the thirty-two-year-old captain was a far from unattractive man. Photographs of the period show him not as the plump, bull-necked figure familiar to us from numerous photographs of the 1930s. Moreover, his heavily scarred cheeks would have been perceived by comrades and lovers more as an honorable badge of courage than a physical blemish; one has only to think of the disfiguring scars that dueling fraternities regarded in the same light. Hans Frank, a former Freikorps comrade of Röhm, described him thus: "Until then I had thought of homosexuality merely as a characteristic of unmanly, soft, self-indulgent, parasitic weaklings. But Röhm was the absolute prototype of a brave, daredevil soldier. Purely outwardly and in his whole appearance, with his war-scarred features and brisk, resolute manner, he looked a 'regular fellow.' There was always a bright, humorous light in his eyes. He had moreover been a loyal, self-sacrificing comrade and . . . highly qualified officer with socially assured manners."[30] Kurt Lüdecke, an associate of Hitler during the early Munich years, also recalled Röhm's appearance as being "the living image of war itself." At the same time, he was a man of "exceptional and quite instinctive courtesy. . . . I liked his keen, open gaze and his firm handclasp."[31] So that was how Röhm, the central figure of the paramilitary scene, was seen by his "comrades in arms": as a war horse, but also as a "cultivated" man with a very definite personal aura. Not that it detracts in any way from the abhorrent nature of his political ideology and criminal vigor, this shows that the reasons for Röhm's success were not confined to his unscrupulous willingness to resort to violence.

Some sources suggest that Röhm and Hitler had a sexual relationship. This is referred to, for example, in the diary of an unnamed Reichswehr general, extracts from which were published abroad in 1934,[32] and the possibility of such a liaison cannot be entirely ruled out. They must have spent some time together in private, for nothing else could have accounted for their intimate and thoroughly informal relationship, but were they lovers? I consider that improbable. The memoirs of Hitler's close friend Ernst Hanfstaengl do contain a hint that, sometime around 1923, the "friendship between Hitler and Röhm" developed "a greater intensity that transcended the fraternal *Du* and gave rise to rumors of a more far-reaching mutual affection." But Hanfstaengl, too, considered such rumors to be "highly exaggerated."[33]

Hitler, who recognized Röhm's talent for planning and organization, was here dealing with someone whose personal authority could keep a large body of soldiers under control. Furthermore, Röhm was a straightforward character and not, according to Rudolf Diels, the first head of the Gestapo, "an underhanded man."[34] When Röhm fought he displayed a "manliness" that Hitler liked to emulate. Watching Röhm, he soon learned how to reconcile a self-assured, masculine manner with homosexual tendencies. It was not long before he could demonstrate "manliness" so convincingly that even hard-boiled soldiers were taken in.

Conversely, Röhm recognized Hitler's talent for politics. He saw Hitler as the charismatic prophet, the leader and seducer who could beguile the masses with rousing speeches and imbue them with something they themselves would have thought impossible: rapturous enthusiasm.[35] Thus the two men knew that they complemented each other. They got on well as comrades and brothers in arms, each in his own sphere. They were also united by their love of music. Finally, the fact that they were both homosexual, which can hardly have escaped them, would have been conducive to a great sense of attachment.

"Hitler and I," Röhm wrote in his memoirs, "were linked by ties of sincere friendship." He had felt obliged "to speak candidly to my friend, like a loyal comrade" even when they fell out in 1925. But what underlay this conflict? The two men had drawn different conclusions from the failed putsch of November 1923. When Röhm was released from detention in April 1924, Hitler had appointed him commander of the SA. In that capacity Röhm founded the "Frontbann," a new edition of the pre-putsch Combat League. Now that the Weimar Republic was becoming consolidated, Hitler soon realized that an updated version of the Freikorps strategy would be a political blind alley. In December 1924, therefore, he removed the SA from the "Frontbann"—and Röhm, who categorically demanded that the National Socialist movement recognize "the primacy of soldiers over politicians," felt that he had been overridden. Their conceptions of the requisite political tactics were diametrically opposed, so their ways parted in the spring of 1925. But it was a parting devoid of intrigues and public recriminations. Röhm forbore to attack his erstwhile protégé even in the years that followed. On the contrary, in 1928 he expressly reemphasized his "attachment to the harbinger and sustainer of the political struggle, Adolf Hitler."[36] He remained loyal, his personal relationship with Hitler intact.[37]

DIETRICH ECKART

Discounting his friendship with Röhm, Hitler owed his entry into Munich politics mainly to one man: the aging bohemian Dietrich

Eckart. He is reputed to have been an archetypal Bavarian who was as good at playing the intellectual as the socialite. In Hitler he acquired an admirer, but also a pupil whom he thought he could mold, inspire and send into the fray of public opinion for his own ends, which he conceived of as ideological rather than political.

In order to gauge what attracted thirty-year-old Hitler to this writer turned politician, who was two decades older than himself, we must first of all take note of an article which is reliably reported to have sent Hitler into a rage and had dire repercussions on its author, who went to prison in consequence.[38] In 1943, on the seventy-fifth anniversary of the long dead Eckart's birth, the *Frankfurter Zeitung* was bold enough to publish an account of his character and career that wholly conflicted with the Nazi myths about Hitler's former mentor.[39] It spoke of a man "who, tossed around by the vicissitudes of the years, tried again and again to secure public recognition." A man whose stage plays had been "brusquely rejected," and whose material circumstances had for years been "very poor." "He had lodgings at the rear of a Berlin tenement, and he sometimes slept on a bench in the Tiergarten." No, Eckart's was no picturebook career, and his prior history sounded equally questionable. In 1893, after dropping out of medical school, quarreling with the members of his dueling fraternity and being unsuccessfully treated for morphine addiction, Eckart had tried his hand at journalism until his financial straits were finally eased by the death of his father. "With the fortune he had now inherited, young Eckart went out into the world: to Leipzig, where he maintained a large house and surrounded himself with artists—actors, musicians, and painters. He went to Berlin for a short time, . . . then moved to Regensburg. He was free and unattached. He suffered from liver trouble, but he lived according to his inclinations and moods, a slave to no one." In 1899, when his money ran out, Eckart moved back to Berlin, where he lived from hand to mouth for a good ten years. His stage version of Ibsen's *Peer Gynt* did at last bring him a

measure of success—in the long term, at least, because at first "everyone attacked him for his presumption," and he had to defend himself
against fierce criticism. In the end, the controversial playwright's
friend and patron Count Hülsen-Haeseler, general manager of the
Royal Theater, gave him an advance for a new stage play on which he
worked in a Blankenburg sanitarium from the fall of 1913 on. In
1915 he moved from the Harz Mountains to Schwabing, Munich,
where the ignominious collapse of the German Empire in the winter of
1918/19 propelled him into the political arena. There he "soon made
the acquaintance of Adolf Hitler."

One can readily imagine why the dictator was infuriated by the
Frankfurter Zeitung's portrait of Eckart. It must have seemed like a
picture puzzle in which he could recognize elements of his own career
and his own characteristic traits: an obsession with living like an
"artist"; a dependence on the help of others; a greater degree of sem-
blance than reality; a thirst for recognition and urge for self-justification; an almost uncontrollable desire for self-assertion; and, last but
not least, an abrupt transition from art to politics. As an artist, Eckart
had experienced precisely what the young Hitler could only dream of,
but that was why he felt a bond with the man from Schwabing: a
social outsider like himself, but one so permeated by—indeed,
obsessed with—a belief in his own superiority that he had finally won
through. To Hitler, Eckart must have seemed like a guarantor of his
own self-made image.

The "classical" bohemian and the pseudobohemian had met in the
political obscurity of postwar Munich. The elder possessed a superabundance of what the younger lacked: confidence, a self-assured
manner, connections and a sense of vocation. But Hitler, as Eckart
saw at first glance, had something of his own to offer. He was not
only tough, determined and an exceptionally gifted orator, but willing
and able to learn and appreciative of advice and encouragement.
Hitler was a promising talent whose public speeches had audience

appeal, and Eckart knew that he himself could never arouse such mass emotions.

This instinctive mutual recognition developed into a close friendship. Eckart felt "drawn to his [Hitler's] whole being," he later confided, "and my relationship with him became more intimate."[40] Hitler, too, was bowled over at their very first meeting—not least, as he rhapsodized ten years later, by "the wonderful cranium of that best of Germans. . . . A mighty forehead, blue eyes, the whole head like that of a bull. And, in addition, a voice of wonderfully honest timbre."[41] They drew closer geographically as well in 1921, when Eckart moved to Thierschstrasse, only a few doors from Hitler's humble lodgings. From now on, Eckart effusively referred to the younger man as "my Adolf."[42] Hitler, in his turn, revered Eckart and looked upon him as a role model—indeed, as his "Pole Star."[43] To one who was in many respects his inferior, Eckart's affectionate sentiments were flattering. It not only did Hitler good to be courted by someone who passed for a literary lion; it positively puffed him up.

Hitler gladly followed Eckart's lead into areas conducive mainly to self-improvement. Roaming around with the literary bon vivant was very much to the taste of an adept with a lot of ground to make up. Eckart had a great gift for self-presentation. Ever intent on having fun and making an impression, he radiated an undoubted charm—outside politics as well—that captivated and endeared the younger man to him, whether in Munich's restaurants, wine bars and beer halls,[44] at carnival time in Schwabing,[45] or in private. "How nice it was at Dietrich Eckart's when I . . . went there!" Hitler once exclaimed, twenty years later.[46] They would sometimes retire to Berchtesgaden for a few days.[47] His friendship with Eckart, Hitler confided to his secretary, "was one of the best things that had fallen to his lot during the 1920s."[48]

Where the inner core of the relationship is concerned, attention must be drawn to something not spelled out by the *Frankfurter*

Zeitung article: Eckart was an inveterate misogynist. Alfred Rosenberg pointed this out in 1927, perhaps naively, perhaps with an ulterior motive, when he made a small compilation of Eckart's "legacy."[49] "I know," he wrote, "that I . . . am here alluding to something that constituted a profound tragedy in Dietrich Eckart's life. Eckart saw a penchant for triviality as the essential feminine trait, declared that women were incapable of truly grasping profundities, and sometimes flatly denied their wish to do so. He was particularly antipathetic to womanly courtesy and pronounced it symptomatic of our feminine age. Woman, he said, was nature, little more." According to Rosenberg, the manner in which Eckart's plays refer to the nature of womankind—they speak of cowardice, submissiveness, cunning, sensuality and treachery—was undoubtedly rooted in a "spiritual abyss" to be found in the "purely personal sphere." That apart, however, Eckart believed in general that "lack of manliness" entailed "a tendency to decadence," and he consequently depicted the intensification "of the feminine-poetic urge by unstable men" as an omen of cultural disaster.[50]

This background may also explain why Eckart campaigned against Magnus Hirschfeld with positively pathological loathing. In 1922 one of his notorious pamphlets branded Hirschfeld an "apostle of sodomy" determined to "drag the vice even further out onto the street. He means to poison young people through and through, and the proletariat are to act as catamite to this satiated Galician Jewish rogue." Eckart would have preferred the "filthy old beast" to have his "skull stove in."[51] Anyone who fulminates with so much froth on his lips and lashes out in so brutal a fashion renders himself suspect, especially as Eckart was anything but an apostle of morality and monastic asceticism in other respects. He clearly launched his emotional attacks on Hirschfeld because he felt personally affected by the latter's endeavors to promote a sexual revolution—indeed, because he felt personally *wounded* by them.

By condemning the "feminine-poetic urge" in man, Eckart was

probably combating a part of himself. At the age of twenty-seven he had made the following confession in verse to a friend of his youth: "You often saw me deep engrossed in dreams, / and saw me ever struggle, wrestle, strive; / you saw me oft exultant, drunk with love, / and saw my young life sullied with self-hate. / . . . / True to myself I've never truly been, / save only in my own true love for you."[52] These lines do convey at least a hint of what a longtime friend of Eckart, Guido Karl Bomhard, could have meant when he wrote, long after Eckart's death, that he was loath "to divulge things that show him [Eckart] in a false light." He went on to say, alluding to their own relationship, that these things were highly personal matters "which stemmed from our common originality, and are to be indulged in only by bohemians."[53] This is consistent with what we know about Eckart's only ally and close friend among Germany's theater managers, Count Georg von Hülsen-Haeseler, who was often accused of being homosexual.[54] But for the steadfast support of Hülsen-Haeseler, Eckart would never have achieved his artistic breakthrough as a playwright.[55]

In view of all this, it is hardly surprising that Eckart did not have the makings of a devoted husband. He was forty-five when he married Rose Marx, a wealthy widow from Blankenburg. According to Rosenberg, it was the "exclusively male company" Eckart kept that destroyed his childless marriage within a few years.[56] Although the relevant documents are missing, the couple got divorced in 1920, the year in which Eckart met Hitler.

Eckart had drawn attention to himself during the winter of 1918/19 by bringing out the periodical *Auf gut deutsch* [roughly: "In Plain German"], which warned against a "Pan-Jewish world conspiracy," advocated genuine socialism and accorded influence only to those of "pure German blood."[57] Whatever it was that made the professional agitator in Hitler prick up his ears, Eckart's inflammatory rag or his first encounter with Eckart himself, the two men were kindred spirits from the winter of 1919/20 on, and not on the political plane alone. Eckart felt "really *inwardly* . . . attached" to Hitler, reported his friend Bomhard, who also felt quite sure "that Eckart's relationship with Hitler was deep-rooted and sincere."[58] Referring to it in one of his monologues, Hitler himself said something that probably goes to the heart of the matter: "In those days I was . . . still an infant."[59] Although he was actually speaking of his own stylistic immaturity compared to Eckart's "brilliant" writing, this conveys better than any other form of words how he must have felt toward an older friend who was in many respects his superior.

By easing Hitler into the higher reaches of Munich and Berlin society, Eckart enabled his "whiz kid" protégé to benefit financially as well as socially. Admission to these circles, whose acceptance he had craved for decades, gave Hitler more self-confidence. Eckart taught him the social conventions, improved his literary style and encouraged him to pay more attention to his appearance.[60] He taught Hitler to be as proficient at drawing-room conversation as he was at holding forth in beer halls. Eckart also helped him to gain the leadership of the NSDAP and made a substantial contribution to Hitler's successful acquisition of dictatorial powers in the summer of 1921. Shortly afterward he pointedly defended the party leader against internal critics who disapproved of his obscure lifestyle. He could swear from his "precise knowledge of the facts" that Hitler was a man of impeccable character: "I firmly believe that no one could serve a cause with greater selflessness, self-sacrifice, devotion, and integrity."[61] Eckart was recompensed at around the same time with the post of editor in chief of the Party's own *Völkischer Beobachter*.[62] This was the high-water mark of the two men's political symbiosis: Eckart was now the spiritual mentor of a movement totally committed to the leadership of a man whose "vigor, energy, and passion" he fervently extolled. Until 1922 he looked upon himself and Hitler as a political unit, a belief in which he seems to have been strengthened by his opponents.[63] Although Hitler initially had no problem with his allotted role of junior partner, it became less easy, as time went by, to see which of them was the horse and which the rider.

There is no doubt that Eckart at first called the tune in ideological matters. His biographer Margarete Plewnia has shown, for example, that Hitler's antisemitism became radicalized under Eckart's influence; more precisely, it was not until early 1920 that he based his attempt to represent the Jews as "the bane of Germany" on something like a "chain of reasoning" cribbed from the inflammatory writings with which Eckart had made his name in the world of politics from 1919 on.[64] Generally speaking, Eckart can probably be credited with the intellectual authorship of almost all the political ideas Hitler evolved up to the mid-1920s.

What Hitler and Eckart meant to each other, and how closely allied they were, is also apparent from their attempts at mutual defense. In the summer of 1922, for instance, Eckart told a meeting that he would, even if alone, "draw his revolver" to defend Hitler against any police intervention.[65] And early in 1923, when the state prosecutor's office was going to call Eckart to account for insulting the Reich president, Hitler promptly sent Premier Knillig of Bavaria a written request "to prohibit the detention order, or the combat organization would offer resistance to his arrest."[66]

But the exceptional feature of Hitler and Eckart's relationship may have been the way in which it combined what they considered necessary with what was psychologically important to them. For both men, politics was an ideal medium of self-fulfillment which they really conceived of as *artistic*. Hitler's friendship with Eckart reawakened his old dream of two artists living in close communion. When the Schauspielhaus revived Eckart's *Peer Gynt* after the revolutionary turmoil had subsided, he naturally took his new friend with him to Berlin.[67] He also rhapsodized to Hitler about the wonderful atmosphere at Bayreuth, which he had formerly experienced as a critic.[68] Theater and opera must therefore have occupied a permanent place in their friendship. Eckart made a habit of introducing Hitler to leading figures on the cultural scene—in 1920, for example, to the former general manager of Munich's Königliche Hofbühnen, Clemens von Franckenstein, who then lived in the famous Lenbach villa. One malicious observer wrote that Hitler was "gratified and inhibited in equal measure" by the invitation, and that he "kitted himself out" for the visit "with riding breeches, quirt, German shepherd, and slouch hat." Although he gratefully seized on his host's "kindly but cool" remarks, it was not long before he completely dominated the conversation and was "preaching like a divisional chaplain."[69] We are not told the precise subject of the conversation, unfortunately, but it is evident how anxious the rising political star was to make an impression, not only in beer halls, but in more exalted social circles.

Hitler clearly needed to hone his image, or so one or two contemporary accounts suggest. The Freikorps officer Gerhard Rossbach, for example, described the Hitler of those days as follows: "soft but wanting to be hard, semieducated but wanting to be omniscient, a bohemian who had to become a soldier if he wanted to impress real soldiers. A man mistrustful of himself and his abilities and, consequently, abrim with inferiority complexes toward all who had already gotten somewhere or were in the process of outdoing him. Deferential and insecure, but often brusque when he sensed some limitation."[70] If this description is accurate, Hitler really did have much to learn and practice. He had already managed to copy a good deal from Röhm, but he still lacked total mastery.

This is evidenced by his meeting with the chairman of Heinrich Claß's Pan-German League in Berlin during December 1920. Apparently, Hitler declared himself a loyal pupil of the nationalist politician and went so far as to kiss his hands, making an extremely "obsequious" and pushy impression.[71] To quote Claß's own memoirs: "The man was a political wildling who had an urge to render the persuasive power of his effusions still more forceful, even when addressing a single individual, by shouting and gesticulating with his arms or hands." He realized after only a quarter of an hour that he was dealing with "a thoroughgoing hysteric." But Claß also recognized that Hitler was someone who represented "something entirely new in the political life our nation"; someone whose "absolute faith in himself and in his own powers of persuasion" differentiated him from the average party leader.[72]

But Hitler soon learned to disguise his weaknesses and convey the image of an experienced politician. As 1922 wore on, Eckart's role as mentor and prompter became redundant. Hitler was now eager to stand on his own two feet, and he succeeded. In the fall of 1922, when Rudolf Pechel, editor of the *Deutscher Rundschau*, returned to Munich after an absence of several months, he was told on all sides that Hitler had become a "megalomaniac."[73] Outside observers of the political scene, too, noticed a change in him. One of them was the British consul general in Munich, William Seeds, who had dismissed Hitler as unimportant in May 1922. By November he was writing to London that Hitler's role had far transcended that of a "scurrilous and rather comic agitator"; many people already regarded him as a German Mussolini, and his popularity had for some time surpassed that of the legendary General von Ludendorff.[74] Hitler's growing importance,[75] objective as well as subjective, made him feel that he was sustained and animated by the whole tide of history, and it was that which seems to have detached him from Eckart. He had become an agile performer on the political stage, calculating and many-faced. He could not only control his emotions but use them for his own ends, and his connections with the political establishment were now adequate. He had no more need of Eckart's help.[76]

But he still preserved some affection for the person who had been largely responsible for his success, so theirs was a parting by installments, accompanied by jealous scenes and mutual recriminations. Eckart probably initiated the process when he responded to Hitler's aloofness by ostentatiously flirting with a woman some thirty years younger than himself, well knowing how much anger and hurt this was bound to cause.[77] To begin with, however, Hitler showed none of this. He assisted Eckart when he was sought by the judicial authorities and took refuge in the mountains at Berchtesgaden, even to the extent of visiting him there in person in April 1923 after a long and tiring walk. There is no doubt of Hitler's concern for the fugitive from justice, who was "genuinely touched" by his unexpected visit. In 1942 Hitler told his intimates more about this meeting at the "Pension Moritz" on the Obersalzburg, which had left a deep impression on him: "We knocked at a door. 'Diedi, Wolf is here!' He came out in his nightshirt, bristly legs and all. Salutations. . . . Eckart introduced me to the Büchners [the boardinghouse keepers, at breakfast the next morning]: 'This is my young friend Herr Wolf!' . . . When noon came, Eckart told me: 'Now you must come with me to the Turk's inn. Being an Austrian, you'll get a genuine goulash there.' . . . I had to return to Munich ere long, but I used to sneak up there whenever I had a bit of time to spare, and we would go on excursions. . . . One afternoon we moved him to the little Göll house. He had his bed and his coffee mill with him, as he always did when moving."[78] So much for Hitler's recollection of the last few months of his relationship with Eckart, which cannot be said to have turned sour at that stage.

This had changed by May 1923, as the U.S. Secret Service was subsequently informed by Ernst Hanfstaengl.[79] When he visited Hitler and Eckart in the Berchtesgaden Mountains early in June, Eckart bitterly complained to him in private that Hitler refused to listen to him anymore and was well on the way to becoming a megalomaniac. Eckart was particularly incensed by "Hitler's exhibitionism," complaining that he danced attendance on Frau Büchner all day long with a dogwhip in his hand, and that he ceaselessly harangued the "silly cow." His self-important manner was such that he already compared himself to Jesus Christ. The next day, when Hanfstaengl went for a walk in the mountains with Hitler, he had to listen to the latter's complaints about Eckart. Eckart had become a "senile weakling" who had, at his advanced age, fallen in love with "this girl Annerl," a woman thirty years his junior. He was irresolute and had no idea what he wanted. Schopenhauer had turned him into a "doubting Thomas"; all he yearned for now was a "Nirvana." Hitler continually reviled Eckart for being an old fool, reserving his special wrath for the latter's attachment to the aforesaid young woman.

The spring of 1923 brought a final parting of the ways.[80] Although Eckart was thoroughly "sick" of party politics, he continued to believe in "his Adolf," notwithstanding all their differences. "Believe it or not," he is reported to have told a friend in December 1923, shortly before his death, "Hitler is the coming man."[81] His last publication was a "Dialogue between Adolf Hitler and Myself"[82]—an attempt to commemorate their relationship in literary terms. And the dedication in which Hitler extolled Eckart as "one of the best" at the end of *Mein Kampf* in 1925 shows that he, too, preserved an affection for his erstwhile companion.

ERNST HANFSTAENGL

In March 1923 many members of Hitler's circle were struck by his sudden intimacy with Ernst Hanftsaengl. Hitherto perceived merely as a kind of "social secretary" in the party leader's café society retinue, Hanfstaengl had now, quite clearly, become a close friend of Hitler.[83] It was not until some years later that he made a name for himself as the "Führer's" foreign press chief. More will be said elsewhere about the career that briefly took Hanfstaengl to the hub of Hitler's power structure. Suffice it to say that a former associate of Goebbels regarded Hanfstaengl as someone who had "the courage to be an original and remain one in Hitler's entourage." And: "Hitler was somehow attached to that man Hanfstaengl, no doubt about it."[84]

Not a great deal is known about the early life of this scion of a respected Munich family of art dealers, who was born in 1887, but some of its main features are documented. From 1905 to 1909 Hanfstaengl was at Harvard, although he had only gained his junior high school diploma after eight years at the Königliches Wilhelmgymnasium in Munich.[85] It is probable that his student years in America were largely a form of escape from these educational problems, whose background is obscure. Even at Harvard, where he claimed to have studied subjects including "psychology, German and English literature, as well as the history of art and music," he was admitted only as a "special student." A Harvard contemporary later recalled that, although Hanfstaengl always mixed with the "right people," he never managed to secure admission to one of the university's exclusive "final clubs."[86] In 1909 he returned to Munich to do his military service as a one-year volunteer. After that, in the late summer of 1910, he went abroad again—to Vienna, Grenoble, London, Paris and Rome—for purposes of study. At the end of 1911 he took over the management of the Hanfstaengl art gallery in New York, where he succeeded in making its salesrooms a meeting place for numerous well-known artists and art enthusiasts. Until World War I he avowedly felt very much at home there. What united the Manhattan social set in which he moved was contempt for "Anglo-Saxon moral hypocrisy" and "puritanical pseudomorality"[87]—in other words, a taste for libertinism. This is demonstrated by, among other things, Hanfstaengl's friendship with Hanns Heinz Ewers, the author and epicurean.

Hanfstaengl tried to play down the importance of their relationship after World War I,[88] but Ewers's second wife refused to let him get away with it, as witness an irate letter of hers: "I'm as well aware as you are of the longtime friendship that existed between you and HHE [Hanns Heinz Ewers]. By denying that friendship today, you make yourself a hypocrite and a cheat. It was through HHE that I got to know you in New York City in 1919. You were on very friendly terms even then. Later on, in Germany, you were a guest in our home on countless occasions, and we were close for years . . . *for HHE was your friend!*"[89] Hanfstaengl conceded to "dear Josephine" that his friend Ewers had been a "warmhearted, patriotic, courageous German and a genuine artist," and that he, Hanfstaengl, had felt very much "drawn to him."[90] Be that as it may, we would do well, for present purposes, to take a closer look at this close friend of Hanfstaengl from his time in America.[91]

By the beginning of the 20th century, Ewers had already made something of a name for himself with his unconventional literary works—for instance, *Die Alraune* [The Mandrake]—and his equally unconventional lifestyle. His friends included artists, politicians and occultists, and he moved in homosexual circles. His reputation was that of a flamboyant snob who suffered from wanderlust and needed alcohol (absinthe) and drugs (mescaline) to remain productive. His play *Enterbt* [Disinherited] dealt with the trials and tribulations of homosexuals far more frankly than was customary in the Germany of his day. It could in general be said that Ewers was regarded, even before World War I, as an expert at handling awkward subjects.

In 1914 he went to New York, where he made friends with Hanfstaengl. They led a dissolute existence in a milieu in which sex and drugs played a prominent part. Ewers described this period in his novel *Der Vampyr* (1919), which some condemned as an amoral "maze of paths through a sexually pathological swamp" and others as "a divine comedy and satyr play combined."[92] Young Hanfstaengl was quite at home in the high society scene it portrayed.

Ewers, as we have already said, felt particularly attracted to men in an erotic and sexual way—and this despite two marriages (which failed partly on that account) and sundry affairs with women. This inevitably sheds a certain light on his longtime friendship with "PH," as he used to call "Putzi" Hanfstaengl. The bond that existed between these two extravagant personalities was something akin to a spiritual affinity combined with a common desire for homoerotic experiences. And liberal New York of the early 20th century was a very suitable place in which to fulfill that desire.[93]

It was Ewers who in 1920, when Hanfstaengl was thirty-three and still unmarried, "procured" him a wife: Helene Niemeyer, the daughter of a German American businessman. Writing to his mother at the time, Hanfstaengl said that this young woman's unexpected interest had saved him from disaster.[94] Their marriage was an overnight decision. Hanfstaengl seldom referred to his attractive wife, with whom he lived for nearly sixteen years, and then only in a far from affectionate manner. Their son Egon, who is still alive, states that the couple's sex life was definitely not a success, and that his mother had contemplated divorce at a very early stage.[95]

In the summer of 1921 Hanfstaengl and his wife returned to Germany with Egon, then six months old, and tried to make a life for themselves in Munich. This proved harder than they had thought, because Hanfstaengl's brother Edgar, who considered him incompetent and feckless, stubbornly refused to make him a partner in the family firm. Accordingly, Hanfstaengl looked around for other professional openings. He took up writing, considered producing feature films and worked on screenplays with friends old and new. At the same time, he attended historical seminars at Munich University, where he had enrolled as a regular student in October 1921. Thanks to the strong dollar, the nest egg he had accumulated in America enabled him to keep his head well above water.

Hanfstaengl cherished no political ambitions until 1922. "After all," he wrote a decade later, "I was an artist; a musician or writer, but—God knows—no politician."[96] But then he suddenly fell for politics, or, to be more precise, for one particular politician. Kurt Lüdecke claimed to have introduced this tall man with the long, thin face to Hitler in November 1922 with the aim of securing Hanfstaengl's putative fortune for the "movement."[97] Hanfstaengl managed to endear himself to Hitler so swiftly that he gained his complete confidence. Before long, many NSDAP members came to regard him as a kind of "camarilla."[98] "In 1923," the *Münchener Post* wrote some years later, "it was an open secret that Hitler listened to no one more readily than to E. Hanfstaengl."[99] The remarkably rapid growth of their relationship cannot have had anything to do with politics. Already a power in the land, Hitler was firmly resolved to lead the *völkisch* movement in accordance with his own ideas. In any case, how could Hanfstaengl have been useful to him politically?

What Hanfstaengl found fascinating about Hitler were his "peculiarly luminous eyes," his "rather dainty hands" and "the fluency with which he expressed himself." When appearing in public he impressed Hanfstaengl as "a man of immense mental energy" whose "fiery" language exerted an incredible "power of attraction." But even in private Hitler had "an endearing quality, a directness" that greatly appealed to Hanfstaengl. Hitler had been "far from conceited"; on the contrary, he was "friendly, unpretentious, and appeared modest and not entirely sure of himself."

That gave Hanfstaengl the scope he needed to cut a glamorous figure, and it was not long before Hitler became addicted to the company of this unconventional sprig of the upper middle class, who played a special role for him. "I enjoyed chaffing him, and I was probably the only member of his inner circle from whom he would tolerate a certain amount of teasing."[100] Hitler evidently didn't mind what other people found affected, quirky and exasperating[101] about Hanfstaengl—in fact, that may have been just what appealed to him. In Hanfstaengl, he wrote in April 1925, he had come to know "a man whose fanaticism is divided into love of the movement and hatred for its enemies." And he added: "He had become a friend to me personally."[102] If we substitute "me" for "the movement," we may have summarized the nub of their relationship.

From January 1923 at the latest, Hitler was a regular visitor to Hanfstaengl's small Gentzstrasse apartment on the edge of Schwabing. Although the two men now saw each other almost daily, the time never dragged because of their common interest in art, music and history. Hitler also liked playing with little Egon, and there may even have been times when he felt like one of the family. The Hanfstaengls welcomed Hitler's company although they lived in a relatively small apartment. Helene Hanfstaengl was very fond of him. She rhapsodized decades later about the "expressive, vibrant quality"[103] of his voice—the same voice whose "immense power" had also appealed to her husband, who found its "unique sound effects" profoundly moving.

But Hanfstaengl and Hitler would sometimes meet in the latter's private quarters on Thierschstrasse or spend the evening at a movie theater. If they visited Party members outside Munich and stayed overnight, they often shared the same bedroom. In 1922/23 Hanfstaengl was privileged to accompany Hitler on many such trips as a "mood maker," for instance, to the Starnberger See, or to Berchtesgaden, Neuschwanstein, Murnau, and Berlin. He enjoyed these excursions very much, because Hitler was "an exceptionally entertaining traveling companion." They also went on walks together "through holiday-hushed streets to the Oberwiesenfeld."[104] Hitler could be "captivating" and "evolve great ideas." He often demonstrated his "mastery of acting," especially when he gave such "cabaret-ripe" imitations of other people that Hanfstaengl could not stop laughing. In short, they were happy in each other's company.

Hitler particularly liked it when Hanfstaengl, with his "rather effervescent temperament," pounded the "somewhat rickety piano" in his furnished room on Thierschstrasse "with Lisztian *fioriture* and fine romantic verve." And "Hitler almost yelled with delight: 'Oh, Hanfstaengl . . . Wonderful!'"[105] One female listener, who called Hanfstaengl's style of playing "exciting and flamboyant," described how the big man had played himself into a state of complete exhaustion and positively overpowered his audience as a result.[106] Hanfstaengl naturally scored his greatest successes with Hitler by playing "Wagner music," notably the "*Meistersinger* prelude" or the "Liebestod" from *Tristan und Isolde*: "That was it! I must have played from it hundreds of times, and he couldn't have enough of it" because "it did him good physically"—to such an extent that Hitler "chuckled with pleasure." Haenstaengl's playing brought him the "relaxation" he craved.[107] That was why "he later kept urging me by telephone to come and play the piano." And "although his imperious claims on my time didn't suit me, I set off for Thierschstrasse regardless."[108] (Thanks not least to Thomas Mann's research, we are familiar with the "liberating effect" and "safety valve function" that Wagner's music had, especially for homosexuals.)[109]

Hanfstaengl later told his son Egon—Hitler's godchild—that he had found Hitler extremely attractive sexually.[110] The sexual component of their relationship, however, manifested itself or sought an outlet in public speaking and piano playing, respectively. Hanfstaengl clearly perceived this: "The whole fabric of leitmotifs, of musical embellishments, contrapuntal melodies and contrasts, was precisely reflected in the layout of his speeches; they were constructed like symphonies and culminated in an immense outburst like the sound of Wagnerian trombones."[111]

All this shows that, to begin with, politics were a secondary factor in Hanfstaengl's relationship with Hitler. They were never entirely unimportant, however. His "Hitler Song Book" of 1923–1924, for example, was meant as a personal contribution to *völkisch* propaganda, and Hitler must have felt flattered by it. Hanfstaengl's opus was a compilation of all the clichés of contemporary Hitlerian rhetoric, from a Jewish conspiracy aimed at "Germany's downfall" to the "resurrection" of the Reich under the auspices of the swastika. The lyrics brimmed with racist invective, and all that could "save" Germany, according to Hanfstaengl, was—needless to say—"Hitler medicine."[112] There is no doubt that, despite his years in the land of the free, this scion of the middle classes had become a genuine National Socialist within a very short space of time. Hanfstaengl's peppy songs commended Hitler not only to the masses, but also to the reaches of Munich's educated bourgeoisie. He is even said, as a leading member of the National Socialist students' group, to have engaged in "zealous and effective propaganda" in the seminar conducted by the historian Hermann Oncken.[113]

Although the relationship between Hitler and Hanfstaengl was primarily of an erotic nature, this did not preclude the latter from hoping that professional advantages would accrue from it, or from being "convinced that his [Hitler's] brilliant gifts would take him to the top."[114] The opposition press was already referring to Hanfstaengl as Hitler's "in-house foreign minister."[115] Alfred Rosenberg believed that post to be reserved for himself, however, so internal conflicts were inevitable.

It annoyed Hanfstaengl—and adversely affected their relationship—that his friend's activities were always "shrouded in an atmosphere of conspiracy and intrigue:" "Hitler . . . led a shadowy existence; one never knew exactly where he was. At bottom, he was a bohemian who never put down firm roots anywhere."[116] Hitler's henchmen within the NSDAP leadership criticized their boss in very similar terms: "What we rather miss in you is a desire for closer contact with your associates, and with other men who work along the same lines." Hitler was too inaccessible, they said, and had no time for important Party matters; he clearly overdid his "relaxation in artistic circles and in the company of good-looking women," thereby occasioning "rumors" detrimental to the Party.[117] Hitler's landlady, Frau Reichert, described him to Hanfstaengl as a "thorough bohemian."[118] All this suggests that Hitler must have been leading a double life that not even his close friends could fathom. Why was he so secretive? What underlay his behavior?

SECRET FILES

The six-volume file on Hitler kept by the Munich police would undoubtedly have provided an answer to this question, but Hitler ensured that it was confiscated as soon as he became Reich Chancellor.[119] We may, however, have some small compensation for this irreparable loss in the shape of Eugen Dollmann's account of some secret papers in the private safe of Otto von Lossow, the Reichswehr general.[120]

That Dollmann's statements are worthy of credence is suggested by the circumstances of his life—more precisely, by his close proximity to the events and matters he describes.[121]A lawyer's son born in 1900, he lost his father at an early age and grew up in the care of his mother, Paula (née) von Fischer, whose grandfather had been personal physician to Empress Elisabeth of Austria. In 1914 mother and son moved to Munich, where Paula Dollmann's excellent social connections enabled them to consort with the Bavarian capital's political and cultural movers and shakers. This continued to be so even after the monarchy fell in 1918, when Eugen Dollmann enrolled in Munich University as a student of history, art history and Romance languages and literature. He was guaranteed access to influential members of Munich's upper crust by his mother, whose contacts in the early 1920s extended to Premier von Knillig of Bavaria and the papal nuncio, Eugenio Pacelli (later Pope Pius XII). From 1922 on, Dollmann was a frequent guest at the home of Otto von Lossow, the Bavarian Reichswehr commander, who evidently became something of a surrogate father to him. At Lossow's suggestion, Dollmann attended Hitler's rallies, and the sensational new party leader seems to have become one of their main topics of conversation.

In 1926 Dollmann graduated magna cum laude under the tutorship of the well-known historian Herman Oncken. Through the good offices of another friend of the family, Ambassador von Preger, Bavaria's envoy in Berlin, the Kaiser Wilhelm Gesellschaft awarded him a three-year scholarship to study in Italy, where he moved early in 1927. He did not, however, lose touch with von Lossow, his fatherly friend. In 1934/35, when he returned to Munich for a good year, the two men resumed their lively discussion of political matters, which was now colored by Dollmann's membership in the NSDAP and Hitler's brutal settlement of accounts with his close friend Röhm. Lossow, wrote Dollmann, had spoken accusingly of Hitler as follows: "He had known it all for years but never dared to intervene until Röhm became a deadly danger to himself—you know why!"[122] Dollmann seems to have been in possession of excellent firsthand information about Hitler's private life, and may even have been authorized to pass it on if so required. This is indicated by some fragmentary notes preserved in Dollmann's literary remains and entitled: "The Third Reich and Homosexuality."[123] They comment on Hitler's proclivities as follows: "Those privy to his past were as little in doubt about this tendency of his as the scholarly or non-scholarly reader of sexological works." And one of those "initiates," according to Dollmann, was the "temporarily all-powerful Reichswehr commander in Munich, General Otto von Lossow. . . . I well remember how, one day in 1923, the general asked me to give him my impression of Hitler. . . . When I had concluded my account, in which I had drawn particular attention to the fanatical enthusiasm displayed at these rallies by young people, Lossow . . . said that the was not surprised at this special contact, this almost mystical power of attraction, because 'men of *that kind* always succeed in casting an extraordinary spell over young people.' What then emerged in the course of an hourlong conversation was a shocking insight into Hitler's 'special proclivity,' which the general blithely defined in a stentorian, parade-ground voice."

Although Dollmann's subsequent employment as Hitler's interpreter and membership of Reichsführer-SS Heinrich Himmler's staff[124] may have given him some additional insights into Hitler's private life, his most authoritative inside information remained that which his fatherly friend had imparted to him with such steadfast certainty between 1922 and 1935. Only this would have emboldened Dollmann to pass it on, in his turn, when the Nazi regime collapsed.

Time: Christmas 1923. Place: the Bavarian war ministry. Among the guests at a dinner party given there by Lossow was Dollmann himself, then a young history student, whose mother was an old friend of the commander in chief. After dinner the host invited a group of men to his office to talk about Hitler's unsuccessful putsch and justify his own part in firmly putting it down. According to Dollmann's notes, Lossow's actual words on this occasion were as follows: "Ever since the putsch was crushed I have been receiving threatening letters from Nazis old and young, and my officers are abused and spit at wherever they show their faces. But nothing will happen to me or to them. Fortunately, I learned in China and Turkey how to behave in the face of abuse and coercion from Braunau [Hitler's birthplace]. Since November 9, Hitler and his supporters have been well aware that any attempt on my own life or those of my officers would cause a European scandal.[125] I still have some good friends in the world, and Adolf would lose that game just as he did on November 9." So saying, Dollmann goes on, "the general produced from a desk drawer a police file containing secret reports and depositions about the private life of Herr Adolf Hitler dating from the time when he again turned up in Munich after the war—all from the vice squad or police headquarters on Ettstrasse." Everyone present immediately grasped "what a dangerous weapon Otto von Lossow had forged during the years when he was at the height of his authority in Munich." Then, in a caustic voice, the general proceeded to read aloud from some of the interrogation transcripts:

"On December 19 . . . on Rosenheimer Landstrasse, I, Michael, eighteen years old, met a man of youngish appearance who invited me to have a meal with him and—in return for payment—to spend the night with him. Having been unemployed for months, and because my mother and brothers were also suffering from hunger, I accompanied the gentleman to his home. In the morning I left." Signed: Michael. Another sample: "I, Joseph, was approached while out walking by a man with whom I went to a movie theater, and then he wanted to take me with him to his room after giving me food and cigarettes. Because I told him that I had been a keen soldier when younger and would have liked to become a noncommissioned officer, he spoke to me for hours about a new German army and urged me to engage in propaganda among my comrades in behalf of a new military formation founded by himself. He talked a great deal, but did not wish me to smoke in his room. I spent the whole night with him and . . ." Signed: Joseph . . . , twenty-two years old. And again: "In a café near the university, I, Franz . . ., an apprentice, made the acquaintance of a gentleman who spoke in Austrian dialect and told me a great deal about Vienna. When he saw I was interested in his remarks, he proceeded to explain the need for the reunification of Germany and Austria. He asked if I would be willing to devote myself to that end. He then wanted to get me some books and periodicals on the subject, which was why we went to his home. And since it was already late and the streetcars had stopped running, he invited me to stay the night with him, and I accepted. . . . The gentleman's name is Adolf Hitler; he wore a pale gabardine overcoat, and one of his distinctive features is a lock of hair that kept flopping onto his forehead." Signed: Franz. . . .

Lossow cited more young men, all of whom had testified that a man named Adolf Hitler had invited them to meals in small restaurants and taverns in the Munich area. He was eager to talk politics with them, and had declared that Germany and the world belonged to them, the young. Such conversations had gone on until after nightfall, "and these young men of the postwar period, with nothing awaiting them at home but hunger and destitution, were then prepared to sleep beside Adolf Hitler, the good friend who never tired of promising to help them."

Dollmann went on to say that Lossow had concluded his readings from police files by making the following statement: "He had ensured through trustworthy intermediaries that Hitler was aware that this [incriminating] material had already been conveyed abroad. In the event that he, Lossow, or his officers were attacked [by the Nazis], these documents would at once be published by the international press. He also strongly advised all present, in their own interests, to keep quiet about this information." In fact, Lossow lived on unscathed until his death in 1938, whereas his political ally, Bavarian State Commissioner von Kahr, was liquidated in the course of the Röhm murders in July 1934. The fact that his life was spared is striking indeed, in view of Hitler's well-documented hatred of the "traitor" Lossow.[126] It would thus have been logical to take revenge on Lossow, as well as on Kahr. Dollmann's memoirs also confirm his close ties with Lossow.[127] Since the young student was himself a homosexual, he must have known exactly what he was talking about when he published these disclosures. In short, there is no valid reason to doubt the existence of such a file on Hitler. Lossow had acquired these compromising documents because he thought they would be useful to him. This is confirmed by other official documents still in the Lossows' family archives. The Reichswehr general was doubly well advised to take out insurance because of his remarkably courageous joust with Hitler at the latter's trial for high treason.

"My best time was the time when nobody knew me," Hitler said later, during one of his nocturnal monologues. "Everyone took me for something, but not for Hitler." And: "No picture of me existed. Those who didn't know me couldn't know what I looked like."[128] It was not until 1923 that his notoriety in Munich became such that he could no longer afford to make advances of the kind recorded by the Munich police. The transcripts quoted above must thus have related mainly to the years 1920–22. This does not, however, mean that Hitler stopped seeking new contacts. It is simply that we cannot tell what form his sex life took after he rose to political prominence.

Great interest attaches to what the author Peter Martin Lampel had to say about Hitler's private life at this period in his unpublished memoirs *Niemandes Knecht*,[129] namely, that he and other former Freikorps men knew "a lot about Hitler's homosexuality from back in Munich," for instance, his liaison with young Edmund Heines, whom Goebbels propaganda branded, like Röhm, as a degenerate homosexual after his murder in 1934. "That is why I was not surprised," Lampel goes on, when Magnus Hirschfeld, a good friend of his, later told him "in confidence " that he possessed "two original transcripts, which he had preserved with special care, and which embodied the statements of two seventeen- or eighteen-year-olds from the time of the SA's foundation, including photographs of those two young men; Hirschfeld also cited the particulars described therein. . . . These transcripts pinpointed Hitler perfectly, in the most personal way possible." Hirschfeld had apparently sent them to Moscow "via a special courier." Lampel was "absolutely convinced" that Hirschfeld's information was accurate, and he believed at the time of writing—the early 1950s—that "sufficient witnesses [to its veracity] are still alive today."[130]

This renders it thoroughly understandable that Hitler, to quote Hanfstaengl, should have kept "different groups of his acquaintances . . . apart as if in watertight compartments. He told no one where he had been or where he was going; nor did he bring them into contact with each other." That is precisely the way to lead a double life. Admittedly, Hanfstaengl went on to say that, in the "sexual no-man's-land in which he lived," Hitler never found "the man who could have brought him release."[131] Maybe, maybe not.

———

So was it pure chance that the Hitler of the early 1920s found and won over men who could hasten his ascent? Surely not. His relations with Ernst Röhm and Dietrich Eckart, protagonists of two different worlds, show that homoeroticism can efface social boundaries. Hitler was able to emulate and confide in such friends, who were superior to him in many respects. But for Röhm's and Eckart's wholehearted support, he would probably have come to grief. They recognized him as a "talent" and smoothed his upward path. Hitler's own contributions to his political career were at first only twofold: his persuasive, aggressive rhetoric, and an ability to style himself a political savior and the finest possible representative of the "leadership principle." Extraneous impulses and stimuli did the rest. In short, Hitler's public career cannot be comprehended without regard to the phases in his private life.

CHAPTER FOUR

Love's Labor's Lost

IN NOVEMBER 1923, when Hitler was arrested two days after the failure of his attempted putsch, he had reached a critical stage in his existence. Within a few months, however, all his self-doubt had evaporated and he was undergoing a kind of rebirth. Detention in the fortress at Landsberg had made a different man of him. When he was prematurely released in December 1924, he resumed his political career with renewed vigor and self-confidence, certain that he alone could dictate the objectives and orientation of the *völkisch* camp. This presupposed a change in political strategy whose ideological structure he had laid down in *Mein Kampf*.[1] In place of his "old revolutionary" stance, he now advocated the legal, parliamentary route to power. For this he required an overall change of image: a less scurrilous, semirespectable public conception of the movement and its leader. By 1930 this had been achieved: the NSDAP was regarded as a relatively well-knit political force—indeed, as the "Hitler Party."[2]

Hitler also succeeded, during his political ascent, in acquiring new comrades in arms. The most politically important of them, beyond doubt, was Joseph Goebbels, in whom Hitler gained not only an ardent admirer but a demagogue as talented as himself. But Goebbels, who was preparing the ground for the Party from the Berlin end, could pay only brief visits to Munich. Hitler was in close contact during these years with three other men.

A photograph taken in 1932 shows him with two of these close associates:[3] Rudolf Hess, his private secretary from 1925 on; and Julius Schreck, his chauffeur since 1928. The only one missing from this group photo—for reasons to be explained later—is Emil Maurice, Schreck's predecessor. Hess, Schreck and Hitler are pictured on an embankment beside the North Sea, wearing fashionable slouch hats and looking quite nonchalantly in the direction of Heinrich Hoffmann's camera. No sign here of "Führerlike" aloofness; the whole scene conveys that three friends are spending a few exuberant hours in each other's company. And Hitler's relations with Hess, Schreck and Maurice really were like that: sustained by an awareness of mutual affection and loyalty.

These "employer-employee relationships" could not on any account be allowed to look like homosexual partnerships, however. This was probably why, during the post-Landsberg years, women suddenly appeared in Hitler's life, his public life included. But care is indicated here: accounts of the period are extremely vague and in many cases apocryphal. The only certainty is that Hitler made ostentatious attempts to establish contact with women at this time. This requires explanation, but from a perspective centered on "Hitler's men," not "Hitler's women."

RUDOLF HESS

On December 25, 1924, Hitler was pacing restlessly up and down in Ernst Hanfstaengl's apartment. Finally, he groaned: "Ah, my Rudi, my Hesserl. . . . Isn't it terrible that he's still locked up?"[4]

Rudolf Hess, who was released from detention only nine days after Hitler, never left his side from then on. This marked the beginning— not only for Hess himself, one presumes—of a "most beautiful human experience," of "shared joy and sorrow, cares and hopes, hatreds and loves; of all the manifestations of greatness—and also of all the little signs of human weakness required to make a person truly lovable."[5] The friendship sealed in 1924 endured until Hitler's death.

Many contemporary observers thought Hess an "almost patholog- ically sensitive, weak, and impressionable person"[6] and detected markedly feminine traits in him. He soon acquired this reputation and was variously nicknamed "Fräulein Hess" (Otto Strasser), "Fräulein Anna" or "Fräulein Gusti" (Ernst Hanfstaengl), "Black Paula" (attributed to Ernst Röhm), "Black Grete" (Bella Fromm) and "Black Emma" (Erich Ebermayer).[7] In 1934, "in full cognizance of the legal consequences," Strasser accused Rudolf Hess "before the German people and the world, of homosexual sentiments and unnatural sexual activities," even citing Hess's own wife in support of his contention.[8] Kurt Lüdecke, on the other hand, could not understand, after meeting "Fräulein Hess," how the man had come by such a nickname. To him, the "Führer's deputy" appeared to be "masculinity personified." Like many other people, however, he found Hess unapproachable; he had never once looked Lüdecke in the eye.[9]

It was clearly hard to fathom the nature of this reserved and taci- turn man. What is more informative is the self-portrait Hess drew in a letter to his future wife, Ilse Pröhl, in 1923: "I am, I think, a strange mixture, generally speaking, hence the tensions that sometimes make my life so difficult. Today I need a harmonious atmosphere, want to work quietly in seclusion and hear nothing of politics and martial clamor, yearn with every fiber of my being for a cultured environment, for Mozart, piano, and flute; tomorrow, I go marching through tem- pest and splashing puddles, plunge into turmoil, public oratory, fierce debates, almost despising what was dear and sacred to me yesterday; today, hypersensitive; tomorrow, rough, gruff, boisterous.—I don't know what to make of myself. Is it modern cultural nerves to an extreme degree, or something unresolved that vainly seeks an outlet? I don't know."[10] This is the self-revelation of someone similar in type to Ernst Röhm: a soldierly "fighter-nature" with aesthetic leanings. Hess discerned this spiritual dichotomy in Hitler, too: "Outwardly so hard, he is touchingly soft within."[11] And: "What a mixture of cold, mature calculation combined with unbridled boyishness!"[12] If this was not an elective affinity, what was it?

What do we know about Hess's life before he met Hitler? A businessman's son born in 1894, he spent his childhood in Alexandria, the Egyptian seaport. When he was thirteen his parents sent him off to a boarding school in Bad Godesberg. Three years later he went to Switzerland, where he attended a commercial college. In October 1912 he embarked on a commercial apprenticeship in Hamburg and volunteered for military service in August 1914. Early in 1919, when he was twenty-four, he was discharged from the army and moved to Munich. His intention had been to study economics in the Bavarian capital, but his wartime comrade and friend Max Hofweber soon introduced him to the extreme right-wing scene. Through Hofweber, Hess joined the *völkisch*, antisemitic Thule Association. He participated in acts of sabotage against the Councils Republic and, ultimately, in its military defeat. The personal contacts he formed during those months were crucial to the future course of his life. He got to know Dietrich Eckart, Ernst Röhm and Karl Mayr, but also Karl Haushofer, the university teacher and geopolitician. From May to October 1919 he served under Epp, the Freikorps commander, and it was then that he must first have met Hitler.[13]

According to Ilse Hess, her husband's life was then governed by twin poles: the university and the Party. The embodiment of the former was Haushofer, his "fatherly friend"; of the latter, Adolf Hitler.[14] Hess had developed a close relationship with Haushofer, who was twenty-five years older than himself.[15] The two of them often spent whole nights sitting together in Haushofer's home, and they also made joint excursions. "He's a wonderful person,"[16] Hess enthusiastically told his parents, and Haushofer dedicated to his "young friend Rudolf Hess" a hymn reminiscent of Stefan George, which spoke of "his eyes festively illumining closed doors" just as "a sunset is reflected in a spring."[17] Ilse Hess later confessed, in a restrained fashion, that she had "long been almost a trifle jealous" of Haushofer, who seemed to have positively "absorbed" her boyfriend.[18]

But Hess was preoccupied at this period not only by his relationship with "Karli,"[19] but also by his work with and for Hitler. Although he formally joined the NSDAP on July 1, 1920, he had probably been active within its orbit since the beginning of that year. He built up its "intelligence service" and attended to problems of organization. What was doubtless more important was the fact that Hess soon sensed a special affinity with Hitler. "He has become a dear friend of mine," he wrote to a girl cousin in April 1921. "A splendid person!"[20] And in August he inveighed against those within the Party who criticized Hitler's lifestyle: "You spend too much time sitting with Eckart and young Hess in the Fledermaus Bar," they admonished the party leader. "It isn't good for you!"[21] Writing in the *Völkischer Beobachter*, Hess retorted that he "knew Hitler very well," had been "with him almost daily for eighteen months" and thus knew best how unjustified these charges of idleness were.[22] A letter in which Hess had defended his friend to Premier von Kahr of Bavaria a few months earlier used similar language: "I know Herr Hitler very well at first hand, since I speak with him almost daily and am also on close personal terms with him."[23]

We may therefore assume that the ties between Hess and Hitler were very close even during the initial phase of Hitler's political career. As Ilse Hess saw it, "well-nigh magical" forces were at work,[24] and Captain Karl Mayr later reported that Hess often worked Hitler up into an emotional state, and that the latter transposed these states of excitement into political agitation. Mayr also said that the party leader sometimes went into seclusion with Hess for days before an important speech, and that Hess "in some unknown way" managed to get Hitler "into the frenetic state in which he came forth to address the public."[25] Hess was soon second to none in his enthusiasm at having finally found "the Führer personality that alone can carry the struggle to its conclusion." And again: "Hitler's nature is willpower in its purest form."[26] Such was the language in which he proclaimed Hitler a cult figure as early as 1921. Thanks to his upper-middle-class origins, officer status and social graces, he also enjoyed the confidence of influential people, and could thus provide Hitler with valuable contacts. Karl Mayr went so far as to call him the future party leader's "earliest and most successful mentor."

In 1921/22, when Hitler became increasingly attached to Dietrich Eckart and Ernst Hanfstaengl, Hess withdrew into the background for a while. He resumed his studies and spent some months at Zurich's Technische Hochschule.[27] His relationship with Ilse Pröhl also became more intimate at this time.[28] In the fall of 1923, when the Munich putsch loomed, he was staying at his parents' country house in the Fichtelgebirge. A few days before the attempted coup d'état he received personal instructions from Hitler to come to the Bavarian capital without delay. Consequently, he was back at Hitler's side on the evening of November 8, when they stormed the Bürgerbräukeller together. Hess fled to Austria when the putsch failed, but soon returned in secret to Munich, where he took refuge with his friend Haushofer. In the middle of May he gave himself up to the authorities and was imprisoned at Landsberg shortly thereafter.

There he was reunited with Hitler, or "the Tribune," as he now called him. He soon became Hitler's leading associate. They were both housed in the so-called Feldherren Wing, together with Hermann Kriebel, the Kampfbund commander, and Friedrich Weber, leader of the Bund Oberland. Emil Maurice acted as a liaison man between the

"Feldherren" and the "Landsknechten" groups of detainees. Subsequent descriptions given by Hans Kallenbach, a fellow prisoner, convey the kind of society that existed within the prison walls: a lively, militant community in which the atmosphere was a cross between an officers' mess and a men's hostel. Not a hint of dejection or regret. The agenda included sporting contests and rowdy evening get-togethers. In general, the putschists enjoyed their "detention center's" amenities. In a letter to his mother[SvE1], Hess enthused about the "hot baths always available to us in the modern bathroom reserved for us alone"[29]—a luxury the inmates often made use of and enjoyed.[30] However, many of their modes of behavior brought the governor down on them from time to time: "Nudity outside the fortress living room (in the communal antechamber) is not allowed. The proprieties have to be observed everywhere, especially when several fellow inmates share a room with you"[31]—a telling remark.

Hitler's months at Landsberg were certainly no real punishment—indeed, they gave him a chance to rest and relax. "The Tribune is looking grand," Hess wrote to his girlfriend. Hitler was bathing and exercising, he reported, and since he drank "hardly any alcohol aside from a little beer, he must be healthy in the absence of the usual hustle and bustle, what with ample sleep, fresh air, and a state of mind that is far from despondent. On the contrary! He has plenty of plans for the future."[32]

Hitler was, in fact, experiencing a high, and Kershaw is perfectly correct in stating that "his almost mystical faith in himself as walking with destiny, with a 'mission' to rescue Germany, dates from this time."[33] It was Rudolf Hess who persuaded Hitler to believe in his vocation and helped him to project himself into the role of "Führer of the German people." Although Hitler had already developed a definite messianic mania by 1923, it was Hess's tireless work on the "myth" that created the requisite political stagecraft. The first part of *Mein Kampf* originated at Landsberg in dialogue with Hess. In writing this book, Hitler was not only ideologically defining his political program; he also intended it to market his life to date as the prior history of his mission. With Hess he could test the plausibility of his lies before he went public with them. At the same time, Hess exerted an influence on the ideological orientation of the whole book. The Lebensraum [territorial expansion] concept, for example, derived from him and/or his friend Haushofer, who often visited Landsberg to talk with the detainees.[34]

As time went by, Hitler and Hess quite deliberately evolved a certain role-playing relationship: Hitler was the "Führer" and Hess the faithful "Hagen"[35] willing to serve him unto death. Theirs was a very close relationship, and Hess was better acquainted than anyone else with "the Tribune's inner thoughts, his attitude to matters of every conceivable kind, his whole nature." They trusted and empathized with each other to the nth degree.[36] It was only logical, therefore, that Hess turned down Haushofer's offer of an assistant's post and—despite the lower salary—became Hitler's personal adviser. Joseph Goebbels described him at the time as the ideal assistant: "calm, amiable, shrewd, reserved: the private secretary."[37] He arranged appointments, dealt with the mail, accompanied Hitler on his travels, organized meals and overnight accommodations. The two men spent a great deal of time together in the seclusion of the Obersalzberg, and in 1926, in the "Kampfhäusl," a small cabin on the edge of the woods, Hitler wrote the second part of *Mein Kampf.*[38]

There is no indication that the friendship Hitler and Hess had sealed at Landsberg was ever in jeopardy during the years that followed. No ill feeling resulted, even when Hess decided to marry his longtime fiancée in December 1927—in fact, Hitler himself had advised him to take this step. On the day of the wedding, however, Hess noticed that he was "pale and trembling." The "good Tribune" was unable to eat anything "for sheer agitation," and had not relaxed "with friend Maurice until after the ceremony was over."[39] This possibly indicates how deeply affected Hitler must have been by his friend's decision, even though the wedding was little more than the beginning of a marriage in name only.

Although Hess sometimes referred in very affectionate terms to his wife Ilse, that "companion in all my thoughts and feelings," she ultimately remained no more than "a good comrade." Echoing Schopenhauer, he used to say that he had fished a stray eel out of a sackful of snakes.[40] It is hardly surprising that Ilse Hess later complained that she had gotten no more out of her marriage than a "girl confirmand,"[41] and she even compared herself, where "the pleasures of matrimony" were concerned, to a "convent schoolgirl."[42] Although Hitler had nothing to fear from Frau Hess, he is said to have cherished a profound dislike for her. According to one of his inner circle, what particularly incensed him was that she "was forfeiting her femininity" and becoming "hermaphroditic"[43] because she aspired to dominate her husband. It is interesting that Hitler scented competition in the masculine aspects of her behavior, not the feminine. As he must have known, Hess was insusceptible to the latter.

Goebbels, too, was eager to make "a friend" of Hitler once he had gotten to know him personally. He regarded him as a "hothead" but felt convinced that he had "a lot of heart." This manifested itself after Goebbels had made a speech in Munich's Bürgerbräukeller: "At the end Hitler embraced me." Goebbels was "happy" and moved to tears. Later, when they were sitting with a few others, he found Hitler "splendid. Could drive one insane." In short: "I love him."[44]

Hess had shown himself similarly overwhelmed by Hitler's sentimental impulses back in Landsberg. When the "Tribune" started to "sob" while recounting some episode from his time in the war, Hess, too, broke down. "I'm more devoted to him than ever! I love him!"[45]

"He has taken me to his heart like no one else,"[46] declared Goebbels. But Hitler had given others the same feeling—deliberately so. He knew how to woo and ensnare, how to make his associates feel genuinely wanted. Ideological indoctrination apart, few could hold a candle to Hitler when it came to soft-soaping people. He was familiar with the human hunger for appreciation—which had, after all, propelled him into politics—and he did his best to assuage that hunger in his immediate circle. He sensed that this alone could bring him something on which he himself was vitally dependent: devoted donkeywork and an implicit belief in his mission.

Was homoeroticism involved in all this? In Hess's case, most certainly. His wife revealed that she and her husband were "preoccupied"[47] with elements of the youth movement, notably the "ideas and impulses" propagated by Hans Blüher and Gustav Wyneken. Many men regarded Blüher's two-volume work *Die Rolle der Erotik in der männlichen Gesellschaft* [The Role of Eroticism in Male Society], published in 1917 and 1919, as a gospel. Wyneken, a school principal suspected of pedophilia, had in 1921 published *Eros*, a sensational apologia in which he spoke in behalf of "pederasty" and "platonic eros."[48] In essence, Blüher's and Wyneken's concerns were the same. According to Wyneken, a boy could experience "no greater happiness or good fortune . . . than to meet the man to whom he can entrust himself: the man who comprehends his yearning; the man to whom he can give his love because he feels love emanating from him; the man who opens his heart to him, who permits him to share in his life, and who becomes symbolic of a more exalted, more divine existence."[49] As for Blüher, he wrote that even in a Wandervogel's early years, one could detect "genuine cries of longing for the beloved man"; changing the world by means of "creative acts" entailed that those acts be inspired by the "eros" directed at "the hero or demigod."[50]

We do not know the extent to which Hess addressed such ideas, but there are many indications that this man who confessed that he "didn't know what to make of himself"[51] may have derived some support from them, and that they gave him a chance to accept his homoerotic tendencies—indeed, to view them favorably. At all events, it was consistent with what contemporary writers had to offer in the way of justification that Hitler should have become his "hero" and "demigod." And to Hess he remained one of the "last true ideals in this . . . world."[52] Hitler never forgot that. Writing to her husband in 1954, Ilse Hess described a conversation she had had with Erich Kempka, Hitler's last chauffeur. Apparently, he had told her about a "very remarkable talk" he had had with the "Führer" in 1945, just before the war ended. Hitler had observed "rather ruefully, rather resignedly, rather ironically, but with infinite affection, that it had at least proved possible, in all those years, for *one* idealist of the first water to gain an ineradicable place in history," namely, Hess.[53]

Hess continued to serve Hitler with undiminished devotion until his spectacular flight to England. On the personal level, however, their relationship cooled a little during 1930. Hitler was now faced with problems to whose solution Hess could contribute little or nothing. Their private lives were diverging. Thus Hess found it a doubly moving moment when, on January 30, 1933, the new Reich Chancellor summoned him, "out of all the leading figures in the reception room, to his bedroom in the 'Kaiserhof.'"[54] With this gesture, Hitler was symbolically reemphasizing their old bond, but that was its only significance. There was no doubt that the new head of state would duly reward his longtime friend for loyal services rendered, but when he made Hess his "deputy" in April 1933 and appointed him a minister some months later, he was merely formalizing their respective positions, not resuming their former close relationship. At the same time, Hess could rest assured, and even publicly proclaim, that "I probably know the Führer and his every last thought better than anyone else."[55]

HITLER, EMIL MAURICE AND GELI RAUBAL:
AN ETERNAL TRIANGLE

"Hess's solemn gravity," Hitler is reported to have told Heinrich Hoffmann in the summer of 1927, "gets on my nerves occasionally." Much as he appreciated his favorite disciple's introverted character, there were times when Hess was simply not cheerful enough for his taste. Not so Emil Maurice, the high-spirited daredevil to whom he became increasingly attached. Maurice received his first public accolade in January 1922, when Hitler enthusiastically referred to him as "our greyhound."[56] On that occasion the party leader was recalling a public brawl in the Hofbräuhaus, which he later described as the SA's "baptism of fire." It was then, in November 1921, that he had been instantly struck by the slim young man's vigorous and pugnacious appearance.

Born near Eckernförde in 1897, Emil Maurice had trained as a watchmaker in his native North Germany before moving to Munich in 1917. After World War I, in which he saw a few months' military service, he became politically active. In 1919 he joined Hitler's party, and before long he was commanding its "Gymnastic and Sports Section"—in other words, the bouncers who saw off political opponents at public meetings. At some stage in 1921 he became Hitler's chauffeur and, thus, one of his closest associates.[57] That he was now one of the initiates is confirmed by Julius Schaub, who described Maurice after the war as the man who "probably knew more than anyone else about Hitler's early days up to 1925."[58] Together with Hitler's "Assault Squad," he took part in the November 1923 putsch, was duly convicted and served his sentence at Landsberg from April 1924 until the end of January 1925.[59]

While there he acted as Hitler's liaison officer and confidential agent, dealt with his correspondence and produced the fair copy of his *Mein Kampf* manuscript.[60] Maurice was no more disheartened by his months in detention than were Hitler and Hess. On the contrary, the young man's sense of well-being is quite apparent from a snapshot taken at the time, which shows him standing immediately behind Hitler. Both men are smiling at the camera, wearing outfits that recur in later photographs of Hitler and his entourage on informal occasions. According to Henriette von Schirach, Hitler and Maurice often wore "lederhosen, white linen shirts, and faded, pale blue linen jackets with staghorn buttons"[61] while traveling—somewhat incongruous attire for a couple of non-Bavarians. In 1926, when Goebbels encountered his boss "in mountain dress," he commented: "Looks quite droll."[62] Hitler evidently liked his North German chauffeur to wear this quaint get-up.

At Landsberg, if not before, the two men became close friends. Hitler called Maurice "Maurizl" or "Mosel"; Maurice addressed the "Führer" simply as "my dear Hitler," a very self-assured form of address for a henchman eight years younger and without any political services to his name. It occurs in a letter dated January 1925 in which Maurice expressly requested the party leader to see him in person, "as promised," on the day of his release: "Looking forward to a happy reunion in freedom, yours, E. M."[63] In the years that followed, Hitler granted his chauffeur access to the innermost reaches of his private life. Maurice had a key to Hitler's Thierschstrasse lodgings, took care of his clothes and laundry and performed many other mundane chores that would normally have been undertaken by a housekeeper.[64] But Maurice was also there when things got tough and never shirked a fight[65]—something for which Hitler officially commended his "good Maurice."[66] As an automobile fan, Hitler took a special delight in Maurice's driving. They "always zoomed along at top speed," Rudolf Hess recalled later. "'Maurice, supercharger!'—that was how we used to race around."[67]

But Maurice also had a romantic, aesthetic side. One of the photographs taken at Landsberg shows him holding a guitar in his hand, like a personal attribute. Many members of Hitler's Munich set cherished pleasant memories of "Mauritzl's" contributions to social gatherings. One of them was Heinrich Hoffmann's daughter Henriette, who described how he used, on outings, to "fetch his guitar from the trunk, sit down on the forest floor with his back against a tree, and sing Irish folksongs while we hummed along." She thought him "a sensitive person, not an ambitious slugger; tenderness underlay his affable exterior."[68] It was doubtless this mixture of panache and charm that Hitler, too, found so appealing.

Like Hitler, Maurice was attractive to women, the difference being that he did not spurn the attentions of the opposite sex. In his recollections of the months in detention at Landsberg, Hans Kallenbach tells of a romance that blossomed over the prison wall. Apparently, the "pining swain" used to exchange nightly hand signals with a young woman who lived in one of the apartments across the way.[69] Thanks to his fellow detainees' incessant teasing, "the Führer himself discovered handsome Emil's sentimental secret. He dismissed the matter with a forgiving smile."[70]

Hitler kept something of a jealous eye on his "handsome Emil." He probably envied his easy-going relations with the opposite sex. If Hitler had been similarly inclined, he would have been spared the embarrassing situation that arose on New Year's Eve 1924. Heinrich Hoffmann, who was giving a party at his home, recalled how one of the employees from his photographic studio, an attractive young woman, lured Hitler into a doorway with a sprig of mistletoe above it. There, in keeping with custom, she clasped the unsuspecting "Führer" around the neck and gave him a passionate kiss. "I shall never forget the look of surprise and dismay on Hitler's face!" wrote Hoffmann. An awkward silence fell. "Bewildered and helpless as a child, Hitler stood there, biting his lip in an effort to master his anger." Thoroughly upset, he left the party soon afterward.[71] His attitude to the opposite sex was still pubertal. Even the prison staff at Landsberg had noticed that "women and girls left him cold."[72]

As someone who would soon be forty and aspired to rule Germany, Hitler had to sort this problem out, not only because he was in the limelight but for reasons of self-esteem as well. He may even have believed, by analogy with Maurice, that he could do one thing without abstaining from the other. But to find this out he needed help and encouragement, and Maurice refused him neither. "We sometimes followed girls together," he recalled. "I was like his shadow."[73] He confided to Christa Schroeder, Hitler's secretary, what used to happen when he and his boss were on trips away from Munich. He had to devote the time Hitler spent in meetings to "picking up girls." They "sat with them and talked. Hitler gave the girls money, too, but he never asked for anything in return."[74] Then again, Maurice recalled, Hitler and he sometimes went to the art college together "to admire the nude models."[75] What can Hitler have hoped to get out of this? He probably wanted to cure his excessive shyness, but these isolated endeavors were an insufficient remedy.

For all that, Hitler is recorded as having made advances to various women in the post-Landsberg years: initially to the daughters of families he consorted with in private,[76] and later—according to Christa Schroeder—to Ada Klein, a staffer on the *Völkischer Beobachter*, whom he met several times in 1925/26—significantly enough, at Emil Maurice's apartment. But "no intimacies ever took place";[77] Hitler was still too bashful for that. This did not, however, apply when he made the acquaintance of sixteen-year-old Maria Reiter at Berchtesgaden in the fall of 1926.[78] Although not everything "Hitler's beloved" told *Der Stern* in 1959 should be taken at face value, she certainly did not invent their relationship. The couple really did meet often in 1926/27. Hitler called her "Mimi," "Mizzi" and "Mizerl." They exchanged letters and gifts. However, Hitler's declarations of love make a false, hollow, uninvolved impression,[79] like the wooden phrases in manuals of advice for courting couples: "Ah, child, you really don't know what you mean to me and how fond of you I am." When she knew him better, he said, she must get down to reading *Mein Kampf*: "Read the books, then you'll be able to understand me."

Although Hitler led Fräulein Reiter to hope that they might become an item, at least for a while, his affection for "the dear child" waned in the course of 1927. A previous episode had already made it apparent that no genuine love affair could result. Having on one occasion chauffeured the couple into the woods, Maurice remained discreetly seated in the car while Hitler and his "Mizerl" set off. They eventually came to a clearing, where he stationed her in front of a tall fir tree. He "turned me to the left, to the right. He stepped back a few paces—gazed at me the way a painter poses his model. . . . 'A glorious picture,' he blurted out." Finally, he clasped her to him and said: "'Mimilein, dear, sweet girl, now I simply can't help myself.' He hugged me really tightly around the neck. He kissed me. He didn't know what to do." How could he have known, in default of any physical desire to guide him? It was only his quirky imitation of a painter that had lent him the courage to venture as far as he did.

Hitler once paid court to Lotte Bechstein, the daughter of his patroness Helene Bechstein. In later years she told her husband the reason why she and Hitler had never gotten together: "He couldn't kiss."[80] His fixation on his own sex was too strong and his self-imposed heterosexuality too dependent on an effort of the will. All his attempts to start a love affair with a woman had come to nothing.

Hitler thought he had disposed of this worrisome problem when his niece Angela Raubal, nicknamed Geli, turned up in Munich in the latter half of 1927. The relationship that developed between him and the daughter of his half sister Angela remains a highly controversial subject to this day.[81] In my opinion, any interpretation of it must include Maurice as a key figure, because the relationship was a three-cornered one. To put it another way, Hitler's woman problem was here combined with his love for a man.

It is not entirely certain when Hitler and his niece first met. Their initial encounter probably occurred in the summer of 1924, when Angela Raubal visited her half brother at Landsberg with her two children, sixteen-year-old Geli and son Leo. Niece and uncle did not become more closely acquainted until 1927, when Geli came to Munich on a school trip and took some classmates to see her famous relation. She graduated from high school the same year and moved to Munich in the fall. But before she enrolled as a medical student and moved into lodgings near the university,[82] Hitler took her, her mother and a girlfriend of hers on a tour through Germany. A letter from Rudolf Hess, who had joined the party "as a favor to the Tribune," is informative on the subject. Hitler had invited him along so that he didn't have to be "alone with the 'womenfolk.'" They visited Dresden and Berlin, went to the opera and the theater. Hess described "the Tribune's young niece" as a "tall, pretty girl of nineteen" who was "always cheerful and as little at a loss for words as her uncle." Indeed, "The latter is hardly a match for her ready tongue." Hitler was "convinced that she won't last more than two semesters, but will get married first. Other people, including the young niece, share his opinion."[83] Although meant as a joke, this forecast soon took on a different complexion.

For Hitler's niece promptly fell in love with Maurice. We do not know whether her love was reciprocated, but it is apparent from a letter she wrote to her "dear Emil" on Christmas Eve 1927 that Hitler at first refused to countenance the liaison. Two days before Christmas he had given the girl a thorough telling-off, even threatening to send her back to her mother in Vienna. Geli wrote that she had "never experienced such suffering before. But it had to happen, and it was definitely good for us both. I now feel that these past days have united us forever." The fact that Hitler did not yet categorically prohibit the liaison was due largely to Ilse Hess's intervention. Hitler had nonetheless insisted, Geli went on, "that we wait two years. Think of it, Emil, two whole years in which we can kiss only now and then and always under O.A.'s [Onkel Adolf's] supervision. You must work to make a life for us, and we'll be allowed to see each other only with other people around." Furthermore, their love was to remain "entirely secret" and she was to go on with her studies. Still, Geli was "glad that I can be with you. We'll see each other often, and often on our own, Uncle A. has promised. He really is a dear."[84]

It seemed that Frau Hess was "the only person" who "believes that you really love me." Hitler probably knew better, because he knew his "Mauritzl" and did not credit him with any serious intentions, but he put a good face on the matter and ended by being "awfully nice" about it. To this extent, Geli's letter may be construed as an all-clear, a sign that a modus vivendi had been established. In a rather patriarchal fashion, the uncle had returned his lovesick niece to the fold of bourgeois morality and evinced a remarkable—indeed, scarcely credible— willingness to compromise. Hitler's ulterior motive becomes discernible when we ask ourselves what he really hoped to gain from the solution he had brought about: first, he did not have to dispense with either Geli or Maurice; and, second, he retained the ability to dictate the future course of developments.

But a three-cornered relationship of this kind cannot survive indefinitely. The two men had a serious falling-out in the months that followed. Maurice stated subsequently that his boss had dismissed him at Christmas 1927 "because of a personal dispute."[85] He said that Hitler had not approved of his betrothal.[86] It was Hitler's jealous love of his niece that had set him against Hitler: "He loved her, but it was a peculiarly unavowed love."[87] However, Maurice's assertions are quite inconsistent with the fundamental tone of Geli's letter to him. Nothing suggests that Hitler was at the time consumed with jealous love for his niece—in fact, a letter he wrote to his friend Winifred Wagner at the turn of the year struck a very confident note and said that he took a thoroughly "cheerful" view of the future.[88] So how had the dispute arisen? Did the conflict between the two men have anything at all to do with Geli Raubal? Less, perhaps, than is commonly supposed.

The fact is that in April 1928 Maurice went to court to claim RM 3000 in arrears of salary. He won his case: his employer was ordered to pay up, although only to the extent of RM 500.[89] But that did not settle the matter as far as Maurice was concerned. He now applied further pressure. Geli is reported to have told Otto Strasser that she had overheard a fierce altercation between him and Hitler. "You'll never set foot in this house again!" Hitler had shouted. "If you throw me out," Maurice retorted angrily, "I'll go and tell everything to the *Frankfurter Zeitung!*"[90] That he was on course for blackmail is shown by the way in which he made a mountain out of the "Mimi Reiter" molehill.

As early as 1927, Party headquarters had received some anonymous letters accusing Hitler of seducing a minor. It later transpired that their author was a certain Ida Arnold, a girlfriend of Maurice, who had invited "Mimi" to coffee and skillfully pumped her for information. Feeling cornered, Hitler requested Maria Reiter to make a sworn deposition to the effect that she had had "no relationship of any kind" with him.[91] Although this amounted to flagrant perjury, it must have seemed Hitler's only possible recourse in the summer of 1928. He was clearly under extreme pressure, because nothing could have presented a greater threat to him, as party leader, than revelations about his private life—and who knew more about that subject than Emil Maurice?

At all events, Hitler feared that his woman problem would be dragged into the light of day—so much so that he was already making preparations to defend himself in court. In this he was greatly assisted by the senior Party judge, Walter Buch, whom he invited to his home at the beginning of July 1928 and entrusted with "a personal matter." Buch had to promise "on his word of honor" not to reveal the contents of his secret brief. Everything suggests that Hitler was currently threatened with a scandal, a court case involving shady episodes in his private life. The Party judge invited Geli and Hitler to spend some time at his home to "help them get over their grievous experience [of Maurice's disloyalty?]."[92] Instead, they decided to make a trip to North Germany, where they spent some "happy days" in Hamburg and on Helgoland in the company of Joseph Goebbels.[93] It is doubtful whether this diversion helped Hitler to get over his "grievous experience." Buch, at all events, was "extremely concerned" by the "contempt for humanity" that Hitler had displayed in the fall of 1928. At the same time, he could well understand why he had been "plunged into such a mood by bitter experience of people on whom you long believed you could rely." But he counseled a clean break, not revenge. "You must not burden yourself with those who have abused your trust and lied to you (albeit after periods of seemingly loyal devotion)"—"Faith in the Führer" would be strengthened only "if the public see that he is strong enough to repudiate unprincipled weaklings, notwithstanding their long years of service."[94]

Although Buch's oblique language sheds no light on the real background to the dispute, it does show how dramatically matters had come to a head. Hitler's associates evidently had to exert all their influence to dissuade the furious party leader from doing something rash. Their attempts at conciliation bore fruit, because the dispute was settled—sans public scandal, court case or bloodshed—before the year was out. But the aftershocks must have continued for some time, to judge by a diary entry Goebbels made in October after a conversation with Gauleiter Karl Kaufmann. The latter, he wrote, had told him some "crazy things about the Chief": "He and his niece Geli and Maurice. The tragedy of woman. Must one lose heart? Why must women make us all suffer so? I firmly believe in Hitler. I understand everything. True and untrue."[95] So Goebbels, too, was uncertain how to classify this "craziness." He construed the affair as a fight over a woman, and Hitler could only welcome that interpretation, because his dramatic breach with Maurice might have rattled skeletons in a closet that had to remain inaccessible at all costs, even to his closest associates.

On August 1, 1928, Hitler wrote Maurice an unobjectionable reference.[96] The latter now described himself as an "outlaw" who had to live "in complete seclusion" and carve out a new life subjected to "many severe privations."[97] He was not too badly off, however, because he soon opened a watchmaker's shop in Munich—even though it was years since he had worked as a watchmaker and he still lacked his master's diploma. He must also have required a substantial amount of starting capital, and who but Hitler could have provided such a cash injection? Otto Strasser claimed that Maurice was paid RM 20,000 in hush money.[98] He now quit the stage. Although he did not leave the Party,[99] he and Hitler were through.

And Geli Raubal? She had lost her betrothed but was "compensated" by Hitler. From the end of 1928 she was his constant companion. He took her out in public—they were seen shopping together, at the opera, at the movies, at the theater—and made her take singing lessons. She not only accompanied him on his travels but was even privileged to enliven his male get-togethers—at the Café Heck, for example—with her jaunty presence. In the fall of 1929 she moved into a room in Hitler's apartment on Prinzregentenplatz. Hitler undoubtedly enjoyed this simulacrum of an engaged couple's existence, for Geli was a pleasant companion. Almost everyone in Hitler's entourage thought the same. Hess took to her from the start, and Julius Schaub described her as "a big child you couldn't help liking," extraordinarily "vivacious" and devoid of "inhibitions."[100] Her manner appealed to Hitler, who made a point of "showing her off everywhere" so as to "impress his Party comrades."[101] Hanfstaengl even wrote that "for a while, Hitler behaved like a youngster in love."[102] One can only speculate as to what really went on between him and Geli, but it is unlikely that he became intimate with her. Christa Schroeder, for example, was convinced that he had "no sexual relations with her."[103]

Be that as it may, Hitler wielded an ever greater measure of control over the lively, venturesome young woman, until he finally had her completely enmeshed in the leading strings of his own selfish interests. Hoffmann reports him as saying: "Right! I love Geli, and I could marry her; but you know my views and you know that I am determined to remain a bachelor. Therefore I reserve to myself the right to watch over the circle of her male acquaintances until such a time as the right man comes along. What Geli now regards as restraint is in reality a wise precaution. I am quite determined to see that she does not fall into the hands of some unworthy adventurer or swindler."[104] This is consistent with what Christa Schroeder inferred from his accounts of their relationship, namely, that he had "intended to school Geli for a life together."[105] That made sense because, having at last found a woman in the person of his attractive niece, he had solved a problem affecting his reputation. The outwardly "marital" appearance of their relationship caused rumors to circulate, and they, too, were more than welcome to him.

But Hitler had reckoned without Geli herself, who did not envision her future in the same light, or not permanently. The life she had initially enjoyed became an irksome golden cage. She wanted to be more than a mere showpiece. As Henriette von Schirach wrote, "during the years when she lived in such close proximity to Hitler, she became withdrawn and serious."[106] The consequences are common knowledge: fits of depression, attempts to escape, fierce rows and an early death effected with a bullet from Hitler's revolver. Many have tried to reconstruct what actually happened to the twenty-three-year-old

woman in September 1931, but their efforts have always been
thwarted by lack of firm evidence.

Some eighteen months after Geli Raubal ended her young life, her
former fiancé suddenly reappeared. When the National Socialists
came to power in the spring of 1933, Emil Maurice reentered his
"dear Hitler's" service. He later justified this rapprochement by claim-
ing that Himmler had threatened and harassed him for weeks before-
hand.[107] This may be true, because Munich's new police chief was
eager to settle many scores dating from 1928. Maurice further stated
that he had approached Hitler in person "with deep concern." As luck
would have it, the latter had immediately shaken hands "in token of
reconciliation" and told him: "Mosel, I did you an injustice."[108] What
Maurice does not say is that he had to pay for this "mark of favor"
with a complicity that may also have been intended to test his courage
and reliability. On March 9, 1933, the day the Party assumed power
in Bavaria, he stormed into the offices of the *Gerade Weg*, which was
edited by Hitler's opponent Fritz Gerlich, with Max Amann and a
squad of Brownshirts. "Where's that bastard Gerlich?" Amann kept
shouting. When he eventually found his victim, he dealt him several
brutal blows in the face.[109] Four days after his *Gerade Weg* performance, Maurice received Hitler's handwritten confirmation of his
appointment as a Munich city councilor.[110] A portrait photograph
taken in 1933 shows him proudly wearing an SS officer's uniform
with his councilor's chain around his neck.[111]

Maurice had an opportunity to prove his renewed devotion to
Hitler during the latter's sanguinary settlement of accounts with
Röhm in 1934.[112] In recognition of "his services in putting down the
criminals' revolt"[113] he was appointed an SS-Standartenführer
[colonel]. He had finally and completely effaced the stain of his defec-
tion. Now, if not before, he and Hitler revived their old acquaintanceship. In October 1934 Maurice was invited by Hitler to join him on

an excursion to Landsberg, and he was also present at the annual commemoration of the Munich putsch: a photograph taken that year shows him outside the Feldherrenhalle, standing in the front row immediately behind Hess and Hitler.[114] It transpired after the war that the two men were not only reconciled but on friendly terms once more: Maurice's denazification papers record that he was Hitler's "constant companion"[115] whenever the latter came to stay in Munich, and his attorney conceded that "the Führer liked to see him when present in Munich."[116]

From now on, Hitler was unstinting with his solicitous gestures of friendship. In 1935, when Maurice decided to marry a medical student fourteen years younger than himself, Hitler attended their engagement party at the Hotel Vierjahreszeiten. He was "extremely charming to me," Hedwig Maurice recalled later: "Not a practiced charm, but one that comes from the heart."[117] It was ostentatiously announced that the "Führer" was making his apartment available for the forthcoming wedding reception.[118] Although Hitler had to cry off at short notice, he visited the newlyweds' new home soon afterward and made them a wedding gift of RM 1000.[119]

Their marriage was, however, associated with certain difficulties. Being an SS officer, Maurice had to submit a family tree before marrying, and Himmler's zealous genealogists discovered the existence of a Jewish forebear. The Reichsführer-SS proposed to expel "non-Aryan" Maurice from his organization, but Hitler ruled that "in this one, exceptional case" Maurice and his brothers could remain in the SS, "because he was his very first companion, and he and his brothers and the whole Maurice family had served with rare courage and devotion during the Movement's earliest and most difficult months and years."[120]

It was remarkable, the treatment to which Hitler subjected Emil Maurice within the space of ten years: affection, condemnation, compromise, rehabilitation, protection. There are two possible explanations for these abrupt ups and downs. Either Hitler had never stopped loving his "greyhound," all disappointments and irritations notwithstanding, or he was so afraid of him that it seemed wiser to bribe him than risk the imponderable results of liquidating him. Once again, the truth probably lies midway between the two.

HITLER'S WOMEN:
MAGDA QUANDT, LENI RIEFENSTAHL, EVA BRAUN

For Hitler, Geli Raubal's death in 1931 was a disaster. His woman problem, which had receded into the background thanks to his liaison with her, reared its head once more. There was no immediate solution in sight—or none that would have seemed convincing, either privately or publicly. This situation threatened to jeopardize the sensational boost Hitler's political career had received from the Reichstag elections of September 1930. As a public figure he could not leave his supporters or his opponents permanently in the dark about the reason for his avoidance of marriage. Moreover, because he owed his aura largely to autosuggestive forces and had no wish to appear a failure in his own eyes, he felt bound to tackle the problem.

So let us examine his behavior in the months succeeding his niece's tragic death—more precisely, his behavior toward women. There were some whom he manifestly liked (and vice versa), and who were not only attractive but would have been willing and able to embark on a relationship with him. The first of these was Magda Quandt, the second Leni Riefenstahl. He could have married either of them in 1931/32—if he had wanted to. Instead, he staged his reluctance in such a way as to create a publicly effective, long-term palliative.

Magda Quandt, the private secretary and lover of propaganda chief Goebbels, got to know Hitler better in the fall of 1931. She was so "entranced and excited" by the party leader's public speeches that she called on him at his Berlin headquarters, the Hotel Kaiserhof, in mid-October.[121] This encounter aroused such emotions in both of them that a closer relationship seemed within the bounds of possibility.[122] Hitler's female admirer frankly admitted to Leni Riefenstahl that she was deeply in love with the "Führer"—indeed, that she was "smitten" with him: "It was not until I realized that, discounting his niece Geli, whose death he will never get over, Hitler cannot love any woman, but only, as he always says, 'his Germany,' that I consented to marry Dr. Goebbels, because now I can be near the Führer."[123]

Here, for the first time, we meet a formula that was to become an important part of Hitler's sexual camouflage: his post-Geli "inability to fall in love." What utterly negates it, of course, is the fact that the ostensibly inconsolable man was paying court to another woman only four weeks after Geli's suicide. Moreover, these advances may have continued for somewhat longer than our scanty information suggests. They resulted in the three-cornered Quandt-Goebbels-Hitler relationship, which the SA's chief of staff, Otto Wagener, had arranged at Hitler's behest. Kurt Lüdecke records a significant remark made by Magda Goebbels: at her wedding on December 19, 1931, Hitler was "the best man" whereas Goebbels was "only the groom." The unmistakable stress laid on the former is consistent with another remark she made six months later: "We like to have Hitler think of this [i.e., our] apartment as his second home."[124]

By early 1932, when he was forty-three years old, Hitler had at last attained what he may have dreamed of: he could enjoy the devotion, admiration and solicitude of a charming woman without having to commit himself in any way. He had also made one of his leading henchmen happy by helping him to contract a marriage to which Madga Quandt might otherwise never have consented.[125] At the same time, he could—by citing Geli's death—proclaim that he could never love another woman—indeed, that he had "overcome the urge to possess a woman physically."[126] Seven years earlier he had sold Rudolf

Hess an entirely different line: he avoided "any strong attachment . . . to a person of the female sex" because he had to be able "without the slightest human, personal considerations, to expose himself to all dangers and, if necessary, to die."[127]

But Hitler would not have been Hitler had he not promptly tried in 1931 to make political capital out of this personal situation. Geli Raubal's death afforded him an opportunity to adorn his self-invention as the German people's political savior with yet another embellishment, namely, the myth that Germany was the true and only bride for whom he had to make personal sacrifices. This was little more, at first, than a theatrical exaggeration of what may have been the relatively genuine sorrow he felt after his niece's suicide. But the more often he trotted out this sob story for other people's benefit, the more artificial and affected it seemed.[128] His dramatically grief-stricken pose became a diversionary maneuver cloaking the lie that, from now on, the Führer could contemplate no love other than that of Germany.

Leni Riefenstahl's memoirs describe an encounter with Hitler on the North Sea coast at Horumersiel[129] that gives us an insight into the nature of this personal myth—a myth based ultimately on the inner resistance of a homosexually inclined man with heterosexual aspirations. An almost summery evening beside the sea in late May 1932 provided the romantic backdrop to a scene that Riefenstahl describes as follows: "Quite relaxed, Hitler spoke of his private life and of things that particularly interested him. Foremost among them were architecture and music—he spoke of Wagner, King Ludwig, and Bayreuth. After he had talked of them for a while, his expression and voice suddenly changed. Fervently, he said: 'But what fulfills me more than anything else is my political mission. I feel that it is my vocation to save Germany—I cannot and may not evade it.' . . . It was dark, and I could no longer see the men behind us. We walked along in silence, side by side. After a long pause he came to a halt, gave me a lingering look, slowly put his arms around me, and drew me to him. . . . He looked at me excitedly. When he saw how averse I was, he at once let go of me. He turned away a little. Then I saw him raise his hands and say imploringly: 'I cannot love any woman until I have completed my task.'"[130] Riefenstahl was quite manifestly seeking the favor of Germany's coming man.[131] Even if she was not quite as "averse" as she would like one to believe, this is precisely how we should conceive of Hitler's attitude toward women in love with him: the self-abnegation of a Don Juan denied fulfillment because of his higher calling. He had developed his instinctive aversion to physical contact with a woman into an extremely persuasive technique designed to present him as a man capable of love—a man to whom women were entitled to feel thoroughly attracted. It is impossible to overestimate the extent of the self-confidence Hitler gained from this theatrical gambit, whose effect on other people seldom failed.

In August 1932, when Lüdecke tried in the course of a private conversation to elicit the real reasons for his failure to marry Magda Quandt, Hitler retorted that he had been "the happiest man in the world"[132] in Geli's company. Lüdecke, who was clearly unaware that the Quandt affair had started only four weeks after Geli's death, felt thoroughly disarmed, especially when Hitler burst into tears. As for Goebbels, who had learned that some "lousy girl"—the daughter of Gauleiter Karl Weinrich—had become Hitler's new "crush," his diary for October 1932 contained the following, surprised, entry: "How great must be Hitler's yearning for a woman?"[133]

Hitler enjoyed playing this role. "It's quite true that I love flowers," he declared in oracular tones, "but that's no reason why I should become a gardener!"[134] Nebulous pronouncements such as these were a quite deliberate way of encouraging speculation. Hitler told Kurt Lüdecke that he kept hearing about his, Lüdecke's, involvement in "scandalous affairs with women," but all he could say about such rumors was that it was better "to have women than men."[135] This turn of phrase was a significant linguistic borrowing by Hitler from the German-Italian author Curzio Malaparte. In his book *Der Staatsstreich* [The Coup d'État], which appeared at just around this time, the author had for the first time submitted Hitler's "profoundly feminine ethos" to detailed public scrutiny, and he left his readers in no doubt as to the result of his studies: "Hitler's feminine side accounts for his success, his power over the masses, and the enthusiasm he arouses in German youth. [. . .] 'Not a single affair with a woman is currently ascribed to him,' states one of his biographers. It would be preferable to say of dictators that not a single affair with a man is currently ascribed to them."[136] Hitler could not have been indifferent to this malicious innuendo, the more so since his opponents promptly seized upon it with gusto.[137] He was quick to learn from the pressure exerted by such experiences. He had quickly learned that it could only benefit him to be gossiped about in connection with women. In 1932/33 his closest associates did the spadework for him in this respect by effecting numerous introductions, but it eventually became too much of a good thing, and he started to evade their matchmaking endeavors. "I'm no misogynist," he allegedly told Leni Riefenstahl late in 1933. "I'm very fond of the company of beautiful women, but I can't stand people trying to force things on me."[138] Now that he had come to power, he could afford to cut down on his ostentatiously paraded conquests.

———

Only one of Hitler's women seems to have been fully aware of her theatrical role: Eva Braun. This is at least implied by a remark she is reported to have made to Eugen Dollmann in 1938: "'Always the mission, the mission, the mission, self-sacrifice and renunciation. In this way,' he [Hitler] observed with a smile, 'we have happily created the authentic masculine Reich.' People naturally believe that my life [at Hitler's side] takes quite a different form: if only they knew!"[139] His relationship with Eva Braun, whom he had gotten to know in 1929, and with whom he was probably on close terms from early 1932 on, was the belated fulfillment of a long cherished idea: platonic cohabitation. With the pretty young employee from Hoffmann's photographic studio he continued what he had begun with Geli Raubal, the difference being that this time he seemed to want to conceal the fact. From the outset, however, there were enough people in the know to make their liaison an open secret. And that suited Hitler perfectly.

Symptomatic of their strangely indeterminate relationship is Julius Schaub's evasive response when interrogated after the war as to why Hitler had failed to marry his "Fräulein Braun" long before those final hours in the Chancellery bunker: "That was the view he took. We often wondered why—we didn't understand it. He simply had his own ideas . . ., more than that I can't say about it." And, when asked what Hitler's "own ideas" were: "He didn't explain why. He never went into details."—"Did he love her very much?"—"He was very fond of her."—"What does it mean in Munich when you say 'He was very fond of her?' Did he love her?"—"He was fond of her."[140] They liked each other.

Herbert Döring, Hitler's majordomo on the Obersalzberg, likewise recalled that it was just an "easygoing, good relationship, with highs and lows." When asked whether it was sexual in nature, he replied: "No, there was never anything like that. Their relationship never went that far. Never! Never!"[141] This confirms a remark made by Heinrich Hoffmann: "Given the whispered gossip that went on in Hitler's entourage, I would have been bound to hear something, be it only from the chambermaids."[142]

When Christa Schroeder complained that Eva Braun lacked the stature to be the "Führer's" partner, Hitler retorted, "But she's good enough for me!"[143] The same applied in reverse, because Eva eventually came to the conclusion that her status as Hitler's "girlfriend" had its "good sides and advantages." As she said to Dollmann: "Just think how convenient it is for a woman never to have to be jealous of any other woman."[144] She was jealous for quite a while, in fact, as her two attempts at suicide demonstrate, but then she realized that she was tilting at windmills and tried to make the best of her situation. She may possibly have overcome her sorrow at not being genuinely loved in the company of her women friends, just as she preferred female society in general.[145]

This could not have worried Hitler unduly. As long as Eva kept up appearances and played the role of his mistress, what she did in other respects mattered little to him. And so she led a dual existence: on the one hand, she lived with Hitler, who not only marginalized her but pampered her with gifts of all kinds—jewelry, nice clothes, Ferragamo shoes; on the other, he left her free to enjoy herself as she pleased—although not with other men, for that would have humiliated him. This arrangement, which became established back in the mid-1930s, remained in operation to the bitter end.

HITLER'S RIGHT-HAND MAN: JULIUS SCHRECK

The scene in the Neuer Friedhof at Gräfelfing, near Munich, on May 19, 1936, resembled a state occasion. The Nazi elite had turned out, almost to a man, to pay their last respects to Hitler's chauffeur, Julius Schreck. No chauffeur can ever have been escorted to the grave with greater ceremony, but Schreck was more than just a faithful retainer. Hitler personally laid the first wreath, which was dedicated to "my faithful old fellow fighter and beloved comrade." Even when he arrived, noted a reporter from the *Völkischer Beobachter*, his face reflected "all the emotion of a man who had lost his comrade, his right-hand man in a long, hard life of struggle."[146] Hitler was profoundly distressed by the death of this "right-hand man"—so distressed that he had to leave the cemetery after Heinrich Himmler's brief eulogy.[147]

Hitler himself spoke no farewell words during the ceremony, nor did he speak much in general at the time. He was not seen again in public until May 30. The commemorative addresses and eulogies delivered by his closest associates indicated what he was either incapable of saying or reluctant to show, namely, how hard-hit he had been by the loss of this "tough but warm-hearted old war-horse." Schreck's "love for the Führer" had been boundless, wrote Rudolf Hess. Similarly his "indefatigable solicitude for the Führer," whose "supreme trust" he had always enjoyed.[148] Himmler, too, alluded in his graveside address to Schreck's knack of "reading [the Führer's] every wish and thought in his eyes and fulfilling them."[149]

Julius Schreck was only in his late thirties when he unexpectedly died of an infection.[150] He had made Vize-Feldwebel [roughly: staff sergeant] in World War I and had joined the Freikorps Epp in May 1919.[151] In the spring of 1923 he and Josef Berchtold jointly founded the "Stosstrupp Hitler" [Hitler Assault Squad].[152] Schreck's police record for this period lists various offenses ranging from fraud, breaches of the peace and the use of offensive language, to grievous bodily harm. When the November putsch failed he fled to Austria but was arrested at the frontier early in 1924 and received a suspended sentence of fifteen months' detention. In 1925 the Stabswache [literally: Headquarters Guard] was formed under his command, and he was its first commander when it was renamed the Schutzstaffel (SS).[153] In April 1926, however, when Berchtold, the former Stosstrupp commander, returned from exile in Austria, Schreck was relieved of his command in short order. The SS chiefs were of the opinion that "Schreck is not equipped with the requisite talent for leadership and organization, nor does he possess a reputation which guarantees that the SS will become an elite formation of the Movement."[154]

This setback did not deter Hitler from employing Schreck as his chauffeur, in other words, Maurice's successor, two years later. Although Schreck had occasionally driven the party leader before that,[155] he was at his service around the clock from 1928 on, for private trips as well as political engagements. When Hitler became better known, not least because of the countless political tours he undertook, "Schreck of the Highroad" also acquired a certain notoriety.[156] "He always knew at once whether to bring his physical strength, or his cunning, or his driving into play," wrote Schaub,[157] thereby intimating that Schreck was far more to Hitler than a willing chauffeur. His skillful piloting of Hitler's speedy, eye-catching Mercedes limousine suited his boss's taste for effective publicity. Not only must Hitler have found their fast and frequent trips by car extremely pleasurable,[158] but they undoubtedly helped to enhance his image and symbolized the advent of a dynamic new era.

Even members of the Nazi inner circle turned to Hitler's constant companion when they wanted to gain swift, direct access to the "Führer" or inform him of something in confidence.[159] Albert Speer recalled that Schreck rather impudently took advantage of his position to make "caustic remarks [to Hitler] about the fawning courtiers who surrounded him. He was the only person who was allowed such liberties."[160] Rumors circulated after his death that he had fallen prey to an attempt on Hitler's life, the assassins having erred in their aim because the two men looked so much alike.[161] They did, in fact, display strong outward similarities. Although Schreck was somewhat more thickset and fuller in the face than Hitler, they resembled each other in height and hair coloring. Like his boss, Schreck parted his hair on the right and—the most conspicuous feature of all—sported the same clipped mustache.

The two men had developed an unceremonious relationship on their innumerable trips across the length and breadth of Germany. Hitler would lovingly "feed" his chauffeur en route "by passing him pieces of bread"[162]—a trivial gesture, but highly indicative of their informal manner with each other. Moreover, far from all their joint tours were undertaken because of political commitments. They would frequently set off into the blue just "to enjoy the German countryside away from the main roads." Excursions of that kind had been simpler when Hitler was less well known, Schreck wrote in 1935. "Many a time one could stay the night at some inn or have a meal without being recognized."[163] Few details of these trips are on record, of course, but at least one episode from 1931 is documented. Hitler had announced his intention of spending Christmas at Haus Wahnfried in Bayreuth, but the Wagners awaited his arrival in vain. A phone call to Munich elicited that Hitler and Schreck had indeed set off, but it was not until a few days later that Hitler informed his friend Winifred Wagner that he had preferred to be alone and made an excursion into the countryside.[164] Hitler and Schreck had stopped off at Bad Berneck, a health resort some 20 kilometers from Bayreuth, and spent the holiday at the Hotel Bube, a favorite with Hitler's entourage ever since 1923. They were the only guests.[165]

Julius Schreck had married in 1920. Officially, he and his wife Maria lived in Munich with his mother, Magda Schreck, until the 1930s. He then moved to Gräfelfing, leaving his wife behind with his mother but without divorcing her. A few weeks after his death, Magda and Maria Schreck approached Hitler for money. Magda's letter to him stated that she had had to share her home with her son's wife at his "express wish." His death had rendered this arrangement defunct, and she now wished, as she had "long intended," to split up with her daughter-in-law. Since she no longer received the allowance her son had paid her hitherto, she viewed the future "with deep concern." In short: "The favor you showed my son encourages me to hope that you, my Führer, will regard this letter of mine in the same light."[166]

Maria Schreck couched her demands in far less deferential language. Her cool and forceful letter came straight to the point. Her husband had never given her more than the bare necessities. Since she now wished to set up a home on her own but possessed no household effects—all the ones in her former home belonged to her mother-in-law—she required, in addition to maintenance payments, "an apartment and the requisite furniture, kitchen, bedroom, and living room. Trusting to your goodwill, I look forward to an appropriate settlement of my financial situation." She went on: "I never, in all these years, took any steps against my husband so as to obtain my entitlement to adequate financial support because I had no wish to put any difficulties in the way of his career. He always said he would never forget the fact that I had so courageously shared the hardest years of his life with him. Death has prevented him from keeping his promise and thereby fulfilling a natural obligation. I am confident that the authorities will not completely ignore my legitimate request and compel me to lead a life that would enlighten the public on the actual state of affairs."[167] If this ordinary woman so boldly squared up to the omnipotent dictator in 1936, she must have been very sure of her ground. Maria's unmistakable allusion to her peculiar marital circumstances at once bore fruit: Hitler decreed that his late chauffeur's salary should, until further notice, be paid to his mother and his wife in equal shares.[168] As Albert Speer noted, a photograph of Julius Schreck hung beside the likeness of Hitler's adored mother in his private quarters on the Obersalzberg.[169]

THE MUNICH CLIQUE

In Munich Hitler maintained a small, two-room apartment on Thierschstrasse, which he had first rented in 1920. He seldom stayed there, however. The novelist Hans Grimm, who visited him there in April 1928, formed the impression that these lodgings were merely a *"pied-à-terre."*[170] Hitler's modest living conditions did not change for the better—and radically so—until quite late, in October 1929, when he moved into an imposing nine-room apartment on Prinzregentenplatz, in the fashionable neighborhood of Bogenhausen.[171]

From the mid-1920s on the party leader was constantly shuttling to and fro between Munich and Berchtesgaden, a remote little alpine town near the Austrian border. He had been a frequent visitor to the area ever since his tours with Eckart. Until 1928 he stayed mainly in boardinghouses and hotels, but in October of that year he rented an idyllic retreat in the shape of Haus Wachenfeld, a small house on the Obersalzberg.[172] Aside from Berchtesgaden, his favorite private destinations during the 1920s were Weimar, Bayreuth and occasionally Bad Godesberg.[173]

Hitler seldom went anywhere alone. Whether in Munich, in the Bavarian Alps or on his nationwide tours, he always surrounded himself with members of his peculiar "court," the entourage that later became known as the "chauffeureska."[174] Typical of many contemporary observers' perception of them is the astonishment with which Goebbels reacted to an encounter with Hitler's Munich clique in 1930: "Oh, that bunch of philistines. . . . How can a person like Hitler endure them, even for five minutes?"[175] One does indeed wonder why he spent so much time with such people. What did he need them for? What had he looked for—and clearly found—in them?

At first sight, Hitler's entourage really does appear to be a crude mixture of taciturn and rather obtuse aides, stalwart bodyguards, dashing chauffeurs and vulgar court jesters. In the very early years his close companions included characters such as the former horse trader and bouncer Christian Weber, the bodyguard Ulrich Graf and the veteran beer-hall brawler and talented rabble-rouser Hermann Esser. From around the mid-1920s, three men—Max Amann, Heinrich Hoffmann and Julius Schaub—became crystallized into an inner circle that retained its undisputed status until 1945. They evidently had no fixed pecking order or areas of responsibility. Because each of Hitler's faithful henchmen could be employed for any purpose, they were to some extent interchangeable. Although none of them was as important to Hitler as seminal figures such as Ernst Röhm or Dietrich

Eckart, they fulfilled an important function as members of his head-quarters staff: they all helped to secure him some private leeway.

Special mention should here be made of Julius Schaub, second only to Julius Schreck as Hitler's chief factotum, who organized Hitler's private life from early 1925 until the spring of 1945. He accompanied him on his travels, handled his finances and ran his household. He welcomed guests, got rid of unwelcome visitors and thus controlled access to Hitler.[176] Of all the men in his immediate circle, it was Schaub who had the most detailed "information about all of Hitler's intimate and personal affairs."[177] Speer considered him "the Führer's most faithful henchman,"[178] and Schaub himself stressed after the war that he was "Hitler's shadow, his daily companion, his constant retainer . . ., perhaps the only person who could, outspokenly but with impunity, tell him anything that came into his head."[179]

In addition to the qualities required of a personal aide—notably, discretion, reliability and circumspection—Schaub could offer his master something else: he was a great movie and theater fan and a connoisseur of the vaudeville scene. Hitler's weakness for movies is legendary; he attended screenings "with remarkable punctuality and regularity"[180] and was also "extremely partial to the theater," as Schaub stated during one of his postwar interrogations. If the "Führer" was prevented from seeing a picture, Schaub had to go on his own and tell him about it at breakfast the next morning.[181] He had numerous personal contacts in the Munich theater and film world.[182] Sometimes he invited ballerinas and actresses "to the Führer's home for an informal chat." On such occasions, Christa Schroeder saw first-hand that Hitler's usually aloof and "grouchy" aide could display an "astonishingly amiable" side.[183]

Common to all the men in Hitler's inner circle were an ability and an absolute readiness to cater to his personal needs and weaknesses. By guaranteeing him a measure of seclusion and privacy, they became a sort of surrogate family. With them, Hitler had no need to dissemble; with them, he could happily indulge his taste for the vulgar and trivial. Being inured to his mood swings and eccentricities, these confidants accepted him just as he was. Although many observers were repelled by their uncouth manners, Hitler exploited their vulgarity because he had no need to soil his own fingers when there was dirty work to be done.

Hitler's favorites were intellectually far inferior to him. They had little desire or ability to influence him politically. The only time they engaged in intrigue was when jobs were at stake. They were certainly not a camarilla. As well-paid stooges, they diligently and perseveringly helped to spin a protective cocoon around Hitler's private life. Self-sacrificing and discreet, loyal and utterly dependable: such was their outward appearance. In most cases, however, close scrutiny would have revealed personal shortcomings, and this explains something about the team's internal structure: Hitler wanted assistants with shady antecedents. Only a detailed knowledge of embarrassing and incriminating incidents in his henchmen's past lives could guarantee his ability to keep them under control at all times. Ernst Hanfstaengl was convinced that he held a "moral bargaining chip and means of coercion" over nearly every one of them.[184] His intimates had to be vulnerable and, thus, compliant. That alone enabled him to envelop them in a dense web of multifarious dependences from which no escape was possible.

Police records have some rather unpleasant things to say, for instance, about Julius Schaub's private life. In April 1923, NSDAP headquarters received a letter accusing his wife of prostitution and procuring: "Are you aware of this woman's activities? Certainly not, or you would very probably have fired them both, because Herr Hitler would [i.e., would *not*] be grateful for [Party] members who ought to be under vice squad surveillance."[185] In May 1925 the marriage was dissolved. The court found that Schaub's wife had entered into an adulterous relationship with the boxer Edmund Schneider, a fellow inmate of her husband at Landsberg.[186] But the divorce decree also stated that Schaub himself had badly neglected his wife and displayed a "gross lack of affection."

Schaub did not marry again until 1931. Hitler was a witness and made his home available for the wedding reception.[187] But this marriage evidently proved just as little of a bar to Schaub's escapades.[188] One of his weaknesses was drink. At parties he always "behaved atrociously," but when this was reported to Hitler he merely made "a despairing gesture" and sighed: "Yes, I know, it's sad, but what can I do? He's the only aide I've got."[189] Schaub was eventually rumored to be mixed up in a "nasty bribery affair" and even fell out with Hitler for a short time.[190] Despite this, Hitler soon afterward remembered "my old Julius Schaub" in his will to the tune of a lump-sum payment of RM 10,000 and a monthly pension of RM 500.[191] That was in 1938. Five years later Schaub received a "Christmas gift" of no less than RM 300,000.[192] Hitler wanted his loyalty to endure, even after his own death, and took care of this in good time.

No less important than such material rewards was Hitler's ability to cast an indissoluble spell over the most competent members of his inner circle. He imbued them with a sense of absolute loyalty and commitment to the "Führer." The finest proof that he really could count on their loyalty was supplied at the end of April 1945, once again by Julius Schaub, who left the flaming ruins of Berlin at the last possible moment and set off for Bavaria, where he emptied the safes in Hitler's Munich apartment and on the Obersalzberg and burned their contents.[193] What these documents were, Schaub doggedly refused to divulge until the day he died. All he once volunteered, in a mysterious tone of voice, was that their disclosure would have had "disastrous repercussions."[194] Probably on himself, but most of all, beyond doubt, on Hitler.

CHAPTER FIVE

The Röhm Campaign

AFTER WITHDRAWING from the clique that headed the National Socialists in the mid 1920s, Hitler's old companion Ernst Röhm was at first compelled to subsist on odd jobs, initially as a representative of the Deutscher Nationalverlag and later as an employee of Nobel, the manufacturers of track-laying machinery.[1] He also wrote his memoirs, which he entitled *Die Geschichte eines Hochverräters* [A Traitor's Story] and published in 1928.[2] For a soldier as keen as Röhm, however, these were only occupational stopgaps. Consequently, when offered the post of military adviser to the Bolivian army in December 1928, he promptly accepted. It was there in South America in the fall of 1930 that he received a letter from Hitler inviting him to become chief of staff of the SA. Having accepted this offer with equal alacrity, he took up his new post on January 5, 1931.[3] He soon acquired political power, and late in 1933 Hitler appointed him a government minister. Within a few months, however, he fell victim to an unparalleled bloodbath—a crime committed at the "Führer's" behest. What lay behind this remarkable development, and what accounted for it?

RÖHM'S RETURN

Why Hitler should have recalled Röhm at all and offered him command of the SA, despite their earlier differences, is a question that cannot be answered without an eye to the political situation prevailing in 1930/31. After Röhm's withdrawal from the NSDAP leadership in 1925, Hitler had initially succeeded in getting the Party to endorse his new conception of the SA as an electoral strong-arm force specializing in public intimidation and propaganda. It made a substantial contribution to the electoral victories gained in the years that followed. In January 1930 the NSDAP acquired its first provincial government minister in Thuringia, Wilhelm Frick, and in June it became the second strongest party in Saxony. Finally, having scored some spectacular gains in the Reichstag elections on September 14 of the same year, it became a political force to be reckoned with from then on.

From then on, too, if not before, the leader of the National Socialist movement had to think and act on a "macropolitical" scale. This meant, first and foremost, harnessing the traditional elites and using them as a route to further support. Hitler tackled this problem with instinctive flair and considerable success, as witness his skillful maneuvering with the German National camp.[4] He realized from the first that, if he was to gain power, he would have to make political concessions and go some way toward accommodating the old elites' conception of political morality. The SA clearly failed to see the need for this. It continually overdid things in its clamorous way, not only in public but inside the Party. In the middle of the election campaign in August 1930, the commander of the Berlin SA, Walter Stennes, had openly rebelled against the Party's Munich leadership. His ostensible reason was a demand for better pay and more SA candidates on the

NSDAP's electoral list. In reality, however, he and many other members of the NSDAP's fighting force disliked the strategy whereby power was to be obtained by legal means.[5] This eventually led to a grotesque incident in which rampaging SA stormtroopers occupied Party headquarters in Berlin. Hitler, who had hurried to Berlin in person to deal with the crisis, did succeed in getting the situation under control. On September 2, 1930, he assumed supreme command of the SA and immediately awarded it a pay raise,[6] but the political damage was considerable, especially as similar disputes between the SA and the Party organization were smoldering throughout the Reich.[7] The so-called Stennes crisis became so acute that Hitler eventually called on Röhm for help.

Given the situation prevailing in the winter of 1930/31, he could not have made a shrewder decision. Röhm hailed from the male-bonded milieu from which SA men were largely recruited. He spoke their language and shared their outlook. Because of his "illustrious" service in the Freikorps he was reputed to be an intrepid fighter, and as one of the early activists of the National Socialist movement he naturally carried considerable weight within the Party. These twin anchorage points afforded the best guarantee that the SA and the Party would not disintegrate further, and that the "brown battalions" would be politically disciplined. Röhm also provided the Party with access to an important ally: the senior officers of the Reichswehr, among whom, as a former staff officer himself, he had many excellent contacts. In short, Röhm was the man who could render the SA "presentable" without alienating the simpler souls in its ranks. Furthermore, his *Geschichte eines Hochverräters* made him a popular figure with the rebellious young, and there were good reasons why the canon of official Nazi literature ranged it alongside Hitler's *Mein Kampf* and Alfred Rosenberg's *Mythos des 20. Jahrhunderts*.[8] The fact that Hitler contrived during 1930/31 to persuade prominent bluebloods such as August Wilhelm of Prussia, the ex-kaiser's son, and Prince Philipp von Hessen to join the SA, rather than the elite SS, demonstrates on another level how serious he was in his efforts to improve the SA's capacity for integration. Röhm rendered him vital assistance in this regard.

But Hitler knew he was running a political risk by reinstating Röhm, who had, by contemporary standards, been remarkably frank about his homosexuality and was thus vulnerable to attacks by opponents inside and outside the Party. Hitler had been expressly warned of this danger and requested at least to make a public statement of his views on the subject of homosexuality—without success, needless to say.[9] Instead, he tried to protect himself and the SA commander in a more noncommittal way. As early as February 3, 1931, he issued a remarkable decree concerning "attacks on the private lives" of "very senior and senior SA officers." These, as Hitler saw them, were based mainly on circumstances "wholly extraneous to the context of [their] duties in the SA." He "vigorously and on principle" rejected all requests to "rule" on these. Quite apart from the fact that it would "pointlessly waste time more essential to the fight for freedom, I am bound to state that the SA is a body of men assembled for a specific political purpose. It is not a moral institution for the education of refined young ladies, but a formation of tough fighting men. . . . Their private life cannot be an object of scrutiny unless it runs counter to vital principles of National Socialist ideology."[10] Hitler wanted to show that he was above the matter and, at the same time, to offer Ernst Röhm the protection he needed. This did not suit homophobic Goebbels at all: "The Party as the El Dorado of the 175ers [homosexuals]?" he wrote in his diary on February 27, 1931. "That can't be allowed. I shall oppose it with all my might."[11]

Politically, Röhm soon fulfilled all of Hitler's expectations. He managed to put a stop to excesses like those of recent months and reduced the tension existing between the SA and the Party organization, even though it never entirely disappeared until 1934. The SA recruited members in increasing numbers, not only from its traditional Freikorps base but from elsewhere as well. Even Goebbels unreservedly conceded this: "Chief of Staff Röhm has accomplished the miracle of molding loose, scattered groups into a tightknit, tearproof organization."[12] Outwardly at least, the SA had now joined Hitler on his "legality course" and renounced any idea of a putsch.

But Röhm owed his successes not only to his reputation as an efficient officer but also to his arbitrary personnel policy. He assigned key positions within the SA mainly to men of homosexual bent, and they, in turn, installed friends in certain posts. One example was Edmund Heines, Röhm's lover of the 1920s, with whom Hitler is also reputed to have been on close terms.[13] He was appointed Röhm's deputy in Silesia with the rank of SA-Obergruppenführer [roughly: general].[14] The extremely important post of SA-Gruppenführer in Berlin-Brandenburg went to another Röhm intimate from the Freikorps days, Count Wolf Heinrich von Helldorf, who was said to have links with the Berlin homosexual scene and extremely close ties with his superiors.[15] Until 1933, at all events, he was regarded as Röhm's "confidential agent" in Berlin.[16] Another man who enjoyed a sensational career in the SA was Karl Ernst, who had gotten to know Captain Paul Röhrbein, the SA's first Berlin commander,[17] at the "Eldorado," a favorite haunt of the German capital's homosexual community. In 1931 Röhrbein introduced Ernst, who soon acquired the nickname "Frau Röhrbein," to his old friend Röhm and did his best to further his career. By April of that year Ernst had become a favorite of Röhm and was commanding SA Subgroup East, and a year later he was in the Reichstag.

The result of such wirepulling was that the SA gradually acquired the reputation of a fraternity devoted to homosexual excesses. Goebbels thought its future "very bleak. The shadow of Paragraph 175 looms . . . over it."[18] As the homosexual art historian Christian Isermayer recalled in an interview not many years ago: "I also got know some people in the SA. They used to throw riotous parties even in 1933. . . . I once attended one. Someone I knew had taken me along. . . . It was quite well-behaved but thoroughly gay, men only. . . . But then, in those days the SA was ultra-gay."[19] Eugen Dollmann, a student in Munich at the time, said much the same. According to him, it was common knowledge "what went on in Röhm's houses and in those of his aides."[20]

Homosexuals acquired political influence even in the "Braunes Haus," headquarters of the SA's supreme command, one of them being Röhm's close friend Count Spreti, Du Moulin-Eckart's successor, although there were conflicting accounts of his proclivities.[21] Hitler was later compelled to state (for internal, government consumption only) that the "inferior manning of senior SA posts" had been due "to the [former] chief of staff's regrettable disposition."[22] From the Nazi leadership's point of view, the SA's homoerotic orientation became an unprotected flank exposed to attack by political opponents, internal Party rivals and Nazi moralists. Not even Röhm's successes could alter that.

RÖHM IN TROUBLE

One of the most urgent tasks Hitler entrusted to Röhm was the removal of Walter Stennes, commander of the Berlin SA. At the end of March 1931, when Stennes once again defied the Party's Munich authorities, Röhm summarily relieved him of his post.[23] The NSDAP had been threatened by a genuine crisis the previous August, whereas this time the whole affair was swiftly resolved in Hitler's favor, mainly because of careful spadework on the part of Röhm, who had weaned the most senior SA commanders away from Stennes in good time. The political situation in the capital of the Reich, which was so important to the National Socialist movement and its public image, had been stabilized once and for all—thanks to Röhm.

Gauleiter Joseph Goebbels of Berlin, who had tried to play a game of his own throughout this dispute, leaving his position vague until the last possible moment, was also obliged to come to heel. In the spring of 1931, whether resentful of being ignored or inspired by a genuine fear that the National Socialist movement was becoming "sexualized," he openly attacked the man who had implemented Hitler's wishes with such success. He ensured that the rumormongers were kept busy by cracking malicious jokes about Röhm's homosexuality at every opportunity.[24] He also betrayed increasing concern about "Paragraph 175. I don't trust some people in this respect. Röhm? Hitler must be warned in good time. That would be the beginning of the end."[25] According to a report in the communist *Rote Fahne*, the Berlin gauleiter's offices were "a hotbed of corruption and intrigue" dedicated to bringing Röhm down by every available means. Compromising information about the SA boss was not only being disseminated but sold to the highest bidder.[26] At an editorial meeting of *Der Angriff* attended by Hitler's faithful henchman Max Amann, who had come from Munich for the occasion, Goebbels demanded that the latter "request Hitler, on behalf of the Party members of North Germany, to dismiss the chief of staff" because embarrassing press disclosures—in the Social Democrat *Münchener Post*,[27] among other papers—had rendered Röhm "utterly intolerable."[28] And the gauleiter of Berlin was not alone in this opinion.

Captain (ret.) Paul Schulz, Stennes's successor and a former member of the counterrevolutionary Ehrhardt Brigade, was particularly active in supporting the Party's anti-Röhm front.[29] Immediately after his appointment as (acting) SA Commander East he sought to make common cause with Gauleiter Goebbels, who, in his currently groggy condition, thoroughly welcomed this approach: "Schulz means to take the political initiative. If so, my position in Berlin would be splendidly clarified at a stroke."[30] At the end of May Goebbels and Schulz called on Hitler at the Hotel Kaiserhof in the hope of gaining his support for their plans to reform their "political work" in Prussia. They urged "the Chief" to "bring his personal influence to bear up here more than hitherto." But Hitler wouldn't take the bull by the horns, Goebbels noted later, adding: "We'll have to pay dearly for it someday."[31] Schulz, too, was "very annoyed with Munich." On June 2, 1931, probably immediately after a "talk" with Goebbels,[32] he wrote Hitler a stinging letter. He may well have sent a copy to Gregor Strasser, his friend and superior, because late in June Strasser's brother Otto leaked his letter to the editor of the *Münchener Post* with the avowed intention of "dealing a blow at Hitler and the Movement."[33] When it was actually published,[34] Goebbels described the mood at the Party's Munich headquarters as one of "utter confusion."[35] As for Röhm, he found it "shocking to be confronted by such attacks from within one's own ranks."[36]

Schulz sought to draw Hitler's attention to "the dangers . . . necessarily entailed, in my opinion, by the employment of morally objectionable persons in positions of authority." In addition to the SA boss himself, Schulz named the chief of staff of the Berlin stormtroop detachment, Karl Ernst, his former partner ex-Captain Paul Röhrbein, Röhm's aides, Reiner and Count Du Moulin-Eckart, and the "V-Mann" [confidential agent] Dr. Meyer. Röhm's close friends, Schulz went on, now formed a "homosexual chain" that extended from Munich to Berlin and emanated from Röhm himself. In Berlin's homosexual haunts "every male prostitute" was already talking about "the excellent relations of 'friend' Röhrbein, via Röhm, with Hitler." What aggravated the situation was that "Captain Röhm makes absolutely no secret of his disposition; on the contrary, he prides himself on his aversion to the female sex and proclaims it in public." Even though he, Schulz, considered the SA commander "a highly qualified officer incapable of any vile act," he could not but object to his "exalted position as chief of staff in view of his homosexual proclivities." Given the public talk about this, "the supreme leader of the NSDAP" could not and should not "overlook it. Things have now reached the stage where rumors are being spread in Marxist quarters that you yourself, my most esteemed Führer, are also homosexual. Widespread incomprehension reigns, among the intelligentsia as well, that there are far more homosexually inclined officers in the Braunes Haus."

If the letter itself sailed close to the wind, its publication was a minor disaster for Hitler's party. The Nazis had no real interest in bringing the matter before the courts, all their denials notwithstanding, because the legal proceedings they instituted "made no headway."[37] In other words, they were deliberately spun out, and the case against the *Münchener Post* was eventually dropped. Instead, the National Socialist press published some halfhearted and unconvincing rebuttals and inveighed against the "Red gutter press" in a manner that unmistakably conveyed that the "November criminals'" shaft had found its mark.[38] Schulz had not only hit a nerve but, for the first time ever, established a link between what Goebbels called the National Socialist "175ers' El Dorado" and the "Führer" himself. Hitler, who was in a bind, thought it preferable to keep quiet about the matter just as he had in 1928/29, when Wilhelm Hillebrand, the former Reich director of music, urged him to reprimand homosexual Nazi functionaries such as Gauleiter Kube and SA-Standartenführer [colonel] Götting.[39]

The *Münchener Post* published further articles on Röhm's homosexual disposition. It cited, inter alia, information supplied by the aforesaid Dr. Meyer, one of Röhm's companions from the early 1920s and a sometime informer of his, who was now marketing his knowledge of the SA chief's coterie of homosexual friends.[40] However, this principal witness was unable to testify in court; on December 15, 1931, he was found hanged in his cell while remanded on a charge of fraud. Official cause of death: suicide.[41]

But Röhm was not yet out of the woods. He now directed all his odium at Paul Schulz and made strenuous efforts to eliminate him, but without any immediate success. The SA commander's position within the Party remained precarious until early 1932, because Hitler made no move to quell these intrigues by exerting his authority and preferred to leave the matter in abeyance. No reaction from him was forthcoming throughout 1931, nor did he do anything in terms of personnel policy that might have been of help to Röhm. Although, according to Heinrich Hoffmann, he declared that he would "never reproach" Röhm for his homosexuality or "act accordingly,"[42] the political imponderables were too great for him to adopt a public position on the matter. He thought it wiser to let Röhm pull his own chestnuts out of the fire. He may even have regarded "the Röhm case" as a kind of trial balloon that would enable him to gauge public reactions to a charge of homosexuality. Was he, perhaps, exposing his personal "problem" to public debate without endangering himself? Although such instrumentalization will remain Hitler's own secret, of course, he could not manage without accomplices, and further examination of "the Röhm case" will disclose how the whole arrangement worked.

––––––

In order to understand the following events, we must view them against the power-political situation prevailing toward the end of 1931, which was dominated by the presidential election scheduled for the coming spring. The Brüning government had tried to effect a two-year extension of Hindenburg's term of office by means of a constitutional amendment, but had failed to obtain the requisite two-thirds majority in the Reichstag. Thus the turn of 1931/32 saw the beginning of the election campaign, whose critical nature was further intensified by five Landtag [provincial parliamentary] elections including one in Prussia, where the Social Democrats would be defending their most important political power base. Hitler began by maneuvering: he left the question of whether the NSDAP would support Hindenburg long unanswered.[43]

His position was difficult, his decision a matter of far-reaching importance. To stand for election against Hindenburg, who was generally and undoubtedly perceived as a unifying figure, would—despite his associates' encouragement—have carried a great personal risk, for this much was clear: a candidate for the office of head of state, in other words, a would-be representative of the entire nation, had to fulfill criteria quite different from those of a party leader. His life would be closely scrutinized. Many people refused to buy the curriculum vitae Hitler had set forth in *Mein Kampf*, so he would have to supplement it in some way. Torn between his supporters' expectations and an awareness of his own vulnerability, Hitler agonized for weeks before bringing himself to make a decision—one that his ongoing dispute with the *Münchener Post* could not have made any easier. It was not until February 22, 1932, that Propaganda Director Goebbels could announce Hitler's candidacy and finally launch the campaign. Its essential purpose was to extol the Nazi leader not only as a brilliant politician but, in addition, as a man of integrity.

This it did on two quite different political levels, of which one has often been described and analyzed: the brilliant staging of the Hitler myth. Joseph Goebbels wrote a series of scenarios for public appearances by the "Führer," who avoided any direct confrontation with Hindenburg.[44] Representing the NSDAP candidate as Germany's last hope, the propaganda chief saw to it that he winged his way to mass meetings in an airplane adorned with the slogan "The Führer over Germany." To Hitler's growing band of supporters it seemed as if the Holy Ghost was descending on them from above.

The other way in which Hitler lent his self-made image a semimythical aura is less well known but no less important: he underwrote his chances of gaining power at the expense of a close friend. On March 7, 1932, the left-wing liberal *Welt am Montag* printed three letters written by SA Chief of Staff Röhm. Two days later they appeared in the *Münchener Post*,[45] and other Social Democrat newspapers poured fuel on the flames.[46] The letters in question, which dated from 1928/29, were extremely intimate in tone. They were addressed to Röhm's friend and personal physician Karl-Günther Heimsoth, who was also in contact with other homosexual Nazi leaders. Röhm had tried to regain possession of them in the spring of 1931, or so, at least, the informer Dr. Meyer told the Munich Social Democrats.[47] Shortly after they appeared in the newspapers they were reprinted as a pamphlet, two of them even in facsimile form.[48] Their authenticity was beyond doubt—in fact, Röhm himself soon acknowledged it.[49]

The publisher of the pamphlet was a certain Helmuth Klotz.[50] A naval officer during World War I, he joined the Freikorps thereafter and had been one of the joint founders of the SA. He was also a close friend of the Party's future chief justice, Walter Buch, and had taken part in the Munich putsch of 1923. In 1924 he stood for election to the Reichstag as a representative of the *völkisch* right wing. In the ensuing years, however, his political views underwent a transformation; he became a staunch champion of the Weimar democracy and drew close to the SPD [Social Democratic Party of Germany]. His publication of the Röhm letters had been preceded in February 1932 by that of another pamphlet, "Wir gestalten durch unser Führerkorps die Zukunft" [We shape the future by means of our leadership corps], which took a National Socialist slogan as its title.[51] In the latter Klotz presented a meticulously researched list of the SA commanders' previous convictions, its purpose being to give the reader a picture of the morals of those members of the Nazi elite. The two pamphlets, which the SPD used as propaganda material in the presidential election, achieved a combined circulation of 300,000 copies.[52]

The letters, which appeared under the title "Der Fall Röhm" [The Röhm Case], publicly exposed the SA commander.[53] Röhm's first letter to Heimsoth stated that certain passages in his memoirs, *Geschichte eines Hochverräters*, had "naturally opposed Paragraph 175"; he had even, "in the first draft, gone more closely into this subject," but had, "on the advice of friends who consider this way of writing more effective, altered it in the present version." He was "at daggers drawn with Herr Alfred Rosenberg, that blockheaded moral athlete. His [homophobic] articles are directed primarily at me because I make no secret of my disposition."[54] Röhm's second letter, written in La Paz, the Bolivian capital, on February 25, 1929, included references to his "homosexual feelings and acts" and his abhorrence of "unnatural intercourse" with women.[55] In his third letter, dated August 11, 1929, and sent from Uyuni, Bolivia, he exclaims: "What you wrote about Berlin awakened all my nostalgia for that unique city. Lord, I'm already counting the days until I can return, and I genuinely intend, if at all possible, to save up here so that I can get something out of life there. The steam bath there is, in my opinion, the acme of all human happiness. At all events, I particularly enjoyed the way things are done there. . . . And now, give our mutual friend Fritz Schirmer my warm regards and, in my behalf—worse luck—a kiss. Now that you're happily married to him, as I hope, I do, of course, strongly advise against a change of abode and the separation necessarily associated therewith. Incidentally, I take definite exception to the fact that your husband (or wife?) omitted to enclose a picture of himself. People here are extremely susceptible to such things. (In this connection, I have a great favor to ask. You once showed me an enchantingly lovely collection of pictures on the relevant subject. If you should have one or two little pictures to spare, or could obtain some for me, be sure to send me them. I'll be eternally grateful to you.)"[56] How had Helmuth Klotz obtained these explosive documents? What interests were involved, and what did it all have to do with Hitler?

———

Hitler's assumption of power in 1933 drove Helmuth Klotz into exile in Paris. When France was occupied in 1940 he fell into the clutches of Himmler's Sicherheitsdienst and was brought back to Germany, where he was tortured into giving an account of what had happened in 1932. His statements are credible, since the SD could check their veracity at any time.[57] According to Klotz, the publication of the

Röhm letters was instigated by the Prussian ministry of the interior, or, more precisely, by three senior civil servants: Undersecretary Wilhelm Abegg, Regierungsrat [senior executive officer] Rudolf Diels and press chief Hans Hirschfeld. He had been urged "shortly before the presidential election of 1932" to publish the letters, of which photocopies were submitted to him. He claimed to have resisted their efforts at first: "I said . . . I did not take the view that such things should be exploited in the political arena and in public. Abegg stated that he shared my opinion, but Hirschfeld and Diels would not give way." In fact, a sexual denunciation of this kind was incompatible with the German Social Democrats' claim to political morality. But then "Diels—in support of his demand for drastic action—produced an original order, signed by Röhm himself, which stated, among other things, that the SA had no room for homosexuals; he also produced documents emanating from the National Socialist parliamentary caucus which demanded that special laws against homosexuals be enacted in the Reichstag." It was not until he adduced this evidence of the National Socialists' hypocritical double standards that Diels eventually overcame Klotz's reluctance.[58]

It is probable that Klotz's decision to accept the "assignment" was also sustained by personal indignation, notably at the potential threat to "German youth." This is at least implicit in his foreword to a new edition of his pamphlet published in September 1932: "The 'Röhm case' has long ceased to be a private matter affecting Hitler's chief of staff. Rather, the 'Röhm case' has become a public scandal of the first magnitude and a German disgrace. A disgrace, above all, to the National Socialist Party—a party which, in its programmatic pronouncements, has the audacity to call for the most draconian 'penalties' for homosexuals, even extending to enforced castration, while continuing to tolerate and support a man like Captain Röhm in his position as a leader of young people. To repeat: I do perhaps feel some pity for Herr Röhm, whether or not he deserves it. But as for those who—despite their long-standing awareness of Chief of Staff Röhm's militant homosexuality!—have reappointed him to his post, I profoundly despise them and will fight them tooth and nail. I accuse them of having deliberately and wantonly abetted the contamination of the youth of Germany!"[59]

Klotz also told the SD how Rudolf Diels had reacted, during their conversation at the ministry of the interior, when he finally gave in: "Diels congratulated me and observed that women would be eternally grateful to me." Furthermore: "But for the active cooperation of the then Regierungsrat Diels and his persistent pressure, the Röhm campaign would never have been undertaken. . . . Diels was its true instigator."[60] Why was this senior civil servant so interested in publicly demolishing the head of the SA?

As head of section in the political department of the Prussian ministry of the interior, Rudolf Diels was responsible for the combating of left-wing radicalism (i.e., the German Communist Party) and for counterespionage. He wielded far more influence within the Prussian administration than his rank would suggest. The ministry was headed by Carl Severing, one of the Weimar Republic's most prominent Social Democrat politicians, and one whose uncompromising opposition to the National Socialists and Communists had rendered him positively symbolic of "the Weimar system." He was profoundly detested in both extremist camps. A remark in his autobiography indicates that he, too, was privy to the "Röhm letters" affair, even though he remained behind the scenes.[61]

But to revert to Diels, whose political stance Helmuth Klotz outlined as follows: "Abegg described Diels to me as a devout republican and democrat who greatly admired Severing. . . . Above all, Diels was a sworn foe of the National Socialists. Diels more than once spoke to me very contemptuously, indeed, cynically, about National Socialism. . . . He simply failed to understand how such an otherwise rational person as myself could have taken part in the 1923 putsch."[62]

This was a skillful act, because Diels was not the ardent republican and democrat his colleagues imagined. A curriculum vitae he wrote in 1935, when he was an SS-Standartenführer [SS colonel], sheds light on this: "In 1930 I was appointed to the ministry of the interior, where I at once became head of the department responsible for combating the communist movement. After June [actually July][63] 20, 1932, the scope of my authority to combat communism was substantially widened, and I was able, even at that stage, to devote myself to preparations for the overthrow of communism in Germany in very close conjunction with leading members of the NSDAP. Having been appointed head of the Geheimes Staatspolizeiamt [Gestapo] and vice-chief of the Berlin police by the prime minister [Göring] after the seizure of power, I was in a position, thanks to the preparations already undertaken in Prussian territory in expectation of the seizure of power, to assist, under the orders of Prime Minister Göring, in swiftly and completely eliminating the communist threat. In mid 1934, pursuant to my repeated requests to the prime minister and the Führer, I relinquished command of the Geheime Staatspolizei and became Regierungspräsident [chief administrator] of Cologne."[64] But the picture remains incomplete until we learn that in March 1932, or around the time when Helmuth Klotz published the Röhm letters, Diels was a "subscribing member" of the SA, and that in 1933 the supreme commander of the SA appointed him an honorary officer of that organization. And since September 1930, as we already know, the supreme commander of the SA had been Hitler himself!

Diels maintained remarkably close personal contact with the "Führer." This can be inferred even from his heavily embroidered autobiography, *Lucifer ante portas*, which appeared in 1949. He describes, for example, how he collected evidence against Röhm on Hitler's direct orders, and how he and the "Führer" discussed the subject of homosexuality in detail. He also enlarges on anti-SA operations.[65] Although he claims that his activities were limited to the years 1933 and 1934, he was an expert at laying false trails.

Diels's memoirs are silent on the question of how so staunch a republican could so soon have established a close working relationship with Göring and, above all, Hitler; on what could have prompted the "Führer" to entrust him with such delicate assignments; and on why the two Nazi bigwigs appointed him, a putative Social Democrat, to build up the Gestapo. The answer is that, probably on instructions from Hitler himself, Diels had been an unofficial collaborator with the NSDAP since 1932. This is implied by the evidence against Diels submitted by the public prosecutor to the postwar denazification tribunal at Bielefeld.[66] In that capacity he developed contacts with both the SPD and the SA.[67] He had, for example, become friendly with Karl Ernst, commander of the Berlin SA and an intimate of Röhm, and it never occurred to either organization that they were dealing with an informant working for the "Führer."[68] A colleague of Diels, Hans Bernd Gisevius, later described his motivation as follows: "When the brown [Nazi] tide came rolling inexorably in, or from around 1931," Diels was "overcome with uneasiness. Had he backed the wrong horse, careerwise? Diels began to pass his police information to the opposition, first to the Nationals, then to the Nazis."[69] Diels's "treacherous role" was not lost on another colleague of his, Walther Korrodi, who considered him a person "shockingly devoid of principle and conscience."[70] It is almost impossible that Diels would have been unscrupulous enough to grasp such a hot potato in the absence of an express order from Hitler. Only the year before, the leader of the NSDAP had loudly proclaimed: "Nothing happens inside the Movement . . . without my knowledge and without my approval. Indeed, more than that, absolutely nothing happens without my wanting it."[71] Coming from Hitler, that can be taken at face value.

How did Diels obtain the documents that enabled him to engineer the plot against Röhm so efficiently? To answer this question we must first go back to 1931, when the public prosecutor's office in Berlin was investigating Röhm for "unnatural sexual offenses"—obviously in response to the rumors that were being circulated about the SA boss by the NSDAP's Berlin headquarters.[72] On July 13, 1931, acting on a tip from Otto Strasser, the authorities searched Dr. Heimsoth's home and confiscated the three outspoken letters that would later appear in the pamphlet.[73] These were handed over to the Munich public prosecutor's office, which was also investigating Röhm. Before long, however, the whole affair petered out because it was impossible to prove that Röhm had actually committed an offense under Paragraph 175. True, he had admitted being "bisexually inclined" and having "often had to do with young boys in that direction," but "I do not engage in criminal intercourse as defined by Paragraph 175"[74]— the standard argument advanced by all accused men, and one that was hard to refute.

It was not until February 1932, just prior to the announcement that Hitler would stand for the presidency, that the Röhm affair came alive again. This emerges from a report by Dr. Kreismann of the Prussian ministry of the interior to the effect that his superior had instructed him "forthwith" to request delivery of the documents pertaining to the case of "Röhm and associates," those in Munich included. The Munich public prosecutor's office initially stated that it could not relinquish these documents, whereupon Kreismann was instructed to "telegraphically request the Munich documents, together with all their appendices, and ensure their return within one week."[75] Berlin was obviously after something specific—something known to be in the Munich files, namely, Röhm's compromising letters. Although public prosecutors' offices were subordinate to their respective ministries of justice, mutual assistance and reciprocal access to documents were quite customary within the civil administration, so Diels was able to conduct his interview with Helmuth Klotz at the Prussian interior ministry only a few days after the Munich papers reached Berlin.

It was in February 1932, when the presidential election was impending, that Hitler must have made common cause with those who were denouncing Röhm. He did so not only—as I contend—in order to gain a hold over the SA commander, but also, and more importantly, to insure himself against similar attacks. For rumors were circulating that Hitler himself had homosexual proclivities, and some including Albert Grzesinski, the Berlin police chief, were convinced of their authenticity.[76] Furthermore, it is noteworthy that Hitler had been taking an interest in the Heimsoth papers since 1931, although his informants had to disappoint him at the time: "The letters confiscated on Dr. Heimsoth's premises," stated a confidential report addressed to Party headquarters, "cannot be obtained from the public prosecutor's office (not even by means of a break-in)."[77] Only six months later, things looked different. Diels was now procuring all he needed for his elaborate scheme: incriminating evidence, willing stooges and a line of argument that made the planned campaign of sexual denunciation acceptable even to the Social Democrats.

He must have managed to commend this operation even to Otto Braun, the Prussian premier. Only that can account for the latter's attempt to play politics with the "Röhm letters," of all things, by sending "photographic copies" of them to Chancellor Heinrich Brüning on March 4, 1932. Braun justified this step as follows: "I shall here forbear even to hint at the contents of the letters. I would ask you, however, to take doubly careful note of the letters themselves, and should be grateful if they were brought to the notice of the Reich President, so as to give him a picture of the character of the man who, as commander of the National Socialist storm detachments, enjoys the particular esteem of Party Leader Hitler."[78] Although fascinated by the affair, Brüning maintained a low profile.[79] He was probably chary of hitching himself to the Social Democratic wagon,[80] but he may also have been deterred by Reichswehr Minister Groener and Major General von Schleicher, who "thoroughly disapproved" of the anti-Röhm campaign.[81]

But that is secondary in this context. The question we must address is: What did Hitler hope to achieve by this whole, conspiratorial scenario?

A few contemporary observers already guessed what was going on, among them the former head of the SA, Franz Pfeffer von Salomon, who had been dismissed over the Stennes crisis. "Hitler," he said after the war, "did not appoint Röhm in spite of his proclivity, but probably because of it as well." He went on to say that Hitler preferred key posts to be occupied by men "with a flaw or weak point, so that he could apply the emergency brake whenever he deemed it necessary." Furthermore, this was how he had been able to keep the whole of the SA in check: "The more consolidated Röhm's popularity and status in the SA became, the harder hit the SA was bound to be by his dishonorable dismissal."[82]

Hitler's calculations must really have been of this or a similar nature—in fact the "Röhm case" perfectly exemplifies the behavioral strategy he adopted toward his closest associates: he entrusted them with "great" assignments and influential positions, guaranteed them wide discretion in the day-to-day running of their departments, sought out their "flaws or weak points" and, finally, threatened them with the "emergency brake." The effect on his henchmen was total dependence, indeed, subjection. If one examined each member of the Nazi leadership in turn, exactly the same pattern would emerge in almost every case: fascination, flattery, corruption, coercion.

In 1932, in a mood of profound resignation, Röhm frankly admitted to Kurt Lüdecke that his "vulnerability" had "delivered me into his [Hitler's] hands." This was "a terrible thing" because he had lost his independence for good. Lüdecke knew himself how Hitler could wear a person down. "And we, *we ourselves*, have made him what he is." His, Röhm's, position was extremely precarious. "I stick to my job, following him blindly, loyal to the utmost—there's nothing else left me."[83]

Hitler himself had incurred suspicions of homosexuality because of the so-called Schulz letter, and they were still around in 1932. For that reason, senior Party functionaries such as Konstantin Hierl implored him to dismiss Röhm rather than fall prey to developments himself:

"Our opponents are far from primarily interested in Röhm himself, but in hitting the Movement in a fatally sensitive spot and, above all, in casting a stain upon you personally, and that is what we all find the hardest thing to bear."[84] It became known in the spring of 1932 that some within the Party were actually planning to murder Röhm and his clique.[85] Hitler dissociated himself from the affair in quite another way, namely, by exacerbating the threat to Röhm. Röhm's opponents wanted to bring him down, whereas Hitler wanted to hold onto him for as long as possible. Although he stepped up the character assassination campaign, he did not, for the time being, intend to abandon his chief of staff. Instead, he preferred to pose as a comrade and man of honor who profoundly abhorred such scabrous attacks—indeed, he wanted to demonstrate that, to the "Führer," loyalty was no empty word. On April 6, 1932, or shortly before the presidential election's decisive second ballot, he publicly declared: "Lieutenant Colonel Röhm remains my chief of staff, now and after the election. Nothing can alter this, not even the dirtiest and most disgusting smear campaign, which does not shrink from misrepresentations, contraventions of the law, and malfeasance."[86]

Hitler's cunning ploy was directed less at his henchmen, who could only shake their heads at his course of action,[87] than at the general public. This affair had, after all, coincided with a phase that was vital to the National Socialist movement's political breakthrough. The *Völkischer Beobachter* declared that Germany was "on the verge of the National Socialist assumption of power."[88] From the aspect of moral discredit alone, it seemed absurd to make political capital out of the Röhm scandal just when the election campaign was at its height in the spring of 1932. Hitler could not hope to enhance his image just by publicly demolishing his chief of staff. Remarkably enough, however, his popularity increased in the course of the Röhm scandal. Why?

On the emotional level, those on the left of the political spectrum fought the election exclusively by campaigning against "Röhm and associates."[89] They avidly fell on the documents that were fed them, hoping that evidence of the SA chief's homosexuality would destroy their hated opponent, and failed to see that Hitler was throwing them this bait as a means of self-promotion. This was probably asking too much of them, because the disclosures in their possession were the kind of thing political enemies dream of. And so, while the National Socialists' opponents were concentrating exclusively on Röhm, the victim of scandal, the "Führer" could pose as a national Messiah far removed from such interparty squabbles. The Social Democrats were soon alone in their offensive. As *Vorwärts* wrote despairingly: "One might suppose that this opinion [indignation at the SA's sexual excesses] is common property in political circles. But neither the parties of the right nor, above all, the Protestant clergymen who beat the drum for Hitler, take any offense at Röhmosexuality!"[90]

The campaign missed its mark. No one expressed this more clearly than Klaus Mann, who in 1934 explained the political ineffectiveness of this "misconceived and undignified campaign" as follows: "Of those whom one tried to recruit against him [Röhm], some did not believe the story and some thought nothing of it; but the others, who were indignant, had probably disliked him in the first place. The fact that Hitler stood up for him and continued to protect a man who was compromised, in a petty bourgeois sense, shed—for the first and last time—an almost sympathetic light on that detestable bunch. The most simple-minded observer was bound to say: That's fine. Hitler is standing by his soldier, no matter what the newspapers blather about his private life."[91]

Thus the moral strictures on the SA leadership simply bounced off Hitler, who had spent those weeks constructing a statesmanlike façade with great recourse to propaganda. Skillful manipulation of the media enabled him to keep out of the line of fire. More than that, Goebbels now transformed him into "a man who, not only as a politician but as a human being, enjoys the greatest love and veneration from all who know him."[92] The "Führer's private side" was a synthetic product of propaganda, of course, but the well-staged scenes that presented him to the public as a "loyal comrade" and emphasized his "qualities of character" did not fail in their effect: the political cartoonists devoted far more time to "Röhm and associates" than to the "Führer."

Hindenburg was reelected, but Hitler, who in comparison to the old man personified youth, strength and the future, managed to garner many more votes than ever before. In April he succeeded in eroding the last major bastion remaining to the defenders of the Weimar Republic, the Prussian Landtag, and in the Reichstag elections of July 31, 1932, the NSDAP gained another brilliant victory. It was now by far the strongest political force in Germany, and to many people Hitler's accession to power seemed merely a question of time.

HITLER'S ENFORCED CONCESSIONS

How did Röhm react to these attacks on his person, and how did he deal with the intrigue whose author was unknown to him? Although he realized how precarious his position was, he began by seeking an injunction against Helmuth Klotz.[93] But the latter had already, on September 7, 1932, obtained a judgment of the last instance that permitted him "to publish Captain Röhm's letters for the purpose of protecting the young people of Germany from homosexual degeneracy."[94] Klotz gained an equally clear-cut victory over Goebbels' own Berlin daily, *Der Angriff*; on November 13, 1932, Berlin's supreme court expressly reconfirmed "the authenticity of the Röhm letters" and directed the editor to "publish this judgment on the newspaper's main page."[95]

By current standards of public morality, Röhm's career would now, if not before, have been at an end.[96] Hindenburg is said to have remarked in private that, in the kaiser's day, an officer like Röhm would have had a pistol left on his desk, and that, if the scoundrel had refused to take the hint, he would have been hounded out of the service in disgrace.[97] But nothing of the kind happened. By the time the courts passed judgment on the whole affair, homosexuality in the SA had long disappeared from the headlines, nor had there been any repercussions on the Nazi leadership. Ernst Röhm, who in his own estimation had had his back to the wall during the first half of 1932, was firmly back in the political saddle by the end of that year. What accounted for this?

Part of the answer can only be that Hitler needed the SA for purposes of general intimidation because of the obstacles placed in his path by Hindenburg's camarilla since the summer of 1932. For in the fall of that year, despite Röhm's serious fall from grace, Hitler rehabilitated him to such an extent that it infuriated some of his most loyal adherents.[98] The decision to lend his "friend" renewed backing was more or less his alone, and he must have taken it for purely personal reasons.

Hitler may well have raised the "Röhm case" during a meeting in Munich on November 8, 1932, at which he assigned his foremost associates their new party-political tasks after the Reichstag elections.[99] (Hans Mend had, incidentally, threatened him with disclosures only the day before.) Hitler's statement that he would "stand or fall with Röhm"[100] also dates from this period. There followed "the Führer's personal appointment of Dr. Luetgebrune to be senior legal adviser to the SA Supreme Command."[101] Luetgebrune was the attorney whom Hitler had curtly reprimanded, only a few weeks earlier, for his defensive policy in the Röhm affair.[102] Hitler now did his utmost to reinforce Röhm's position, and he succeeded: by 1933 the SA commander was once more numbered among the most powerful figures in the Nazi hierarchy.

Attorney Luetgebrune laid the propagandistic foundation stone for his official rehabilitation with "Ein Kampf um Röhm," which appeared early in 1933. This underlined the steadfast friendship existing between Röhm and Hitler, "who has never for a moment left his comrade in the lurch."[103] "As the attorney and friend of the publicly assailed chief of staff," Luetgebrune was ostensibly at pains "to clarify matters aired in public on countless occasions and presented to the German people in a deliberately distorted manner." What was at issue was not "whether it is correct to credit Röhm with a particular sexual bent." It must rather be stated "quite clearly, that a person's sexual *disposition* has absolutely nothing, in itself, to do with morality and decency." Least of all in the case of a character like Röhm: "In time of trouble and disgrace, impotence and defenselessness, it matters more to the Fatherland's welfare that a person should be a fighter and a real man than that, for fear of giving offense, he pay universal consideration to the moral hypocrisies of a dying social class." The use made of "the characteristic imputed to this most manly of men" had been character assassination of the most disgusting and disgraceful kind. "Marxist circles" and "the entire Jewish press" had been guilty of "exploiting sexual accusations." Equally reprehensible was the political "abuse of justice" with which Prussia's SPD government had made the smear campaign possible in the first place. This "exceedingly mean and spiteful campaign" had been bound to fail, however, because Röhm had defied the unworthy attacks on his person "with soldierly equanimity and unconquerable fighting spirit"—and this although "it would have been easy for the chief of staff, by the same means, to transform a defensive operation into a similarly directed offensive operation. He would indeed have had plenty of material with which to silence those self-appointed moral arbiters once for all."

This gave Ernst Röhm a clean bill of health. The Party's senior judge, Walter Buch, made a final attempt to dissuade Hitler from this change of tack in May 1933, but he failed despite the "thick wad" of letters of complaint and accusation he had brought with him. The "Führer" dismissed these as defamatory and went so far as to claim that Röhm "took far too much pleasure in women to fall prey to such things."[104]

It was remarkable how often Röhm appeared at public functions and ceremonies throughout the year, not only at Hitler's side but rivaling him as a leading representative of the "Movement." At the NSDAP's annual convention in September 1933 it even looked as if the National Socialists now had two "Führers." Shortly afterward Röhm published a spectacular declaration of war[105] on the "hypocrites, goody-goodies, and victims of suppressed complexes" inside and outside the Party. His display of indignation at their "ludicrous excesses of prudishness and worse" would have been quite unthinkable the year before. Now, however, the commander of the SA could blithely pose as a free thinker. His forty-sixth birthday, November 28, 1933, was celebrated like a national holiday, and a month later Hitler persuaded Hindenburg to appoint Röhm a minister. To confirm the SA boss in office must have come hard to the elderly Reich president, who had declared, only a year before, that he had found it "positively nauseating" to shake hands with "that breechloader" in the course of an audience.[106]

At the turn of the year Hitler wrote Röhm a letter which the *Völkischer Beobachter* published together with other letters of good wishes to sundry Nazi bigwigs. It was markedly cordial and familiar in tone.[107] The "Führer" had obviously taken trouble over it: "When I appointed you, my dear chief of staff, to your present post, the SA was undergoing a grave crisis. It is primarily to your credit that, within a few years, this political instrument was able to develop the strength that made it possible for me finally to win the struggle for power by overcoming our Marxist opponents. Now that the year of the National Socialist revolution has ended, therefore, I feel impelled to thank you, my dear Ernst Röhm, for the imperishable services you have rendered the National Socialist movement and the German people, and to assure you how grateful I am to destiny to be privileged to call men like you my friends and comrades in arms. In cordial friendship and grateful appreciation, yours, Adolf Hitler." Hitler's effusive letter not only certified that Röhm had played an important part in constructing the Third Reich but contained a hidden message whose gist was: Anyone who attacks Röhm attacks the "Führer." This seemed to have secured Röhm's position of power once for all. A man whom "decent" German society had ostracized only a few months before—a man who was still exposed to public ridicule—had been rehabilitated.[108]

Nor did Hitler have any qualms about promoting Röhm's (former) intimates. One such was Karl Ernst, whom he appointed to command the SA's Berlin-Brandenburg detachment, thereby investing an erstwhile "waiter" from the homosexual scene with a rank roughly equivalent to that of general. Ernst was also reputed to be "the Reich Chancellor's favorite SA officer," so Göring promptly made him a Prussian councilor of state as well. There was considerable surprise within the Party at Hitler's decision "to confer such a visible distinction on that nasty piece of work," because many regarded Ernst as an "amoral individual."[109] However, it was probably clear to everyone that Hitler would nip any renewed opposition to his Röhm policy in the bud. Only that can account for the brazen way in which Röhm and Ernst ventured to advertise their proclivities, for instance, at a reception at the Turkish embassy in October 1933.[110] This is consistent with what Hitler is reported to have told Hermann Rauschning at lunch in the Reich Chancellery in the early summer of 1933: "I won't spoil any of my men's fun. If I demand the utmost of them, I must also leave them free to let off steam as *they* want, not as churchy old women think fit. . . . I take no interest in their private lives, just as I won't stand for people prying into my own."[111] That was precisely the attitude Röhm had always propagated. Thus the man whom Kurt Lüdecke had found in the depths of despondency in the summer of 1932 now had every reason to exult that he had suffered enough on account of his homosexuality, and that this "Damocles sword" was not "going to hang over" him any longer.[112]

From the spring of 1933 on, the "homosexual clique centered on Röhm," as it was described in the highest circles, notably by Reichsbank President Hjalmar Schacht, was not only socially acceptable but a political power factor.[113] This surprising development requires explanation, the more so since it was followed only a few months later by the abrupt overthrow of Röhm and his associates and their public moral condemnation. As Hanfstaengl wrote in an unpublished passage in his reminiscences: "Ernst, another homosexual SA officer, hinted in the 1930s that a few words would have sufficed to silence Hitler had he complained about Röhm's behavior."[114] There seems to be something in this. There is evidence to suggest that, after the campaign against him, Röhm abandoned his hitherto steadfast loyalty to Hitler and decided to pursue a policy of his own. For this he needed allies, spies and informants. As early as April 1931 he had instructed the agent Georg Bell to build up an SA intelligence service—and also to fend off attacks on his person.[115] All this entailed at first was the intimidation of "politicians inside the NSDAP who wanted to exploit Röhm's predicament," either by counterdenunciations or by "armistice" negotiations such as those conducted with Gregor Strasser and Paul Schulz, the latter being—according to Rosenberg—a "staunch opponent of the homosexual Röhm."[116]

In the spring of 1932, or after the publication of the "Röhm letters," a change of tactics occurred. Now at daggers drawn with the NSDAP leadership, Röhm came to terms with opposition forces.[117] Bell arranged a meeting with a former Reichswehr comrade of Röhm, the onetime intelligence officer Karl Mayr, who had since joined the SPD.[118] With his help, the SA commander tried to discover the real authors of the campaign and take countermeasures. Mayr lent himself to such a marriage of convenience partly because he and Röhm shared many a secret about Hitler's early days in Munich in 1919/20. The fact that Röhm agreed with Mayr "to treat their conversation as confidential"[119] does not conflict with his subsequently published statement under oath that he reported it to Hitler "immediately" after the meeting.[120] All it shows is that he was now deliberately maneuvering with a view to intimidating "the Leader of the Movement."

By the time the "secret negotiations between Nazi Röhm and Reichsbanner Mayr" became known at a Munich court hearing in October 1932, and were delightedly pilloried by the Communists,[121] Röhm seems to have been apprised of the background to the intrigues against him, insofar as it was known to Mayr.[122] According to the latter, Röhm had been anxious "to seek support from me against his opponents in his own camp."[123] And the SA boss now knew what to do: he had to exert pressure on Hitler in his turn.

Walther Stennes, Röhm's mortal foe in 1930/31, reported that he must have "privately severed his links with the Party" in 1932; "because he got in touch with me and told me that conditions inside the Party were becoming more and more intolerable. He regretted that he had misjudged the situation on his return from Bolivia and had sided against me. He . . . proposed that we secretly cooperate. I did not trust Röhm at the time, because I was aware of his friendship with Hitler and feared a trap, so I declined to cooperate in any way. Subsequent developments warrant the conclusion that, astonishing though his proposal sounded, it was seriously intended."[124]

Moreover, Röhm had discussed the same matter with Schleicher only the day before his conversation with Mayr.[125] This is confirmed by the memoirs of Carl Severing, the SPD politician, who even alleges that Röhm initiated a cordial correspondence between the two men in 1932.[126] Röhm, it later emerged from a book on the "background" to the "Röhm putsch" murders, "positively conspired with Schleicher," who "did his utmost to deride Hitler" within the Hindenburg camarilla.[127] He evidently had more luck with this influential schemer than he did with Stennes.[128] This may possibly be connected with the fact that rumors were then circulating to the effect that Schleicher himself was "abnormally inclined."[129] Admiral Magnus von Levetzow, too, expressly warned Göring against this "ethically and morally debased individual," about whom he had heard bad things.[130]

At all events, Röhm found in Schleicher an ally who, being Reichswehr minister, not only had access to Hitler's military record but possessed an efficient secret service in the shape of the Abwehr.[131] That they developed a mutually advantageous trade in potentially explosive information is not mere speculation but is documented by a reliable source: according to Bredow in *Hitler rast*, Schleicher "privately intimated that Röhm had informed him of certain matters, and that those matters were of such a nature that their publication could inflict severe political damage on Hitler."[132]

The fact that Röhm now parted company with Paul Röhrbein and Georg Bell and declared his former confederates fair game, as it were,[133] was another weapon in his arsenal of shrewdly gauged preventive measures. The two men had concentrated on Hitler's private life, and Bell had "gone to the lengths of shamelessly exploiting" his information in public and "spreading it around."[134] His behavior did not suit Röhm, who wanted this inside information, not as the makings of a campaign, but as an instrument that would enable him to resume the political offensive. In other words, he was preparing a counterattack from the summer of 1932 on, and his direct access to the "Führer" rendered threatening letters or a smear campaign superfluous: his warnings could be most effectively conveyed in private. Above all, he refused to be intimidated by Hitler. "If Hitler shouted," recalled his then attorney, Luetgebrune, "Röhm shouted louder still."[135]

Fritz Günther von Tschirschky, an associate of Vice Chancellor Franz von Papen, unexpectedly overheard such an altercation from Hitler's outer office at the Reich Chancellery early in 1934. "It was clear that a very heated argument was in progress in Hitler's room. After a short while I said to Brückner [Hitler's aide-de-camp]: 'Who's in there, for God's sake? Are they killing each other?' To which Brückner replied: 'Röhm's in there. He's trying hard to talk the Old Man (he always called Hitler that) into going to the Reich President and forcing him to grant his requests.' So I waited. The door was relatively thin, and one could catch isolated, particularly loud scraps of conversation—indeed, whole sentences. . . . Again and again I heard: 'I can't do that, you're asking the impossible of me!'" But: "I learned from the Reich President's palace a few days later that Hitler had, in fact, submitted Röhm's requests to Hindenburg, but had met with a very curt and brusque refusal."[136]

This highlights the way in which Hitler's spectacular "revaluation" of Röhm after the end of 1932 should be assessed: as the result of enforced concessions. That Röhm compelled Hitler to discuss the so-called second revolution and the future of the Reichswehr, which was associated therewith, even though Hitler's own position on the subject differed from his entirely, points in the same direction.[137] The SA chief had had to pay a high price for his political naivete in the past; he now wanted compensation.

Röhm was not only acquainted with the shady beginnings of Hitler's political career;[138] he was also one of the very few people who knew about his homosexuality. It must have been Hitler's nightmare that he would one day launch a smear campaign. The "Führer" was in a quandary. Had he himself not been so vulnerable because of his homosexual proclivities, he could have countered Röhm's attacks in another, more rational way, for instance, by admonishing or dismissing him. Although his standing within the Party would readily have enabled him to do so, this route was now closed.

When asked a few days after the "Röhm putsch" whether he could not have adopted "another procedure," Hitler gave the following significant reply: "Only someone who is acquainted with the facts and has closely followed the clandestine maneuvers and intrigues of recent months . . . is entitled to explain by what methods the threat might have been averted."[139] One person who was "acquainted with the facts" was the then head of the "National Defense Agency against Communist Intrigues," Walther Korrodi, who managed to escape to Switzerland in 1935. From there he also conveyed these facts in an anti-Hitler pamphlet.[140] Korrodi's suspicions had been aroused in the fall of 1933 by an encounter with Röhm's friend Edmund Heines, whose response to Hitler's criticism of his lifestyle was as follows: "Adolf hasn't the slightest reason to open his trap so wide—one word from me, and he'll shut up for good!" This remark, Korrodi told Hitler in his pamphlet, "clearly shows that Heines, who was one of your oldest comrades in arms . . ., is in possession of a secret about his Führer. He wasn't the only one, though, was he, Herr Reich Chancellor? The other person who knew the secret was your close friend Ernst Röhm, with whom you kept 'faith' . . . in so remarkable a manner."[141]

Such, more or less, must have been the field of tension that had grown up between the "Führer" and the SA in 1933, a strained atmosphere fraught with mistrust and marked by numerous attempts at blackmail. As Hitler himself put it, he was faced with "a crisis that could only too easily have had truly devastating consequences for the foreseeable future."[142] His political instinct for self-preservation, if nothing else, compelled him to escalate matters. At the same time, he was urged on by the prospect of concealing his own homosexuality forever by the elimination of dangerous witnesses, and right at the top of the list of potential blackmailers was Ernst Röhm. If Gestapo chief Rudolf Diels is to be believed, he was engaged in spying on Röhm from January 1934 on.[143] The Reichswehr is documented as having done so from February of that year,[144] and in April, if not before, Reichsführer-SS Heinrich Himmler—freshly invested with new and wide-ranging powers—and his sidekick Reinhard Heydrich also took a hand in the Röhm affair.[145] Finally, in mid-May, largely with an eye to forthcoming events, a new "decree on the imposition of terms of imprisonment" was issued. By abolishing the judicial review of appeals against detention and placing other severe constraints on the ability of defense counsel to intervene on their clients' behalf, this opened the door to Gestapo tyranny.

Röhm and his senior SA officers posted their own sentries and armed their men as best they could.[146] On May 16, 1934, the chief of staff instructed the SA to make a systematic compilation of reports on the subject of "hostile acts against the SA."[147] According to his Berlin deputy, Karl Ernst, Röhm began at this time to deposit "important evidence" in "a safe place" because "we must be ready for anything."[148] So Röhm knew what was brewing. He had spoken quite bluntly and declared war on the Hitler government even at Ernst's wedding in February. According to one eyewitness, he had said that "SA men are not just poor devils privileged to sweep the street clean for grand gentlemen." He was now "turning his bunch into an army, and—he slammed a gleaming dagger down on the table—'This is the watchword!' We gazed in silence at the short, sharp knife, the SA's dirk of honor instituted by Röhm himself, whose blade was engraved with the words 'All for Germany!'"[149]

But the SA's chief of staff had overreached himself, in particular by planning to build up an army of his own. This conflicted with the interests of the Reichswehr, which now became Hitler's principal ally in his contest with Röhm. Moreover, Hitler got the other Nazi big shots on his side. He had something for everyone: for Himmler, who did not want his SS to be overshadowed by the SA any longer; for Heydrich, who was banking on a meteoric career; for Goebbels, who had had a score to settle with Röhm since the days of Stennes; for Göring, who was intent on becoming the regime's number two. In mid-April 1934, Hitler is said to have made it clear to Göring and Himmler that the whole of the police must be brought under unified command if—in his own words—"we want to get rid of Röhm."[150] In the early summer of 1934, having largely isolated his former friend and patron from the rest of the Party, he was in a position to lure him into a lethal trap.

Early in June 1934, Hitler extracted a promise from Röhm that he would send the SA on four weeks' furlough. The relevant order clearly betrays how uneasy the chief of staff felt about this step: "If the SA's enemies delude themselves that it will not return from furlough, or not at full strength, let us indulge them in that short-lived hope. They will receive the appropriate answer at such a time and in such a manner as seems necessary."[151] Hanfstaengl noted that an equally belligerent basic mood prevailed when he encountered Röhm, "clearly already drunk," at a soirée at SA headquarters on June 6, 1934: "He lapsed into the wildest bout of swearing I'd ever heard; he cursed, shouted, threatened. . . . I wondered what sinister game was afoot behind the scenes."[152]

By getting the SA sent on furlough Hitler had managed to deprive his adversary of his principal means of protection. He also talked Röhm into taking several weeks' vacation at Bad Wiessee on the Tegernsee. Then he went over to the offensive. Only a few days after Hitler's conversation with Röhm, Rudolf Hess ordered the SA intelligence service to be disbanded.[153] At Hindenburg's Neudeck [now Nejdek] estate on June 21, Hitler personally obtained the president's approval of his plan to proceed against the SA leadership by force.[154] Next, the SS under Himmler evaluated its "incriminating evidence" and compiled death lists in which other Party bigwigs like Göring and Chief Justice Buch also had a say.[155] On June 25 Goebbels delivered a long and menacing speech, broadcast by every German radio station, in which he referred to a virulent power struggle. But: "One person remains exempt from all criticism, and that is the Führer!"[156] This completed the requisite preparations. Within four days everything had been agreed, and without involving the army in this civil-war-like scheme. "The army has nothing to do with the whole affair," Hitler is said to have informed a Reichswehr officer in Munich on June 30, 1934. "We'll wash our dirty linen by ourselves."[157]

Recent estimates indicate that Hitler had a total of some 150 "opponents of the regime" murdered between June 30 and July 3, 1934.[158] Even while the operation was in progress, Hermann Göring decreed the destruction or confiscation of all the relevant documents, and immediately thereafter the Reich government enacted the "Law Relating to National Emergency Defense Measures," which simply declared the murderous operation to have been "lawful."[159] This deprived the legal authorities of any grounds for investigations after the event.

The startled public naturally stood in need of explanation and justification, however, so the National Socialists' most unscrupulous demagogue after Hitler, Joseph Goebbels, was obliged to "enlighten" the German people on the background to the massacre. On July 1, or while the murders were still going on, he broadcast a speech whose length suggests that most of it had been drafted before June 30.[160] Goebbels portrayed the speed of the whole operation as a skillful tactic: "The Führer has once again, as so often in grave and difficult situations, acted in accordance with his long-standing principle, which is to say only *what* must be said, to *him* who must know it, *when* he must know it." What had been at issue was the suppression of "traitors." Far from disclosing any conspiratorial plans to overthrow the government, however, Goebbels strayed off into stereotyped attacks on a "small clique of professional saboteurs" which had refused to "appreciate our indulgence." The Führer had now "called them to order" with due severity. "A clean sweep is now being made. . . . Plague boils, hotbeds of corruption, and symptoms of moral degeneration that manifest themselves in public life are being cauterized— drastically, what is more."

What had mainly prompted this deliberate escalation was, of course, something else; something to which Goebbels alluded rather casually but with remarkable directness when he claimed that the SA leaders "were on the point of exposing the entire leadership of the Party to suspicions of shameful and loathsome sexual abnormality." We should not be too quick to pass that sentence by. In the first place, no one in the Third Reich had ever heard of any "suspicion" that the "entire" leadership of the NSDAP might be homosexual. Second, who was supposed to have spread such a rumor, if even the Social Democrats had failed to do so while freedom of speech still prevailed? And what did "were on the point of" mean? Had they been acting deliberately? Negligently? Involuntarily? No, that sentence was no piece of sophistry, no demagogue's punch line; it was a reflex reaction to a very real threat—one to which, in the summer of 1934, Hitler's only possible response was lynch law.

A quite similar example of involuntary self-betrayal was provided by the Reich Press Office's first press release, which stated: "His [Röhm's] unfortunate proclivity generated such unwelcome pressure that it imposed grave conflicts of conscience on the Leader of the Movement and Supreme Commander of the SA himself."[161] The report that Hitler submitted to his cabinet on July 3, 1934, likewise conveyed his true motives for the murderous operation of recent days. The "clique headed by Röhm," which had been "held together by a particular disposition," had "slanderously attacked" him, and he charged the former chief of staff with "insincerity and disloyalty." Röhm had threatened him, ostensibly with his retirement, and that threat had been "nothing more nor less than barefaced blackmail." The "object lesson" he had now administered would serve to make it clear to each of his men "that he risks his neck if he conspires against the existing regime in any way."[162]

In other words, Hitler could defend himself only by going to extremes, so the few people who knew that he, too, was homosexual had to be either murdered or thoroughly intimidated. This is revealed by a closer look at the individual victims. Those who were murdered or locked up included the homosexual SA commanders Röhm, Ernst and Heines, all of whom were on personal terms with Hitler; Gregor Strasser, who had hitherto been "an intimate friend" of Hitler and had even chosen him to be "the godfather of his sons";[163] Karl-Günther Heimsoth and Paul Röhrbein, who had been close friends of Hitler's former intimates, even though they had long ago distanced themselves from "Röhm and associates"; senior civil servants privy to potentially explosive documentary evidence about Hitler, for instance, Erich Klausener, head of the police department at the Prussian ministry of the interior, and his head of section, Eugen von Kessel;[164] Reichswehr Minister and ex-Chancellor Kurt von Schleicher and his right-hand man, Ferdinand von Bredow; the Munich police chief August Schneidhuber; the ex-premier of Bavaria, Gustav Ritter von Kahr, whom Hitler probably suspected of being in possession of the material Lossow had preserved;[165] the attorneys of Röhm, Strasser, Lüdecke and other senior Nazis, who had learned dangerous things from their clients and from trial documents, among them Walter Luetgebrune, Gerd Voss, Robert Sack and Alexander Glaser; and, finally, the Munich journalist Fritz Gerlich, who probably knew more about Hitler and his inner circle than any other newspaperman of this period.

Anxious to prevent himself from being compromised at all costs, Hitler took his revenge in a positively fanatical manner on the "conspiratorial clique" that had harbored designs on his "life," thereby endeavoring to cut the ground from under any future conspiracy. Potentially incriminating witnesses were ruthlessly dispatched. A few examples will serve to demonstrate his mode of procedure.

Karl Zehnter, thirty-four years old, was the landlord of the "Nürnberger Bratwurstglöckl," a hostelry situated a stone's throw from Munich Cathedral. Politically naive, Zehnter belonged to Röhm's homosexual set and sometimes went on excursions with him,[166] but he was also a close and longtime friend of Edmund Heines. Both SA leaders were regular patrons of his establishment, which Hitler, too, frequented on occasion. An upstairs room in the "Bratwurstglöckl" was permanently reserved for private meetings between these Nazi dignitaries, and Zehnter made a habit of serving them himself, so he inevitably overheard things—not least about Hitler. That, and that alone, was why he had to die.

Also murdered was Martin Schätzl, a twenty-five-year-old Munich painter who had accompanied Ernst Röhm to Bolivia.[167] Although their relationship did not blossom into the love affair Röhm had hoped for, Schätzl had for two years been his closest companion in a foreign land. They remained in touch thereafter. Schätzl joined the SA when Röhm assumed command and was appointed to his staff on February 1, 1934. The two men must have talked a great deal together, not least about Röhm's friendship with Hitler. That was why the young man could not, under any circumstances, be permitted to survive.

General Ferdinand von Bredow, who had been living in retirement at his Berlin home since Hitler formed a government, was bludgeoned to death in a police van and his body thrown into a ditch. What proved his undoing were his activities as head of military intelligence during Heinrich Brüning's chancellorship.[168] A close friend of Schleicher, Bredow had also been the Reichswehr minister's right-hand man in the six months prior to Hitler's assumption of power. As such he got to read some spicy documents, for instance the report of a meeting of the Jungdeutscher Orden[169] on July 3–4, 1932. This stated that the main subject under discussion had been as follows: "Reichswehr Minister Schleicher supports the NSDAP because that movement is headed mainly and exclusively by homosexuals, and, according to evidence submitted by Otto Strasser, the Reichswehr minister is also abnormally inclined. This evidence dates from the Reichswehr minister's time as an officer cadet. Herr Otto Strasser had gone to see Mahraun [the grand master of the order] to inform him of these matters. Furthermore, while Herr Hitler was spending a longish sojourn at his home, Otto Strasser observed things that lead one to infer an abnormal disposition in that gentleman too. Reich Chancellor von Papen must also be accounted a member of this circle. . . . The gentlemen's club close to the Chancellor is also composed largely of men of 'abnormal' disposition. . . . The Jungdeutscher Orden . . . will, once questions of power have been resolved, proceed within the Reich on the basis of its evidence."[170] The various files that passed across Bredow's desk would have contained further items of compromising information. That explains why this essentially irreproachable Reichswehr general had to die like his boss, who was known to have taken a "precious possession" into retirement with him, namely, copies of confidential files. "But it was dangerous possession as well as a precious one."[171]

The star Nazi attorney, Dr. Alfons Sack, was kept locked up for the whole of July 1934 so that Gestapo officers could search his law office and his home at their leisure.[172] He had doubtless been targeted by Himmler merely because SA commanders such as Röhm, Heines and Ernst were among his frequent visitors.[173] Sack himself was also reputed to be homosexual. Röhm's attorney, Walter Luetgebrune, was likewise detained and, on his own submission, "roughed up." Luetgebrune had "always lived well," but a client who visited him in 1935 was shocked to note that he had "lost everything."[174] Strasser's attorney, Gert Voss, fared still worse. When he refused to open his safe, he was summarily shot dead by a raiding party and the safe forced.[175]

Equally typical was the fate of Röhm's young aide, Du Moulin Eckart, who had been forewarned by friends and managed to hide during the bloodbath. When he thought it safe to reappear he was promptly arrested and consigned for years to Dachau concentration camp. Even Winifred Wagner was unable to help this son of Wagner's celebrated biographer, who was a close friend of the Haus Wahnfried set. "Don't plead for that boy," Hitler told her firmly. He was "the worst of the lot" and would remain in Dachau.[176]

One last feature of the June 30 scenario was the cynical way in which many survivors were informed that they, too, had been on a death list and could count themselves lucky to have survived. Not even Rudolf Diels was spared this threat. Heydrich is said to have told him to his face that Göring had unfortunately crossed his name off.[177]

It may readily be inferred from these few examples that the operation carried out on and around June 30 was considerably more than a preemptive strike against the SA leaders and a few of those "putschists'" reactionary accomplices. It was a carefully planned campaign against people who knew, or were suspected of knowing, too much about Hitler. The violent imposition of a "state of emergency" was intended to enable the authorities to gain possession, at a stroke, of documents considered dangerous by Hitler and his regime. Of the more than 1,100 persons detained in the course of the purge, thirty-four were still behind bars in the fall of 1934.[178] Their arrest made it possible to seize private papers and sift them with the utmost care. Hitler's speech to the Reichstag on July 13, 1934, revealingly disclosed that most of his time since the "Röhm putsch" had been spent looking through countless files, diaries and other "shocking documents"[179]—in other words, confiscated material.

His principal motive for taking action against "Röhm and associates" was fear of exposure and blackmail. What additionally confirms this is that the mountains of confiscated documents were not to be used in trials of any kind—Hitler had firmly rejected any such judicial proceedings from the outset[180]—but handed over to Himmler's Gestapo and, thus, to Hitler himself. The elimination of witnesses and evidence—*that* was the real purpose of this act of terrorism, which was carried out, not by some gang or other, but by flying squads drawn from an already largely centralized national police force.

When Hitler appeared before the Reichstag on July 13, or nearly two weeks after the bloodbath, he must have dreaded for days that, somewhere abroad, safes might be opened and evidence of a devastating nature produced. But nothing of the kind had happened. It was only now, when he felt relatively secure, that he ventured to render an account before "the nation's most authoritative forum." His speech was considered by many to be among the most rhetorically skillful of his career. Hitler's initial hesitancy gave way to an irony and sarcasm which, as the stenographic record of the Reichstag session noted, evoked "hilarity" and even "laughter"[181] from his audience—a remarkable feat of unscrupulousness. He did, for all that, frankly concede that it was only the rift between himself and Röhm and the disastrous disintegration of their close friendship that had conjured the swiftly escalating political conflict into being. At the same Reichstag session Göring even made a sibylline allusion to "the Führer's terrible hours of sorrow" at the fact that "his trust was abused by the man whom he himself had held up to us all as a paragon of utter fealty."[182] In stating that the personal had preceded the political, Hitler had told the truth. It was only half of the truth, of course, because no one was informed what had really destroyed his relationship with Röhm. But Hitler had wriggled out of a tight spot yet again. He had succeeded, not only in retaining his supporters' trust, but in actually reinforcing it. "You've done it," Göring is reported to have exclaimed at the time, and not without reason. "You possess that trust, and based upon that trust you can do what is needful for Germany's resurgence."

A Preventive War on His Own Behalf

Although Hitler had managed to petrify his remaining enemies inside the Third Reich, the press in exile was harder to control. On July 5, 1934, for example, the Paris-based communist *Deutsche Volks-Zeitung* announced that Hitler had eliminated "initiates who had become dangerous"—initiates privy "not least to the private life of the Führer, who is himself homosexual."[183] Otto Strasser, too, must have known what he was talking about when he gave an article in his expatriate newspaper *Die Deutsche Revolution* the following headline: "Does Paragraph 175 apply to the dead alone? A question addressed to Adolf Hitler." Indignation leveled by the Nazi press at the murdered SA leaders' "abnormal disposition" was "disgusting hypocrisy," the article went on. "Anyone who—like us—has drawn attention to these abuses for years, and anyone who—like us—has sought and implemented judicial clarification thereof, is immune to any charge of condoning such matters. But was it not precisely Herr Hitler and his party who, notwithstanding all the complaints from within their own camp and all their opponents' attacks on this open wound, protected Röhm and his homosexual friends again and again?" What was more, the "Führer" was continuing to do this in the case of "surviving ministers."

Strasser consequently announced that he would publish "a preliminary list of incumbent senior dignitaries of the Hitler system" and, "in full cognizance of the legal consequences, charge them before the German people and the world with homosexual sentiments and unnatural sexual activities."[184] This list was actually published a week later. In its "preliminary" form, it comprised the following names: Rudolf Hess; Baldur von Schirach, the Reich Youth Leader; Helmuth Brückner, gauleiter of Silesia; Karl Kaufmann, gauleiter of Hamburg; and Wilhelm Brückner, Hitler's aide-de-camp. The credibility of this disclosure was enhanced by a postscript: "As witnesses in support of our allegation, which we are willing and able to affirm under oath in court, we name (since the two principal witnesses, Captain Röhm and Gregor Strasser, were regrettably eliminated in good time) Minister Dr. Frick, Oberpräsident Erich Koch, General von Heinemann (ex-chairman of Uschla [the so-called Investigation and Arbitration Committee, alias the NSDAP's supreme court]), Major Buch (the current chairman of Uschla), Frau Minister Hess, Premier von Killinger, and others, on whose direct evidence (and on their personal inspection of secret Party documents) our accusation is based."[185]

Thanks to the Third Reich's strict press censorship, this information found its way only into a few foreign newspapers. Hitler was able to dismiss it as part of the wave of protests to which he was anyway subjected after the Röhm operation, although not, of course, without complaint, as witness a *New York Herald Tribune* interview with him published on July 11, 1934. It was, he said, "a misfortune for us all that wild and unfounded rumors about us are being constantly disseminated in America and other countries," because such rumors were doing "immense damage."[186] Above all, though, they made him feel uneasy. He could never be sure what his own "people" were saying about his homosexuality,[187] and this sense of inadequate control continued to exercise him even after his preemptive strike on June 30. Because he saw the hub of his dictatorship—the Führer myth—threatened by rumormongers, he feverishly searched around for further precautionary measures.

Only six months after the Röhm murders, the so-called Malicious Practices Act[188] came into force. This act penalized any remark that might "seriously prejudice the welfare of the Reich or the reputation of the Reich government or that of the NSDAP or its organizations." The same went for "remarks about leading members of the government or the NSDAP that are openly malicious, inflammatory, or indicative of base sentiments." Most of the relevant regulations were carried over from the decree "for the countering of malicious attacks on the government of national revolution" signed by Hindenburg in March 1933. These were now extended to Hitler's party and enshrined in the law, but their special feature was that prosecution was made dependent on the approval on the Reich minister of justice, which meant ultimately by his boss, Reich Chancellor Adolf Hitler. His self-made image as "the German people's supreme judicial authority" was thus to take effect in an area that the "Führer" clearly deemed to be more ticklish than most: disrespectful remarks about him uttered by members of the public.

To the best of our knowledge, most of the remarks the courts had to deal with related to Hitler himself and his homosexuality.[189] Whether or not the accused was in sympathy with the National Socialist movement or had actually rendered it some service seems to have been immaterial from the aspect of prosecution and verdict. Here is an example from Nuremberg.[190] In the summer of 1935, a homosexual engineer who had worked for the NSDAP since the mid-

1920s was alleged by an informer to have importuned a young man as follows: "Look at our Führer—he also pleasures himself with gentlemen." In spite of the plea for clemency which the accused man's wife addressed to the minister of justice, drawing attention to his "National Socialist sentiments," he was sentenced to the maximum penalty, or two years' imprisonment. "His vile and outrageous slandering of the Führer precludes any token of clemency," ruled the judge. Other cases, too, reveal the exceptional sensitivity with which the special courts reacted to any remarks that alluded to a homosexual disposition on Hitler's part.[191]

But despite—or because of—all these threats and penalties, gossip about Hitler's sexual orientation persisted. In 1937 an SA trooper who had let slip a remark to the effect that Hitler was "a 175er," like Röhm, spent the next two years behind bars.[192] Berlin provides another example of infinitely greater relevance dating from the fall of 1942.[193] No less a person than Julius Schaub, Hitler's personal aide, denounced the editor Hans Walter Aust, who was a member of the Reich Press Chamber and exempt from military service. Aust had told Schaub's female informant "that the Führer keeps a young girl named Everl [i.e., Eva Braun] on the Obersalzburg; the Führer keeps this girl solely for the purpose of concealing his homosexuality from those around him." Although Aust claimed that he had only been repeating what he himself had been told "by a well-known lady," the court showed no mercy and sentenced him to two years' imprisonment. Its judgment clearly reveals how difficult it was for judges to substantiate their verdicts: "Even though the Führer's person is far too exalted to be affected by such rumors, one should not, especially in wartime, underestimate the danger that threatens the German people if widespread faith in the leadership is undermined by such idle talk." This "vile slander is all the more serious in that it imputes to the Führer precisely those unnatural proclivities which he himself had rigorously condemned on the occasion of the Röhm incident in 1934." However, not even these judicial contortions were enough for Hitler: from 1943, remarks to the effect that the "Führer" was homosexually inclined were punishable by death.[194]

But to revert to 1934. Three months after the Röhm operation, Hitler instructed the Reichsführer-SS, Heinrich Himmler, to decree that a register be kept of all "homosexual misdemeanors" throughout the Reich, especially those committed by "political figures,"[195] and that a special department be established at the heart of his tyrannical organization. Hitler's interest in illuminating every corner of the homosexual scene in Germany shows how uneasy he still felt *after* he had gained some leeway by brutally crushing "Röhm and associates." He wanted to get such a grip on the "problem" of homosexuality that it could never again present a threat to his position of power. But for this he required comprehensive information, continuous intimidation and, last but not least, more stringent penal laws that gave the police and the judiciary a free hand.

A few months after the enactment of the Malicious Practices Act, therefore, drastic steps were taken to strengthen Paragraph 175.[196] From now on, mere suspicion of "indecent acts" was sufficient to justify an arrest. This opened the door to arbitrary police procedures. Hitherto still partly intact, the homosexual subculture—of major cities in particular—was destroyed during the latter half of the 1930s. A campaign of systematic persecution was launched against homosexuals, who were threatened with torture, detention in concentration camps and even death.[197] They were registered throughout the Reich, with the result that more than 30,000 persons were under surveillance, so to speak, by 1939. But matters did not stop there. As early as 1935 the number of cases brought under Paragraph 175 rose sharply, as did the percentage of convictions. For a substantial number of those concerned, intensified repression had fatal consequences. Not all escaped with terms of imprisonment; many of them—estimates vary between 5,000 and 15,000—were permanently consigned to concentration camps, where they were not only harassed but persistently

tormented to such an extent that the death rate among inmates wearing the "pink chevron," who were always concentrated in special
groups, was exceptionally high. Only selective research has been
devoted to the number of men who actually succumbed to this policy
of repression, which was perverted from many points of view. However, the suffering inflicted on those whom Hitler's persecution mania
prompted him to take hostage, as it were, should certainly not be
underestimated.[198] Hitler was mortally afraid of the obscurity of the
homosexual milieu, which he himself had experienced firsthand in
Vienna and Munich. He knew that this demimonde could at any time
yield up disreputable secrets—even some, perhaps, that might affect
him personally. He wanted to nip this potential threat in the bud
throughout the Reich, and his only way of doing so was to entrust the
task to Heinrich Himmler, the head of his terror apparatus. Although
not interested in a policy of repression toward "ordinary" homosexuals, he was doubly so in cases where definite interests were involved.

One graphic illustration of this relates to Oberpräsident and
Gauleiter Helmut Brückner, the man whom the press in exile had
accused of homosexuality in the summer of 1934. A Nazi veteran,
Brückner had been under suspicion since 1932/33,[199] but had evaded
the SS's savagery and survived the so-called Night of Long Knives
unscathed. A month later he was denounced as a "175er" to the attorney general's office in Breslau by Himmler's representative in Silesia,
Udo von Woyrsch.[200] In October 1934, Brückner naively sent Hess,
Göring and other senior Nazis a "memorandum"—not extant in the
original—in which he sought to compromise Woyrsch, Himmler and
possibly other leading members of the regime by imputing the same
tendencies to them.[201] He was promptly arrested by the Gestapo and
taken to Berlin, where, in December 1934, Himmler's thugs bullied
him into confessing his homosexual "misdemeanors." He was duly
expelled from the Party and removed from office.

But that was not the end of it. On express orders from Hitler, who followed the affair with remarkably close attention and even found time for a one-hour conversation with Brückner's wife, his old comrade in arms had to remain in prison despite his assurance that he would keep his oath to Hitler "outside the NSDAP as well."[202] Although Göring had promised Frau Brückner that it would not come to a trial, Hitler evidently wanted to lure the man out of his shell and ordained that the public prosecutor's office hold a formal inquiry under Paragraph 175. Brückner promptly warned against "settling his case in court, because he would then have to raise matters that would gravely damage the Movement and the government."[203] But these matters were just what Hitler wanted to hear—in closed session, of course—so the trial went ahead in October 1935. At a preliminary stage in the proceedings, Brückner cited the following arguments in his defense in an (intercepted) letter to his attorney:

His "bisexual disposition" stemmed from "formerly practiced mutual masturbation," but he categorically denied having committed a penal offense thereby. The Reich Supreme Court had not ruled that mutual masturbation came within the ambit of Paragraph 175 until the summer of 1935, and his own "activities" antedated that—the argument successfully employed by Röhm in 1931. As for the charge that his conduct had harmed the Party, Brückner firmly rejected it on the following grounds: "My inhibitions recurred more strongly when, on June 30 [1934], there occurred within the National Socialist Party itself a sudden, radical transition from non-existent toleration to the most drastic eradication. . . . The Reich Supreme Court's decades-old judgment and ruling, which applied to the postwar period as well as the prewar, was, after all, common property in nationalist Germany. This view was expressly confirmed by the NSDAP in the Röhm case, not only in 1932, in connection with the Röhm letters, both within the Party and by the Party leadership, but also after the assumption of power in 1933, notably when Hindenburg, at the Reich Chancellor's suggestion, appointed Chief of Staff Röhm to be a minister at New

Year 1934. This dispelled of any uncertainty. National Socialism not only authoritatively and manifestly endorsed the Supreme Court's traditional view of mutual masturbation, but expressly approved it—indeed, eliminated any inhibitions by acknowledging its incidence in society!"

It is clear how disconcerted Brückner had been in 1934 by the NSDAP leadership's "radical transition" from homophilia to homophobia. But he soon realized that "political considerations" were at work. The public prosecutor's office was merely the "stooge of a judicial system," and: "We were lied to." At the main hearing on October 22, 1935, however, he did not speak his mind or paint any picture of the homosexual culture to which the NSDAP leadership had granted such latitude until the summer of 1934. Instead, he fell back on his services to the Party and pleaded his innocence under the law. The court sentenced Brückner to fifteen months' imprisonment, but he lodged an appeal.

On November 1, 1935, having already exerted an influence on the trial through Reich Minister of Justice Gürtner,[204] Hitler received a personal report on "the Brückner affair" from Himmler. As the Reichsführer-SS noted a few days later, he ruled that "the public prosecutor's office should not put any obstacles in the way of the appeal proceedings. After the second hearing, the Führer continues to reserve the right of decision."[205] In other words, the validity of legal provisions was dependent solely on the man for whose personal safety they had been laid down in the first place. Hitler could arbitrarily dictate the course of events in what was, de facto, a legal vacuum. When Brückner had served the first part of his prison sentence, the "Führer" was lenient enough, or so it seemed, to suspend the remainder. He may have hoped that this would assure him of Brückner's loyalty, especially as he instructed Himmler and Göring in 1938 to find him suitable employment outside politics.[206]

The "Führer's" Monopoly

As head of state, Hitler had plenty to do apart from taking a personal interest in the trial of a bisexual Party member. He never concerned himself in detail with the harassment of "opponents of the regime," a task he entrusted to Himmler and the SS. But as soon as the subject of "homosexual politicians" cropped up, and especially when politicians in his own ranks were involved, he insisted on being consulted from the outset. In such instances, his personal ruling was all that counted. He displayed an equally keen interest in learning what people heard or said on the subject of homosexuality with reference to himself. Reports of relevant investigations, even from the most remote corners of his domain, were forever passing across his desk. This reflected the paranoia of a man who, although he had probably come to believe in the "Führer" myth himself, sensed that it did not fit him. It was also symptomatic of the unconquerable dread of exposure that continued to haunt him even after the "Röhm putsch," the Malicious Practices Act and the strengthening of Paragraph 175.

Moreover, the "Brückner case" shows that Otto Strasser's disclosures were not mere fabrications. Even at the end of 1934, it is probable that the Nazi top brass still included one or two homosexual politicians, namely, Rudolf Hess, Baldur von Schirach and Hans Frank, in whom Gilbert, the American forensic psychologist at Nuremberg, later detected "homosexual tendencies,"[207] or Karl Kaufmann, about whom similar things were said in the course of various postwar trials.[208] But Brückner was the only one who broke the unwritten law that prevailed inside the National Socialist movement: Never mention homosexuality; above all, never name names! It was that blatant breach of the rules, not his homosexuality, that cost him his job. After Röhm's murder, of course, almost every homosexual officeholder lived in fear of Himmler's SS and Reinhard Heydrich's blacklists.[209]

The result was total dependence on Hitler's favor. By 1935 his paladins' knowledge of his sexual orientation had become worthless as an insurance policy. The dictator had made homosexuality a privilege reserved for certain chosen associates and, in addition, a personal monopoly that brooked no competition. He was the only one against whom legislation in respect of homosexuality could never be used. Germany's "Führer" had become a "savior" in his own behalf.

But Hitler was also pursuing a political policy. He had realized in 1934 that homosexual advances within his movement could no longer be tolerated, if only for his own sake. His experience of the public mudslinging campaign against Röhm was of inestimable importance: it had shown him that nothing could prevail over the stigmatization of homosexuality, not even inside his own party. He could see no alternative but to yield, more and more, to conformist pressure, and his hopes were fulfilled: once he had taken action against "Röhm and associates," his courage and initiative were extolled by public and social elites alike.[210] The fact that he had ostensibly crushed a "putsch" enhanced his power-political standing, and his approaches to the Reichswehr commanders and harnessing of the conservative elite, who seemed fascinated by his determination to instill "order," enabled him to polish his image as "the savior of the nation." To this extent, the Röhm affair not only consolidated Hitler's dictatorship but generated a renewed surge of admiration that rapidly drowned the harsh criticism leveled at his course of action by foreign observers.

Thus, three months after this major breakthrough, Hitler could count himself extremely fortunate and feel able, in private, to venture the following exclamation: "I think my life is the greatest novel in the history of the world!"[211] That is precisely how it appears to historians. But his life was governed by a brutal maxim which, in another political context, the "Führer" had bellowed into the microphone only a few weeks earlier: "Absolutely nothing will force us into submission! We shall not surrender under any circumstances!"[212]

CHAPTER SIX

Posthumous Revelations: Erich Ebermayer and His Sources

THE SYSTEMATIC destruction of definite source material relating to Hitler's homosexuality has not prevented information on the subject from being passed on by persons whose interest in transmitting their knowledge was not only political but sometimes quite personal. One of them was the homosexual lawyer and novelist Erich Ebermayer (1900–1970). If his statements are correct, and there is much to be said in their favor, they constitute a genuine discovery.

In 1959, Zsolnay-Verlag published Ebermayer's "personal and political diary" for the years 1933/35.[1] Among its most interesting passages are the entries dealing with the "Röhm putsch" of the summer of 1934.[2] At the time, wrote Ebermayer, he was "paralyzed with terror," and his initial comments on the official announcements betray the helplessness and fear he felt at the possibility of further incursions by the authorities. Before long, however, we detect a sense of outrage, which culminates in Ebermayer's conjecture that the operation was designed "to eliminate unwelcome initiates from the Führer's own past and the Movement's time of struggle." And Ebermayer could cite good reasons for that suspicion: "The most interesting and shocking thing of all is the slant—or, rather, the twist—the affair is now taking on: the campaign against homosexuality. It goes without saying that this campaign is spurious and disingenuous. According to the Führer's military record, which was seen by Dr. Külz, the former Reich minister of the interior, homosexual activities precluded him from promotion to sergeant despite his bravery in action. . . . During its time of struggle, the National Socialist movement—and not just the Röhm clique—was a 'fraternity' such as Blüher portrayed in his books, its motive force being homoeroticism. In the view of all who have an intimate knowledge of the circumstances, Hess, known in Party circles as 'Black Emma,' was for many years the Führer's partner, especially during their joint detention in Landsberg. . . . My exceedingly trustworthy sources of information about these confidential matters . . . have hitherto . . . *proudly* stressed the homoerotic orientation of the Führer and his inner circle, and have stated that the Führer himself no longer indulges his inclinations now that politics are absorbing more and more of his energies. Only occasionally, on car journeys, notably at the Hotel Bube in Berneck in the Fichtelgebirge, does he get an opportunity to relax during trips from Berlin to Munich. However, they say he still views this problem with the greatest sympathy and understanding, as witness his toleration—indeed, his advancement—of Röhm and his associates."[3]

Having read this passage, one regards those parts of the book which contain far more discreet allusions to Hitler's private life in a different light. The speech Goebbels delivered to mark Hitler's forty-fourth birthday in April 1933 was devoted to his "fantastic ascent from the depths of the people." Commenting on this, Ebermayer wrote: "Napoleon's career is nothing in comparison. He was an officer, after all, whereas our man was an unemployed (or work-shy?)

painter who survived by scrounging, and sometimes, no doubt, by pursuing a more distasteful trade." With reference to Röhm's astonishing rehabilitation, Ebermayer hazarded the opinion that "the 'Führer' is entirely in the hands of his friend Röhm, who is said to be one of the few people acquainted with his private life." Finally, he comments on Hitler's countless attempts to present an acceptable curriculum vitae: "This wondrous tale did not bring the walls tumbling down. What I find most miraculous of all, however, is that he himself clearly believes in the legend of his life. If someone recounted his life to him as it actually was, he would, with the most devout conviction, call him a liar. . . . As a writer, I can well understand this. I often believe in my own invented stories—I have to, or I couldn't tell them reasonably convincingly."[4]

All in all, Ebermayer's information about Hitler is a remarkable mixture of insider's knowledge, guesswork and literary assimilation. It is regrettable that he was never cross-examined as closely as Albert Speer, for example. Today, just over thirty years after Ebermayer's death, it is far harder to gauge the veracity of his statements. An attempt must be made, however, because he put into words what many insiders dared not utter. Let us begin, therefore, by asking whether he could have known that what he wrote was true.

ERICH EBERMAYER

Erich Ebermayer was the only son of Ludwig Ebermayer, an extremely well-known and politically influential lawyer who had been senior attorney at the supreme court in Leipzig and was, at the turn of the century, a highly respected advocate of penal reform.[5] He attained the peak of his career between 1910 and 1930, serving as adviser to several ministers of justice and the interior. He also kept open house in Leipzig, and his regular visitors included many prominent politicians.

This left its mark on young Erich. "Through my father," he recalled, "I got to know many intelligent, well-known people, and saw, with a mixture of revulsion and amusement, what went on behind the political scenes during and after the war."[6] Having served on numerous parliamentary and ministerial committees over the years, Ludwig Ebermayer had a detailed knowledge of Germany's political structures, and his special field, penal reform, was in many respects highly controversial. Even before World War I, for example, discussion had been devoted to reforming Paragraph 175, a subject on which Ebermayer adopted a decidedly progressive position. He argued in favor of decriminalizing straightforward homosexuality, and continued to espouse that widely respected view during the 1920s.[7]

His liberal approach to this question was not, however, an automatic pointer to his party-political stance. He never joined any party despite his friendly relations with leading politicians, although he probably favored the right-wing, middle-class camp. This is indicated by his close relations with Curt Joël,[8] a politician of conservative reputation who was minister of justice in 1931/32 and a leading government adviser. Joël was one of the Weimar system's *éminences grises*; anyone whose friend and confidant he was had access—at least until the Brüning government fell—to the *arcana imperii*. But Ebermayer himself, having led for the prosecution at trials of extremist enemies of the republic, possessed certain confidential information.[9]

Another "old friend and colleague of my father's," Erich Ebermayer wrote to Alfred Rosenberg,[10] had been Franz Gürtner. This conservative, nationalistic advocate of authoritarian government had been Bavarian minister of justice in the 1920s,[11] and it was he whom Hitler had to thank for having gotten off so lightly after his various breaches of the law during that period. When Hitler assumed power, therefore, it seemed only natural to reward him accordingly. Gürtner was appointed Reich minister of justice, and it was in this capacity that he and Hans Frank, the Bavarian minister of justice, are said to have requested Ludwig Ebermayer—"in the Führer's name as well"— to collaborate on planned amendments to the penal code. When Ebermayer Sr. died shortly thereafter, Gürtner came to Leipzig in person for the funeral and, after delivering a brief eulogy, laid a wreath on behalf of the Reich government.[12]

Although Ludwig Ebermayer's cordial relations with Joël and Gürtner do not, in principle, call his independence into question, they do show that he was well provided with political inside information— thanks also to his contacts with the left-wing bourgeois camp and, in particular, with Wilhelm Külz.[13] A leading representative of the German Democratic Party, Külz became Reich minister of the interior in January 1926 and retained that post for over a year. He resolutely opposed the militarization of political organizations, especially those on the nationalistic right wing, thereby earning himself the odium of the National Socialists.[14] He perceived Hitler as a political threat even in the mid-1920s. That was why, when Hindenburg gave Külz temporary charge of the Reichswehr ministry for three months in the spring of 1926 (as a stand-in for Otto Gessler, who was ill),[15] he must have seized the opportunity to look at Hitler's military record—a source of information to which a "civilian minister" like himself would not normally have had access.[16] It is not surprising that ministry records contain no reference to his having done so,[17] as Erich Ebermayer mentions, because it was a semilegal action bordering on espionage. That the diarist knew of this becomes quite understandable when we learn that the sons of the senior state attorney and the Reich minister of the interior were on even closer terms than their fathers,[18] and had been since the summer of 1934, when Erich Ebermayer was desperately seeking an explanation for the events of June 30. In 1959, when he finally disclosed his knowledge of the Hitler documents Külz had seen, the latter's son Helmut was senatorial chairman of the Federal

Administrative Court. If Ebermayer's statements about so delicate a matter had been false, Helmut Külz not only could but—in view of his position—should have rebutted them.

These circumstances would also explain why the National Socialists took Wilhelm Külz into so-called protective custody at the end of 1934. Although they gave no reason, their manifest purpose was to intimidate him. But the crucial information about Hitler's military record had seeped into another bureaucratic channel. In Frankfurt an der Oder in March 1937 a district court official was denounced to the Gestapo for having claimed that he "knew from a very reliable source that the Führer, despite being awarded the Iron Cross 1st Class, had not been promoted because he was homosexual. Himmler, accompanied by an SS detachment, had tried to get the Führer's military papers from Blomberg [the then Reichswehr minister], but Blomberg had refused to surrender them."[19]

———

Young Erich Ebermayer had taken an interest in the subject of homosexuality ever since he became a law student in 1919. Like Thomas Mann in *Death in Venice*, he tackled the theme in his own literary efforts and used his draft novellas as a means of getting in touch with his celebrated exemplar.[20] The favorable interest shown him by Thomas Mann and others encouraged Ebermayer to publish his first novel, *Dr. Angelo*, in August 1924. Contemporary critics commented that it was an ill-disguised form of self-disclosure.[21] Foremost among those who hailed Ebermayer's literary debut was the homosexual emancipation movement, the more so because the author was the son of Germany's senior state attorney.

But Ebermayer must have been particularly proud of a letter of "sincere congratulations" from Thomas Mann, who was convinced that his "fine publication . . . will undoubtedly earn your talent many friends."²² Drawing on his fairly undisguised homoerotic inspiration from then on, Ebermayer wrote a number of short stories and stage plays which had, by the end of the 1920s, assured him of a well-established place in the relevant literary canon.²³ What also contributed to his reputation as a pioneer of the "new eros" was his close friendship with Gustav Wyneken, the educational reformer.²⁴ In 1923 Ebermayer came out openly in support of Wyneken and, thus, of his "Pedagogic Eros" ideology, and in 1925 he accepted election to the chairmanship of the board of governors of Wyneken's scandal-enshrouded school.²⁵

Meanwhile, after graduating and obtaining his doctorate, Ebermayer worked as an attorney in Leipzig, "but, wisely, in an office where I had nothing to do and . . . only [took on] the occasional defense assignment,"²⁶ for instance, in cases brought under Paragraph 175.²⁷ His commitment is particularly manifest in "Jugend und Eros" [Youth and Love], an essay published in 1926, in which he called on his readers "to help to do away with the injustices" associated with Paragraph 175. This, he wrote, was "a mission and a call to the young that affects everyone, of whatever erotic orientation. For the campaign against Paragraph 175 of the Penal Code is no longer a 'homosexuals' war of liberation,' as it is often mistakenly regarded, but a fight for the social recognition of a variety of human nature, for humane and equitable freedom, and for the state's magnanimous and wise restraint in matters which, because of their purely private and naturally occurring character, cannot be subject to its authority."²⁸ In this remarkably frank plea for homosexual love, which all those affected "perceive, not as a regrettable, pitiful curse, but . . . as a blessing and distinction," Ebermeyer was not only resorting to Gustav Wyneken's arguments. Also discernible are lines of reasoning in favor of male homosexual eroticism inspired by Hans Blüher. Although we have no correspondence that might furnish us with detailed information about any personal exchange of ideas between Blüher and Ebermayer, a careful perusal of *Kampf um Odilienburg* (1929), a roman à clef that contrasts "male" eros with "feminine" homosexuality,[29] leaves one in no doubt that Ebermayer was very well acquainted with Blüher's writings. Seen against this background, Ebermayer's citing of Blüher as a principal witness on behalf of his diagnosis of the National Socialist movement, which we quoted at the beginning of this chapter, acquires clarity and relevance.

Furthermore, Blüher left behind a manuscript, published posthumously in 1966, which characterizes Hitler's party in much the same way as Ebermayer: "What informs the conscientious observer of a person's sexual orientation is not particular acts, which might be interesting from the aspect of sexual scuttlebutt, but the *atmosphere* in which he lives. Where Hitler is concerned, it is not hard to define this. In his case the diagnosis reads . . . orientation toward a fraternity. No one who has observed all this and knows it can be in any doubt that Hitler thought and acted homosexually; that he was a definite man's man [the German is a play on "lady's man"] who transformed his original male society into a political party, and thus founded a fraternity of unique proportions—a fraternity in which, under Ernst Röhm's direction, communities of young men and couples linked by erotic friendship played a politically important role of which Hitler was not unaware. . . . In the immediate aftermath of the so-called 'assumption of power,' many advocates of male homosexuality believed that the time had finally come to abolish Paragraph 175, because they and their kind had . . . provided their Führer with powerful forces, rooted in eroticism and derived therefrom, for the establishment of his powerful new regime. . . . So all the penal regulations that defamed and endangered their love life must finally and permanently disappear. I heard such voices raised. But I warned one or two credulous homosexuals against unmasking themselves too soon, and advised them to bide their time."[30]

Although Ebermayer did not consider joining the Nazi movement, he too was one of the "men's men" who believed in 1934 that the "Führer" and his loyal henchmen would not betray the homoeroticism that had been one basis of their political success. He must have been pretty convinced of this, because he was exceptionally well informed about the arcane subject, notably through his cousin Philipp Bouhler, who had been on Hitler's personal staff since 1925, and with whom Ebermayer was in close touch from 1930 on.[31] "As I heard from my cousin, the NSDAP's Reich business manager, not long ago," Ebermayer informed Herr Costa, a director of Zsolnay-Verlag, the Viennese publishers, "my books have for years been among the works the Führer and his circle enjoy reading."[32]

To Ebermayer, of course, homoeroticism was not just a subject for literary assimilation but a part of his daily life as well. In 1925 he formed a friendship with Klaus Mann, with whom he occasionally collaborated.[33] It was then, if not before, that he became acquainted with the value of culturally refined male relationships as exemplified by Thomas Mann's high-strung son. At the turn of 1932/33, when the collapse of the Weimar Republic seemed imminent, the two men planned a new joint project: a dramatization of Antoine de Saint-Exupéry's *Vol de nuit*. By late January 1933 this project was taking shape, and the two friends met in Leipzig to arrange when and where to put it into effect.[34] Their meeting coincided with Hitler's assumption of power, not that this event caused any immediate disruption in their plans. Mann had only just returned to Munich when he wrote to say how much he was looking forward to working with Ebermayer. Employing a truly remarkable turn of phrase, he added: "Incidentally, may the German Reich Chancellor graciously protect us. Sincerely, Klaus."[35] What did he mean? Had he been assured at Ebermayer's home that the new head of government took a thoroughly open-minded, indeed, sympathetic view of homosexual love among men of letters?[36] On the other hand, was he being mordantly sarcastic? We do not know.

At all events, Klaus Mann's antifascist sentiments did not at first deter him from pursuing his and Ebermayer's joint literary project. It was not until after the Reichstag fire and the March elections that a fundamental change in the political and cultural climate threatened his entire family and jolted him out of his sense of security. He went into exile "more from instinct than 'conviction'"[37]—precisely the motive that prompted his friend Ebermayer to remain in Germany. It did not affect them that their reactions to the political situation differed so greatly, and they continued until the end of 1933 to exchange cordial letters in which Klaus sent his "regards to your boy [the last word in English]."[38] But it was not fear of homophobic repression that had driven Klaus Mann from Germany, and his friend was certainly free from any such apprehensions.

———

After Hitler came to power, Ebermayer observed him at very close quarters in Berlin's Hotel Kaiserhof, nicknamed "the headquarters of the Movement." Knowing that Hitler still, even as chancellor, took his afternoon coffee "in a corner of the lobby," he went there "a few times" in February 1933. Sitting down "right beside the table reserved for Hitler," he saw confirmation of what he had long been told: "There are only men at his table. . . . The whole scene calls to mind a master eating with his disciples. . . . Then a new 'disciple' comes in and makes his presence felt at his lord and master's table. Remaining seated, Hitler returns his salute with raised hand bent far back and little finger extended sideways. There's something feminine about this salute. Very soft, very Austrian. The accompanying expression is grimly serious and hard as stone. . . . Remarkable how many cakes he eats! I count up to eight! . . . I'm struck, again and again, by his airy, graceful gestures. The way he raises the cup to his lips, dissects his cake—it's all so un-Prussian, so soft and southern, so feminine."[39]

His impression was confirmed a few weeks later by Hans Severus Ziegler, the newly appointed chief dramaturge of the German National Theater at Weimar. In May 1933, Ziegler invited him and his partner Peer Baedeker, with whom he had had a liaison since 1932, to a performance of one of his, Ebermayer's, plays. Ebermayer described Ziegler not only as "one of the Movement's earliest champions in Thuringia" but as an "artistic, sensitive, likable man" whom he had known since 1929. A devout adherent of Hitler, Ziegler had tried even then to persuade Ebermayer to join the Movement. "You belong with us," he had said. "The sooner you realize it, the better for you— and us! The opportunities you would have with us are immense. . . . As a cousin of Bouhler's, a son of your father's, a lawyer, a writer, and someone with your racial characteristics, you're better predestined than almost anyone to go straight into the Party's supreme leadership. You need only say yes, and tomorrow I'll call the Führer and Dr. Goebbels, and we'll arrange an interview."[40]

Ziegler was himself homosexual. This was probably why, for all their ideological differences, the two men were united by "a certain affection"[41] that had not evaporated four years after Ziegler's original offer and a few months after Hitler came to power. "A wave of genuine goodwill flows toward me," Ebermayer noted. What particularly pleased him was the unaffected way in which Ziegler included his partner in his amiable remarks. "We celebrate with the actors and a group of Weimar theaterlovers until dawn. After midnight Ziegler plays Wagner, Liszt, Chopin, all freely and tastefully extemporized. Sparkling wine flows like water. Not a word about politics, thank God. When we leave the cellar the sun has just risen. . . . Ziegler doesn't want to go to bed yet, so we drive out to Belvedere. Stroll in the park for an hour. . . . While we're sitting on the terrace high above Weimar, looking down at the eternal city, which is still thinly wreathed in morning mist, Ziegler puts his arms around M's [Peer Baedeker's] and my shoulders and says: 'You blockheads, why on earth haven't you joined us? Don't you regret it yourselves, now? But then, you can't be aware that the Führer is the most splendid person in the world.'"[42]

Early in June 1934, during a visit to Schloss Zeesen near Berlin, which Gustaf Gründgens had acquired not long before, Ebermayer gained a similar impression of the carefree way in which prominent homosexuals were at liberty to lead their lives until the summer of that year. Being members of the Klaus Mann circle, he and Gründgens had known each other since the late 1920s. Gründgens was now a protégé of the regime's most powerful men and a personal "acquaintance" of no less a person than Hitler himself.[43] Ebermayer was profoundly impressed by the luxurious property and the stage star's lifestyle. "We go out into the grounds. Stroll along the lakeshore. Swimming there are some shapely youths, guests of the director's [i.e., of Gründgen], who don't venture to interrupt us because we're in mid conversation. . . . We lunch on the shady terrace. . . . And now the young swimmers also appear, charming and agreeable [youths]—and among them the great artist of the stage and of life."[44] Gründgens, too, urged Ebermayer to join the Party and spoke of the "great opportunities" it presented. He raved about Göring, who had "once more proved himself an 'incredible gentleman'" and had apparently told him, in so many words: "Put on Ebermayer's play, and I'll have all the journalists who review it inappropriately arrested the day after the première."

In view of these enlightening experiences, Ebermayer had no doubt that the Third Reich would in some respects adopt a liberal attitude, at least toward homosexuals. This being so, one can well understand how profoundly puzzled and dismayed he must have been, even in retrospect, by the events of June 30, 1934. Not so Blüher, who made a largely ignored attempt, after the downfall of the Third Reich, to analyze Hitler's settling of scores with Röhm and point out its repercussions on the Nazi attitude toward homosexuality. "Röhm, who had organized Hitler's fraternity for him, was a troublesome accessory to be eliminated once he had become redundant and was obstructing the fulfillment of other plans. It was his mistake to have concentrated far too much on the sexualization of that fraternity, to have promoted it too zealously and thereby neglected the politically sustaining idea. With Röhm, the old spirit of the Hitlerian fraternity based on erotic friendship disappeared, to be replaced by one of total suppression leading to fanatical hatred. That was how the unexpected happened. Benevolently tolerated hitherto, love of man for man was pilloried overnight as abominable homosexual vice. . . . Hitler now gave his fraternity by another name a different face, and, at the same time, instituted his moral double standards. Within the fraternity, sex was to play no further part: all his men had to conduct themselves like their (impotent) Führer. . . . Off duty, they were granted complete freedom, particularly in sexual matters. Under Röhm's tuition, Hitler had doubtless perceived that male homosexuality was a fundamental force conducive to the establishment of political regimes, especially those of a revolutionary nature. That was why he ensured that this fundamental force could be instantly destroyed, if it manifested itself in potential opponents, by strengthening Paragraph 175 and setting up a body of police specially trained to combat homosexuals. On the other hand, special dispensations enabled it to survive . . . without restraint among his tried and trusty henchmen. Although the double standards instituted by Hitler were regarded and treated as a state secret of the most confidential kind, it was inevitable, in view of the many men who benefited from those double standards and were privy to them, that this state secret became very much of an open secret." Thus Hitler "succeeded in harnessing the politically creative, elemental force of homosexual eros and fully exploiting it for his own ends. At the same time, he managed to employ the same force as a scourge and transform it into a source of nerve-racking torment."[45]

Blüher's analysis is to be regarded not as an empirically certified account of historical reality, but as an interpretation that may help us to discern the crude logic underlying Hitler's regime, especially as regards its impact on sexual policy and, in particular, on the changed situation in the post-Röhm period. It offers one possible explanation for the seemingly paradoxical fact that, in the Third Reich, homosexuality was simultaneously proscribed and protected: Hitler had tailored it to his political and personal requirements. What helped to guarantee his absolute sovereignty was that the homosexual lifestyle possible in Germany was subordinated to an extremely arbitrary raison d'état. How this worked is exemplified by Ebermayer and, more particularly, Ziegler.

TOLERATED HOMOSEXUALITY: TWO CAREERS

In May 1933, impending upheavals in cultural policy were drastically highlighted by the public burning of books on campuses all over Germany. Erich Ebermayer, too, being a "decadent" writer from the so-called system [i.e., Weimar] era, fell into disfavor for a short while, mainly because of his supposedly close association with the hated "bolshevik" literary circle centered on Heinrich Mann, whose *Professor Unrat* he had adapted for the stage in 1931.[46] However, he soon averted this threat with the help of Philipp Bouhler, his influential cousin, and by his own efforts. "My relations with the new Germany and the new government," he wrote to his Viennese publisher in October 1933, "are now, after initial mistrust, as good as can be. I'm currently being staged by wholly National Socialist theaters in Weimar, Cassel, and Meiningen. . . . After the assumption of power I was offered, through intermediaries, two theater directors' posts in Central Germany, which I declined because of my literary activities. I tell you this, not to brag, but to dispel any misgivings on your part."[47] Three days later, with some complacency, he noted in his diary: "I everywhere encounter the greatest surprise that I'm not yet 'really big in Berlin,' since it's my fantastic good fortune to be the cousin of two such grand gentlemen as Bouhler and Todt."[48] It was not surprising that, early in 1934, Ebermayer felt emboldened to embark on a new phase in his life by purchasing a villa in the Grunewald, a select Berlin suburb, and moving into it with his partner Peer Baedeker. "Personally," he wrote to his exiled friend Klaus Mann, he was doing "very, very well. No money, but love."[49]

But then, a few months after the so-called Röhm revolt and the first police raids on the homosexual subculture,[50] Ebermayer came under fire once more. Early in May 1935 he was "mercilessly and bluntly" rebuked for his literary misdemeanors by *Das Schwarze Korps*, the SS's notoriously polemical newspaper, which was particularly vitriolic in its homophobic agitation at the time. The reviewer described his oeuvre, ranging from *Dr. Angelo* to the novel *Jürgen Ried* (1931), the most recent literary work in which Ebermayer had dealt with the theme of homoeroticism, as "an unbroken series of pathetic scandals" that reflected Ebermayer's "abysmal delight in the revolting, perverted, disgusting, and depraved."[51] Proof that the reviewer was not just a scheming individual who had exceeded his authority is supplied by a file in the records of Himmler's Sicherheitsdienst, in which Ebermayer was numbered among "those authors who try to lend expression to eroticism, perversion, and exoticism. He fastens on the problem of sex with almost boyish excitement. Here, in a mood of torment, in sexual fear and distress, he conveys a plethora of sensual experience, which he heightens to a pitch of pathological ecstasy. . . . All of Ebermayer's literary work displays a strong tendency toward harsh extremes which is very often questionable from the aspect of sexual morality, for the spirit his works exude is not at all wholesome, but morbidly erotic."[52]

Without protection from very influential friends, no author in the Third Reich could have survived such an attack unscathed. As it was, nothing untoward happened to Ebermayer. He managed to secure the personal intervention of his cousin and, through him, of Goebbels, with the result that by the fall of 1935 he could confidently inform Vienna "in the first place, that I'm politically completely unobjectionable, and, secondly, that Minister Dr. Göbbels [sic] and Reichsleiter Bouhler rebuff these old troublemakers and opponents of mine by stressing that fact at every opportunity."[53] But other Party authorities continued to include Ebermayer in their blacklists. One such was the "Office for the Cultivation of Literature," which wrote as follows to the "NSDAP's Central Training Office" in the summer of 1939: "Although no official obstacles are currently being placed in the way of Ebermayer's activities, and although he is freely pursuing his career as a screenwriter, there is still reason for the Party to reject him, or at least to withhold its support."[54]

This did not, however, damage Ebermayer's career. He scored his greatest financial and social successes in the second half of the 1930s,[55] not least because of his close collaboration with Emil Jannings. His "abnormal inclinations" were well known to Himmler's Security Police, but the fact that "his outward appearance and whole manner" stamped him as "a typical representative of such circles"[56] was clearly no bar to his participation in the Third Reich's cultural activities. He and his partner survived the war years without a finger being laid on them. He was exempted from military service and permitted to travel abroad, and by 1939 he could afford to buy the small baroque château near Bayreuth in which he lived until the war's end. A conformist and an opportunist, Ebermayer managed to adapt so perfectly to the conditions prevailing under Hitler's dictatorship that he remained unscathed despite his notorious homosexuality and compromising literary past. This differentiated his career—like those of other prominent persons—from the disastrous fate of ordinary homosexuals in the Third Reich.

———

Another member of this privileged minority was the aforesaid Hans Severus Ziegler. He not only remained a devotee of Hitler until his

Adolf Hitler and his friend August Kubizek, with whom he had a close liaison during 1905–1908. The drawing is most likely from 1905, the photograph from 1907. © Süddeutscher Verlag, Bilderdienst, D – Münche; © Leopold Stocker Verlag, A – Graz

Rudolf Häusler who became Hitler's friend in Vienna in 1912 and then moved to Munich with him in 1913. The photo is probably from 1914. © Marianne Koppler, A – Hobersdorf

Caricature of Goethe and Schiller
with an anti-Semitic bias in
Jugend(ITAL), the Munich
intellectuals' magazine. It regards
the efforts of the sex researcher
Magnus Hirschfeld to make
homosexuality palatable for
society. The original caption read
'Panic in Weimar. "Wolfgang,
let go of my hand! Dr. Magnus
Hirschfeld is coming!"'

Hitler cheers for the German mobilization on August 2, 1914, at Odeonsplatz in Munich.
© Scherl / Süddeutscher Verlag, Bilderdienst, D – München

Field Soldier Hitler (far left) visibly enjoys a musical performance by his comrades who formed the "Kapelle Krach" [Noise Orchestra].
© AP / Süddeutscher Verlag, Bilderdienst, D – München

Hitler (middle) and his friend "Schmidl" (Ernst Schmidt); these two runners were inseparable between 1914 and 1919. They are pictured here with Karl Lippert (right). © Scherl / Süddeutscher Verlag, Bilderdienst, D – München

Hitler and Schmidl kept in personal contact even after Hitler rose to become the "Führer and Reich Chancellor," as is evidenced by this photograph probably from 1935 which was found in Eva Braun's photo album.

Title page of the propaganda publication of Hitler's former war comrade Hans Mend which Hitler launched in 1932. It stylizes Hitler as a model combat

Caricature about Hitler's failed attempt to get the courts to silence the many people who doubted his heroism during the war; here with a reference to a trial against the social democrat paper *Hamburger Echo* from 1932.

Hitler's propagandist in Munich: Ernst Hanfstaengl, son of a publisher, in this picture about 36 years old. He is pictured here with his wife Helene, his daughter Hertha and his son Egon. © Egon Hanfstaengl, D – München

Thirty-one-year-old staff officer Ernst Röhm and his spy Hitler in 1919. © Bundesarchiv, D – Koblenz; © Anton Joachimsthaler

Hitler's friend and "foster father": the antisemitic writer and ideologist Dietrich Eckart in the early 1920s.

Hitler and his two favorite disciples, Rudolf Hess and Julius Schreck, in
1932. © Fotoarchiv Heinrich Hoffmann, Bayerische
Staatsbibliothek, D –München

Hitler and Rudolf Hess on the
Obersalzberg near Berchtesgaden,
probably in 1929. © Heinrich
Hoffmann

"State funeral" for Hitler's companion Julius Schreck in 1936. © Heinrich
Hoffmann, Bildarchiv Preußischer Kulturbesitz, D – Berlin

Hitler and his "Mosel" (Emil Maurice)
during their detention in the Fortress at
Landsbers in 1924. © NYP 68040,
Imperial War Museum, GB – London

Hitler's niece Angelika Raubal, the
woman who stood between Hitler
and Maurice.

Eva Braun in one of her roles.
The man next to her is
unknown.

The young historian Dr. Eugen Dollmann in the early 1930s. He later became a top agent of the Reichsfuhrer SS, Heinrich Himmler, in Rome. © Lothar Machtan, D – Bremen

Hitler's agent, senior servant Rudolf Diels (right), here after he was promoted to Gestapo chief and SS-Officer in conversation with Heinrich Himmler (left).

Enriched by drastic caricatures, the "Ballade vom Armen Stabschef" [Ballade of the Poor Chief of Staff] written by Bertolt Brecht in the Summer of 1934 was circulated in Nazi Germany as an illegal KPD pamphlet starting in the Fall of the same year. © Bertolt Brecht: Ballade vom armen Stabschef. Stiftung Archiv der Akademie der Künste; Bertolt-Brecht-Archiv 1649/03, D – Berlin

Hitler with Julius Schaub (left)
and Wilhelm Brückner, later
his senior aide, during a
propaganda tour in 1932.

Hitler and his factotum Julius
Schaub (second from right) in
front of the Braunes Haus in
Munich around 1932.
© Deutsche Presse-Agentur,
Bilderdienst, D – Hamburg

"Steadfast friendship." Hitler and his chief of staff Ernst
Röhm during the so-called Seizure of Power (1932/33).
© Scherl / Süddeutscher Verlag, Bilderdienst,
D – München

The German exile press tried to dismantle the homosexual head of the SA, Ernst Röhm, with caricatures such as this one from December 1933.

Even before Hitler settled the score with Röhm, there are several hints of Hitler's effeminateness in the foreign press; here a caricature from the Prague paper "Der Simplicius."

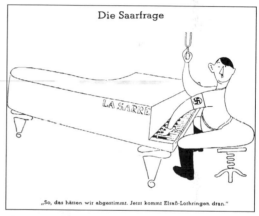

Die Saarfrage

„So, das hätten wir abgestimmt. Jetzt kommt Elsaß-Lothringen dran."

Done! With Hitler's accession to power in January of 1933, Röhm could briefly consider himself the second man behind, if not next to, Hitler; much to the dismay of his rival Joseph Goebbels. © Bundesarchiv, D – Koblenz

The poet Erich Ebermayer during the mid-1920s. © Schiller-Nationalmuseum, Deutsches Literaturarchiv, D – Marbach am Neckar

Hitler privatissime. In front of the Hotel "Bube" in Berneck near Bayreuth, Hitler's favorite flophouse during his incognito travels before 1933.
© Eta Jobst, D – Bayreuth

Hitler in sculptor Josef Thorak's studio, where he may also have found his own aesthetic ideas fulfilled (mid-1930s). © Bayerische Staatsbibliothek, D –München

Private politician Kurt Lüdecke during a picnic with Hitler; a snapshot from 1933.

Drawing by the famous Munich
caricaturist Thomas Theodor Heine for
the leftist intellectual magazine *Tage-Buch*
from 1930.

Hitler in his favorite pose as the
virile "Führer"; here a photo
from 1938. © Fotoarchiv
Heinrich Hoffmann,
Bayerische Staatsbibliothek,
D – München

Hanfstaengl has ideas about culture.

Hitler's "Putzy" Is Here

DR. ERNST "PUTZY") HANFSTAENGL, intimate friend of Leader Hitler and Harvard-educated head of the Nazi Foreign Press Department, is in London.

He is staying at Claridge's Hotel.

Dr. Hanfstaengl holds emphatic opinions on the subject of culture.

When he visited Harvard last month he gave busts of Goethe and Schopenhauer to his old university.

Recently William Ormonde Thompson, one-time partner of the great American lawyer Clarence Darrow was shown through the Nazi "People's Court" by Dr. Hanfstaengl.

According to the account in the Journal "Time," of September 19.

"When persistent lawyer Thompson started quoting the opinions of British jurists on the subject of Nazi justice, harassed Harvardman Hanfstaengl grew highly excited and finally incoherent:

"'Roared he, 'Damn those Oxford professors! I'll send some of our swine to burn down their Oxford!'"

(handwritten German letter — third page)

meiner Angelegenheit bitten. Seit vollen zwei Jahren haben mich verschiedene Persönlichkeiten der Partei mit allgemeinen Versicherungen abzuspeisen gesucht, um mich zur Heimkehr nach Deutschland zu bewegen; die erbetene Rehabilitation durch Sie, Herr Hitler, ist mir jedoch bis zur Stunde konsequent verweigert worden.

188

Will ich nun im kommenden Prozess meine u. damit Ihre Ehre verteidigen, muss ich zum Mindesten wissen, ob ich als ein von Ihnen verleugneter Exilant oder als ein, in seiner Ehre und seiner Stellung voll rehabilitierter Nationalsozialist vor Gericht stehe. Sollte ich daher bis Anfang März Ihre diesbezüglichen, eindeutigen Weisungen samt umfassender Rehabilitation nicht in Händen haben, so müsste ich zu meinem Leidwesen daraus folgern, dass Sie noch immer nicht gesonnen sind mir Gerechtigkeit werden zu lassen. Ich müsste aber daraus noch weiterhin den Schluss ziehen, dass Ihnen, Herr Hitler, nicht nur meine seit Jahren bewiesene Anhänglichkeit und Treue sondern auch meine Ehre u. Zukunft total gleichgültige Dinge sind. Sollte sich dies als Ihre Einstellung erweisen, so werde ich wissen, was ich zu tun habe.

Mit deutschem Gruss!

Ernst Hanfstaengl

Tear sheet from the English paper *Daily Express* with a very suggestive article about Ernst "Putzy" Hanfstaengl dated September 19, 1934.

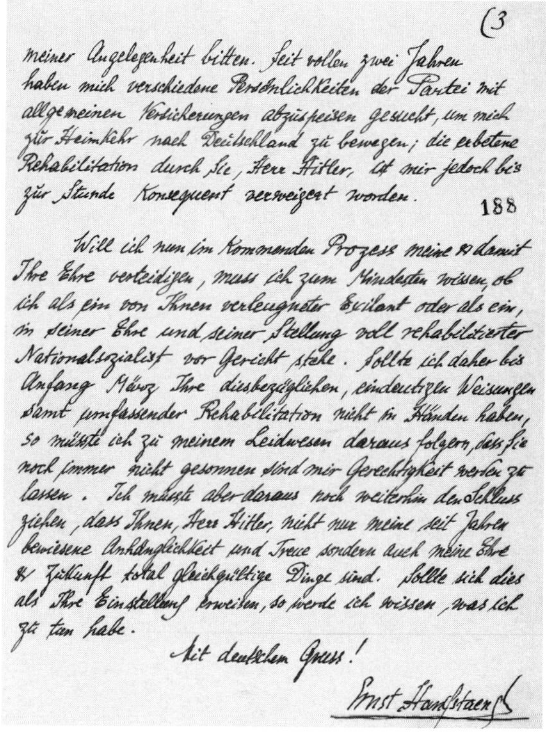

Third page of a handwritten threatening letter Hanfstaengl wrote to Hitler on February 12, 1939. © Bestand NS 10 – Persönliche Adjutantur des Führers und Reichskanzlers, Band 149 (Bl. 185–188), Bundesarchiv, D – Koblenz

Foreign press chief Hanfstaengl (second from left) among friends in his Berlin apartment, probably in 1933; in the photo, to the left of him, is Truman Smith, the military attaché at the U.S. embassy. © Süddeutscher Verlag, Bilderdienst, D – München

Hitler and his favorite, Albert Speer. © Bayerische Staatsbibliothek, D – München

Hitler and "Fräulein Braun" on the steps of the Berghof, probably photographed a few months before their obscure marriage.

death in 1978 but in 1964 published *Adolf Hitler*, an interesting but disconcerting tribute based on his personal experience of the man.[57] His unregenerate attitude becomes comprehensible only when we trace the course of his life.[58] A banker's son born in 1893, he received a thorough musical training and majored in the history of literature and art. In 1923 he went to Weimar, where it took him only a few years to attain a prominent position in the field of cultural policy. He sought an answer to the disaster of 1918/19 in the nationalism of the *völkisch* right wing, and from there it was only a small step to the NSDAP, which he joined in February 1925. A month later he met Hitler in Weimar. During the latter's many visits there[59]—discounting Bayreuth, the Thuringian cultural metropolis was Hitler's most frequent port of call during the period 1925/33—Ziegler soon became his constant companion. According to him, Hitler looked upon Bayreuth and Weimar as "oases" that he "had to visit as often as possible,"[60] even for no specific reason. "Sometimes, while on the way to Munich by car, the Führer would treat himself to a break [there]. Those were the Weimar days, which he profoundly enjoyed, and on which we all gained our most direct impressions of him as a human being."[61] Ziegler introduced Hitler to the city's social life and also to local figures such as Nietzsche's sister or Carl B. N. von Schirach and his son Baldur.

What Hitler liked about Weimar was the theater, the snug artists' cafés, the comfort of the Hotel Elephant, Belvedere Park—in short, the delightful but homely atmosphere of a world remote from the hectic bustle of everyday life. But this does not entirely explain why "the few days of leisure the Führer can permit himself keep bringing him back to Weimar"[62]—a phenomenon even his contemporaries found puzzling. Ziegler, who claimed to have been present during "approximately forty" visits by Hitler, naturally conveyed the insights he gained from "frequent and intensive experience of Hitler the man" in a discreet and allusive manner. As Ziegler himself put it, those insights would prove informative mainly to those readers who "really know how to read everyday jottings and correctly arrange the mosaic stones assembled here."[63] That is why we should not dismiss Ziegler's Hitler apologia simply as a neo-Nazi effusion—which it undoubtedly is as well—but try to discover what it leaves unsaid and latent. Ziegler was no ordinary observer, after all; he was a homosexual National Socialist who rapturously venerated Hitler—indeed, one could say, loved him. He never tired of "watching, sensing, and experiencing" the man, and he obviously got something back from him that reinforced his enthusiastic perception of him.

"Whenever Hitler stopped off at the 'Elephant' in Weimar, he would send for the hairdresser immediately on arrival and get the latter to give him a massage after his bath, and I remember that the young master craftsman in question described Hitler's body to me as being not only well-groomed but well-proportioned, supple, and well-exercised."[64] Hitler's physicians are on record as saying something quite different, namely, that he was averse to baring his body and had an unathletic physique.[65] Ziegler further stated: "Anyone close to him could tell him the unvarnished truth, whatever his predicament. 'I'm familiar with every aspect of human nature. Tell me what's on your mind.' Such were the words with which he once encouraged one of my closest friends, who had a serious confession to make." Generally speaking, Hitler preferred the company of "men to whom he was personally attached" and with whom he could "pleasurably converse with shining eyes in humorous, cheerful vein." But Ziegler's "intensive experience" of Hitler was not confined to their joint visits to the theater or their conversations with artists and other congenial males. It also embraced "confidential talks" during which "the most intimate and personal matters" were discussed, and "solitary walks à deux"[66]—occasions on which Hitler's face had "glowed" with excitement. And so on and so forth.

The reminiscences of this Nazi-addicted aesthete make embarrassing reading. Was he merely bragging, or indulging in sentimental

Hitler nostalgia? What militates against this is not only the author's level of education but, more especially, the fact that such descriptions were bound to offend postwar German sensibilities. Political regeneracy cannot altogether account for this outmoded glorification of Hitler; its cause must be sought in Ziegler's profound emotional attachment to him, which survived his disastrous downfall. One is bound to ask whether his affection was returned. There are definite indications that it was.

Immediately after Hitler came to power Ziegler was appointed artistic director and chief dramaturge of Weimar's German National Theater and state commissioner of the Thuringian regional theater. This appointment overrode fierce opposition from influential local interests centered on Carl B. N. von Schirach, who not only coveted Ziegler's post himself but enjoyed direct access to Hitler through his son and daughter-in-law. His bitter reaction to Ziegler's advancement: "Thanks to these tiresome Party considerations, I cannot get at Dr. Ziegler as I would like, unfortunately, because he should really be brought before an honor board and expelled from the artists' association. We have jointly decided to treat him coolly and with extreme caution, because he is very dangerous. One never knows what he is spreading about other people behind their backs. His conduct here is so outrageous, he'll probably dish himself before long"[67]—an unmistakable allusion to Ziegler's homosexuality. By April 1934, however, Ziegler was (temporary) director general of the German National Theater,[68] which Hitler funded extremely generously, even to the extent of making "personal" contributions.[69] But his greatest mark of favor was a private invitation to spend two weeks on the Obersalzberg in August 1932. As Ziegler wrote over thirty years later: "I think I got to know him better during those unforgettable days than many other people did in years."[70]

Hitler's guest devoted an appropriate amount of space to those "unforgettable days" in his memoirs. The retrospective stress he lays on them is in keeping with an entry in Ernst Hanfstaengl's guest book: "For me, the Hanfstaengl home seems to be a place filled with yearning. I shall come again. Hans Severus Ziegler, Weimar. Midnight, after 'Tannhäuser,' on my way to the Obersalzberg."[71] Immediately on his arrival at Haus Wachenfeld, Hitler invited his guest from Weimar to accompany him to three Wagner Festival performances in Munich. He did so during an "evening walk," needless to say, "just as the full moon emerged from a bank of cloud."[72] When the operatic cycle opened on August 17, Hitler conveyed his guest "in a new car" to his Prinzregentenplatz apartment, where he showed off his "extensive library." "The two hours before the performance passed quickly." Hitler had given his aides "time off." At the theater the two men were joined by Eva Braun, and after the performance they sat together in the Café Heck. "After a stimulating conversation with Hitler lasting roughly three quarters of an hour, he asked me to stay there and wait while he took Fräulein Braun home, and ordered a taxi. . . . After a quarter of an hour he returned, ordered himself a glass of tea and me another glass of wine. Before long we drove home . . . to the Obersalzberg. This routine was repeated three times during that festival week." One wonders why the two men did not simply stay in Munich, but the city probably lacked "the intimate atmosphere . . . captured on the Obersalzberg." Very few of Hitler's henchmen—even those of the first rank, to which Ziegler did not, admittedly, belong—were granted the privilege of a two-week vacation there in his company. Sadly, his guest from Weimar does not give a detailed account of how they spent their long hours together.

After the Obersalzberg experience the two men saw each other almost monthly until May 1933. They met less often thereafter because the party leader and head of government had other commitments,[73] but Ziegler continued to regard him as "the most wonderful person." Then came June 30, 1934, which seemed to offer Ziegler's habitual enemies in Weimar a welcome chance to settle old scores. We do not know exactly what he was accused of, but the charges must have been sufficiently grave for the Thuringian interior minister to issue a public statement in support of his theatrical consultant. "Unqualified authorities," he declared, "have presumed, pursuant to Point 7 of our Führer's decree of 30 June [calling for the Movement to be purged of homosexuals] to institute inquiries into the person of State Commissioner Dr. Ziegler. I have taken the opportunity to look into all such rumors myself, and have, after a thorough investigation, ascertained beyond doubt that no acts covered by the Führer's decree under Paragraph 175 of the Reich Penal Code have been committed. In view of this statement, I expect the dissemination of these baseless rumors to cease, and will take ruthless action against all who contravene this directive."[74] No regional minister would have dared to express himself so categorically in such uncertain times without orders from higher authority. Had Hitler intervened in person? That he stopped off at Weimar on July 9, 1934, on his way from the Obersalzberg to Berlin and stayed the night there would suggest so.[75]

However, the evidence Ziegler's enemies had collected was clearly so overwhelming that not even the "Führer" could sweep it under the carpet just like that. In Ziegler's own words, he continued to be "hated and persecuted." "I can't tell anyone what I've been through these past months," he wrote to Ebermayer in January 1935. But he had "taken preliminary steps toward clarifying the *fundamental* side of the problem, and will make the final and most profound confession to the Führer himself, and then request a clear-cut decision. I am the only Party member in the Movement able to speak like that, from the aspect from which the subject must be treated."[76] Ziegler's last sentence intimated what liberties he, as an "avowed" homosexual, could still take inside a movement "purged" of "Röhm and associates." His optimism sprang from an unshakable belief that Hitler would not, in the last resort, abandon him. And so his letter to Ebermayer concludes in a rather upbeat fashion with some words of advice that the hard-pressed Ziegler may even have been given by an authoritative source: "Don't take my diplomacy amiss; sentiment must sometimes be overridden by political considerations. This presents no danger to genuine characters. . . . As far as possible shun the public, whose lewd and vulgar gaze profanes the lives of all who have style and class. Calm and reason will return, and so, in the end, will clarity."

The surprising thing is that Ziegler's optimism was justified. By early in March 1935 his troubles were over: public reference was once more made to the "baseless rumors" about him and another warning issued against "the continued dissemination of malicious rumors about Staatsrat Dr. Ziegler."[77] This meant that Ziegler was under political protection. All he wanted now was a heart-to-heart talk with the Führer.[78] He was not granted one, not in spite of, but probably because of his earlier intimacy with Hitler, who had to distance himself inwardly as well as outwardly. Ziegler now felt the effects of Hitler's policy of double standards under different auspices: its aim was to protect people like himself but, for the moment at least, to keep them at arm's length. This subjected even protégés like him to the "nerve-racking torment" of which Hans Blüher wrote.

Ziegler waited in vain for a sign of life from Hitler. He possessed his soul in patience until the fall of 1935, when he tried a direct approach in the shape of a semiformal letter sent via Brückner, Hitler's aide. He felt, he wrote, "that I may, in this particular matter, be permitted to choose this unusual route and beg this personal favor." The pretext for his letter was the impending appointment of a new theater director in Dresden, a post for which he recommended himself, but his real purpose was to bring about "a personal discussion," which would make him "infinitely grateful and happy."[79] But Hitler, who refused to abandon his new line, informed the petitioner by way of Gauleiter Sauckel of Thuringia that he should remain at Weimar.[80] This brushoff did not end Ziegler's career, however. In September 1936 he was appointed director general of Weimar's German

National Theater, and two months later Goebbels appointed him to the Reich Cultural Senate.

At some stage in 1937, Ziegler got his long-awaited audience. "He received me on my own, with a kindliness that deeply gratified me. His tone was as intimate and familiar as it had been in the Weimar days."[81] Their conversation was only superficial, however, being concerned with "cultural matters affecting Weimar and Thuringia that required his decision." In any case, their meeting was possible only because a great deal of water had flowed under the bridge since the events of "June 30," and because the dictator's double standards had become firmly established. Homosexual eros was outwardly proscribed and discriminated against, a policy to which Hitler's tolerated homosexual associates conformed. If they wanted to secure their influence and steer clear of danger, they had to accept his perverted, bigoted sexual morality—a price they were prepared to pay. That applied as much to Ziegler as it did to Gustaf Gründgens and Baldur von Schirach, to cite two other examples.[82]

THE BAYREUTH "EL DORADO"

Ebermayer, as we have already mentioned, wrote that Hitler's only opportunities to indulge his homosexual inclinations in the early 1930s occurred on "car journeys, notably at the Hotel Bube in Berneck in the Fichtelgebirge." And Ziegler tells how he once helped Hitler to slip out of Weimar unobserved. He had wanted "to catch his breath for twenty-four hours in nearby Berneck on the edge of the Fichtelgebirge. . . . Sometime, somewhere he needed an El Dorado." Between 1925 and 1933 Hitler "now and then made private visits to Bayreuth, as he did to Weimar, to relax in the company of the Wagner family and gather the spiritual energy he needed for his grueling activities."[83] As Joachim Fest informs us in his notes of the conversations he had with Speer, the latter could think of no reason for Hitler's frequent excursions from the Hotel Bube to Haus Wahnfried other than an affair between him and Winifred Wagner. "'He was,' he said, 'quite convinced of it at the time by countless revealing little signs.' He had also heard that Hitler always looked 'peculiarly uplifted' on his return, with 'a certain light in his eyes—blissful, in fact.' . . . This, more or less, had been the opinion of nearly all who took part in his trips. Sometimes, when Hitler had been in a bad mood for days, they 'jokingly' said the Führer needed another 'Bayreuth cure.'"[84] (Brigitte Hamann's forthcoming biography of Winifred will demonstrate in detail that there was nothing between Hitler and the widow of Wagner's son that could in any way confirm such a suspicion.)[85]

Whatever the truth, Hitler was certainly not the only person in Bayreuth to have homosexual proclivities. He shared them, for instance, with Richard Wagner's son, who pursued his passion until he died in 1930—so overtly that he was forever being subjected to blackmail and other importunities.[86] Hitler must, in fact, have drawn encouragement from Siegfried Wagner's lively friendships with young men, especially after he himself had been admitted to this circle. At their very first meeting, Siegfried rhapsodized about the "love-force" in Hitler's eyes and laughingly told him to his face: "You appeal to me, you know."[87] This was how there developed that "intimate relationship between Hitler and Siegfried" which Syberberg has documented with the aid of relevant correspondence.[88] Hitler must have been particularly impressed by "the great family discipline observed at Haus Wahnfried;" Goebbels stresses this in connection with Siegfried's "homosexuality," about which Hitler showed himself "thoroughly well informed."[89] Under these circumstances he could not have found self-disclosure a very hard step to take, "for in those days," said Winifred, "he doubtless had no one in whom he [. . .] could confide."[90]

It seems, therefore, that the Wagners and Hitler developed a close and intimate relationship. "I was on familiar terms with them," Hitler said later. And: "I love those people."[91] As Winifred saw it, theirs was no politically motivated relationship,[92] but "a purely human, personal, and intimate bond between us." She added: "Politics were never discussed at all."[93] Although this is undoubtedly true, homoeroticism's role in their relationship was a subject on which she remained silent until the day she died. It is relatively easy to detect, however, because it was not only obvious in terms of family history. Magnus Hirschfeld, in his day, knew that Bayreuth was "a rendezvous much favored by uranians, some of whom come on their own and others with their friends."[94] Certain of the artists performing there were also homosexual. The most prominent example was Max Lorenz, Hitler's favorite tenor, who remained unscathed even though legal proceedings against him were pending for offenses under Paragraph 175, whereas his sexual partners were prosecuted.[95]

It is not surprising that Hitler's recollections of the early years of his enthusiasm for Bayreuth sounded euphoric when he spoke of them much later on. He had had a "sunny time" there, and not only at Wahnfried with the Wagners. "It was a wonderful life there in other respects as well. When I went to the 'Eule' I was in immediate contact with all the artists." He had often enjoyed sitting with the artists in the 'Anker,' too, "or we would drive to the 'Bube' at Berneck."[96] This is a reference to the pre-1933 years, be it noted, when Hitler, in his own words, "so often passed through Bayreuth" and "always paid a visit." An unpublished photograph, probably taken in 1930, shows him leaving the Hotel Bube looking quite informal and rather abstracted. The daughter of the then owner of the hotel, Frau Jobst, states that this was a common sight, and that she saw Hitler three or four times a year prior to 1933, not only alone but in the company of men, his close friend Julius Schreck in particular. There were never any women around.[97] Winifred Wagner told a British journalist that Hitler was a lonely man at this period, which was why he turned up so

often. "But he was not in search for [sic] a wife."[98] The evidence at
hand suggests that the motivation for Hitler's frequent visits during
these years to the "magic triangle" of Weimar-Berneck-Bayreuth was
rooted more in his sexual inclinations than his cultural interests. After
1934, however, he could no longer indulge his inclinations there, and
visits to the area decreased significantly. From then on, his one
remaining refuge was the Obersalzberg.

BETWEEN CONJECTURE AND FICTIONALIZATION

In light of the above, one of the most important "exceedingly trustworthy sources" to whom Ebermayer owed his secret knowledge of
Hitler's homosexuality must have been Ziegler, but he, of all people,
was not immortalized in *Das Buch der Freunde*, which appeared on
Ebermayer's sixtieth birthday, a year after the diaries. One can only
conclude that Ziegler must have been very annoyed by Ebermayer's
disclosures, but he did not have the courage to assail them openly,
thereby ultimately corroborating them. On the other hand, Ebermayer's memoirs did receive the blessing of Winifred Wagner, who
addressed the following informative words to "dear Erich Ebermayer" on his sixtieth birthday: "You yourself revered Siegfried Wagner as a youth. We have known each other for forty-three years—and
now we have long been linked by a quiet, firm, faithful friendship. So
good luck for the new decade!"[99] A warm and friendly greeting of that
kind cannot be dismissed as meaningless, so this important figure in
Hitler's private life should probably be accounted another of the birthday boy's well-informed "sources"—the more so since Ebermayer
maintained his very close links with the Wagner family after 1945.[100]

Yet another of Ebermayer's informants, of course, was Philipp
Bouhler, the "faithful cousin" through whom he had tried to gain
access to Hitler from 1930 on.[101] Contact between the two bachelors,

who were almost the same age (Bouhler married in haste after "June 30"),[102] was probably far closer than Ebermayer's diary suggests, even prior to 1935. Bouhler had grown up in Hitler's male-bonded circle since the beginnings of the Nazi Party, so we may take it that his good connections, and especially his long-standing friendship with Max Amann, made him privy to detailed inside information.[103] So there are reasons for taking Ebermayer's remarks about Hitler's homosexuality seriously, even when his information had been obtained secondhand. Nor does it invalidate his disclosures that his diary entries, originally "inscribed in oilcloth notebooks," did not undergo their "literary molding" until ten years later and were not published for another fifteen.[104] On the contrary, Ebermayer was able to check his view of events, as they receded into the past, against other accounts. He could also, where necessary, interpolate items of information gleaned subsequently, not only from Winifred Wagner, but also from Emmy Göring, whose defense he had undertaken in 1946.[105] Admittedly, the reworking of his notes enabled him to appear more critical of the regime than he actually had been, but being a lawyer as well as a writer, he must have carefully considered the substance and form of what he was publishing. One can hardly blame him for not venturing to come clean about his homosexuality, because that would have been too risky in the Germany of 1959—indeed, quite impossible. Even so, we must regard his own disposition as the prime mover of his courage in "outing" Hitler. Ziegler could not do any such thing, or only obliquely, because he would have deemed it tantamount to disloyalty. Ebermayer had no such scruples: he intended his "outing" to unmask the self-disavowing hypocrite in Hitler and, thus, to dissociate himself further from the dictator and his regime.

Although reviewers differed widely in their reactions to this attempt in 1959/60, none of them cast doubt on the author's validity as a source. "Ebermayer's diary is impulsive, sensitive, vain, engaging, enthralling, unwitting; it is unabashed and therefore genuine," was the verdict of *Die Welt*. The *Berlin Telegraph*, too, credited the book with "great significance," describing it as "honest and informative." The *Süddeutscher Rundfunk* reviewer declared that it was a "very important document . . . which will not acquire its true value until historians insert it, like a mosaic stone, in a totality." The harshest verdict on Ebermayer's book came from *Das Parlament*, which said that although it conjured up "a certain impressionistic picture" of the years when Hitler came to power, this was "only blurred and obscured by the embarrassing features of the remaining impression," among which were his "peculiar symbiosis . . . with a young man," the "exalted portrayal of which, like his predilection for handsome youths, pervades the entire book." The reviewer of the *Mitteldeutsches Jahrbuch* also had problems with the mélange of personal and political, erotic and cultural: "No reflection on the relationship between the historical and the personal takes place." Only the *Frankfurter Allgemeine Zeitung* pronounced the spicy details supplied by Ebermayer relevant: "Among politically significant matters, one gains a closer insight into the role of male friendships in the Hitler, Röhm, Hess clique."[106]

Ebermayer's documentary collage, with all its allusions, broodings and apologias, was clearly too much for contemporary critics. It is indeed sometimes difficult to penetrate his mixture of disclosure and obfuscation, although easier today, no doubt, than it was in the Adenauer era. His deliberately subjective reconstruction of the Nazi past makes certain features of the German dictatorship seem farcical, which they doubtless were. Ebermayer played no real part in that pantomime, but as an extra and stagehand he had a quite different view of the direction and stagecraft than the audience, and we must give him full credit for having passed on at least some of his impressions in such an undisguised form.

As far as I can see, Ebermayer never attempted to develop his detailed knowledge of Hitler into a genuinely literary portrait, probably because, being a homosexual himself, he did not come to terms with Hitler's homosexuality. He liked to idealize this eros in his literary works, but a figure like Hitler, whose homoerotic side could not have been simply ignored, resisted such an approach. The author obviously thought himself incapable of resolving the attendant difficulties. Not so his old friend Klaus Mann, who must have felt positively challenged to perform such a feat. What makes his literary treatment of the subject so interesting is that his prerequisites were much the same as Ebermayer's. He too was homosexual, he too could fall back on a similarly well-founded knowledge of Hitler's private life, and he too had once observed him at close quarters. He recorded this encounter in Munich's Carlton Tearoom in a diary entry dated July 13, 1932: "At the very next table: Adolf Hitler in the most doltish company. His positively conspicuous mediocrity. Extremely ill endowed; the fascination he exerts is the greatest disgrace in history; a certain sexually pathological element cannot account for everything."[107] This impression accords with the general verdict of Munich's old established families on the Nazi leader and his hordes: vapid, stupid, intellectually inferior, dumb. As for Hitler's "sexually pathological element," Mann had clearly known about it before he set eyes on the man at the next table.

After that chance encounter, Klaus Mann made no further reference to Hitler until December 1932. A snippet of his in the periodical *Das Tagebuch* reported that he had come across a picture of Hitler in, of all places, the window of the Sexological Bookstore on Berlin's Wittenbergplatz. "Was this the storekeeper's way of externalizing internal associations that have always, it is true, been apparent to us? At all events, I denounce it as scandalously provocative. A pretty state of affairs! Any more of it, and we'll be put off sexual pathology altogether."[108] However, underlying this witticism was a genuine problem that the German dictator posed even to so staunch an opponent of his as Klaus Mann: where homosexual intellectuals were concerned,

Hitler's homosexual orientation made him "one of us," so to speak. Psychologically, this was hard to take. Mann's initial response to this presumption was "Die Linke und das Laster" [The Left and Vice], an essay that appeared in 1934.[109] It was quite wrong, he said, "to identify homosexuality with fascism purely because there are reputed to be many members of National Socialist organizations who love young men rather than women." There had always been "hundreds of different types of homosexuals, extremely inferior and disastrous ones included." That one of them was an "uncouth, cynical rogue" like Röhm meant nothing: "Sharing one's erotic disposition with a few bandits does not make one a bandit oneself."

Klaus Mann's pamphlet amounted, generally speaking, to a defense of homosexuality against current prejudices. His underlying purpose, however, was to banish "Brother Hitler," as his father called him soon afterward, from the homosexual domain: "what matters is intellect alone . . ., not erotic adhesive."

Apropos of "Brother Hitler": if we take seriously the latest tendency of Thomas Mann scholars to detect, even in the most mythical examples of his literary oeuvre, a real, that is to say, autobiographical core and tortuous confessions,[110] we should reconsider the "brother argument"—the "exceedingly embarrassing affinity" that so "ashamed" the great writer—in his brilliant demolition of Hitler in April 1938. Thomas Mann's biographer Klaus Harpprecht opines that "the most fervent and effective resistance to the dictator" entailed "a measure of proximity—an understanding that stemmed from a sense of affinity and could arouse an all the more fervent hatred."[111] But in what did the "sense of affinity" and "measure of proximity" consist? Did not the laboring of "artistry" as an explanation of their common ground amount, when all is said and done, to camouflage? How did the "magician" contrive to assimilate that "sorry idler, genuine ne'er-do-well, and fifth-rate 'visionary'" to such an extent that he could lay bare Hitler's "disastrous spiritual life" with such conviction? What did he know of the man who could do nothing "that men can do . . . , not even beget a child"[112]—the man whom, a few months before writing his essay, he had associated with an "absolutely revolting, catamitic Siegfried"?[113] I shall leave better qualified scholars to answer those questions.

Two years after the appearance of "Brother Hitler," Klaus Mann likewise felt an urge to undertake a literary approach to this "murky figure" in his autobiography *The Turning Point*. He considered its portrayal of Hitler so important that he enriched it for the benefit of the German reader with a few new colors after the war.[114] The result was a text that alternates between approximation and repulsion, disclosure and encipherment.

The relevant passages in the most recent (German) edition are these:

"I couldn't get it into my head that the Germans could seriously have regarded Hitler as a great man, indeed, as the Messiah. Him and great? One only needed to look at him! I had several opportunities to study that physiognomy. Once at very close quarters for about half an hour. That was in 1932. . . . There were two questions that mainly exercised me during those thirty minutes of sinister proximity: first, what was the secret of his impact, his fascination; and, secondly, whom did he remind me of, whom did he resemble? Without doubt, he looked like a man with whom I wasn't personally acquainted, but whose picture I had often seen. Who could it be? Not Charlie Chaplin. Certainly not! Chaplin has the little mustache, but not the nose, the fleshy, nasty—indeed, obscene—nose which had instantly struck me as the vilest and most characteristic feature of Hitler's physiognomy. Chaplin has charm, grace, wit, intensity—characteristics of which nothing could be detected in my lip-smacking, whipped-cream-guzzling neighbor. He, by contrast, seemed to be of extremely base substance and composition, a malicious philistine with a hysterically turbid look on his pallid, puffy face. Nothing that might have hinted at greatness, nor even at talent! It certainly wasn't a pleasant sensation to sit near such a creature, yet I couldn't look at his repulsive visage enough. I had never found him particularly attractive, neither in pictures nor on the illuminated rostrum; but the ugliness confronting me surpassed all my expectations. The vulgarity of his features soothed me, did me good. I looked at him and thought: You'll never win, Schicklgruber, not even if you shout your head off. You aspire to rule Germany? You want to be a dictator with that nose? Don't make me laugh! You're so lousy, one could almost feel sorry for you—if your lousiness wasn't of such a repulsive nature. . . . While I was summoning the waitress to pay for what I'd consumed, it suddenly occurred to me whom the fellow reminded me of. Haarmann, of course. Why hadn't I thought of it long ago? Yes, of course, he looked like the boy-murderer of Hanover whose trial had recently caused a sensation. Was he, the Austrian operetta habitué at the next table, as proficient as his North German doppelgänger? That homosexual Bluebeard had succeeded in luring thirty or forty boys into his hospitable parlor, where he bit through their throats during the act of love and made tasty sausages out of their corpses. A stupendous achievement, particularly when one reflects that the industrious pedophile lived in a cramped tenement house among watchful neighbors! Where there's a will, there's a way: one carries out the apparently impossible with dogged determination. . . . I was struck by the resemblance between those two men of action. Mustache and lock of hair, the clouded gaze, the simultaneously self-pitying and brutal mouth, the stubborn brow—yes, even the repulsive nose. They were all the same!"[115]

There are three main messages here. First: yes, Hitler was a homosexual, but his sexual fantasies were inspired by the bestially murderous desires of the most notorious psychopath of the early 20th century, Fritz Haarmann,[116] or—supertemporally, as it were—by the knight in the cruel fairy tale, although the latter's victims were women. The second message: Hitler was certainly no "brother," however embarrassing; he was a "Schicklgruber,"[117] a hick from Bohemia, an escapee from humble circumstances, a magnet for the mockery and derision of all sophisticated men and women. And, finally, it was right to detest Hitler before he ruled the German Reich and to credit him, even then, with every conceivable form of malice.

Klaus Mann's rhetorical rather than analytically acute endeavor to explain the Hitler phenomenon is a prime example of the desperate and futile attempts made to get to the bottom of it by means of invective, albeit of a stylishly presented kind. No, it was no "homosexual Bluebeard" with the aura of a gruesome fairy-tale figure whom the German establishment helped to gain power in 1933, to the rapturous acclamation of his followers, who were already millions strong. But homosexual he really was. Klaus Mann did not wish to leave that unsaid, even though he would sooner not have known it and been able to present Hitler as a straightforward Bluebeard—a metaphor from his childhood, incidentally, and one that was current among other members of the family.[118] Read what Heinrich Mann says on the subject in *Der Hass*, which he published in exile: "He [Hitler] quite rightly began with mature women. . . . Although he did not spurn them for his mission's sake, he much preferred the virile daredevilry of boys. He himself captivated mainly with feminine charms of a special kind." And: "Some of his people know precisely what they are dealing with. It is clear to them that he himself, like his brilliantly successful movement, has derived from ambivalent areas of human nature that would ill withstand elucidation."[119]

It is at this point—the Manns' ever similar but ever veiled allusions to Hitler's homosexuality—that the wheel comes full circle and the deeper reason for people's unremitting interest in the subject becomes discernible. For, as Countess Mathilde von Schönwörth confided to

Erich Ebermayer in 1935, the old established Munich families knew "absolutely *everything*, even of the most intimate nature, about the 'leadership corps.' . . . Nothing is hidden from these old Müncheners. They smile at the grandiloquent speeches and innumerable lies with which the German people and the world are being deluged by the new masters. They cannot, with the best will in the world, take it all seriously; they simply cannot grasp that this clique of political adventurers, charming blatherers, and erotic 'inverts,' who passed muster as leaders of a radical opposition party and could even be amusing, are now the absolute rulers of Germany."[120] Thomas Mann's diaries of the period 1921/33, which he destroyed, could have provided us with much information on what the Manns' Munich household knew about Hitler before 1933, but he evidently preferred to draw a veil over it.

Be that as it may, all the authors quoted above make the same fundamental statement, the Manns in an oblique and encoded literary manner, Ebermayer far more bluntly and straightforwardly: Hitler was a homosexual, and we knew it.

CHAPTER SEVEN

Dangerous Machinations:
Kurt Lüdecke and Ernst Hanfstaengl

IN 1922 Ernst Hanfstaengl and Adolf Hitler were close friends. Just two decades later, the former "disciple"[1] described the "Führer" to U.S. intelligence as "a type of egocentric and masturbic [sic] Narcissus" who had, owing largely to intense sexual frustration, taken refuge in an "artificially dramatized public life."[2] We can trace the way in which Hanfstaengl reached this verdict, but it is a long story, and one that is closely linked with that of a man who got to know Hitler around the same time as Hanfstaengl and was a no less equivocal character: Kurt Lüdecke. Although mistrustful of him at first, Hitler quickly recognized his qualities. If Lüdecke was "a spy," he said, "he is not only one of the craftiest but also one of the most dangerous ever to have operated in Germany."[3] He was still enthusing about him nineteen years later: "The fellow spoke French, English, Spanish, and Italian as well as he did German. He would have been the right man [for tricky foreign assignments]; there's nothing he wouldn't have sniffed out."[4]

Ernst Hanfstaengl did not share this assessment of Lüdecke. In 1937 he declared that "anyone who still dared to stand up for that stinker, directly or indirectly, in earnest or for a joke, [was] an abject rogue, a male prostitutes' pimp, a plague on the Party, and a traitor to the Fatherland."[5] What had aroused his ire was *I Knew Hitler*, the sensational book Lüdecke had published in exile in America after making an adventurous escape from Germany. Hanfstaengl dismissed it merely as the figment of "a blackmailer's imagination." Rudolf Diels, the former Gestapo chief, intimated after the war that underlying this so-called figment of the imagination was a very real story, albeit one known only to "the most intimate and discreet circle [of initiates]." He added, in an equally meaningful way, that "in the Lüdecke case, the suspicion had arisen that Hitler, too, had homosexual tendencies."[6] Reason enough for us to take a closer look at where and how Lüdecke's and Hitler's paths crossed.

WHO WAS KURT LÜDECKE?

Born in Berlin in 1890, Lüdecke spent his childhood in Oranienburg, where his father ran a chemicals factory. His secondary education in Berlin ended in disaster: he was expelled and had to switch to Braunschweig, where he graduated in 1907 with only a middle school certificate. After doing his military service he went to London, then moved on to France, where he claimed to have gambled so successfully in 1910 that he could thereafter afford to lead a life of footloose luxury.[7] The records of the public prosecutor's office attached to Berlin's Royal Regional Court tell a different story. In January 1911, Lüdecke came under investigation on a charge alleging "extortion on a homosexual basis." He was said to be known in "homosexual circles" for seeking out wealthy friends and then, after having sexual intercourse with them, coercing them into paying him.[8] Just when the charge was brought, Lüdecke disappeared from Berlin. Thus the simple explanation for his extravagant lifestyle is that he had made his fortune, not at the roulette table, but as a gigolo and blackmailer. He drifted across Europe in this way until World War I brought his conman's career to an abrupt end. Even then, however, he managed to secure his release from the military after only two years, and without ever having heard a shot fired in anger.

Although we cannot effect a precise reconstruction of the private ventures that took him all over the world until 1920, they earned him a Mexican passport and two substantial dollar accounts. In May 1921 he settled in Munich, where he made preparations to hold "an exhibition of German pictures in New York."[9] A police report stated that "the exhibition was not a commercial success," but that, thanks to the sale of various objets d'art, "he still had at his disposal, on his return to Munich at the beginning of April 1922, a balance of $1,400."[10] At such an inflationary period, this was a fortune.

But Lüdecke not only dealt in art and antiques in the United States. He also worked for that legendary capitalist Henry Ford, who had set up a kind of private secret service.[11] Since 1920 this organization had, among other things, conducted a smear campaign against influential American Jews. In order to expose their private lives, a detective bureau had been opened in New York and funded so generously that a whole band of zealous sleuths could be hired. Having come into contact there with close associates of the powerful industrialist, Lüdecke discovered that there was money to be made out of militant antisemitism. It may well be that he was assigned to recruit influential German allies for Ford's campaign, and that it was on this secret mission that he was sent back home with the requisite financial backing.

At all events, his baggage contained a copy of Henry Ford's tract, "The International Jew: The World's Foremost Problem," when he returned to Germany in April 1922.[12] Armed with detailed knowledge of the background to Ford's antisemitic campaign and the prospect of American slush money, he now planned to cast bait on *völkisch* waters. During a visit to Berlin in May he made the acquaintance of Ernst von Reventlow, who, as editor of *Der Reichswart*, a periodical highly regarded in right-wing circles, had the ear of people with whom Lüdecke, too, wished to get in touch. Early that summer he was introduced to the leading representatives of the extreme right-wing camp, Hitler among them. However, not even Ernst von Reventlow's personal introduction sufficed to overcome the suspicion Lüdecke aroused in many quarters.[13] Hitler's "first impression," for example, was thoroughly "unfavorable, the more so since we now recalled having already been warned against him. But because Lüdecke had, in the meantime, more or less gained access to all the associations, his brusque rejection no longer seemed expedient." Even so, Hitler instructed his closest associates "to record their conversations with Lüdecke in writing."[14]

Max Amann, Hitler's specialist in shady transactions, recorded the following impression of Lüdecke after their first meeting: He was "a very shrewd, thoroughly crafty con man who doubtless has all manner of dirty tricks to his credit. I infer from his sophistication and his self-assured manner that, if he has been infiltrated into our movement as a spy, as I believe he has, he is certainly being well paid for it by his employers."[15] Dietrich Eckart, too, referred contemptuously to Lüdecke because he was "thrusting himself forward so unscrupulously" and "stinks of perfume at six paces. Added to that, he looks like the worst kind of dandy" and was, "in that get-up," well on the way to "thoroughly discrediting the Party."[16]

None of this dissuaded Hitler from hiring Lüdecke. It may be that he employed him to spy on the other leaders of the *völkisch* camp, and that he believed he could hold him in check by stringing him along and keeping him under surveillance. There must, however, have been more to their cooperation, or Hitler would have been more aloof. As for Lüdecke himself, he never made any secret of the fact that he was captivated by Hitler.[17] He even regarded him at one time as a "broadminded person in matters of honor."[18] The drawing of Frederick the Great which Hitler's new admirer gave him for Christmas in 1922 is said to have adorned his private apartment for many years, and he hung a portrait of Henry Ford which Lüdecke had brought with him from America in his office at Party headquarters.[19]

By January 1923 Lüdecke could justifiably feel that Hitler was his "friend,"[20] a status reflected by the political assignments delegated to him. With accreditation from Hitler and Ludendorff, he traveled to Italy to establish links with Benito Mussolini, the up-and-coming leader of the Italian fascists. He was also authorized to "set up an intelligence bureau in his apartment,"[21] having been "entrusted with foreign propaganda."[22] But his pleasure at this advancement was short-lived, because on January 27, 1923, he was, to his complete surprise, remanded in custody on suspicion of treason. That was ten days after Hitler had hinted to the investigating authorities that, if Lüdecke was working as a spy for a foreign power, "given his unquestionably wide knowledge of very important internal affairs, especially those of Bavaria, I consider him to be a really major threat. To detain him without at least definitely neutralizing him for a considerable time might, in my view, be a dire disaster."[23] What had led to Hitler's sudden change of tack?

He must have come to the conclusion during the winter of 1922/23 that his influence over Lüdecke was far less potent than he had originally supposed; that the man was serving several masters and could thus become a danger to himself. Someone may also have enlightened him on Lüdecke's career as a blackmailer. His arrest would not be enough, because only a successful prosecution could "neutralize" him permanently. However, although the Munich public prosecutor's office made resolute efforts to put Lüdecke on trial for treason,[24] he was soon released. Proceedings were quietly dropped.

The prisoner had intimated when questioned that he would return fire if necessary, because, to quote his own words, "my patience is now at an end."[25] Being well acquainted with an official in the political section at Munich's police headquarters,[26] Hitler must soon have learned of these threats, so he called off the whole operation. Lüdecke was even readmitted to his circle, but first the party leader sent him off on a lengthy vacation—to allow the dust to settle, as he put it. Hitler's true purpose, no doubt, was to prevent Lüdecke from investigating the source of his exposure and to encourage him to go on believing that he had been informed on by *opponents* of the NSDAP. That "theory" underlay the statement which "Party Member Lüdecke," as "a devout National Socialist," was permitted to publish in the *Völkischer Beobachter*.[27] Although this settled the matter as far as Hitler was concerned, the Munich press was greatly surprised at the speed with which the "Lüdecke treason case" had come to nothing. "It will doubtless be necessary," wrote the *Münchener Zeitung*, "for the competent authorities to provide a more detailed explanation of the surprising outcome of the affair, notably of how it was possible for the man to be subjected to so grave a suspicion which later proved to be totally unfounded."[28]

Hitler's tactic in the ensuing months was to involve Lüdecke more deeply in his cause. In the late summer of 1923 he met him at a conference of *völkisch* associations in Salzburg, after which he invited him to join him on a brief private visit to Linz.[29] There, after he had dismissed the rest of his entourage, they spent a whole day alone together. Lüdecke's memoirs refer to what followed as an "intimate meeting" but leave the reader in the dark in other respects, calling it "too delicate" a matter to elaborate on.[30] We can, however, form a rough impression of its nature from one or two allusions.[31] Hitler's ostensible reason for the Linz meeting was to brief Lüdecke in preparation for another talk with Mussolini. In Lüdecke's memory, however, it was dominated by things quite other than politics, for he encountered a Hitler known only to very few. He was literally able to "read" Hitler's face, and the language his "friend" had used was not only beautiful but almost "poetic." As they walked together on the Poestlingberg, where Hitler had enjoyed many a romantic stroll with his boyhood friend Kubizek fifteen years earlier, he "revealed still another side of his character." They sat in silence, side by side, and "Hitler gazed over the vast landscape with love in his eyes." In short, Hitler's impassioned manner rendered Lüdecke positively "speechless with emotional excitement." They parted with mutual promises that Lüdecke later elevated to the status of "vows."

We can only speculate about the underlying purpose of this encounter, but reading between the lines one gathers that Hitler had staged a tear-jerker designed to pledge Lüdecke to discretion and loyalty. And their relationship really did change in the years that followed: it became a trifle sentimental and never quite sincere, but they did each other no more damage.

Lüdecke's political mission was to win support for Hitler's plans for a coup d'état, mainly in Italy, and he pursued it during the fall of 1923 with great enthusiasm but only moderate success.[32] The failure of the November putsch seemed to have left him stranded, so nothing could have been more timely, from his point of view, than an encounter in Rome with members of the Wagner clan.[33] Hitler's detention had not impaired their very cordial relations with him. On the contrary, Siegfried and Winifred Wagner proposed to enlist support for him abroad during an American concert tour early in 1924.[34] On learning of these plans, Lüdecke offered to put his knowledge of the language and the country at their service, and in January 1924 he joined the Wagners aboard the *America*, bound for the United States from Bremerhaven.

Hitler had equipped Lüdecke for the journey with a personal letter in which he requested him "to promote the interests of the German liberation movement in North America, and, in particular, to collect financial resources for the same."[35] But the hoped-for success did not materialize. Although Ford granted the Wagners and Lüdecke a personal interview, Hitler's political debacle had made him chary of backing such a desperado, especially as the money with which he had sent Lüdecke to Bavaria in 1922 had proved a dud investment. In May 1924 Lüdecke returned to Munich empty-handed. It soon transpired that, deprived of Hitler's personal protection, he was a nonentity. Those of the NSDAP leaders who were not imprisoned dropped him, Alfred Rosenberg and Ernst Röhm being the only ones who offered him a measure of support.

When Lüdecke visited the party leader in Landsberg, he immediately noticed a change in him. "Hitler was plainly embarrassed, as I was, by the memory of our intimate meeting on the Poestlingberg. . . . Gladly, I eschewed the subject as too delicate."[36] All he got out of their reunion was a signed photograph and a request to continue to make himself useful to the Party.

From now on, however, Lüdecke appeared on the political stage less and less often, and then only when there was a prospect of "doing business" as well.[37] One such occasion was an international congress of antisemites in Salzburg at Easter 1925. Lüdecke made a "bad" impression on Heinrich Himmler, who attended in his capacity as business manager of the *völkisch* bloc. That impression derived from his "bon vivant's" manner, which indicated that "his moral conduct is far from unobjectionable," and from "his diligent and persistent efforts to glean news and intelligence," which rendered him as "suspect" as did "the good information at his command from all countries." Himmler considered Lüdecke "an international political con man" who was, through his "direct influence on the Führer," propelling the *völkisch* movement in the "wrong direction" and using what he learned inside the movement to make money out of "Germany's opponents." To the best of Himmler's knowledge, however, Lüdecke was "still in Hitler's immediate entourage, even today."[38]

Few of the National Socialist leaders trusted Lüdecke an inch. Hitler must also have seen through the man, but he courted him instead of getting rid of him. In February 1925, for instance, he told the *Völkischer Kurier* that Lüdecke was "an idealist," and that he still regretted being to blame for his having been remanded in custody a year earlier.[39] At around the same time he invited Lüdecke to Thierschstrasse for a private visit—another token of his personal esteem.[40] He not only offered him a contract to represent the *Völkischer Beobachter* in Berlin but even requested him to act as his personal informant in the German capital.

One wonders why Hitler should have taken a chance on a man with such dubious characteristics. Lüdecke himself supplied the answer in his memoirs: "I was practically the only one who could give him firsthand information about other than strictly Party matters."[41] This amounted to an admission that he was Hitler's personal spy. Lüdecke was exceptionally valuable because of his shady character and past, not in spite of them. "We must sometimes adopt strange methods and use dubious ways if we want to stay in the race," Hitler is said to have told him.[42] He couldn't afford to antagonize Lüdecke— the man knew too much for that. Lüdecke had felt a "burning curiosity" to discover as much as possible about Hitler's "real self" and true face.[43] In his trade, many had insured themselves by means of such secret knowledge, and the contacts he was seeking at the time,[44] for instance, with Röhm, indicate that he guessed who the likeliest sources of such inside information were.

Before he made use of his knowledge, however, he and Hitler went their separate ways for seven years. In the summer of 1925, unattracted by what the party leader had to offer him immediately after the reestablishment of the NSDAP, Lüdecke decided to try his luck in America once more.

HANFSTAENGL AND HITLER: A LOVE AFFAIR THAT FAILED

Hitler's friendship with Hanfstaengl was still completely intact in
1923. Being aware that he had rivals, however, Hanfstaengl tried to
oblige Hitler even more by toadying to him in the time-honored way,
but also, when Alfred Rosenberg was temporarily appointed the
imprisoned party leader's deputy after the failure of the November
putsch, by engaging in intrigue. He was determined to bring down
that "distasteful individual" with his "countless revolting love
affairs,"[45] and in Hermann Esser he found a no less motivated ally.[46]
He also tried to get Kurt Lüdecke on his side, but Lüdecke rejected
Hanfstaengl's "frivolous" palace revolution methods, stuck with
Rosenberg and thus made an enemy of the person who aspired to
become Hitler's right-hand man.[47] Hanfstaengl carried his plot to
such extremes that Rosenberg eventually thought his only means of
defense against him and Esser, two party members at the heart of the
leadership, would be to sue them for defamation. This would have
caused an embarrassing scandal, and Hitler ultimately managed to
prevent it.[48]

Also in 1924, Hanfstaengl developed a marked interest in learning
more about Hitler's past. He knew that on November 9, like himself
and other prominent members of the Party, the leader of the putsch
"could have escaped to Austria had he wanted." He now made every
effort to discover why Hitler had failed to do so, especially as he had
never succeeded in "getting Hitler to talk about his prewar years."
Hanfstaengl therefore used his enforced sojourn in Austria "to look
up Hitler's family in Vienna. I was interested in finding out as much as
possible about his past." Hanfstaengl's reminiscences do not reveal
how successful he was.[49]

When Hanfstaengl tried to reestablish his influence on Hitler after
the latter's early release from detention in the winter of 1924/25, he
could not help noticing, like Lüdecke, that Landsberg had wrought a

great change in him. Although he happily accepted "Putzi's" invitations to his apartment and was as relaxed and fond of music there as ever, Hanfstaengl detected "a gradual cooling in my relationship with Hitler."[50] Why was this?

From the political aspect, Hanfstaengl was disappointed that Hitler had ultimately thwarted his plot against the detested Rosenberg. What was more, Hitler assured the controversial Nazi ideologist of his esteem in a letter dated April 1925: "Not only do I regard you as one of our movement's most valuable members, . . . but I am absolutely convinced of the personal integrity of your sentiments."[51] At the same time, it had seemed as if Hitler would exclude Rosenberg from the inner circle. The erstwhile interpreter of the Party's program did not show up at its renewal rally on February 27, 1925, and Hanfstaengl took pride, even ten years later, in the fact that "the Führer spent the evening of renewal day with me in my little house on Pienzenauer-strasse."[52] But Hitler retained Rosenberg on his leadership team and once more entrusted him with the editorship of the *Völkischer Beobachter* when it reappeared in April 1925. That temporarily put Hanfstaengl's dreams of gaining an authoritative Party post in the field of cultural or foreign policy on hold.

But privately, too, Hanfstaengl was dissatisfied with the way things were going. He had already noticed on his visits to Landsberg that Rudolf Hess was "reluctant to leave Hitler's side when I was talking with him." Hanfstaengl was "extremely concerned" by how intimate the two men had become because, as he rightly remarked, "the bond between them [was] very close. Here, for the first time, I heard them address each other by the familiar *Du*." His response was a "somewhat clumsy" attempt to persuade Polizeirat Rupprecht's monarchist friends to favor the early release of his "endangered" friend. Born of jealousy, this campaign proved as unsuccessful as his other attempts to reinforce his ties with Hitler. At their very first meeting after his return from Landsberg at Christmas 1924, the latter so clearly betrayed "the emotional strength of the friendship he had developed for Hess" that Hanfstaengl felt neglected.[53]

In 1925 his mood must have been that of a cuckolded lover. That may have been why he spread the rumor that Hitler was about to get engaged to his sister Erna, and it is possible that he really did try to play the matchmaker as a way of "keeping close to" his friend. Be that as it may, when national newspapers carried an announcement of the engagement, Hitler issued a curious disclaimer: "I am so much married to politics that I cannot consider 'getting engaged' as well."[54] More curious still, his "Private Secretariat: signed R. Hess" had to confirm that disclaimer six months later because of "questions about the subject from within our own ranks."[55]

Hanfstaengl was "very disappointed" by all this—so disappointed that he took his revenge: he demanded the return of all the money he had contributed to Party funds over the years. At the same time, he intimated to Hitler that he was "uninterested" in developing closer relations with him "as long as Rosenberg and Hess retained their influence." That, in 1925, ended their friendship: "The relations between us were more or less severed for some time." Having taken his revenge, Hanfstaengl resignedly conceded: "I no longer have his trust."[56] Hitler probably dropped him because his scheming and snooping had become a nuisance, and because he needed less eccentric associates for his new political plans. Hanfstaengl retired hurt, but it was soon borne in on him that "despite all my disappointments, I had far from succeeded in eradicating the impression Hitler had left on me." This brought them no closer, however, and the atmosphere that prevailed at their sporadic meetings was "not governed by mutual affection."[57]

Hitler certainly presented Hanfstaengl with many enigmas, but the greatest of them seems to have been his sexual identity. That question haunted Hanfstaengl for decades, and he almost risked his life in the quest for an answer to it.

Hanfstaengl first pronounced on the subject in the summer of 1942, in a dossier compiled for American intelligence.[58] Although it is debatable whether he divulged everything he knew to Hitler's wartime enemies, his statements must be taken seriously[59] because they are demonstrably based on his own observations and personal inquiries. Even after the war he attached particular importance to the statement that it had taken him years "to plumb the depths of his [Hitler's] most personal problem." And what was Hitler's "most personal problem"? That his self-fulfillment lacked "a very important factor." He did not, in Hanfstaengl's own words, have "a normal sex life."[60]

Hanfstaengl gave his most succinct explanation of what he meant by that statement to the historian Fritz von Siedler in 1951: "Hitler's potency was partly limited and partly perverted into abnormality. The basis of that abnormality must have been developed by his experiences in the men's hostel in Vienna. That he had a liaison with Hess . . . is beyond doubt." This defines the twin poles around which Hanfstaengl's "diagnosis" circled: Hitler's "partial impotence" and his "175er tendencies."[61] He dwelt in a "sexual no-man's-land" where there was no one "who could have brought him release"—neither man nor woman.[62] Elsewhere, Hanfstaengl describes Hitler's stunted sex life as "a sort of bisexual narcissistic vanity."[63] This emotional makeup had disastrous consequences because its "excess of male energy" found "no normal outlet." By "not normal" Hanfstaengl meant that Hitler was "neither completely heterosexual nor completely homosexual."[64] The word "completely" is significant. How did Hanfstaengl know that, if not from personal experience?

But another reason why Hanfstaengl knew so precisely what he was talking about was that his own sensibilities were clearly not unlike Hitler's. This is demonstrated by his friendships with the homosexually inclined Prince "Auwi" of Prussia[65] and with the author

Hanns Heinz Ewers, whom we mentioned earlier. Being reluctant to admit his own homoerotic feeling, Hanfstaengl too had a "sexual problem." It is entirely possible that he thought—perhaps even hoped—that Hitler would help him solve it. It is also possible, conversely, that he imagined he could do the same for Hitler. But the latter did not cooperate, which in turn led Hanfstaengl to surmise that some of this "strange, wavering sexual disposition . . . had been activated at Landsberg . . . in the company of Hess."[66] Whatever the truth, it is this deeply personal background that makes Hanfstaengl's statements about Hitler's sexuality so interesting and valuable. I consider them more credible than almost anything else written about the subject by Hitler's close associates. Why? Because Hanfstaengl reproached Hitler, not for his homosexuality, but for the fact that he failed to fulfill it properly. Indeed, he once refers with positive disappointment to Hitler's "very diluted sexual inversion."

Although Hanfstaengl's "diagnosis" was undoubtedly correct, it needs to be objectivized. Hitler was homosexual, certainly, but he was also interested in women, although he did not desire them physically. Furthermore, his passions were so closely conjoined with his narcissism that his sexuality acquired a strongly autoerotic flavor. Such was the "sexual no-man's-land" of which Hanfstaengl spoke: a world of emotion that remained to a certain extent "pubertal" and, thus, restricted predominantly to persons of his own gender because he was sexually less inhibited with them than with women. This being so, how could he ever have attained emotional stability?

ONE TOO MANY: LÜDECKE AND HANFSTAENGL
VIE FOR HITLER'S FAVOR

In America Lüdecke continued to pursue his two long-standing objectives: personal profit and pleasure. In 1927 he married an American woman,[67] although he had recently, in New York, met and fallen for the pretty young wife of a businessman named Günther Quandt: the future Magda Goebbels. Whether or not they had an affair[68] when he renewed their acquaintanceship during a brief visit to Germany in the summer of 1930,[69] as seems likely, they were on very familiar terms from then on.

Lüdecke also tried to resume contact with the leaders of the NSDAP, but they had heard nothing but adverse things about his activities in America.[70] His request for admission to the Party in the fall of 1931 was curtly rejected: "In view of his highly controversial character, the Reichsleitung [national executive] attaches no value to his membership."[71] In the early summer of 1932 Lüdecke again visited Germany, where he witnessed the advance of Hitler and the NSDAP firsthand. In mid-August, after sounding out the ground, he had a long and confidential talk with his friend Magda, now Frau Goebbels, at her Berlin apartment.[72] He was delighted to hear that Hitler had often referred to him in friendly and appreciative terms and would surely give him a second chance.

Encouraged by this news, Lüdecke pressed on with his plan to set up a kind of NSDAP "foreign office" with Rosenberg at its head and himself as number two. He got a chance to discuss this scheme with Hitler early in September 1932. Hitler did not seem averse but asked him to reach an accommodation with Hanfstaengl. His attempt to do so failed miserably, so he pinned all his hopes on Rosenberg. On September 12 he had another detailed discussion with Hitler at the Hotel Kaiserhof, its subject being foreign policy and the possibility of employing Lüdecke in that field—in the United States, for example. But private matters, too, were raised. Lüdecke frankly admitted to knowing that Magda Goebbels would sooner have married Hitler than her present husband. Hitler was as dismissive of that as he was of Lüdecke's attempt to raise the subject of homosexuality in the SA leadership: "Ach, why should I concern myself with the private lives of my followers! . . . I love Richard Wagner's music—must I shut my ears to it because he was a pederast? The whole thing's absurd."[73] At the end of September Lüdecke was privileged to call on Hitler once more, this time at his apartment. The party leader was his old, senti-mental self, profoundly emotional and even moist-eyed. Lüdecke had every right to feel content. By the time he left for the United States a few days later, he had genuinely achieved something: not only had he been admitted to Party membership;[74] he also had in his pocket a doc-ument, signed by Rosenberg, authorizing him to represent the NSDAP in matters affecting "foreign policy."[75] Above all, though, he had regained access to Hitler.[76]

———

Lüdecke's keenest rival and competitor for Hitler's favor was Ernst Hanfstaengl. Having devoted himself mainly to his study of history during the period 1926–28, Hanfstaengl had not rejoined the NSDAP leadership until 1929. At the Party rally in Nuremberg he made friends with Prince August Wilhelm of Prussia, who was just develop-ing an enthusiasm for National Socialism: "We very soon took to each other," "Putzi" wrote of his feelings for "Auwi," who became a regu-lar and "welcome visitor" of his, sometimes accompanied by Göring. "At all events, it was mainly Prince Auwi who rekindled my hopes for the future of the Party."[77] The extent of this rapprochement in the fall of 1929 becomes apparent from an entry Joseph Goebbels made in his diary after an evening around the fire in Hanfstaengl's villa: "Hanf-staengl is shrewd and witty. . . . While we are debating foreign policy, Göring lies snoring on the sofa." It was not lost on Goebbels how "fiercely" Hanfstaengl "rounded on Hitler" because he "sides with Rosenberg, whom Hanfstaengl detests."[78]

We do not know exactly why Hanfstaengl thrust his way back into Hitler's innermost circle. It was probably because he no longer wanted to stand aside now that Hitler's prospects of gaining political power were steadily improving.[79] But it was also in Hitler's interest to reinforce his links with his former crony, having reached a stage in his career when he was more than ever dependent on securing the loyalty of old friends. After the unpleasant way their relationship had ended, and in view of Hanfstaengl's hotheadedness and unpredictability, he may have considered him a security risk, so he conscripted him, as it were. He would not have done so without making certain promises. There was later talk of a seat on the Munich city council, a Reichstag seat and even an ambassadorship.[80] At all events, Hitler began by appointing his former companion the Party's foreign press chief in November 1931.[81] He also invited him to his home now and then "to perform on the piano," Hanfstaengl recalled, "but not as often as formerly or as generally supposed."[82] For all that, he "belonged" once more and envisioned himself on the threshold of a great career.

Hanfstaengl became an important member of the "Führer's" entourage during the election campaigns of 1932. Hitler needed him to strike the right note with journalists from abroad, where interest in the Nazis had blossomed, and Hanfstaengl was adept at charming them. But he also needed him as a comforter, as someone who could divert and cheer him up when he was depressed.[83] Thus Hanfstaengl was often seen at the "Führer's" side, not only in public but within the Party. Although Hitler never really resumed their intimacy, it seemed that the two men were friends. Hanfstaengl could only welcome the general belief that he "had Hitler's ear,"[84] because he subsisted on being thought influential: financially by arranging interviews with Hitler and selling exclusive stories; and politically by behaving in a self-important way that brought him valuable connections, for instance, Rudolf Diels, who headed the Prussian security police. In a telltale allusion to that shady individual, Hanfstaengl's memoirs once refer to him as "Rudi" and state that he was one of the "most useful contacts" he had at this period.[85]

Hanfstaengl could secure his status only by conspicuous membership on Hitler's staff, so he did his utmost not to sink in the "Führer's"
estimation—especially after the latter's assumption of power, which
brought Hanfstaengl an important position. Many have left sarcastic
accounts of Hanfstaengl's behavior, and all contemporary observers
describe him as an attention-seeking functionary who wouldn't hear a
word said against Hitler.[86] But that was the only constraint Hanfstaengl laid on himself; in other respects, as Rosenberg and Lüdecke
were soon to discover, he carried a dagger beneath his cloak.

Through "Rudi" Diels, Hanfstaengl had obtained compromising
material about his two worst enemies: police evidence to the effect
that Rosenberg, a rabid antisemite, was having an affair with the
daughter of a Jewish publisher, and that Lüdecke had been active as a
blackmailer and con man since 1911. Hanfstaengl was obviously
seeking such evidence because in March 1933 Hitler had appointed
Rosenberg to head the NSDAP's foreign office directly under himself.
Although the new post had yet to acquire any political clout, Rosenberg could now hope to secure an influential and powerful position in
the hierarchy.[87] From Hanfstaengl's point of view, this development
was particularly dangerous because it derived from a renewed initiative on Lüdecke's part.

Word of Hitler's assumption of power had brought Lüdecke hurry-
ing back to Berlin, where he was soon granted a lengthy audience at
the Reich Chancellery.[88] Lüdecke purposely raised the subjects with
which he had tried to coax the "Führer" out of his shell in Munich six
months earlier. "Although Hitler has learned how to control himself
in a marvelous way," he recalled later, "he is by nature too impulsive
to control his eyes and his mouth. . . . Those who have known him
from his early days can infer a great deal from the expressions on his
mobile features." Hitler's man in America had been banking on those
telltale reactions when he quite deliberately reported on American
criticism of the National Socialists: "'The current whispering cam-

paign is especially fond of branding you a homosexual. It—' 'Tsk, tsk!' Hitler broke in, looking annoyed. 'Incredible!' He clearly wanted to hear no more of it." But Lüdecke had attained his objective, which was to remind Hitler of the value of his, Lüdecke's, discretion. He could now move on, all the more directly, to the price of his discretion, namely, an appointment as press attaché at the German embassy in Washington. Accreditation would assure him of diplomatic immunity, and he could also, while there, render useful service as an informant. For that he naturally required a jumping-off point in the Party, preferably a "foreign policy bureau," and a lot of money.

Hitler was not averse to this proposal, and Lüdecke endeavored to clinch matters by calling on press chief Walter Funk, Rosenberg and Hess. Those in favor of setting up the new bureau were naturally aiming to arrogate certain powers, which entailed taking them away from other persons and departments.[89] This was bound to present a challenge, not only to Hanfstaengl, but to Foreign Minister von Neurath and Hermann Göring, who also cherished ambitions in the field of foreign policy. The situation became genuinely threatening when, at the Hotel Kaiserhof in April 1933, Lüdecke succeeded in persuading a large gathering of industrialists to contribute several hundred thousand reichsmarks for expenditure on propaganda abroad. These funds might sooner or later transform the Party's "paper tiger" into an effective and powerful machine.

Accordingly, Hanfstaengl prepared to counterattack. On his own submission, he had come into possession of evidence that Lüdecke had blackmailed a German doctor in New York by threatening to report him for performing an abortion, and had thereby earned himself several hundred dollars. "I duly passed the relevant evidence to higher authority."[90] We do not know for sure whether this was the only thing that prompted Göring to have Lüdecke summarily arrested, but by May 9, 1933, he and Rosenberg's Jewish mistress were behind bars. At the same time, Hanfstaengl tried some character assassination by producing a leader for the *New Yorker Staatszeitung*, which printed it on May 12, 1933, under the headline "Lüdecke arrested on charges of false pretenses and extortion."[91] This seemed to have eliminated his rival once for all. But Hanfstaengl had reckoned without Hitler, who instructed Göring to release the detainees forthwith and apologize for overstepping the mark. Lüdecke's memoirs describe with relish how the mighty Prussian premier performed this distasteful chore. Göring had apparently been astonished at the extent of his credit with Hitler, whose obvious scruples granted Lüdecke his freedom but, at the same time, led him to overestimate the "Führer's" patience.

For Lüdecke was far from willing to disappear to Washington right away, as various people suggested. Although Hitler had by now decreed his appointment to the German embassy in Washington, Lüdecke was insistent that he publicly endorse him to the Party. At their next meeting, however, the Reich Chancellor stonewalled him completely. Their heated exchange of words indicated that Hitler had absolutely no desire to see the "Lüdecke case" investigated in detail or submitted to further discussion.

But the disappointed dupe dug his heels in and tried to obtain satisfaction in another way. The aforesaid leader in the *New Yorker Staatszeitung*, whose authorship he had soon discovered, afforded him the opportunity he was seeking. Hellbent on paying Hanfstaengl back with a libel action, Lüdecke got in touch with the well-known attorney Dr. Alfons Sack and told him quite bluntly that his aim in bringing the case would be to shed light on "a hot zone of Nazidom." The attorney did not balk at this prospect, although both he and his client realized that Hitler would scarcely permit such a potentially sensational case to proceed. However, Lüdecke calculated that his initiative would at least compel Hitler to back him more firmly. If not, he would be a miserable hypocrite. To insure against the latter eventuality, Lüdecke tried to form a kind of secret pact with Ernst Röhm. Meanwhile, the hearing had been scheduled for mid-July 1933. Behind the scenes, Max Amann urged Rosenberg to try to persuade Lüdecke to quit politics and take a lucrative job with the publishing house of Eher-Verlag instead. Rosenberg, who had become uneasy about Lüdecke's escalating course of action in any case, strongly advised him not to drag matters into court. But Lüdecke refused to listen, with the result that on July 5, 1933, he was again taken into protective custody—this time at Hitler's personal behest.

It is apparent from Lüdecke's own account, which we have followed hitherto, that he had been playing politics in his own behalf and with a foot in more than one camp. This would naturally have been reported to Hitler, so he was bound to regard Lüdecke as a dangerous schemer—dangerous because he knew too much, and because his wild ambitions had made him unpredictable. The proper course seemed to be to take him out of circulation, confiscate his personal papers and await developments.

Lüdecke's response was not long in coming. In plaintive letters [not extant] to Hitler, Göring and Himmler, he hinted that he was not as helpless as might be supposed[92] and threatened to publish compromising material about the Nazi leadership that he had deposited abroad. But Hitler kept his nerve. He tightened up Lüdecke's conditions of imprisonment and left him to stew in Plötzensee for a few weeks. It was not until the beginning of September 1933, after he had been transferred to the Brandenburg concentration camp, that an envoy from Rosenberg came to inform him that Hitler had "personally" reserved the right of decision in his case.[93] Lüdecke's only recourse was an about-face: he begged Hitler's pardon for his offenses against the "timing and rhythm of the Movement"[94] and assured him of his absolute loyalty. He also wrote to Party judge Buch in similar terms. But Hitler still made no move to help his onetime associate—indeed, he is said to have told Röhm in December 1933 that Lüdecke was "a dangerous brother."[95] It was deliberate policy on Hitler's part that his prisoner should feel, after eight months' detention, that he was "gradually going under . . . in [a state of] agonizing uncertainty and mental attrition."[96]

But Lüdecke sought other ways out of his predicament. He managed to bribe the guards at the Oranienburg concentration camp, in which he had since been confined, and got the camp commandant on his side.[97] This enabled him to slip away for a few hours after dark, and in January 1934 he even claimed to have succeeded in meeting with Röhm and hatching a plot with him. At the same time, he tried to keep a back door to Hitler open by way of his friend Rosenberg. On February 19, 1934, he was actually granted leave of absence and allowed to travel under escort to Berlin, where he had a long conversation with the Reichsleiter.[98] He did not, however, achieve the real purpose of his visit, which was to submit his plea to Hitler in person, the latter having told Rosenberg that he had forbidden himself, once for all, to intervene in the matter. Lüdecke now knew what he had to do: during a second spell of leave on March 1, 1934, he fled to Czechoslovakia and from there to Switzerland. From Geneva on April 10, 1934, he sent a "personal and urgent" letter to Hitler—with copies to Rosenberg, Amann, Heinrich Hoffmann, Brückner and Magda Goebbels.[99]

Six and a half pages long, Lüdecke's letter expressed a wish to speak with Hitler "frankly and freely, man to man," especially as they had "more than once discussed confidential matters." It seemed to him— and the following passage in his letter was underlined—"that you, of all people, should be especially careful before you allow me to suffer such a cruel injustice." If Hitler did not personally rehabilitate him in short order, he was determined to "enforce" this. He presented an ultimatum: if he did not receive "*complete* rehabilitation and satisfaction" within two weeks, he would have "to draw the appropriate conclusions in every respect," and he admitted "frankly, that—weighing up all eventualities—I have prepared and insured myself accordingly."

It is only in the light of this letter, which might have come from a manual of the blackmailer's art, that we can once more see the "Lüdecke case" in context. It was a strictly confidential, highly classified document, and one which Hitler showed only to a handful of close associates. He knew that Hanfstaengl was mainly responsible for landing him in this mess—he himself would have preferred to shunt Lüdecke off to America—and he suspected that his SA commander was also involved in the affair in some way. That made the situation exceptionally dangerous, because he was already watching Röhm warily, and the struggle for absolute power was far from over in 1933/34. On the other hand, Lüdecke's knowledge of Hitler was a potential threat that convinced him he held the dictator in the palm of his hand. Lüdecke had reverted to the trade he still knew best, so Hitler had to take his blackmailer very seriously. This became clear early in May 1934, when the *Evening Star* published an article, obviously by Lüdecke himself, which described his spectacular escape from Germany and vaguely hinted that influential party leaders might have helped him in the expectation that his activities abroad would benefit their own interests.[100] It is apparent from a later source that the Gestapo questioned leading Nazis who might have aided his escape and compiled "an interesting dossier of special sworn depositions."[101] In October 1934 the case was submitted to a "thorough examination"[102] under Himmler's personal supervision.[103] All this suggests that Hitler was trying to discover what evidence against him Lüdecke was actually holding. The relevant documents have not survived.

Lüdecke kept quiet for the next few months, from which we must infer that Hitler had somehow contrived to seal his blackmailer's lips. Hush money may have aided this, as Hans Mend hints in his "protocol" of 1939. This states that a certain "Liedtke" had "fled to America" shortly before the "Röhm putsch" with some of the SA chief's diaries, "and blackmailed the party leadership from there." Mend goes on: "Rudolf Hess called Hanfstaengl when Liedtke asked for more money, to wit, 50,000 dollars in cash and 50,000 dollars' worth of 'medicaments,' presumably so as to sell them in America at a profit."[104] The garbled name should not surprise us, considering that the *Münchener Post*'s articles on Lüdecke had mistakenly called him "Liedtke,"[105] but everything else fits the picture, from the Röhm diaries and Lüdecke's reputation as a blackmailer to his racketeering and crook's nose for business. The phone conversation between Rudolf Hess and Ernst Hanfstaengl can also be explained, but for that we must first revert to Hanfstaengl's career.

BLACKMAILER VERSUS BLACKMAILER

It far from reinforced Hanfstaengl's position within the Nazi leadership that all his ambitions in the spring of 1933 were focused on eliminating Rosenberg and Lüdecke so as to acquire greater influence in the sphere of foreign policy. Goebbels called him a "scatterbrain" after he had yet again been "terribly" grouchy about Rosenberg.[106] He himself had passed on a definite warning from Hitler at that time: "Hanfstaengl, you carry your criticism of Party Member Rosenberg too far. If you don't stop, I'll dismiss you."[107] In February 1934, despite this admonition, Hanfstaengl made another attempt to distinguish himself by taking a private diplomatic initiative: in Rome he offered Mussolini not only the Italian copyright of a Nazi propaganda film but an early meeting with the German dictator. Hitler's reaction to his foreign press chief's presumption must have been reminiscent of the fall of 1933, when he flatly dismissed a German-Austrian peace program submitted by Hanfstaengl as "idiocy."[108] Even the daughter of U.S. Ambassador William E. Dodd heard on the grapevine that Hanfstaengl was "no longer trusted" in senior Party circles.[109]

He could not have been accused of insufficient political commitment, because he always, in his official function, presented himself as an unswerving National Socialist. Symptoms of this ranged from the Hitler bust on his desk[110] and his advocacy of a nationalistic "blood cure" for the German people[111] to his crassly antisemitic remarks in diplomatic company[112] and simultaneous propaganda on behalf of Hitler's "immense work for peace."[113] It was not lack of commitment to the Nazi regime that caused him to fall out with the Nazi leadership, just overweening ambition.

————

Kurt Lüdecke's flight was just about the worst thing that could have happened to Hanfstaengl, not only because he himself had largely helped to bring it about by provoking his rival, but because Lüdecke's blackmail letter expressly warned Hitler against him. Hanfstaengl, wrote Lüdecke, had "not only plotted and conspired against Rosenberg . . . and against me in an unconscionable and criminal manner, but has, on occasion, adopted a very questionable attitude toward you as well."[114] Hanfstaengl probably guessed that Hitler would read more into that allusion than a cheap retort. There was still the danger that Lüdecke would publicly denounce him abroad and destroy his reputation. It was at this stage, in March 1934, that the situation was given a new twist by an invitation to Hanfstaengl to attend a class reunion at Harvard.

Hanfstaengl accepted with pleasure—only to cry off not long afterward, his sheepish explanation being that urgent official business precluded a trip to America.[115] Possibly Hitler had called him to heel. Ever since Lüdecke's letter, which had been followed early in May by another,[116] Hanfstaengl had been kept on a short leash. But in mid-June 1934 he was suddenly allowed to travel to the States after all, helter-skelter, without any press announcement, and not in the usual way from Bremerhaven, but from Cherbourg, whither he was specially conveyed by air. Sailing from the same harbor at around this time was the Canadian ship that took Kurt Lüdecke across the Atlantic.[117] By the beginning of July 1934, both mortal enemies were in New York, where Voigt, Hanfstaengl's assistant, had been reconnoitering the terrain for some time.[118] It was unlikely to have been a private pleasure trip, therefore, but Hanfstaengl's diversionary maneuvers managed to conceal the real object of the whole undertaking. And that, in my submission, was—on Hitler's orders—to dissuade Lüdecke from doing anything stupid.

Although we have no documentary evidence relating to Hanfstaengl's mission or the way in which he carried it out, there are various pointers indicating that it was a secret assignment. The first is that Lüdecke made no move for months after Hanfstaengl's visit. One possible explanation for such uncharacteristic self-restraint is hush money; another—a psychological factor of equal value—is the fact that his fiercest adversary had come to him cap in hand, for that is precisely what Hitler must have demanded of Hanfstaengl. In the meantime, Hitler's murderous operation against Röhm demonstrated in the most brutal way possible how he dealt with "traitors" from his own camp. When Hanfstaengl learned of these events, he felt like staying in America. "I went weak at the knees, . . . the pictures swam before my eyes," and he felt "utterly bewildered and outraged."[119] But Foreign Minister von Neurath personally ordered him back to Germany. He landed at Bremerhaven on July 14, 1934, and was promptly summoned to Heiligendamm, the seaside resort where Hitler and Goebbels were taking a summer vacation.[120]

Goebbels makes only a brief allusion in his diary to Hanfstaengl's visit on July 15.[121] He was not in the know, presumably, because Hitler saw the visitor alone. Hanfstaengl, on the other hand, gives a very detailed description of this meeting in his memoirs, because in retrospect it marked his definitive break with Hitler. He says not a word about his American mission, of course. The only believable part of his account refers to the frosty detachment—indeed, biting sarcasm—with which Hitler received his report. Whether Hanfstaengl actually told Hitler all that he had done in the States in regard to Lüdecke is an open question, but one thing is certain: it must have been very important, politically speaking, for Hitler to have summoned him at once to his vacation quarters, which he had only just moved into. In those heady days, the "Führer" surely had better things to do than be briefed on a Harvard reunion.

Hanfstaengl concludes his subsequent report by saying that, after the Heiligendamm meeting, he had "nothing left to hope for."[122] He must nevertheless have prevailed on Hitler to give his foreign minister an order. Only this would explain why, the very next day, the foreign office instructed the German embassy in Washington to counter any political machinations on Lüdecke's part by publicizing his criminal career.[123] Hanfstaengl's next step was to enlist the help of William Randolph Hearst, the American press tycoon, who happened to be in Germany.[124] In August 1934 the *Völkischer Beobachter* assigned great prominence to a report that the foreign press chief had conducted "a series of private discussions" with the celebrated publisher "about the current political situation," and was expressly authorized to publish a statement about them. According to this, Hearst had declared himself in sympathy with the German people's "struggle for liberation from the iniquitous terms of the Versailles Treaty." He "wholeheartedly" approved of "all that was beneficial to Germany."[125] Coming after the ruinously bad press the Nazi regime had been receiving abroad since the Röhm murders, such a declaration of solidarity from the lips of an authoritative American opinion-maker was, of course, a considerable prestige boost—not least for Hanfstaengl himself, who promptly followed this up by arranging a meeting between Hearst and Hitler.[126]

As a reward for his good work, Hanfstaengl was permitted to accept a personal invitation from Hearst to spend a few days at his country mansion in Wales. On the way there they stopped off in London, where Lord Beaverbrook, the British press baron, took an interest in the visitor from Nazi Germany. On September 19, 1934, Beaver-brook's *Daily Express* drew a bead on Hanfstaengl with the headline "Hitler's 'Putzy' Is Here" and called him an "intimate friend of Leader Hitler."[127] When interviewed by an *Express* reporter the next day, he took violent exception to the designation "Putzy" because it sounded in English like "Pussy"—and that, he explained many years later, was a "derisive nickname for men of unnatural disposition."[128] But the reporter parlayed his interview into another article filled with spiteful imputations that were bound to create the impression that there was something not quite right about this German visitor.[129] This suggests that Hanfstaengl's homosexual tendencies were a more or less open secret in well-informed journalistic circles. However, the titillating feature of the actual report was that it imputed an intimate relationship with Hitler, the man whose Röhm bloodbath had only just issued a resolute declaration of war on homosexuality.

Hanfstaengl realized that, for all their inconvenience, these attacks presented him with a great opportunity to involve Hitler himself in the affair. Accordingly, he at once and without consulting Berlin took out a libel action against the owner of the *Daily Express*, whose terse response was that he looked forward to the trial.[130] When Hanfstaengl returned to Berlin at the end of September, he at last had a means of exerting pressure on Hitler. We do not know how Hitler reacted, but the very fact that the hearing was continually postponed for months on end and then came to nothing gives one some idea of the tussle that must have gone on behind the scenes.[131]

The "Lüdecke case" also came to life again. A communication dated September 1934 from the foreign office to Gestapo headquarters stated that Lüdecke might soon be publicly questioned by a House of Representatives committee about Nazi propaganda activities in the United States, and that it would be appropriate "to initiate precautionary steps to counter the probable repercussions of Lüdecke's statements." This would require "an exhaustive account of the criminal offenses of which Lüdecke stands accused."[132] That was just the sign Hanfstaengl had long been waiting for, because it seemed at last to provide him with a pretext for destroying his hated adversary.

In October 1934, although no one had instructed him to, Hanfstaengl used his good relations with the Gestapo to carry out an internal reconstruction of "the files on Kurt Lüdecke with Detective Superintendent Braschwitz."[133] In his capacity as a member of the so-called Hamburg-Bremen Information Committee, "a confidential organization available to the Reich ministries for the permeation of the foreign press with articles and news items favorable to Germany,"[134] he also fed compromising statements about Lüdecke to the German-American press.[135]

But unauthorized actions of this kind were bound, sooner or later, to lead to a row with Hitler. At the end of October, Hanfstaengl was dismissed from the Reich Chancellery, because of his "steadfast combating of Lüdecke on the Führer's instructions, with the words: 'The Führer desires you to return to the Reich Chancellery only when the Lüdecke case is resolved.'"[136] This was more than an impulsive bum's rush, because it soon turned out that Hanfstaengl had fallen into permanent disfavor. Although he later sought to attribute his break with Hitler to purely political differences, he himself supplies a detail that betrays the purely personal nature of the dispute. During a heated argument at lunch in the Chancellery over the question of how to behave toward Lüdecke, Hitler, "white with fury," blurted out: "It's all your fault, Hanfstaengl. You should have treated him more diplomatically."[137] It obviously enraged Hitler that Hanfstaengl's initiative had put him in a tight spot, so he used him as his whipping boy and resolved that any further decisions in the matter would be taken by himself alone.

But the Lüdecke-Hitler blackmail case now became a Lüdecke-Hanfstaengl blackmail case as well, and Hanfstaengl thought his only way of averting personal ruin, in spite of Hitler's reprimand, was to continue to hound Lüdecke, if need be on his own initiative. On November 1, 1934, he submitted to the foreign office the report of a Gestapo investigation headed "Reichsleitung der NSDAP" and personally addressed to Hans Dieckhoff, the relevant undersecretary. This report embodied all the major items in Lüdecke's list of sins since 1911 and unmasked him as a "swindler and confidence trickster . . . who has used his questionable activities on behalf of the NSDAP as a means to an end, namely, the procuring of greater sources of income."[138] The official communication which Gestapo headquarters sent the foreign office the next day was almost identical, but it omitted a sentence to which Hanfstaengl clearly attached special importance: his own version had stated that Lüdecke "is reported to have had intimate relations with other men, and to have received payments therefor." This betrayed his real intention, which was to expose Lüdecke as a kind of male prostitute in such a way that any sexual denunciation from *him* would inevitably be dismissed, on principle, as devoid of all credibility.

Hans Frank, the Bavarian minister of justice, who had been variously involved with the Lüdecke case as Hitler's former attorney and an associate justice of the Party court, was also supplied by Hanfstaengl with his Gestapo findings and, thus, harnessed to his campaign.[139] Outwardly, Hanfstaengl always gave the impression that he was working on the case for the "Führer," who was still generally considered to be a good friend of his. This enabled him, for instance, to enlist the foreign office in the service of his campaign against Lüdecke[140] and to urge a senior civil servant at the Bavarian ministry of justice to "hasten inquiries into the Lüdecke case as much as possible, because speed is of the essence."[141] He contrived to examine and get copies made of confidential documents in both ministries. (He also sneaked a look at the file kept on him by Munich police headquarters,[142] which indicates that he was conducting inquiries in his own interests as well.) Furthermore, he collected written depositions in which former acquaintances of Lüdecke had given compromising evidence against him,[143] with the result that by late November he was in possession of a dossier as thorough as any professional secret service could have compiled.

Hitler, by contrast, wanted to maneuver more cautiously in the Lüdecke case. One can well imagine his reaction when, at the end of November, he learned that Hanfstaengl had defied his categorical veto and was conducting his private war against Lüdecke with undiminished zeal. When he instituted inquiries at the Bavarian ministry of justice as to why Hanfstaengl had been given certified copies of official documents, he learned that the latter had justified his access to them by stating that he had "to put the Führer in the picture about Lüdecke's person."[144] Hanfstaengl had deceived him, in other words, and no one knows how he managed to survive such a lapse. At all events, Hitler decreed that all the material on Lüdecke be withdrawn and kept in the "poison cabinet" in his adjutant's office.[145]

But the matter was far from settled even then. In December 1934 Lüdecke made himself heard once more, and in a way that showed, yet again, that he was a master of his craft. He persuaded some American intermediaries to use their contacts with Reichsbank President Hjalmar Schacht on his behalf. Early in January 1935 a whole stack of potentially explosive documents arrived in Berlin.[146] Their author was Lüdecke himself, although some were represented as neutral reports by those who were helping him. The cover letter expressed confidence that Schacht would "use his influence to ensure that Herr Hitler really does see to it that the L. case is settled as suggested." The "suggestion" in question was hot stuff. Lüdecke presented a deadline by which the following demands had to be met: a public apology by the Nazi leadership, printed in the *Völkischer Beobachter*, for having unjustly interned him, coupled with a declaration that he had "performed his National Socialist duties and assignments in an irreproachable manner"; and "an indemnity of $50,000," of which "at least

$25,000" to be remitted in cash and the other half in the form of "first-class, high-quality goods." If his "suggestion" went unheeded, he would "unhesitatingly and ruthlessly proceed by all available means . . . to revenge himself on his enemies." He had it in his power "at a big public trial, . . . to present his whole case to the general public in the most sensational manner, which would naturally be a scandal of the first order." He expressly warned against any attempt "to remove or neutralize" him by violent means, because he had "thoroughly insured himself" with that in mind. The same went for any attempt to portray him as "wholly insignificant or a liar," which would gain no credence "because of his documentary evidence, accompanied by photographs, and because of the events of June 30 [1934]."[147]

The salient feature of this document is undoubtedly its brazen language. What is more significant, however, is the way in which it underpins the credibility of the "Mend Protocol." Hans Mend can only have derived his information from Hanfstaengl, who was obviously engaged in pumping people like him. Hanfstaengl and Hitler reacted at once to the threat from New York. The foreign press chief instructed his confederates in America to publish a pamphlet containing "extracts from German files," his purpose being to broadcast Lüdecke's criminal record to the world at large. These extracts were identical with the Gestapo report mentioned above.[148] Hitler, on the other hand, did something quite different. He got Philipp Bouhler, who headed his personal office, to draft an extremely civil letter to Lüdecke's intermediary asking him to inform "Herr Lüdecke" that "I shall deal with his concern as quickly as possible. . . . You may rest assured that everything will be done here to settle the matter."[149]

Hitler's undertaking left all his options open, for the moment at least, and he must soon have reached some form of modus vivendi, because Lüdecke made no further move for a good two years. Nothing happened—no scandalous court case or sensational newspaper articles and no more blackmailer's letters—even though Lüdecke had made the following public statement in New York early in January 1935: "Unless this court [the NSDAP's own tribunal] pronounces me innocent, I shall know how to clear my name, even if Hitler and his National Socialist Party bite the dust in the process."[150] We shall probably never know how the German dictator managed to defuse Lüdecke's bomb, but he would surely have failed to do so without remunerating him generously.

Hitler was not to know that in 1936, despite all his attempts at compromise, Lüdecke contracted with Charles Scribner's Sons, the New York publishers, to write a book in which he would recount his experiences with Hitler and the National Socialist movement.[151] Faithful to his guiding principle, he wanted to have his cake and eat it as well: pocket hush money while simultaneously selling his knowledge for a high price. Hitler having been prepared to give him only a part of what he felt entitled to, namely, "*complete* rehabilitation and satisfaction," Lüdecke was using his exposé in an attempt to obtain the remainder.

The title of the book, *I Knew Hitler*, was more than a publicity gimmick; to Lüdecke's principal adversary, it must have sounded like a threat. Its deeper meaning becomes more apparent if one takes the subtitle and dedication seriously: "The Story of a Nazi Who Escaped the Blood Purge"; and "In Memory of Captain Ernst Röhm." Lüdecke makes clear, in the very first sentence, that "I can afford to tell the unadorned truth, limited only by my conscience and considerations of good taste." Elsewhere he mentions a confidential talk with Röhm in the spring of 1934, and says that the time is not yet ripe to make the whole of that conversation public.[152] But he is at his most artful in the passages that allude to Hitler's sexuality. What he makes Magda Goebbels say about Hitler's bizarre attitude toward women[153] is so pointed that the reader can only conclude that the "Führer" had a genuine problem with the opposite sex. "Hitler was perfectly charming," declares Frau Goebbels, "but somehow. . . ." The fact that, at that point, Lüdecke abruptly switches to Ernst Röhm's homosexuality is a clear indication of his cunning: he suggests that if Hitler is capable only of platonic relationships with women but shielded and protected Röhm, a homosexual and one of his closest associates, there must be something in the rumors of his homosexual tendencies. This insinuation is reinforced when one reads on and learns that, when Lüdecke questioned Hitler on the subject, his response was brusque in the extreme. Finally, there is Röhm's fury at Hitler's hypocrisy. The SA chief is recorded as telling Lüdecke that his "abnormality" was nobody's business but his own. "I do as I please within my own four walls—like anyone else," he added meaningfully.[154]

Hitler must have seen the publication of Lüdecke's book as a renewed attempt to blackmail him, because it was certainly no coincidence that he promptly dispatched Fritz Wiedemann, his personal aide, to New York.[155] Wiedemann makes no comment on this trip in his memoirs, but the very fact that it was disguised as a private vacation but funded like an official visit makes it more than likely that Wiedemann was carrying out a secret mission in Hitler's behalf.[156] Some months later the German embassy in Washington reported that Lüdecke had, on his own submission, "finally left politics and intended to live for himself in the future."[157] The blackmailer must have been silenced again by some means. An additional indication of this is that Lüdecke withdrew his libel action against the *New Yorker Staatszeitung* at the end of 1937, although the damages under negotiation amounted to $100,000.[158]

That more or less wrapped up the "Lüdecke case" as far as Hitler was concerned. The British press could make little of it—or nothing threatening, anyway.[159] Although *I Knew Hitler* was described as "the most intimate book yet about the Nazis," it was not used as the hook for a campaign against the German dictator.[160] The same applied in the United States, where it received mixed reviews.[161] That was why

Hitler could confidently reject Lüdecke's final attempt to make capital out of his memoirs early in 1939. Lüdecke had seriously suggested to the German ambassador in Washington that the NSDAP should purchase all the rights to the book for a "substantial" sum, pointing out that it would be "in the German interest to prevent further dissemination of the book." The ambassador, who readily perceived that this was "a straightforward attempt at blackmail,"[162] declined to acknowledge receipt of Lüdecke's letter. He did, however, consider it so potentially explosive that he immediately forwarded it to the foreign office, which passed it on to the Reich Chancellery. "The Führer thoroughly endorses the conduct of the embassy in Washington," Hans Lammers, head of the Chancellery, wrote back.[163] Hitler remained unruffled, especially as the annexation of Austria had made it impossible to publish a German edition of the book. As for the foreign office copy, it was kept "in a sealed envelope in the safe."[164]

A SECOND BLACKMAILER

Hanfstaengl had to pay a high price for his dogged attempts to destroy his rival Lüdecke in 1933/34: the loss of Hitler's favor. Rosenberg was heartily glad when, after "several visits to the Führer," he learned in the spring of 1935 that Hitler had "finally dropped a sick and malicious pest like Dr. Hanfstaengl."[165] But Hanfstaengl was not dismissed and still preserved some freedom of discretion, even if he had ceased to belong to Hitler's entourage and his foreign press office was carefully supervised.

All his efforts were now directed toward enforcing Hitler's solidarity. This became very clear at the end of 1935, when he requested the Party treasurer, Franz Xaver Schwarz, that he be simultaneously awarded the "Gold Badge of Honor" and the "Blood Order" on the grounds of his long membership of, and services to, the Party.[166] When

Schwarz snubbed him,[167] he repeated his request. This time he addressed himself in very personal terms to "dear Party Member Schwarz" and justified his approach in the following, thoroughly insidious way: "I attended the renewal of the Party in the Bürgerbräukeller in 1925. At the Führer's wish and with his repeated approval, I refrained for many years from applying for official membership in the Party. The reasons for that must be known to you." He went on: "In this connection, let it be remembered that the Führer spent the late evening of Renewal Day with me in my little house on Pienzauer Strasse."[168] It does not require any great feat of the imagination to discern the outlines here of a threatening posture—an attempt to base claims on their former intimacy. Even though Schwarz remained unimpressed and smugly left it up to the petitioner "to approach the Führer direct in this matter,"[169] we may take it that Hanfstaengl was now about to follow in the footsteps of his arch rival, Lüdecke, and play the blackmailer's card against Hitler.

It was around this time that he must have begun to assemble compromising material about Hitler. The precise circumstances are unknown,[170] but Hanfstaengl's notes on the subject were leaked or somehow conveyed to him. What we do know from Hanfstaengl himself is that he was summoned to the Reich Chancellery by Julius Schaub, Hitler's factotum, and brusquely hauled over the coals. How dare he continue to stir up trouble for Lüdecke with various Party and government authorities? How could he compile such beastly material about the Führer? According to Hanfstaengl, Schaub wound up his fierce accusations by threatening that, unless he watched his step, the authorities would compile a dossier that would finish him once and for all.[171] This was more than intimidation; it was a lethal ultimatum. Fearing a plot traceable back to Lüdecke, Hanfstaengl reacted to his desperate predicament in very much the same way as Hans Mend. He now told everyone the nature of his accusations against Hitler and why he had unjustly forfeited his goodwill.

We know this from a letter about Hanfstaengl that Hertha Frey, a former secretary of Hitler, sent to his aide Fritz Wiedemann in the summer of 1936. In April of that year, she wrote, she had run into Hanfstaengl in Starnberg, where he had given vent to a "positively hair-raising tirade" about Hitler which her "duty to the Führer" now compelled her, "after long deliberation," to bring to Wiedemann's notice. Apparently, Hanfstaengl had explained his attitude thus: "'That swine Lüdecke, whom you know too, has been in Berlin and has made himself at home there in all quarters. You know what a con man, pimp, etc., he is. The foreign office, Herr Meissner [head of the presidential chancellery], the embassy, etc., all know what the fellow is like, yet Hitler keeps him on. Rosenberg, who leads a thoroughly unwholesome private life, . . . protects the fellow because he knows that he [Rosenberg] is or was having an affair with the daughter of Georg Bernhard [the Jewish publisher] and is afraid that Lüdecke will reveal this. Lüdecke is also a frequent visitor to the home of Dr. Goebbels, even though the latter, too, knows about him, because Frau Goebbels formerly had a liaison with Lüdecke, and the concern is that the fellow will take advantage of this.' Dr. Hanfstaengl then employed the following turn of phrase, word for word: 'That's the rotten thing about Hitler, that he tolerates these people around him . . ., that he knows everything and does nothing.'" Wiedemann's informant added: "My fear is that Hanfstaengl naturally says the same things to other people as well."[172]

In his reply, Wiedemann could only confirm that "Dr. Hanfstaengl's intemperate manner is not unknown to us, and I think the Führer has already been informed of it more than once." Trying to play the matter down, he said that he would "inform Herr Hess of the contents of your letter when the occasion arises."[173] In fact, Hertha Frey's denunciation triggered a minor earthquake among Hitler's faithful henchmen. Rosenberg sought an interview with Goebbels, his old enemy, and told him about the "unpleasant Lüdecke business" in which his,

Goebbels', wife was also involved. When Goebbels took her to task, she reluctantly conceded "that the Lüdecke affair is true." Goebbels was thunderstruck. "I shall take a long time to get over it," he wrote in his diary.[174]

Had Hanfstaengl's complaints about Hitler stemmed from self-pity alone, he would probably have been left to his lamentations. But most of what he had said was true, and related to matters that not only required discretion but were actually taboo. To that extent, Hertha Frey's fears were absolutely justified, though not in the way she imagined. "To talk in so vile a way about the Führer and others," she wrote back, "cannot possibly be in the Führer's interest and is dangerous as well." She could not share Wiedemann's conciliatory view that Hanfstaengl had merely made some "intemperate remarks." "After all, the good man is also telling people at great length that he 'was one of the Führer's oldest and best friends, [but that] the latter is now cold-shouldering him and, alas, being thoroughly ungrateful.'"[175] In other words, Hanfstaengl was not only expatiating on subjects which, in the Third Reich, no one could discuss with impunity; he was doing so in his role as an intimate friend of Hitler.

It is hard to gauge whether Hanfstaengl had lost control of himself because of the setbacks he had sustained, or whether he was deliberately taking the bull by the horns. Whatever the truth, he was certainly fighting with his back to the wall. At stake was his whole design for living, the dream of a failed intellectual who had built his career entirely on the swastika, that "sacred symbol of a new Germany,"[176] and, of course, on his personal relationship with Hitler.

But Hitler, too, had to take some action. His foreign press chief was too well known to be simply eliminated. On the other hand, he could not sit back and watch Hanfstaengl's activities in idleness. There was no knowing what else his erstwhile friend might get up to. For a start, Hitler mobilized the cuckolded Dr. Goebbels. The propaganda minister not only cut off Hanfstaengl's source of funds but set the public prosecutor on him. "Hanfstaengl will now be interrogated. A stop put to his game," he venomously noted on August 16, 1936, and five days later he reported: "Hanfstaengl totally broken."[177] And when Helene Hanfstaengl separated from her husband around this time, Hitler is said to have exclaimed: "Well, I'll have to send her a telegram right away and wish her luck."[178] From now on, Hanfstaengl suspected that his life was in danger. This became clear in February 1937, if not before, when Hitler taught him a cruel lesson.

On the eve of Hanfstaengl's fiftieth birthday he was ordered to attend a meeting with German press representatives in Spain, where the civil war was raging. After his plane had taken off from Berlin, however, Hanfstaengl was informed of the "true" purpose of his mission: he was to bail out over the "Red troops" and land behind the lines by parachute. Mortally afraid of an attempt on his life, he managed to escape during an intermediate stop in Switzerland.[179] Although he had been contemplating the possibility of escape since the summer of 1936, he was ultimately rather reluctant to seize his chance. Nevertheless, he was now free to make use of the means whereby he hoped to regain a position of influence in Nazi Germany. What followed was a two-and-a-half-year struggle—a stubborn tug of war.

A few days after Hanfstaengl's escape became known, the startled Nazi leaders tried to lure the defector back to Germany: first Goebbels, who offered him "the bait of a large fee for film music;"[180] and soon afterward Göring, with a letter that his aide Karl Bodenschatz delivered to Zurich in person. This stated that the suicide mission on which he had been sent served him right for his incautious remarks, but that if he now returned to Germany he would be a free man.[181] However, when Hanfstaengl was informed by Göring's envoy that a refusal of this offer would have unpleasant consequences, he promptly launched a counterattack. He was, he said, in possession of secret documents about the Nazi elite dating back to 1922—documents whose publication would compromise the political leadership of the Third Reich. Several copies of them were in safe hands and would, if necessary, be handed to the international press.[182] Hitler, Göring and Goebbels were puzzled and worried: "Let's hope he doesn't emigrate."[183] But they failed to entrap Hanfstaengl with even more generous offers, for instance, the full restoration of his professional and financial position. On the contrary, this told him that he really did possess an extremely effective means of pressure.

In April 1937 Hanfstaengl moved to London, where, as Goebbels noted with great dismay, he threatened to publish "disclosures." "If he spills the beans, it'll put all the other emigrés in the shade." This explains the Nazi leaders' eagerness to change his mind and persuade him to return. "If we get him, we'll have to detain him in short order. And never let him out again." He, Goebbels, had always known the "swine" for what he was; he was "capable of anything."[184] The Gestapo proceeded to confiscate Hanfstaengl's personal belongings, but friends of his had already removed certain items and were able to send them to him.[185] He was also threatened with a charge of high treason, the inquiry being headed by Heydrich in person.[186] In mid-May, however, Bodenschatz brought Hanfstaengl a more conciliatory message from Göring inviting him to Berlin for talks and granting him safe-conduct. An envoy of the so-called liaison staff also turned up in London and implored Hanfstaengl not to be a "bastard." Hanfstaengl retorted that the occupants of the Reich Chancellery were "unclean," Hitler included. A "queer and blackmailer"—meaning Lüdecke, of course—carried more weight than he did, and that was an ample demonstration of the spirit that prevailed there.[187]

After three months, therefore, the respective positions of Hanfstaengl and the Reich Chancellery had crystallized. Hanfstaengl, who remained hipped on Lüdecke, wanted Hitler to issue a public repudiation of the man and then formally apologize to him. Confronting him were the political heads of the Nazi regime, Hitler, Goebbels and Göring, who were mortally afraid of his potential "disclosures." They had to do everything possible to prevent their former foreign press chief from carrying out his threat and, at the same time, save face.

When Lüdecke's book *I Knew Hitler* appeared in November 1937, Hanfstaengl felt completely vindicated. Although he perceived that the author had "not yet fired all his ammunition,"[188] and must also have realized that his arch rival had stolen a march on him once more, he seized on Lüdecke's revelations as a stick with which to beat the Third Reich's Party and government leaders. He had, he said, been the only National Socialist prepared to risk his position in order to rid Hitler's circle of this "bisexual swine" who had now, in addition, turned out to be a confederate of Röhm.[189] Unless he was rehabilitated forthwith, he threatened to publish his Lüdecke file of 1934. When Hitler showed himself unimpressed, Hanfstaengl sent no less than forty-five prominent Nazis a brief digest, entitled "I knew Lüdecke," of what he considered to be the most telling passages in Lüdecke's book. But he was aiming less at the author himself than at "those who have for years misjudged, maligned, fought, and finally, out of 'loyalty' to Lüdecke, deprived me of my position and sent me into exile." There was now only one thing for them to do: "to apologize to me one and all."[190]

To the Nazi leaders, and to Hitler in particular, his lachrymose tone sounded like the barking of a dog that wouldn't bite. "Hanfstaengl would like to return to Germany," Goebbels noted with relief in January 1938. "He hasn't made any move against us to date."[191] Soon afterward, when Hanfstaengl sought support for his request to Hitler from "Dear Herr Himmler," of all people, the latter recorded the dictator's response: "Hanfstaengl to stay where he is. Führer uninterested."[192] By the end of March 1938, the very most Hanfstaengl could expect from the Third Reich was permission to return with impunity, but with his demands for "satisfaction" unfulfilled and "only with the intention of leading a quiet life devoid of any political role."[193] This was a shattering outcome to a yearlong, nerve-racking contest. Even now, however, Hanfstaengl had still not played his best trump card, his knowledge of Hitler's homosexuality, whether because of scruples, fear of the consequences or simply lack of opportunity.

In April 1938 he was presented with such an opportunity by a brief article in *The New Republic*, and he unhesitatingly exploited it with the aid of every trick in the blackmailer's book. The article had stated that "Dr. Hanfstaengl was famous as Hitler's boyfriend until he became the victim of a palace intrigue."[194] The attribution "Hitler's boyfriend" was a welcome excuse to launch the libel action he had wanted to initiate three years earlier because of the designation "Hitler's Putzy." He now decided to resume the offensive, confident that he would hit the German dictator in a sensitive spot.

Hanfstaengl employed various channels in staging his coup. He began by trying to convince the new German ambassador in London, Herbert von Dirksen, that the sentence in question was a "shocking slur on the Führer's character," and that it was probably only the start of a large-scale smear campaign by interested parties.[195] A few weeks later he wrote in quite similar terms to his elderly mother, hoping to persuade her to raise the matter with Göring. The article, he said, was a grave challenge not only to himself but also to Hitler, because it "injured" his "reputation as a man." If the German government abandoned him in his fight to restore his reputation, he would be compelled to take legal proceedings, and that would inevitably cause a scandal of vast dimensions: "Homosexuality in connection with A.H. in the courtroom! My hair stands on end when I think of the press. But what can I do?"[196] His mother, who at once spotted the disingenuous nature of his request, was horrified. A court case such as he proposed could only have the direst consequences for all concerned: "I can't understand your action."[197]

Two days later Göring also sent him a letter. As a friend, he wrote, he could only urge him to return to Germany at once. Hanfstaengl

could live there as unscathed as himself, he gave him his word as a
Reich marshal. He should simply ignore the said article; Hitler's reputation was absolute proof against such "hacks." "I believe I've no
need to remind you that you yourself once made notes about the
Führer of a less than tasteful kind, and that the Führer dissociated
himself from you on that account." Göring's letter concluded with the
following entreaty "Stop this nonsense! . . . Above all, give up this
crazy litigation mania!"[198]

But this time Hanfstaengl stood firm and refused to be intimidated.
His reply to Göring dated September 9, 1938, which he signed with a
"Heil Hitler," stressed his loyalty to the "Führer" and offered to continue faithfully serving the National Socialist cause, but only if Hitler
wrote him a personal letter of apology asking him to return to Germany and offering him an attractive post. If his legitimate claims were
not met, he would remain abroad and conduct a libel action.[199] Four
weeks later, when the German embassy received a check for him in the
sum of RM 20,000, together with a request that he return to Germany
forthwith, Hanfstaengl knew that he had struck the right note and hit
the right nerve. He rejected the bribe and, on November 17, 1938, got
his attorneys to file suit against the publishers of *The New Republic.*
The next day he sanctimoniously wrote to Göring and Ribbentrop
that "the Führer's reputation and private life" would now be the subject of court proceedings, and inquired whether Berlin had any specific instructions on how he should conduct himself.[200]

He now received word, by roundabout routes, that if he returned to
Germany he would be granted a generous lifetime pension. This
emboldened him to disconcert Hitler further by approaching him
directly. Hanfstaengl's letter, of which only a draft is known, warned
him of an "evil attack" that "the opposition" evidently intended to
launch with the aid of incriminating evidence obtained from his former circle of friends. One of the main points at issue was the question
of why he, Hanfstaengl, had been compelled to leave the Reich Chan-

cellery. The Jewish press would be bound to seize on this trial and exploit it in order to mount a relentless campaign of agitation against Hitler. He himself would naturally do all in his power, as he had until now, to protect Hitler's reputation from being "besmirched."[201]

On December 2, 1938, Hanfstaengl received a response to his provocative letter via Bodenschatz, Göring's right-hand man. Bodenschatz informed him that his boss saw nothing offensive in the term "boyfriend," still less any sexual imputation. It was simply a translation of the German word "Jugendfreund," so why the court case? Hanfstaengl's reply, dated December 14, called a spade a spade at last: the court would have to decide whether the opposition could submit genuine proof of the libelous insinuation that he and Hitler had had criminal relations as defined by Paragraph 175 of the penal code. Since that evidence could not be adduced, the opposition would be bound to try an indirect tack, namely, by citing Hitler's homosexual comrades in arms from earlier times (Röhm, Heines, etc.) or those of his current associates whose morals were questionable. His, Hanfstaengl's, task would be to defend Hitler's reputation against such attacks. To withdraw the suit would be tantamount to admitting "that the Führer is guilty of the crime of homosexuality."[202]

This was strong stuff indeed. No member of Hitler's entourage had ever dared to associate the "Führer" with Paragraph 175! Anyone who did so had to feel safe from the clutches of the regime and very sure of his ground. But for Hitler's awareness that Hanfstaengl had some live ammunition for use in an emergency, his letters would have been dismissed as a mere joke, the figment of a deranged imagination. Instead, they became the subject of secret diplomacy at the highest level and involved almost the whole of the Nazi leadership. In short, they were seen as a genuine threat. Unsurprisingly, rumors now arose that Hanfstaengl was blackmailing the German government and being silenced with hush money.[203]

By the end of 1938, Hanfstaengl's blackmail had achieved results.

A cordial letter from Winifred Wagner informed him that she had obtained Hitler's promise that, if he returned to Germany, he would be not only unharmed but permitted to pursue any form of career he chose.[204] But that was not good enough for Hanfstaengl, who wanted a guarantee from Hitler himself. Early in February 1939, therefore, he sent Hitler a handwritten letter: "As you well know, I was some time ago accused of homosexual relations with you. Being unwilling to swallow this insult, I have filed suit. The hearing has been scheduled for mid March. Two days have been set aside for the hearing itself." In court he would have to provide information "about my former and present relations with you. If, at the forthcoming trial, I am to defend my reputation, and, thus, yours, I must at least know whether I am to appear before the court as an exile disavowed by you, or as a National Socialist whose reputation and position have been fully restored. If I do not, by the beginning of March, receive your clear instructions on the subject, together with complete rehabilitation, I shall regretfully have to conclude that you are still unwilling to do me justice. But I should further have to conclude that you, Herr Hitler, are totally indifferent, not only to the affection and loyalty I have shown you for years, but also to my reputation and future. Should that prove to be your attitude, I shall know what I must do."[205]

This letter, too, was a masterpiece of the blackmailer's art, and was promptly perceived as such by all concerned. At the instigation of Göring, who could just as well have made it disappear, it was forwarded to the head of the Reich Chancellery. The latter did not pass it on to Hitler until the end of February, so Hanfstaengl followed it up with another letter, dated February 27, whose text has not, unfortunately, survived. Nevertheless, in February and March 1939 Hanfstaengl's threat galvanized the regime's most powerful men: Hitler, Himmler and Göring and their sidekicks Bormann, Heydrich and Bodenschatz, the last of whom continued to act as an intermediary. The concessions eventually made to Hanfstaengl "on the Führer's behalf" were substantial: reimbursement of all expenses occasioned by his involuntary exile, reappointment to a suitable post in the Third Reich and no sanctions.[206] To Hanfstaengl, the end seemed in sight. The only remaining prerequisite for his return was, in his own words, "a letter of rehabilitation in the Führer's own hand."[207] But Hitler decided to await the court case. Knowing Hanfstaengl as he did, he probably assumed that he would, after all, shrink from making any sensational disclosures. And he was right.

The hearing on May 18 and 19, 1939, went badly for Hanfstaengl. Although the defendants regretted that the relevant passage in the article might be construed as derogatory, it did not constitute a sexual denunciation or a slur on Hitler's private life. Hanfstaengl's claim for damages was rejected on the ground that no offense had been committed, and costs were awarded against him.[208] He had balked at taking the final, crucial step. The predicted press sensation came to nothing. It was now clear to those in the know that his threats were ineffective. Over five weeks went by, during which time he wrote further letters to Hitler's associates, before Hanfstaengl grasped this fact.

Realizing that he had overreached himself, he concluded his desperate attempts to woo Hitler with a letter that harked back to the beginning of their relationship: "You know me, Herr Hitler, and you know as well as I do what led me to you in 1922–1923: that was when I devoted myself to you, and you alone, as being the Elect. No one else has the right to lay a claim to my loyalty and obedience. For as long as you live, I shall listen to your voice alone, and to no other. Only you can recall me. I wrote from the bottom of my heart; do the same. This I ask of you."[209]

That Hitler was still accessible to a personal plea of this nature is documented by a letter from Bormann to Karl Wolff, Himmler's aide, in which he mentions that Hitler "intended to write briefly to Hanfstaengl."[210] This was only a fit of sentimentality, however, because

Hanfstaengl never received a reply. But in September 1939, just after he had plunged Europe into war, Hitler reverted to the subject: "The Führer asks that the foreign mission representing us in London be requested to get in touch with Hanfstaengl at once and prevail on him to return to Germany. Foreign currency, also for the settlement of debts there, is to be made available forthwith.[211] It was too late. The British interned Hanfstaengl a few days after war broke out and later deported him to Canada. Later still, in the summer of 1942, he really did divulge a good deal of what he knew about Hitler—to U.S. intelligence.

Epilogue

FROM THE MID-1930s on, Hitler seems to have fulfilled his homo-sexuality only in very sublimated forms. At least, we know of no sources that would permit us to precisely reconstruct his double life for that period as we can for the three preceding decades.

It has been said of Albert Speer that he was Hitler's "unhappy love," but the facts underlying that form of words are far from trans-parent.[1] True, there are contemporary observers who suggest that the relationship between Hitler and his chief architect was more than just perfervid. To the author Günther Weisenborn, who watched them together in the Münchener Künstlerhaus in the summer of 1939, Speer seemed a kind of "object of admiration, a beloved" of Hitler. The dictator had been manifestly fond of him, wrote Weisenborn, and treated him unlike his other paladins.[2]

But the historian Joachim Fest, who is probably better informed about Speer's life than anyone, warns us against jumping to exaggerated conclusions. "Once, when I spoke to him [Speer] on the subject of homoerotic relations with Hitler, his response was highly indignant. He probably suspected that I was implying a homosexual relationship. That, of course, was certainly not the case. But I don't think he ever rendered an account of the subject to himself. Nor is there the slightest indication in his memoirs that he . . . recognized this aspect of their mutual relations.[3] Fest speaks of an "indubitably homoerotic male friendship" in which Speer was the more dominant and stronger partner and Hitler the more dependent and weaker, but he insists that Hitler's favorite "did not, strangely enough, perceive the erotic elements involved in their relationship."[4] After his barbarous settling of scores with Röhm, Hitler may really have disciplined himself when it came to revealing his sexual orientation. Then again, Speer may have simply found the historical truth too embarrassing. We do not know, and must limit ourselves to conjecturing how and to what extent the Hitler-Speer relationship bore a homoerotic imprint.

One thing is certain, however: for Hitler, the highly emotional nature of their friendship paid off politically until the very end. As armaments minister, Speer substantially helped to delay the total and inevitable downfall of the Third Reich.[5] Even when he clashed with the dictator over the so-called Nero Order, which directed retreating German troops to implement a scorched earth policy on German soil, Hitler talked him around. In general, too, Speer backed Hitler's futile, criminal, manic insistence on holding out to the last. No rift ever developed between them. On the contrary, at their penultimate meeting on March 19, 1945, Hitler handed Speer a photographic memento that testified to his "everlasting friendship." Furthermore, a few days before Hitler committed suicide, Speer made his way—for "romantic" reasons, as he himself put it—to the Führer's bunker in central Berlin, which was already in the thick of the fighting, to assure the vanquished tyrant of his personal loyalty. This gesture, a bizarre leavetaking compounded of submission and affection, is said to have moved Hitler to tears.[6]

This highlight would terminate our account, but for Eva Braun. As stated earlier, Eva Braun seems to have understood the role she was playing in Hitler's life better than anyone with the exception of Hitler himself. Yet it is doubtful whether Hitler attached much importance to their liaison until Eva Braun's first attempted suicide in 1932. And even thereafter, when he not only presented her with a Munich villa but paid her more attention, he had to fend off further demands from his hopeful twenty-year-old "girlfriend" by falling back, yet again, on high-flown allusions to his historic mission.

It was not until 1936, when he granted Eva Braun a permanent place in his "bourgeois" private life at the Berghof, that his "Tschapperl" seems to have accepted her lot. This is at least hinted at by conversations she had with Hitler's interpreter Eugen Dollmann. "'He's a saint,' she told me. 'Even the thought of physical contact with me would be, to him, a contamination of his mission.'" She said that Hitler had often explained to her that "Germany was his only love, and that to forget this, even for a moment, would destroy the mystical energy of his mission." By 1938, if not before, she must have grasped the nature of the stage production she was required for. That she accepted the role of "mistress" and performed it extremely well is an indication of her inability to lead a self-determined existence.

And Hitler? His relationship with Eva Braun was the belated fulfillment of a long cherished idea: platonic cohabitation. This enabled him to approximate a little more to "normalcy": he now had a "girlfriend" who listened to and looked after him, but one who remained as discreet and self-effacing as his requirements dictated. Banal and trivial as it may sound, Eva afforded him many a respite from his public life. But the supposition that Hitler was never infatuated with Eva is confirmed by many other contemporary observers,[7] and her attempts to give the outside world a different impression do not invalidate it. Anything else would have not only compromised Hitler but dealt an even greater blow to Eva's womanly self-esteem than the reality of her life already did.

It is probable, therefore, that Hans-Severus Ziegler aptly described the relationship when he spoke of Hitler's "almost paternally friendly manner" toward Eva Braun. "Eva Braun," wrote Ziegler, "was, as men of a chivalrous, comradely disposition tend to put it, 'a decent fellow' whom everyone liked."[8] Just a female "fellow," nothing more, but that was the crucial point. She had to be close at hand when needed, just as Geli Raubal had been—in fact, she probably reminded Hitler vividly of his late niece. Common to both women were their youthful lightheartedness and love of sports, and both were said to have been "tomboys." One of Eva's childhood friends described her as "a boy *manqué*." She never flirted with youngsters, was very fond of dressing up and liked to play male roles.[9] She also tried hard, no doubt, to copy Geli in matters such as hairstyle and dress.

Eva Braun became a genuine partner of Hitler: they both cultivated the illusion of a self-denying love affair. By 1945, of course, Hitler's mission had failed disastrously, yet he managed even then to wring some meaning out of their relationship. He wanted the illusion he had created to endure after his death, so the partnership that had lasted over a decade was exalted for posterity's benefit into a "genuine" marriage, albeit one that was never consummated. These belated nuptials were not only Eva Braun's reward for loyal service to the Hitler myth but an important contribution to the same: by means of this last, brilliant lie, the "Führer"-turned-husband swathed himself in an aura of normalcy. Or, in the words of Hans Blüher: "His marriage *in extremis* must have been a mechanical tribute to bourgeois respectability; to us it seems to be the end result of the tragicomedy he enacted before the world."[10]

Until he came to power, Hitler's life was governed primarily by persecution mania. Even in 1924 he believed that "my political opponents are now, with loving care, scrutinizing my life, down to and including my . . . boyhood." They were "robber knights" who, in an "infamous Jewish manner . . . delve into the most secret family affairs and do not rest until [their] truffle-hunters' instinct unearths some pathetic incident, which is then designed to finish off their luckless victim."[11] Once he had prevailed over the "slanderers" among his political opponents in 1933, and over the blackmailers in his own camp in 1934, his persecution mania became transmuted into megalomania. From then on he strove feverishly to carry out his plans for world conquest and racial extermination. Meantime, his private life not only receded from view but was more effectively hidden than ever before. By 1936 the protective screen around it was almost impenetrable. Thereafter, discounting attempts at blackmail like those of Lüdecke and Hanfstaengl, the dictator could feel relatively secure.

It was the Third Reich's imminent collapse in the spring of 1945 that once more confronted Hitler with his life's central problem: the need for dissimulation and camouflage. Committing suicide and ordering his body to be burned were not enough. Only the systematic destruction of his personal papers and the documents he had confiscated, his marriage to Eva Braun, his political testament and, above all, the immense devastation for which he was responsible, enabled him to obliterate the traces of his private person more thoroughly than any ruler before him. He had escaped into history—and then returned as a warning to the world. But this must not be the last word: if we can still wrest secrets from the story of Hitler's life, it behooves us to do so.

Postscript:
On The History of a Taboo

THE RELUCTANCE to discuss or explore the subject of Hitler's homosexuality is a phenomenon that has persisted from the immediately
postwar period to the present day.

In 1949 Eugen Dollmann's memoirs appeared in Italy under the
somewhat sensational title *Roma Nazista*.[1] It was not the scholarly
reputation of a trained historian that prompted the publisher to bring
them out, but the inside information available to one of the Third
Reich's most influential representatives in Rome between 1938 and
1945. Dolmann was not only Himmler's personal representative but a
kind of confidential interpreter of Hitler, notably during his talks with
Mussolini. He knew a great deal and was prepared to divulge some of
it for the benefit of posterity. That made his book a sensational success—but only in Italy.

The reviewer of the *Corriere della Sera* pronounced Dollmann "a
genuine and authentic *éminence grise*." His memoirs were "valuable

testimony," and their great advantage was that they described "the outward and inward nature of well-known personalities" by means of "razor-sharp disclosures and comments that bear witness to a profound study of psychology."[2] Dollmann refers to Hitler's homosexuality in his very first chapter.[3] Being one of the few people who avowedly "knew the most delicate secret in Hitler's life," he felt it his duty to "disclose the basic facts." But he promptly added a reservation: "It could not be my task to shed light on the enormity of the National Socialist dictator's aberrations during the first half of his life. . . . If at all, this would be the task of quite different initiates into the Führer's secrets."[4] The surviving "initiates," if they were acquainted with Dollmann's book at all, probably thought his summons unreasonable and felt strengthened in their resolve to disavow their secret knowledge of Hitler. Only Hans Blüher, until 1934 an influential sexual theorist and apologist for homoeroticism, had the courage to address the homosexual context of Hitler's career in 1949.[5]

In the field of literature it was Jean Genet who tackled the theme in his novel *Pompes funèbres*, published in 1947,[6] which bluntly portrayed Hitler as a "prude." His deliberately provocative approach was an appeal for merciless candor (or so, at least, it seemed to Nicolaus Sombart, who was living in Paris at the time.)[7] The same idea underlay Fritz von Unruh's novel *Der nie verlor*, which appeared in 1947.[8] His likewise highly sexualized portrait of Hitler was based on personal experience, however, not on fictional elements alone. Unruh had been a longtime member of the circle centered on the Hohenzollern princes Oskar and August Wilhelm, so he knew what he was talking about.[9] But, although the author's postscript expressly asked that the voice he had given the dictator be heard as a "memento," his literary reconstruction of the "real" Hitler aroused no public controversy.[10] The only comments Unruh attracted were derisive.

This was all symptomatic. Dollmann's book has never been published in German, and the author, who did not die until 1980, was never questioned although his account could, and should, have given a fillip to further research. But the Germans were in denial about the politics of the past, and the "Führer" himself was the last person they wanted to hear about. That was why Erich Ebermayer, who resurrected the subject of Hitler's private life by publishing his diary in 1959, aroused equally little debate.[11]

Many people in postwar Germany must have found it intolerable to think that they had run after someone who was not only a criminal but—in the moral perception of the Adenauer era—a "pervert" as well. To have followed Hitler struck them as unforgivable enough, but this would have compounded their shame with a stigma that threatened to seal their disgrace for all time. To that extent, not-wanting-to-know was an integral part of the postwar Germans' national psyche: a collective refusal to permit any further disruptions of their identity. The Germans found in Hitler's curriculum vitae "only" what they *wanted* to find: his political and ideological motives and, at most, one or another psychopathological reason for his rise and his catastrophic downfall. It was consistent with this that historians of the time attached little importance to the "personal" aspect of historical developments. Much has changed since then, it is true, but anyone who imagines that this applies to the subject of "Hitler's homosexuality" is mistaken. Dollmann, Ebermayer and the rest may lie far in the past, but their evidence is hugely topical.

Critical analysis of Hitler has been hampered by the perpetuation of this postwar taboo. As I said at the beginning of this book, understanding Hitler's sexual orientation does not supply *the* key to his career, but a knowledge of it gives scope for new interpretations—interpretations that in no way mitigate Hitler's crimes and Hitler's guilt or present his policies in a better light, but which can explain aspects of them more precisely. For the personal can be highly political; of that there can surely be no better proof than the story of Hitler's life.

Notes

TRANSLATOR'S NOTE: *Where the Notes relate to English-language editions of works originally in German, many citations from them in the text have been translated afresh.*

ABBREVIATIONS

BAB — Bundesarchiv Berlin
BAB-DH — Bundesarchiv Zwischenarchiv Dahlwitz-Hoppegarten
BAK — Bundesarchiv Koblenz
BDC — Berlin Document Center
BSB — Bayerische Staatsbibliothek
DAF — Deutsche Arbeitsfront
DLA — Deutsches Literaturarchiv
GstA PK — Geheimes Staatsarchiv Preußischer Kulturbesitz
HstA — (Bayerisches) Hauptstaatsarchiv
IfZ — Institut für Zeitgeschichte
NL — Nachlaß
OÖLA Linz — Oberösterreichisches Landesarchiv Linz
StA — Staatsarchiv
StaBi — Staatsbibliothek
VfZ — Vierteljahreshefte für Zeitgeschichte
PAA — Politisches Archiv des Auswärtigen Amtes

INTRODUCTION

1. Joachim Fest, *Hitler. Eine Biographie* (Munich, 2000), 13.
2. *Frankfurter Allgemeine Zeitung*, October 1, 1998.

3. Ibid.

4. Quoted from Hans-Ulrich Wehler in the *Frankfurter Allgemeine Zeitung*, November 23, 1995.

5. See Guido Knopp, *Hitler. Eine Bilanz* (Munich, 1997), 9.

6. John Lukacs, *The Hitler of History* (New York, 1997), 51.

7. Ron Rosenbaum, *Explaining Hitler. The Search for the Origins of his Evil* (New York, 1998), 7.

8. Robert Goldmann recently summarized this credo thus: "To 'rationally explain' the great crime of the 1930s and 1940s . . . would cause us to violate the memory of and degrade history. It will remain impossible to understand, despite all attempts at finding an explanation. And it is exactly this overwhelming impossibility to understand which prevents new disaster." *Frankfurter Allgemeine Zeitung*, July 31, 2000.

9. Alan Bullock, *Hitler. A Study in Tyranny* (London, 1952).

10. Ibid., 324.

11. Ibid., 9.

12. Alan Bullock, *Hitler and Stalin* (New York, 1991), 139ff., 341.

13. Ibid., 937ff.

14. Rosenbaum, *Explaining Hitler,* 89.

15. Bullock, *Hitler and Stalin. Parallel Lives,* 696f.

16. Joachim Fest, *Hitler. Eine Biographie* (Munich, 2000, 3rd printing of the new edition, 1995), 19. See also ibid., the second chapter of Book Six (724–769), which explicitly opens up the "view of an unperson."

17. Ibid., 5 and 29.

18. Ibid., 67.

19. Ibid., 69.

20. Ibid., 467.

21. Ibid., 13.

22. Rosenbaum, *Explaining Hitler,* 135ff.

23. Douglas M. Kelley, *Twenty-Two Cells in Nuremberg. A Psychiatrist Examines the Nazi-Criminals* (New York, 1972), 235f.

24. Bela Grunberger/Pierre Dessuant, *Narzißmus, Christentum und Antisemitismus* (Stuttgart, 2000), 451ff.

25. Rosenbaum, *Explaining Hitler,* 76.

26. As an example of this attempt, I am using two exemplary essays: Hans Mommsen, "Adolf Hitler in der Sicht von Gefolgsleuten und Zeitgenossen. Anmerkungen zur Hitlerismus-Debatte," in: Mommsen, *Von Weimar nach Auschwitz. Zur Geschichte Deutschlands in der Weltkriegsepoche* (Stuttgart, 1999), 73–91 (originally in: *Jahrbuch des Wissenschaftskollegs zu Berlin 1983/84* [Berlin, 1985], 229–246).

Mommsen, "Hitlers Stellung im nationalsozialistischen Herrschaftssystem," in: Mommsen, *Von Weimar nach Auschwitz,* 214–247 (originally
in: Gerhard Hirschfeld/Lothar Kettenacker, *Der "Führerstaat": Mythos
und Realität. Studien zur Struktur und Politik des Dritten Reiches*
[Stuttgart, 1981], 43–72).

27. Mommsen, *Hitlers Stellung im nationalsozialistischen Herrschaftssystem,*
246.

28. Ian Kershaw, *Hitler,* Vol. I: 1889–1936. Hubris. 1st American ed. (New
York, 1999); Kershaw, *Hitler*, Vol. II: 1936–1945. Nemesis. 1st American ed. (New York, 2000).

29. Ibid., xxv.

30. Ibid., xxvi.

31. *Frankfurter Allgemeine Zeitung,* October 1, 1998.

32. Interview in *Der Spiegel,* No. 34/2000, 63.

33. Klaus Hildebrand, "Nichts Neues über Hitler. Ian Kershaws zünftige
Biographie über den deutschen Diktator." im: *Historische Zeitschrift* 270
(2000), 389–397.

34. Paul Matussek/Peter Matussek/Jan Marbach, *Hitler. Karriere eines
Wahns* (Munich, 2000), see especially 25ff.

35. Ibid., 9.

36. Ludolf Herbst, "Der Fall Hitler—Inszenierungskunst und Charismapolitik." im: Wilfried Nippel (Ed.), *Virtuosen der Macht* (Munich, 2000),
172ff.

37. Kershaw, *Hitler,* Vol. I, xxv.

38. October 7, 1998.

39. December 6, 1998.

40. October 29, 1998.

41. October 10/11, 1998.

42. This was the fitting observation of the interviewers (*Frankfurter Allgemeine Zeitung,* October 1, 1998).

43. Manfred Koch-Hillebrecht failed in this with his book *Homo Hitler*
(Munich, 1999)—not to mention the completely exaggerated histori-
copolitical conclusions he feels he can draw from his findings.

44. In this regard and with regard to the following, see Bernd-Ulrich
Hergemöller's introduction to the manual he edited, *Mann für Mann.
Biographisches Lexikon zur Geschichte von Freundesliebe und mann-
männlicher Sexualität im deutschen Sprachraum* (Hamburg, 1998), 35ff.

45. See Helmut Blazek, *Rosa Zeiten für Rosa Liebe. Geschichte der Homosexualität* (Frankfurt a.M., 1996).

46. Even with regard to nonprivate matters, such as Hitler's activities in gov-

ernment, there is a lack of authentic sources. See Martin Moll's introduction to the edition he edited *"Führer-Erlasse" 1939–1945* (Stuttgart, 1997), 9ff.

47. See Henry Picker, *Hitlers Tischgespräche im Führerhauptquartier* (Wiesbaden, 1983), 117f.

48. Ernst Hanfstaengl, *Zwischen Weißem und Braunem Haus. Memoiren eines politischen Außenseiters* (Munich, 1970), 63.

49. See also Ernst Deuerlein (Ed.), *Der Hitler-Putsch* (Stuttgart, 1962), 117ff.; as well as Anton Joachimsthaler, *Hitlers Weg begann in München 1913–1923* (Munich, 2000), 34f. and 361; Harry Slapnicka, *Hitler und Oberösterreich* (Grünbach, 1998), 102ff.; "Der letzte Befehl" (manuscript), in: *IfZ Munich, ED 203* (Schaub), Vol. 2.

50. Rosenbaum, *Explaining Hitler*, 32.

51. Albert Speer, *"Alles, was ich weiß." Aus unbekannten Geheimdienstprotokollen vom Sommer 1945*, Ulrich Schlie (Ed.) (Munich, 1999), 39 and 49.

CHAPTER 1

1. For Hitler's youth, see as most relevant: *Franz Jetzinger, Hitlers Jugend. Phantasien, Lügen—und die Wahrheit* (Vienna, 1956); Bradley F. Smith, *Adolf Hitler. His Family, Childhood and Youth* (Stanford, 1967); Anton Joachimsthaler, *Hitlers Weg begann in München 1913–1923* (Munich, 2000); Brigitte Hamann, *Hitlers Wien. Lehrjahre eines Diktators* (Munich/Zurich, 1997).

2. The account given here follows the information presented by Hamann and Joachimsthaler, who base themselves on the relevant "hard" sources.

3. Draft Board findings dated February 5, 1914, quoted from Jetzinger, *Hitlers Jugend*, 265.

4. For Hitler's "flight from military service," see also ibid., 253–272.

5. See also Joachimsthaler, *Hitlers Weg*, 81, as well as a copy of the registration, ibid., 20.

6. See also ibid., 105ff.

7. In this context, the empirical work performed by sexologist Magnus Hirschfeld proves to be extremely useful. The scientific study entitled "Die Homosexualität des Mannes und des Weibes" in particular, published in 1914, throws light on the situation of homosexuals at the beginning of the 20th century and gives an informative insight into the sociocultural environment; the following is taken from: Magnus Hirschfeld, *Die Homosexualität des Mannes und des Weibes* (Berlin, 1920, 2nd, unchanged edition).

8. Postcard written by Kubizek to Jetzinger on June 11, 1949, in: OÖLA Linz, Zl. 2489/36-1956 (Jetzinger-Materialien), No. 64.

9. Unless otherwise indicated, the short biography follows the information provided by Kubizek in the epilogue of his book: *Adolf Hitler. Mein Jugendfreund* (Graz/Göttingen, 1953).

10. See also Kubizek's "Education and Career," enclosed with a letter to Jetzinger dated August 16, 1949, in: OÖLA Linz, Zl. 2489/36-1956, No. 64. Kubizek states in his book that he graduated in October 1912 (319).

11. This information was received in writing from the city archives in Eferding on July 17, 2000. Hamann himself gives the date of his wedding as August 1 (78). Nothing could be found on Kubizek's wife or his married life.

12. Kubizek's "Education and Career," enclosed with a letter to Jetzinger dated August 16, 1949, in: OÖLA Linz, Zl. 2489/36-1956, No. 64.

13. Examination before the District Court in Eferding on July 4, 1938, in: OÖLA Linz, Safe, File Hitler-Kubicek (emphasis made by the original author).

14. Kubizek, *Jugendfreund*, 322ff.

15. Hitler to Kubizek on August 4, 1933, printed ibid., next to 16.

16. See ibid., 333.

17. Information given orally by the OÖLA Linz on June 28, 2000.

18. See Kubizek, *Jugendfreund*, 335.

19. See letter by Hitler's Adjutant Albert Bormann to Kubizek dated April 29, 1938, in: OÖLA Linz, Zl. 2489/36-1956, No. 60. Kubizek apparently had congratulated Hitler on his forty-ninth birthday.

20. Kubizek, *Jugendfreund*, 336.

21. See BAB, BDC Franz Neuburger.

22. "Declaration of Honor" by Franz Neuburger on October 6, 1938, in: OÖLA Linz, Film No. 349, issued by the state government, Section GR 879.

23. See ibid.

24. Examination on July 4, 1938, in: OÖLA Linz, Safe, File Hitler-Kubicek.

25. Kubizek to Hitler on July 21, 1939, in: BAB, NS 10/453; printed by Beatrice Heiber/Helmut Heiber (Eds.), *Die Rückseite des Hakenkreuzes. Absonderliches aus den Akten des Dritten Reiches* (Munich, 1993), 72f.

26. See Kubizek, *Jugendfreund*, 343ff.

27. See BAB, BDC August Kubizek. Kubizek himself claims he had not joined until 1942; see Kubizek, *Jugendfreund*, 348.

28. See Hamann, *Hitlers Wien*, 80.

29. See Report of Reich Governor Oberdonau to the Reich Minister of the Interior dated May 3, 1943, in: BAB, BDC Reichskulturkammer/

Bildende Künste Gerardine Troost; here quoted from Heiber (Ed.), *Rückseite des Hakenkreuzes*, 100.

30. See Government Minister Meissner to the Reich Minister of Finance on July 5, 1943, in: BAB, R2/17752; first in Heiber (Ed.), *Rückseite des Hakenkreuzes*, 101.

31. See Joachimsthaler, *Hitlers Weg*, 326.

32. For the biography of Franz Jetzinger, see: Harry Slapnicka, *Oberösterreich. Die politische Führungsschicht 1918–1938* (Linz, 1976), 140f.; *Mühlviertler Bote*, No. 12 (March 27, 1965); as well as Jetzinger's own information given in his book.

33. See Kubizek, in a letter to Jetzinger on March 25, 1949, and Kubizek's letter to Jetzinger on August 16, 1949, in: OÖLA Linz, Zl. 2489/36-1956, No. 64.

34. Kubizek in a letter to Jetzinger on June 3, 1949, in: ibid.

35. See ibid.

36. See Rudolf Hans Bartsch, *Schwammerl. Ein Schubertroman* (Leipzig, 1912), 110ff.

37. Kubizek in a letter to Jetzinger on June 19, 1949, in: OÖLA Linz, Zl. 2489/36-1956, No. 64.

38. Kubizek in a letter to Jetzinger on December 20, 1948, in: ibid.

39. Kubizek, *Jugendfreund*, 10.

40. Ibid., 22.

41. The latest such one-sided attempt at interpreting their relationship can be found in Paul Matussek/Peter Matussek/Jan Marbach, *Hitler. Karriere eines Wahns* (Munich, 2000), 119f.

42. The above quotes were all taken from Kubizek, *Jugendfreund*, 305, 26, 180, 130, 29, 285, 183, 184, and 130.

43. August Kubizek, *Erinnerungen an die mit dem Führer gemeinsam verlebten Jünglingsjahre 1904–1908 in Linz und Wien*, Vol. 2: *Wien* (manuscript), 1943, in: OÖLA Linz, Zl. 2489/36-1956, 22. Kubizek later expressly confirms to Jetzinger: "The tragic comedy regarding the winter coat is factual." Kubizek to Jetzinger on June 19, 1949, in: ibid., No. 64.

44. Kubizek, *Jugendfreund*, 39.

45. See ibid., 38ff.

46. Ibid., 195.

47. See Hirschfeld, *Homosexualität*, 689.

48. See ibid.

49. See Oskar Panizza, "Bayreuth und die Homosexualität," in: *Die Gesellschaft* 11, 1895, 88–92.

50. The above quotes were all taken from Kubizek, *Jugendfreund*, 229, 203,

215, and 339. Other relevant passages are found on pp. 139, 305, 328, 333, 341f., and 344.

51. Kubizek, *Jünglingsjahre* (1943), 1.
52. Kubizek, *Jugendfreund*, 186.
53. Ibid., 271f.
54. See ibid., 194f.
55. See ibid., 273f.
56. Kubizek to Jetzinger in May 6, 1949, in: OÖLA Linz, Zl. 2489/36-1956, No. 64.
57. See Hirschfeld, *Homosexualität*, 104ff.
58. The above quotes were all taken from Kubizek, *Jugendfreund*, 165, 167, 13, and 169.
59. Franz Jetzinger, *Das Hitler-Buch Greiners, ein Lügengewebe zur Verunglimpfung Hitlers* (manuscript), in: OÖLA Linz, Zl. 2489/36-1956, No. 146, 19.
60. Kubizek, *Jugendfreund*, 276.
61. See Jetzinger, *Hitlers Jugend*, 143f.
62. Kubizek, *Jugendfreund*, 198.
63. See ibid., 273ff.
64. Ibid., 189f.
65. Kubizek, *Jünglingsjahre* (1943), 2f.
66. Kubizek, *Jugendfreund*, 283f.
67. See Jetzinger, *Hitlers Jugend*, 209f.
68. Kubizek, *Jugendfreund*, 199; see also 239.
69. Ibid., 287.
70. Ibid., 210f.
71. Jetzinger, *Hitlers Jugend*, 218.
72. See Reinhold Hanisch, "I Was Hitler's Buddy." Parts I–III, in: *The New Republic* (April 5, 12, and 19, 1939), here Part I, 239.
73. See Samuel Igra, *Germany's National Vice* (London, 1945), 57.
74. *Illustrierte Oesterreichische Kriminal-Zeitung*, No. 30, November 11, 1907 ("Zum Prozess Moltke-Harden").
75. For the situation in Vienna, see: Magnus Hirschfeld, "Die Homosexualität in Wien," in: *Wiener klinische Rundschau*, Vol. 15 (1901), 788–790; as well as the report of an "Austrian Source" in: Hirschfeld, *Homosexualität*, 543ff.
76. Kubizek, *Jugendfreund*, 275.
77. Stefan Zweig, *Die Welt von gestern. Erinnerungen eines Europäers* (Frankfurt a.M., 1947), 91.
78. *Illustrierte Oesterreichische Kriminal-Zeitung*, No. 17, August 12, 1907.

79. *Illustrierte Oesterreichische Kriminal-Zeitung,* No. 23, September 23, 1907.

80. Regarding these efforts, see: Hirschfeld, *Homosexualität in Wien;* Manfred Herzer, "Hirschfeld in Wien," in: *Capri. Zeitschrift für schwule Geschichte* 24, 1997, 28-38.

81. Adolf Hitler, *Mein Kampf* (Munich, 1930, 3rd Ed.), 57f.

82. See William A. Jenks, *Vienna and the Young Hitler* (New York, 1960), 129. Jenks refers to an article in the *Deutsches Volksblatt* of October 27, 1907. (The entire quote reads: "The commotion he had stirred up in the Viennese 'Jewish' press was compared to scenes in a pigsty when the swill was dumped into the trough. Harden was the pigherd 'from whose mouth flowed a broad stream of those spicy details which his rassial associates greet as the finest of tidbits.'")

83. Speech given at an evening reserved for anyone who wanted to speak, held by the NSDAP in Munich on October 18, 1920, in: Eberhard Jäckel/Axel Kuhn (Eds.), *Hitler. Sämtliche Aufzeichnungen* (Stuttgart, 1980), 248.

84. Speech given at a NSDAP meeting in Munich on February 17, 1922, in: ibid., 577.

85. John Weiss, *Ideology of Death. Why the Holocaust happened in Germany* (Chicago, 1996), 191ff.

86. Adolf Hitler, "Zehn Jahre Kampf" in: *Illustrierter Beobachter* (August 3, 1919), here quoted from Klaus A. Lankheit (ed.), *Hitler. Reden Schriften, Anordnungen,* Vol. III/2 (Munich, 1994), 337.

87. See Jenks, *Young Hitler,* 144. The clashes at the university took place in November 1907.

88. Feature article entitled "L'amour à l'allemande," in: *Der Sturm,* No. 23, August 4, 1910.

89. For greater details, see Hamann, *Hitlers Wien,* 285ff.

90. Hirschfeld, *Homosexualität,* 501f.; for the situation in the hostels for the homeless, also see 715.

91. See the graphic depiction in Emil Kläger, *Durch die Quartiere der Not und des Verbrechens* (Vienna, 1908), 76ff.; otherwise Hamann, *Hitlers Wien,* 232ff.

92. See Joachimsthaler, *Hitlers Weg,* 331.

93. See Hamann, *Hitlers Wien,* 248 and 542.

94. See Joachimsthaler, *Hitlers Weg,* 72 and 331.

95. Joachimsthaler names August 1912 as the date when he returned to his home country (331). Hanisch, however, says it happened in 1913: "Buddy," Part III, 300.

96. See Hamann, *Hitlers Wien*, 265ff.

97. See Hirschfeld, *Homosexualität*, 500.

98. Hanisch, "Buddy," Part I, 240.

99. Statement made by Karl Leidenroth on August 27, 1935, before the District Court in Vienna, in: BAB, NS 26/64. For more about the relationship of Hanisch-Leidenroth versus Hitler, see Hamann, *Hitlers Wien*, 248f.

100. See Joachimsthaler, *Hitlers Weg*, 332f.

101. Hanisch, "Buddy," Part II, 271f.

102. Ibid., 271.

103. See Hamann, *Hitlers Wien*, 245.

104. Hanisch, "Buddy," Part I, 241. Joachimsthaler, *Hitlers Weg*, 69, and Smith, *Adolf Hitler*, 138, claim that Hitler and Hanisch settled down in a hotel, but Hamann speculates that Hitler took Neumann to Waldviertel to visit his "Hanitante" (245).

105. The relationship between Hitler and Neumann didn't last long, either, for Neumann left Vienna as early as July 1910 and went to Germany. He is supposed to have tried in vain to convince his friend to accompany him; see Hanisch, "Buddy," Part II, 272.

106. However, the editorial regarding Hanisch's series of articles in *The New Republic* gives rise to the suspicion that something was odd about this death: "Some time later the public was informed, as might have been expected, that Hanisch had died in prison after a sudden illness. He had died of pleurisy, in three days, the official report said" (239).

107. See Hanisch, "Buddy," Part III, 297.

108. Hirschfeld, *Homosexualität*, 502.

109. See Hamann, *Hitlers Wien*, 232.

110. See Brünner Anonymus [anonymous inhabitant of Brno], *Muj Prítel Hitler* [My Friend Hitler], in: *Moravsky Ilustrovany Zpravodaj* [Moravian Illustrated Observer], No. 40, 1935, 10f. For a review of the source, see Hamann, *Hitlers Wien*, 271f.

111. See Hamann, *Hitlers Wien*, 542.

112. Karl Honisch, "Wie ich im Jahre 1913 Adolf Hitler kennenlernte," transcript dated May 31, 1939, in: BAB, NS 26/27a; this text was also reprinted in Joachimsthaler, *Hitlers Weg*, 52ff.

113. Ibid.

114. Ernst Hanfstaengl, *Adolf Hitler*, in: Franklin D. Roosevelt Library (New York), "Henry Field's Papers," Box 44, 30. (The entire quote reads: "The Men's Hostel called 'Männerheim Brigittenau' in Vienna had, Dr. Sedgwick believes, the reputation of being a place where elderly men went in

search of young men for homosexual pleasures. It is probable that these types of old roués and young gigolos became familiar to the young Adolf at this time which would account for his relative lack of genuine disgust with them up to the present time.")

115. See "Die Erhebung der österreichischen Nationalsozialisten im Juli 1934." Files of the Historical Commission of the Reichsführer SS (Vienna, 1965), 74. The research done by Dollfuss is also mentioned in Fritz Thyssen, *I paid Hitler* (London, 1941), 190f.; as well as in Jetzinger, *Hitlers Jugend,* 289.

116. Il Popolo di Roma, dated July 29, 1934, quoted from Jens Petersen, *Hitler–Mussolini. Die Entstehung der Achse Berlin–Rom. 1933–1936* (Tübingen, 1973), 363. (The entire quote reads: "Che cosa sono i signori nazisti ? Assassini e pederasti.") See also François Broche, *Assassinat du Chancellier Dollfuss* (Paris, 1977), 167f. Igra, *Germany's National Vice,* 66f., also hints in this direction, but without naming any sources.

117. Hitler, *Mein Kampf,* 135.

118. See BAB, BDC Rudolf Häusler; Hamann, *Hitlers Wien,* 273ff., as well as regarding the incident in Czechoslovakia, 608; Joachimsthaler, *Hitlers Weg,* 322f.

119. See Hamann, *Hitlers Wien,* 274f.

120. Personnel questionnaire issued by DAF, dated October 9, 1939, quoted from Joachimsthaler, *Hitlers Weg,* 80f.

121. Hamann, *Hitlers Wien,* 566.

122. See ibid., 566–574.

123. Ibid., *Hitlers Wien,* 515f.

124. Hitler, *Mein Kampf,* 138.

125. See Hitler's letter to Dr. Emil Gansser on November 29, 1921, reprinted in Joachimsthaler, *Hitlers Weg,* 92ff.

126. W. Marchand, *Die Knabenliebe in München! Münchens Homosexuelle. Sittenbild aus der Großstadt* (Munich, 1904), 7f. The journalist's intention in writing this brochure was to bring proof of the "rather scary increase in homosexuals in Munich" (preface) and point the reader's attention to the limited abilities of the police to intervene (12).

127. Erich Mühsam, *Namen und Menschen. Unpolitische Erinnerungen* (Berlin, 1977), 110f.

128. Ibid., 112.

129. This is very well described in Leonhard Frank's autobiographical essay entitled "Links wo das Herz ist" (Berlin, 1955), 17f.

130. For the Munich Bohemian scene during the time before the war, see the

relevant passages in David Clay Large, *Where Ghosts walked. Munich's Road to the Third Reich* (New York, 1997); a depiction of the criteria for belonging to the different groups can be found in Elisabeth Kleemann, *Zwischen symbolischer Rebellion und politischer Revolution. Studien zur deutschen Boheme zwischen Kaiserreich und Weimarer Republik* (Frankfurt a.M., 1985), 13–23.

131.   See Heinz A. Heinz, *Germany's Hitler* (London, 1934), 56ff.

132.   See Paul Kutter, *Das materielle Elend der jungen Münchener Maler* (Munich, 1911), especially 15ff.

133.   The above information and quotes all come from Hitler's letter of justification to the Linz Magistrate in January 1914, in: Jetzinger, *Hitlers Jugend*, 262ff.

134.   During the 1930s NSDAP headquarters was extremely interested in these pictures drawn by the Führer. It bought them back from their owners and collected reports of memories in which these owners described meeting the painter; see the relevant documentation in: BAB, NS 26/25ff.

135.   Report of memory by Dr. Hans Schirmer dated August 14, 1935, in: BAB, NS 26/30; also reprinted in Joachimsthaler, *Hitlers Weg*, 84f.

136.   BAB, BDC Dr. Josef Schnell, here quoted from Joachimsthaler, *Hitlers Weg*, 88.

137.   Report of the director of the NSDAP's main archives, Holtz, dated October 10, 1939, in: BAB, NS 26/43.

138.   In February 2001, a picture drawn by Hitler depicting flowers that he allegedly sold to Hepp's Munich colleague Ernst Doebner was supposed to be auctioned off, see: Frankfurter Allgemeine Zeitung, February 15 and 16, 2001, as well as Doebner's "notes," a copy of which was kindly provided to me by the auctioneers Bloss. Regarding Doebner, also see: HStA Munich, MF 32256 (Personnel File); City Archives Munich, Police Registration Form.

139.   See *Neue Revue*, No. 46, 1952, 39 (Article Series "Das war Hitler").

140.   See Report of the director of the NSDAP's main archives, Holtz, dated October 3, 1939, in: BAB, NS 26/43; Uetrecht to Reichsamtsleiter Schulte-Strathaus on October 19, 1939, in: ibid.

141.   Report of the director of the NSDAP's main archives, Holtz, dated October 3, 1939, in: ibid.

142.   See Hitler to Hepp on February 5, 1915, in: Jäckel/Kuhn (Eds.), *Sämtliche Aufzeichnungen*, 69.

143.   See *Neue Revue*, No. 46, 1952, 39. Regarding this way of living, see

Hermann Wilhelm, *Die Münchener Bohème. Von der Jahrhundertwende bis zum Ersten Weltkrieg* (Munich, 1993).

144. For more detailed information on Schuler, see: Eduard Gugenberger, *Hitlers Visionäre. Die okkulten Wegbereiter des Dritten Reiches* (Vienna, 2001), 19–30; as well as Bernd-Ulrich Hergemöller, *Mann für Mann. Biographisches Lexikon zur Geschichte von Freundesliebe und mann-männlicher Sexualität im deutschen Sprachraum* (Hamburg, 1998), 646ff. For the historical context of the scene, see Large, *Where Ghosts walked*, 25ff.

145. Alfred Schuler, *Cosmogonische Augen. Gesammelte Schriften*, edited, commented, and introduced by Baal Müller (Paderborn, 1997), 219.

146. See Robert Boehringer, *Mein Bild von Stefan George*. Text (Munich/Dusseldorf, 1951), 109.

147. See Hamann, *Hitlers Wien*, 333ff.

CHAPTER 2

1. It has meanwhile been sorted out of Hentig's estate and added to the *Zeugenschrifttum* Collection of the IfZ Munich as No. 2397. Hentig's estate is kept in the Political Archives of the German State Department, the Federal Archives in Koblenz, as well in Munich's Institute for Contemporary History.

2. Werner Maser, *Adolf Hitler. Legende, Mythos, Wirklichkeit* (Munich, 1971), 456 and 139. Maser knows of this document only from hearsay.

3. HStA Munich, Dept. IV, HS 3231.

4. See Susanne Meinl, *Nationalsozialisten gegen Hitler* (Berlin, 2000), 278f. and 428.

5. Friedrich Alfred Schmid Noerr, "Dokument des Widerstandes—Entwurf einer Deutschen Reichsverfassung," in: *Voran und beharrlich*, No. 33/34, 1961, 36.

6. Meinl, *Nationalsozialisten*, 228.

7. Quoted from Heinz Höhne, *Canaris. Patriot im Zwielicht* (Munich, 1976), 370. See also Christian Hartmann, *Halder. Generalstabschef Hitlers 1938–1942* (Paderborn, 1991), 162ff.

8. As a dispatch rider on the staff of the so-called List Regiment from October 1914, to June 1916, Mend was in close contact with the other runners of this unit, which was the unit Hitler belonged to starting in October 1914 as well. In 1918/19, the two of them met again in Munich.

9. "Mend-Protokoll," in: HStA Munich, Dept. IV, HS 3231.

10. The following attempt at reconstructing Mend's life is mainly based on

the relevant material contained in the StA Munich, Staatsanwaltschaften
[District Attorney's Office], No. 9959 and 34513, as well as the
Kriegsstammrollen [Records of Military Service] 13184/6046 and
3040/737, in: HstA Munich, Dept. IV.

11. In a letter to his landlady dated October 27, 1938, Mend called this letter a document that was "irreplaceable" to him, in: BAB, NS 26/64.

12. See BAB, NS 26/9 and 10.

13. "Mend-Protokoll," in: HStA Munich, Dept. IV, HS 3231.

14. Letter of State Police Headquarters Munich to the Head of the Prosecuting Authorities at the Special Court in Munich, dated December 31,
1940, in: StA Munich, Staatsanwaltschaften, No. 9959. See also the
appeal against the warrant of arrest submitted by Mend's attorney Roder
dated January 8, 1941 (ibid.), in which he writes, "He used to get
together with the Führer at Café Heck almost daily during his stay in
Munich, and the Führer always used the fraternal *Du* with him."

15. "Mend-Protokoll," in: HStA Munich, Dept. IV, HS 3231.

16. This publishing house in Diessen is still in existence today but was not
willing to assist in the clarification as to how these two publications
came into being.

17. Press release by Mend on December 1, 1932, in: *Der Gerade Weg*, No.
49, dated December 4, 1932.

18. See articles such as "Kommandierender von Hitlers Gnaden," in: *Münchener Post*, January 8, 1931.

19. See Georg Franz-Willing, *Ursprung der Hitlerbewegung 1919–1922*
(Preußisch Oldendorf, 1974), 68.

20. Balthasar Brandmayer, Hitler's wartime comrade, had been treated very
similarly when he published his book *Meldegänger Hitler* with the
Munich publishing house Franz Walter Verlag around the same time
Mend published his book. Here, too, the issue was to fabricate an
authentic witness for political purposes. It therefore fit the picture that
the last pages of the book were reserved for advertisements for "national
socialist postcards" and "toys."

21. See *Hamburger Echo*, No. 55, February 29, 1932; as well as Egon Erwin
Kisch, *Gesammelte Werke*, Vol. 7 (Berlin, 1992, 4th ed.), 299f.

22. The above quotes were all taken from Hans Mend, *Adolf Hitler im Felde*
(Diessen, 1931), 7ff., 61f., 100, 113, 118, 172, 186, and 191.

23. See Mend's press release dated December 1, 1932, in: *Der Gerade Weg*,
No. 49, December 4, 1932; as well as Amann's letter to Wiedemann
dated March 26, 1935, in: BAK, NS 10/173.

24. Feature article entitled "Der Kriegsheld Hitler," in: *Münchener Post*, No.

235, October 10, 1932. See also the weekly insert to the Social Democratic *Hamburger Echo*, "Echo der Woche," dated March 13, 1932, in which Mend is called "Hitler's own principal witness" and "Hitler's like-minded person."

25. See *Völkischer Beobachter*, November 25, December 3, and December 10, 1931.

26. "Mend-Protokoll," in: HStA Munich, Dept. IV, HS 3231.

27. With regard to Gerlich, see Hans-Günther Richardi/Klaus Schumann, *Geheimakte Gerlich/Bell* (München, 1993), 28–51.

28. *Der Gerade Weg*, No. 41, October 9, 1932.

29. Mend's letter to Franz Xaver Schwarz dated July 8, 1933, in: BAB, BDC Hans Mend.

30. Mend's press release dated December 1, 1932, in: *Der Gerade Weg*, No. 49, December 4, 1932.

31. "Mend-Protokoll," in: HStA Munich, Dept. IV, HS 3231.

32. Letter of State Police Headquarters Munich to the head of the Prosecuting Authorities at the Special Court Munich on December 31, 1940, in: StA Munich, Staatsanwaltschaften, No. 9959.

33. Mend to Franz Xaver Schwarz on July 8, 1933, in: BAB, BDC Hans Mend.

34. "Mend-Protokoll," in: HStA Munich, Dept. IV, HS 3231.

35. Mend to "Reichsleiter Bormann" on March 15, 1935, in: BAK, NS 10/173. In this letter, reference is made to a summer 1934 correspondence regarding the same matter, which did not survive.

36. Copy of the letter Wiedemann wrote to Mend on March 27, 1935, in: BAK, NS 10/173.

37. Letter dated March 26, 1935, in: ibid. The fact that the name "Mend" was well-known in the circle around Hitler is evidenced by a letter Wiedemann wrote to Amann on March 22, 1935 (ibid.), in which he says, "You told me various details regarding Mend back then."

38. See registration papers of Hans Mend in the City Archives, Munich.

39. Minutes taken during the questioning of Franz Schneider on January 15, 1958, in: StA Munich, Staatsanwaltschaften, No. 34513.

40. Letter written by Hans Mend to Michael Mend on January 22, 1934, private collection of Jürgen Kamleiter, whom I sincerely thank for his kind permission to let me have a copy.

41. See Minutes taken during the questioning of Hans Mend on October 27, 1938, in: BAB, NS 26/64.

42. Schaub to Amann on December 9, 1935, in: BAK, NS 10/172.

43. See letter written by Dr. Paulus to the Amtsgericht [municipal court] Starnberg on July 28, 1957, in: StA Munich, Staatsanwaltschaften, No. 34513.

44. Minutes taken during the questioning of Rosl Braunschweig on February 5, 1958, in: ibid.

45. "Mend-Protokoll," in: HStA Munich, Dept. IV, HS 3231.

46. Copy of a letter written by Mend to his landlady Dr. Göringer on October 27, 1938, in: BAB, NS 26/64.

47. Copy of a letter written by Attorney Hermann Alletag to Mend on November 3, 1938, in: ibid.

48. Letter written by State Police Headquarters Munich to the Head of the Prosecuting Authorities at the Special Court in Munich on December 31, 1940, in: StA Munich, Staatsanwaltschaften, No. 9959. See also the letter written by Book Retailers Koehler & Volckmar in Leipzig to the NSDAP's main archives on June 1, 1938, in: BAB, NS 26/64.

49. In this regard, see also the detailed case study performed by Hans-Günther Hockerts, *Die Sittlichkeitsprozesse gegen katholische Ordensangehörige und Priester* (Mainz, 1971).

50. See Mend's handwritten curriculum vitae for the head prosecutor at the Landgericht [district court] Munich, Dr. Rasch, dated January 12, 1941, in: StA Munich, Staatsanwaltschaften, No. 9959.

51. Quoted from the "Kriminalbiologisches Gutachten" [Forensic Expert Report] by Dr. Riedl dated February 14, 1941, in: ibid.

52. See letter written by Gestapo-Headquarters Munich to the head of the Prosecuting Authorities at the Special Court Munich on November 14, 1941, in: ibid.

53. Ibid.

54. Copy of a letter written by Mend to his landlady Dr. Göringer on October 27, 1938, in: BAB, NS 26/64.

55. Dr. Paulus in a letter to the Amtsgericht [municipal court], Starnberg on July 28, 1957, in: StA Munich, Staatsanwaltschaften, No. 34513.

56. Minutes taken during the questioning of Eva König on February 24, 1958, in: ibid.

57. Letter written by the gendarmerie post in Aufkirchen to the chief administrative officer for the district of Starnberg on September 24, 1940, in: StA Munich, Staatsanwaltschaften, No. 9959. Another supporting factor in this is what the then municipal employee Rosl Braunschweig said during her questioning on February 5, 1958. She could "remember that Eva König played a dark role in this matter," in: StA Munich, Staatsanwaltschaften, No. 34513.

58. For details, see StA Munich, Staatsanwaltschaften, No. 9959.

59. The circumstances of Mend's death have never been clarified. After a short investigation, the District Attorney's Offoce at the Landgericht [district court] Munich II declared that a clarification of the case was impossible. One thing was learned by the police: "There is no official paperwork regarding Mend's death in existence." (Letter by the police field office in Fürstenfeldbruck to the District Attorney's Office on June 21, 1958, in: StA Munich, Staatsanwaltschaften, No. 34513.)

60. Mend in a letter to his girlfriend and housekeeper Betty Heinzl on December 15, 1940. This handwritten letter appears to have been seized by the prison warden and thus found its way into the files (ibid.).

61. Express letter sent by the head of the Prosecuting Authorities at the special court in Munich to the department of prisons on March 18, 1941, in: ibid.

62. This conclusion was drawn after seeing the underlying trend of the various witness statements, in: StA Munich, Staatsanwaltschaften, No. 9959.

63. Opinion of the Court dated March 11, 1941, in: ibid.

64. Minutes taken during the questioning of Eva König on February 24, 1958, in: StA Munich, Staatsanwaltschaften, No. 34513.

65. Minutes taken during the questioning of Franz Schneider on January 15, 1958, in: ibid.

66. See, for example, Magnus Hirschfeld (ed.), *Sittengeschichte des Ersten Weltkriegs* (Berlin, 1929); as well as H. C. Fischer/E. X. Dubois, *Sexual Life During the World War* (London, 1937), 288ff.

67. Hirschfeld, *Sittengeschichte*, 219.

68. For the following, see the most detailed description of this phase of his life in Anton Joachimsthaler, *Hitlers Weg begann in München 1913–1923* (Munich, 2000), 98–197. Unfortunately, the analysis and interpretation of the sources collected with great diligence do not meet the standard of scientific research.

69. The following information was taken from the interviews Schmidt gave to Heinz A. Heinz, in, *Germany's Hitler* (London, 1934), 97ff.; from *Neue Revue*, No. 47, 1952 (Article Series "Das war Hitler"); as well as HStA Munich, Abt. IV, Kriegsstammrolle, 3071 and 4424/157; StA Munich, Spruchkammer, Box 1643.

70. "Bericht über meine politische Tätigkeit," July 31, 1948, in: StA Munich, Spruchkammer, Box 1643.

71. See registration papers Rudolf Häusler under "HäHim," City Archives Munich, where the name "Schmidt" is found.

72. So Schmidt told the *Illustrierter Beobachter,* No. 15, April, 1937, 527. See also Balthasar Brandmayer, *Meldegänger Hitler* (Munich, 1933, 2. enlarged ed.), 86ff.; as well as Mend, *Hitler im Felde,* 39, 82, and 141.

73. Heinz, *Germany's Hitler,* 98. (The quote reads, "but three of us in particular seemed to hang together, Hitler, Bachmann and I. Personally I was very much attracted to Adolf"). Bachmann, who was born in 1895 and volunteered for the service, was suddenly sent to the Eastern Front in May 1917 for reasons that are unclear. He died shortly thereafter. In the photographs preserved, he poses as an innocent boy who appears to have entrusted himself entirely to the care of Hitler and Schmidt. It is possible that he is the officer's orderly to the regiment physician Riehl Mend calls "Baumann, who was Hitler's close friend," in *Hitler im Felde,* 163.

74. Brandmayer, *Meldegänger,* 100 and 78.

75. Speech given by Hitler on June 4, 1939, quoted from Max Domarus (ed.), *Hitler. Reden und Proklamationen 1932–1945,* Vol. II/2 (Wiesbaden, 1973), 1205.

76. Friedrich Wiedemann, *Der Mann, der Feldherr werden wollte. Erlebnisse und Erfahrungen des Vorgesetzten Hitlers im I. Weltkrieg und seines späteren Persönlichen Adjutanten* (Velbert, 1964) 28ff.

77. Quoted from Eberhard Jäckel/Axel Kuhn (eds.), *Hitler. Sämtliche Aufzeichnungen* (Stuttgart, 1980), 78f.

78. See Joachimsthaler, *Hitlers Weg,* 158. Mend is not the only one to mention Hitler's subservience toward the officers of his regiment: see also Edgar Stern-Rubarth, . . . *Aus zuverlässiger Quelle verlautet . . . Ein Leben für Presse und Politik* (Stuttgart, 1964), 133f.; Walter C. Langer, *The Mind of Adolf Hitler* (London, 1973), 121f.

79. Egon Erwin Kisch, "Es gilt, Hitler zu begreifen," first published in: *Das Blaue Heft* (Paris), July 15, 1933; here quoted from Kisch, *Gesammelte Werke,* Vol. 10 (Berlin, 1993, 2nd ed.), 356f.

80. See IfZ Munich, ZS 1751; see also *Nürnberger Nachrichten,* No. 178, August 4, 1961.

81. See *Deutsche Allgemeine Zeitung,* August 3, 1933 ("Wie Hitler das E.K. I erwarb").

82. See Friedrich Percyval Reck-Malleczewen, *Tagebuch eines Verzweifelten* (Stuttgart, 1947) 75, who was made aware of this by "an officer familiar with the practice of awarding decorations back then."

83. See Joachimsthaler, *Hitlers Weg,* 110.

84. Hauke Hirsinger gave a first overview of these inconsistencies in his master's thesis: *Hitler im Ersten Weltkrieg. Fakten und Legenden* (Bremen, 2001).

85.   See John Toland, *Adolf Hitler* (New York, 1976), 68, where he bases himself on the personal statements made to him by Ernst Schmidt.

86.   Quote taken from Jäckel/Kuhn (eds.), *Sämtliche Aufzeichnungen,* 82.

87.   See Maser, *Adolf Hitler,* 108.

88.   *Neue Revue,* No. 47, 1952, 37.

89.   See Maser, *Adolf Hitler,* 149.

90.   Adolf Hitler, *Mein Kampf* (Munich, 1930, 3rd printing), 225.

91.   Heinz, *Germany's Hitler,* 101f. (The entire quote reads, "We met, we two, and cemented our old friendship.")

92.   Ibid., 103.

93.   And he remained a hardship case. To bring one example: as someone always willing to hook up with anyone who was even halfway friendly to him, Hitler let a young farmer near Bad Reichenhall feed him for eight days after the two of them had shared a room for a night at a railway hotel in February 1919. This farmer reminded the "dear Führer" of this in 1937 and then requested a short private visit with him, "after you have been so close to [me] once before in my life." The reader may think that the mighty dictator cannot possibly have taken such a letter seriously. Think again. Hitler did not ignore this hint at all but had the admirer "put off until next year" for time reasons. Letters to and from farmer Josef Neumeier dated July 14, September 25, and October 4, 1937, in: BAK, NS 10/370. As can also be seen from this event, Hitler had originally intended to visit his wartime comrade Tiefenböck but he had not been home.

94.   So Hitler said in a speech held before SA men on March 7, 1931, in Munich (police report), in: Constantin Goschler (ed.), *Hitler. Reden, Schriften, Anordnungen,* Vol. IV/1 (Munich, 1994), 229f.

95.   See Katja-Maria Wächter, *Die Macht der Ohnmacht. Leben und Politik des Franz Xaver Ritter von Epp (1868–1946)* (Frankfurt a.M., 1999), 56ff.

96.   See Klaus Bredow, *Hitler rast. Der 30. Juni. Ablauf, Vorgeschichte und Hintergründe* (Saarbrücken, 1934), 5f. This brochure, probably published under a pen name, was written by a journalist who had excellent knowledge of the internal workings of the Nazi movement.

97.   See Joachimsthaler, *Hitlers Weg,* 210ff., who brings evidence from many different sources.

98.   For more details, see Ernst Deuerlein, "Hitlers Eintritt in die Politik und die Reichswehr," in: VfZ, Vol. 7 (1959), 177ff.

99.   See the anonymously published article, 'I was Hitler's Boss,' in: *Current*

History, Vol. 1, No. 3 (November, 1941), 193–199, here p. 193. There is some evidence that this text is based on an interview Mayr gave to Otto Strasser during Strasser's life as an emigrant in France, which he later changed into an autobiographical text and "enhanced" here and there.

100. So Mayr said in the *Münchener Post* on November 13, 1928.

101. The fact that Mayr remained a very controversial character even when he later became involved with the Fighting Union "Reichsbanner" (a group close to the Social Democrats) is evidenced by Karl Rohe, *Das Reichsbanner Schwarz Rot Gold* (Düsseldorf, 1966), especially 189 and 349.

102. So shown by Röhm's (later) biographer Eleanor Hancock, "Ernst Röhm and the Experience of World War I," in: *The Journal of Military History,* Vol. 60 (1996), 56ff.

103. See registration documents regarding Rudolf Häusler and Ernst Schmidt in the city archives of Munich.

104. See Heinz, *Germany's Hitler,* 107; see also "I was Hitler's Boss," in: *Current History,* Vol. I, No. 3, November 1941, 194.

105. So Schmidt told Maser, *Adolf Hitler,* 160.

106. Heinz, *Germany's Hitler,* 98 (The entire quote reads, "To my dear and faithful war-time comrade Ernst Schmiedt, in remembrance, Adolf Hitler."); as well as Fritz Demmel, *Geschichte und G'schichten aus der Gemeinde Garching a.d. Alz* (Garching, 1999), 295.

107. In this regard, see especially the documents for Hitler's suit against *Hamburger Echo* in March 1932, in: StA Hamburg, 213-4 LG-Rechtsprechung, D 1933-2.

108. See Joachimsthaler, *Hitlers Weg,* 143.

109. Series 15, April 1937.

110. See Joachimsthaler, *Hitlers Weg,* 143f. and photograph after p. 96.

111. Minutes taken during various questioning sessions, in: StA München, Spruchkammer, Box 1643.

112. Quoted from Demmel, *Garching,* 295.

113. StA München, Spruchkammer, Box 1643.

114. Quoted from Demmel, *Garching,* 294.

115. See Heinz, *Germany's Hitler,* 97f.

116. Some clues can be found in Joachimsthaler, *Hitlers Weg,* 143ff. Not satisfactory for our question is the book written by Gerd R. Ueberschär/Winfried Vogel, *Dienen und Verdienen. Hitlers Geschenke an seine Eliten* (Frankfurt a.M., 1999).

117. See David Lewis, *The Secret Life of Adolf Hitler* (London, 1977), 52ff.

118. See Langer, *The Mind of Adolf Hitler,* 124.

119. Hitler, *Mein Kampf,* 176f.

120. Ibid., 235.

121. See Hans von Tresckow, *Von Fürsten und anderen Sterblichen. Erinnerungen eines Kriminalkommissars* (Berlin, 1922), 112, 135, and passim; in addition, see the testimony given in Karl-Heinz Janßen/Fritz Tobias, *Der Sturz der Generäle. Hitler und die Blomberg-Fritsch-Krise 1938* (Munich, 1994), 107.

122. Thus the observation of journalist Karl Tschuppik in 1927 in an article for the "Tagebuch," reprinted in: Wolfgang Weyrauch (ed.), *Ausnahmezustand. Eine Anthologie aus "Weltbühne" und "Tagebuch"* (Munich, 1966), 295f.

CHAPTER 3

1. See Ian Kershaw, *Hitler,* Vol. 1: 1889–1936. Hubris. 1st American ed. (New York, 1999), 140 and 154.

2. Ernst Röhm, *Die Geschichte eines Hochverräters* (Munich, 1934, 6th ed.), 115. Römer was the head of the Freikorps "Bund Oberland."

3. See Peter Longerich, *Die braunen Bataillone. Geschichte der SA* (Munich, 1989), 15.

4. For the biography and military career of this unmarried son of a painter, see Katja-Maria Wächter, *Die Macht der Ohnmacht. Leben und Politik des Franz Xaver Ritter von Epp (1868–1946)* (Frankfurt a.M., 1999), 79ff., which mentions the relationship with Röhm only in passing, however.

5. Röhm, *Hochverräter,* 158f. See also Wächter, *Epp,* 87ff.

6. Brigitte Hamann will report more about this—particularly with respect to the visits the couple Röhm–Epp paid to Bayreuth—in her new book about Winifred Wagner.

7. See Otto Wagener, *Hitler aus nächster Nähe. Aufzeichnungen eines Vertrauten 1929–1932,* edited by Henry A. Turner (Frankfurt a.M., 1978), 197. Also, with respect to Röhm's attorney Walter Luetgebrune, see Ernst von Salomon, *Der Fragebogen* (Hamburg, 1951), 449.

8. Epp in a letter to General von Möhl on February 16, 1922, in: BAK, N 1101/92; quoted from Wächter, *Epp,* 92.

9. See Longerich, *Bataillone,* 15ff.

10. Adolf Hitler, *Mein Kampf* (Munich, 1930, 3rd ed.), 391.

11. Gerhard Rossbach, *Mein Weg durch die Zeit. Erinnerungen und Bekenntnisse* (Weilburg, 1950), 215.

12. Hitler, *Mein Kampf,* 391.

13. Röhm, *Hochverräter*, 9f. and 313.
14. For more details, see Ulfried Geuter, *Homosexualität in der deutschen Jugendbewegung. Jungenfreundschaft und Sexualität im Diskurs von Jugendbewegung, Psychoanalyse und Jugendpsychologie am Beginn des 20. Jahrhunderts* (Frankfurt a.M., 1994).
15. Published in *Der Eigene*, No. 10 (1925), 415–425; the following quotes were taken from here as well.
16. Hans Blüher, *Die Rolle der Erotik in der männlichen Gesellschaft. Eine Theorie der menschlichen Staatsbildung nach Wesen und Wert* (Stuttgart, 1962), 28.
17. Hans Blüher, *Werke und Tage. Geschichte eines Denkers* (Munich, 1953), 256.
18. See *Weißbuch über die Erschießungen des 30. Juni 1934. Authentische Darstellung der deutschen Bartholomäusnacht* (Paris, 1934), 124f.
19. Interview with Friedrich Karl Freiherr von Eberstein in 1975, in: IfZ München, ZS 539.
20. Röhm, *Hochverräter*, 356.
21. This bundle of letters from the year 1929 is located in: StA Munich, Staatsanwaltschaften, No. 28791/41.
22. Anonymous, "Nationalsozialismus und Inversion," in: *Mitteilungen des Wissenschaftlich-humanitären Komitees*, No 32 (January/March 1932), 340–345. The following quotes are on pp. 341, 343, and 345.
23. Röhm in a letter to Heimsoth on February 25, 1929, in: *Mitteilungen des Wissenschaftlich-humanitären Komitees*, No. 33 (April/August 1932), 394.
24. See the discussion with General Ritter von Hörauf on November 10, 1951, in: IfZ Munich, ZS 70.
25. See Konrad Heiden, *Adolf Hitler. Das Zeitalter der Verantwortungslosigkeit. Eine Biographie* (Zurich, 1936), 237; see also Heinz Höhne, *Mordsache Röhm. Hitlers Durchbruch zur Alleinherrschaft 1933–1934* (Reinbek, 1984), 80.
26. Discussion with General Ritter von Hörauf on November 12, 1951, in: IfZ Munich, ZS 70.
27. Röhm in a letter to Heimsoth on February 25, 1929, in: *Mitteilungen des Wissenschaftlich-humanitären Komitees*, No. 33 (April/August 1932), 394.
28. See *Münchener Post*, No. 147 (June 30, 1931); Röhm, *Hochverräter*, 269.
29. See Röhm, *Hochverräter*, 362f. and 267ff.
30. Hans Frank, *Im Angesicht des Galgens. Deutung Hitlers und seiner Zeit*

auf Grund eigener Erlebnisse und Erkenntnisse (Munich-Gräfelfing, 1953), 88f.

31. Kurt G. W. Lüdecke, *I knew Hitler. The Story of a Nazi Who Escaped The Blood Purge* (New York, 1937), 245.

32. Published by the Social Democratic emigrant Helmuth Klotz (who will demand our attention in a later chapter), these documents attributed to General Ferdinand von Bredow were first published in early 1934 in the Prague newspaper *Wahrheit,* No. 7-36; see the copies of the article series in: IfZ Munich, ED 86 (Bredow), Vol. 7. These pages were published that same year in London and New York under the heading 'The Berlin Diaries.' They hint at Röhm as "Hitler's better half."

33. Ernst Hanfstaengl, *Zwischen Weißem und Braunem Haus. Memoiren eines politischen Außenseiters* (Munich, 1970), 97.

34. Rudolf Diels, *Lucifer ante portas . . . es spricht der erste Chef der Gestapo . . .* (Stuttgart, 1950), 89.

35. See Röhm, *Hochverräter,* 215.

36. The above quotes are all taken from Röhm, *Hochverräter,* 340, 349, and 348.

37. See the diary entry made by Joseph Goebbels on May 15, 1928, after a visit to Munich where he saw Hitler and Röhm in cozy unity, in: Elke Fröhlich (ed.), *Die Tagebücher von Joseph Goebbels. Sämtliche Fragmente,* Vol. I/1 (Munich et al., 1987), 224.

38. See Margarete Plewnia, *Auf dem Weg zu Hitler. Der "völkische" Publizist Dietrich Eckart* (Bremen, 1970), 113f.

39. *Frankfurter Zeitung,* No. 150 (March 23, 1943); the article signed "hk" (for Herbert Küsel) had the simple title "Dietrich Eckart. Geboren am 23. März 1868."

40. Minutes taken during the police questioning of Eckart on November 15, 1923, in: BAB, NS 26/2180.

41. So Hitler wrote in his article "10 Jahre Kampf" for the *Illustrierter Beobachter* issued on August 3, 1929.

42. So the report of Eckart's friend Fleischhauer included in his letter to a Mr. Ruttke, an employee of the NSDAP archives, on April 7, 1938, in: BAB, NS 26/1311.

43. So Hitler said in his very telling monologue on January 16/17, 1942, in: Werner Jochmann (ed.), *Adolf Hitler. Monologe im Führerhauptquartier 1941–1944* (Munich, 1980), 208.

44. See Hans Hinkel, *Einer unter Hunderttausend* (Munich, 1938), 69.

45. See the notes taken by Franz Xaver Bauer, in: BAB, NS 26/2183.

46. Jochmann (ed.), *Monologe*, 208.

47. See Lüdecke, *I knew Hitler*, 122f.

48. Christa Schroeder, *Er war mein Chef. Aus dem Nachlaß der Sekretärin von Adolf Hitler*, edited by Anton Joachimsthaler (Munich, 1985), 65.

49. Alfred Rosenberg (ed.), *Dietrich Eckart. Ein Vermächtnis* (Munich, 1928).

50. Ibid., 16f.

51. Quoted from Richard Linsert, *Kabale und Liebe. Über Politik und Geschlechtsleben* (Berlin, 1931), 296f. It is rather surprising to read that Hitler had said something very similar about the "Schweinejuden" [dirty Jew] Hirschfeld on October 18, 1920, at an NSDAP meeting, "whom he accused of the spiritual murder of thousands of German national comrades." And he had added, "In such a case the people must help themselves and perform popular justice." Quoted from the documentation entitled "Hitler als Parteiredner im Jahre 1920," in: VfZ, Vol. 11 (1963), 323.

52. Quoted from Rosenberg (ed.), *Vermächtnis*, 15.

53. Guido Karl Bomhard in a letter to Philipp Feldl on August 2, 1935, in: BAB, NS 26/1307.

54. For more detail, see Hans-Günther Reichel, *Das Königliche Schauspielhaus unter Georg Graf von Hülsen-Häseler 1903–1918* (Berlin West, 1962), 3, 34, and 89–94.

55. The partly extant correspondence shows the friendly relationship. In: BAK, *Kleine Erwerbungen*, No. 124.

56. Rosenberg (ed.), *Vermächtnis*, 18.

57. See Plewnia, *Weg*, 29ff.

58. Bomhard in a letter to Feldl on August 2, 1935, in: BAB, NS 26/1307 (stresses made by the writer of the letter).

59. Jochmann (ed.), *Monologe*, 208.

60. See Hermann Wilhelm, *Dichter, Denker, Fememörder. Rechtsradikalismus und Antisemitismus in München von der Jahrhundertwende bis 1921* (Berlin, 1989), 105f.

61. See *Völkischer Beobachter* No. 61 (August 4, 1921), "Der Gaunerstreich gegen Hitler."

62. See Plewnia, *Weg*, 78ff.

63. See Eckart's Article, 'Enthüllungsdelirium der Post,' in the *Völkischer Beobachter*, No. 81 (October 26, 1921).

64. See Plewnia, *Weg*, 94ff. If the oral statement made by Hermann Esser is correct, namely, that Hitler met Eckart as early as the fall of 1919 (ibid.,

66 and 128), then there is something to be said for the argument that Eckart may be the "intellectual author" of the September, 16, 1919, letter in which Hitler stated his "Antisemitismus der Vernunft" [antisemitism of reason] for the first time. The original document can be found in: HStA Munich, Dept. IV, Gruppenkommando 4, Vol. 50/8, Aufzeichnungen, 88ff.

65. Quoted from the *Münchener Post,* No. 177 (August 1, 1922, 'Der getreue Eckart').

66. Quoted from the unpublished "Lebenserinnerungen" of Gustav Ritter von Kahr dated 1928, in: HStA Munich, NL Kahr, No. 51, 1177.

67. See Henry Picker, *Hitlers Tischgespräche im Führerhauptquartier* (Wiesbaden, 1983), 108f.

68. Ibid., 116.

69. Friedrich Percyval Reck-Malleczewen, *Tagebuch eines Verzweifelten* (Stuttgart, 1947), 23f.

70. Rossbach, *Mein Weg,* 215.

71. See Alfred Kruck, *Geschichte des Alldeutschen Verbandes 1890–1939* (Wiesbaden, 1954), 192.

72. BAK, NL 659 Claß, FC 1734 N, Manuscript, 8f.

73. Rudolf Pechel, *Deutscher Widerstand* (Erlenbach-Zurich, 1947), 280.

74. Quoted from Detlev Clemens, *Herr Hitler in Germany. Wahrnehmung und Deutung des Nationalsozialismus in Großbritannien 1920 bis 1939* (Göttingen, 1996), 47. (The entire quote reads, "Herr Hitler has developed into something much more than a scurrilous and rather comic agitator".)

75. For more details, see Kershaw, *Hitler,* Vol. 1, 180ff.

76. In this regard, see the unpublished "Lebenserinnerungen" of Gustav Ritter von Kahr, in: HStA Munich, NL Kahr, No. 51, 1166a/1167.

77. According to Kurt Lüdecke's observation, Eckart's emotions were divided between generosity and jealousy; see *I knew Hitler,* 123.

78. Jochmann (ed.), *Monologe,* 203f.

79. The following was taken from Ernst Hanfstaengl's Memorandum, "Adolf Hitler" dated 1942, in: Franklin D. Roosevelt Library (New York), Henry Field's Papers, Box 44, 34ff. (The entire quote reads, "Hitler's exhibitionism," "silly cow," "a senile weakling," "this girl Annerl," "Schopenhauer has done Eckart no good. He has made him a doubting Thomas, who only looks forward to Nirvana.")

80. And yet, the *Völkischer Beobachter,* No. 49 (March 24, 1923), celebrated Eckart on the occasion of his fifty-fourth birthday still as "the most revered pioneer and the one who spiritually paved the way of the National Socialist movement."

81. Bomhard in a letter to Feldl on August 2, 1935, in: BAB, NS 26/1307.

82. Posthumously published in Munich in 1924 as 'Der Bolschewismus von Moses bis Lenin.'

83. See Lüdecke, *I knew Hitler,* 119.

84. Friedrich Christian Prinz zu Schaumburg-Lippe, . . . *Verdammte Pflicht und Schuldigkeit . . . Weg und Erlebnis 1914–1933* (Leoni am Starnberger See, 1966), 273f.

85. The following information regarding Hanfstaengl's education after his military service was taken from: HStA Munich, Dept. IV, OP 32067; from the documents involving his doctorate, in: Archives of the Ludwig Maximilians University Munich, O N prom 1927/28; as well as from statements his son Egon Hanfstaengl made to the author.

86. Hans von Kaltenborn, *Fifty Fabulous Years. 1900–1950* (New York, 1950), 51. (The entire quote reads, "He always went with the 'right' people but never achieved his ambition of making one of the exclusive final clubs.")

87. Hanfstaengl, *Außenseiter,* 7ff.

88. See Hanfstaengl's version given in the article entitled, 'Ich habe gewarnt' in the *Badische Illustrierte Woche,* No. 50 (December 15, 1951).

89. Josephine Ewers in a letter to Haenfstaengl on December 15, 1951, in: Heinrich-Heine Institut Düsseldorf, Teil-Nachlaß Josephine Ewers (stresses inserted by the writer of the letter).

90. Hanfstaengl in a letter to Josephine Ewers on December 19, 1951, in: ibid.

91. For details with regard to Ewers's biography, see Wilfried Kugel, *Der Unverantwortliche. Das Leben des Hanns Heinz Ewers* (Düsseldorf, 1992).

92. Quoted from ibid., 247.

93. For more details, see George Chauncey, *Gay New York. Gender, Urban Culture, and the Making of the Gay Male World 1890–1914* (New York, 1994).

94. Letter dated May 12, 1920, here quoted from David George Marwell, *Unwanted Exile. A Biography of Ernst "Putzi" Hanfstaengl, Ph.D.* (New York, 1988), 60.

95. The author's conversation with Egon Hanfstaengl in Munich on October 21, 2000.

96. Ernst Hanfstaengl, "Wie ich Adolf Hitler kennenlernte," in: *Der Freiheitskampf,* No. 293 (October 21, 1934).

97. See Lüdecke, *I knew Hitler,* 94f.

98. Letter written by Gottfried Feder to Hitler on August 10, 1923, quoted from Oron James Hale, "Gottfried Feder calls Hitler to Order: An Unpublished Letter on Nazi Party Affairs," in: *The Journal of Modern History,* Vol. 30 (1958), 360.

99. Mümchemer Post No. 260, dated November 11, 1930 ('Eine Rück-endeckung für Hitlers Außenbeziehung. Wer ist Ernst Hanfstängl?').

100. The above quotes were all taken from Hanfstaengl's unpublished reminiscences, written in 1956, in: BSB, NL Hanfstaengl, Ana 405/47.

101. See the impressions of American diplomats and journalists described in: Philip Metcalfe, 1933. (Sag Harbor/New York, 1988), 32ff.

102. Hitler in a letter to Rosenberg on April 2, 1925, in: Archives du centre de documentation juive contemporaine Paris, document LXII–1.

103. According to the "Notes" taken by Helene Niemeyer, the former Mrs. Hanfstaengl, in 1939/40, which her son Egon kindly made available to me.

104. The above information and quotes were all taken from Hanfstaengl, *Außenseiter*, 84, 66ff., 111f., and 124.

105. Hanfstaengl's unpublished reminiscences (1956), in: BSB, NL Hanf-staengl, Ana 405/47.

106. Martha Dodd, *Through Embassy Eyes* (New York, 1939), 44; elsewhere (on p. 69), she speaks of 'vulgarity' as the best way to describe Hanf-staengl's style of playing. (The entire quote reads, "He had a drink, was persuaded to go to the piano, where he tore out several exciting and flamboyant songs.")

107. Hanfstaengl's unpublished reminiscences (1956), in: BSB, NL Hanf-staengl, Ana 405/47. See also Schroeder, *Chef*, 189f.

108. Hanfstaengl, *Außenseiter*, 54 and 81.

109. See the numerous allusions in Klaus Harpprecht, *Thomas Mann. Eine Biographie* (Reinbek, 1995); also, Karl Werner Böhm, *Zwischen Selb-stzucht und Verlangen. Thomas Mann und das Stigma der Homosexual-ität* (Würzburg, 1991), 249ff.

110. Conversation with the author in Munich on November 15, 2000.

111. Hanfstaengl, *Außenseiter*, 56.

112. *Hitler-Liederbuch 1924* (Munich, 1924); in there can be found: 'Hitler-Lied,' 'Deutsche voran,' and 'Die Hitler-Medizin.'

113. Eugenio Dollmann, *Roma Nazista* (Milano, 1949), 25f. (translation; for this and the following translations from the Italian [into German], I thank Bianca Matthäi).

114. Hanfstaengl's unpublished reminiscences (1956), in: BSB, NL Hanf-staengl, Ana 405/47.

115. *Münchener Post,* No. 260 (November 11, 1930).

116. Hanfstaengl's unpublished reminiscences (1956), in: BSB, NL Hanf-staengl, Ana 405/47.

117. Letter written by Gottfried Feder to Hitler on August 10, 1923, quoted from Oron James Hale, "Gottfried Feder calls Hitler to Order: An Unpublished Letter on Nazi Party Affairs," in: *The Journal of Modern History,* Vol. 30 (1958), 360ff.

118. Hanfstaengl's unpublished reminiscences (1956), in: BSB, NL Hanfstaengl, Ana 405/47.

119. With regard to this event, see: StA Munich, Polizeidirektion München, No. 10082.

120. For the following: Dollmann, *Roma Nazista,* 26ff.

121. For more details on the following, see especially the unpublished manuscript, "Mein Leben—in Stichworten" contained in the Dollmann estate which is owned by the Hausleitner family in Zell, as well as the BDC documents regarding Eugen Dollmann in the BAB.

122. Dollmann, "Mein Leben," 5.

123. Three-page typed manuscript privately owned by the Hausleitner family.

124. For more details, see BAB, BDC Eugen Dollmann, as well as PAA Berlin, R 101185; see also his depiction in: *The Interpreter. Memoirs of Doktor Eugen Dollmann* (London: Hutchinson, 1967), as well as Dan Kurzman, *The Race for Rome* (Garden City, N.Y.: Doubleday, 1975).

125. Such assassination plans were reported by the *Münchener Post,* No. 13 (January 15, 1924).

126. Besides Hanfstaengl's unpublished reminiscences (1956), in: BSB, NL Hanfstaengl, Ana 405/47, see especially the unpublished discourse, 'Die Wahrheit zum 9. November 1923' by Jobst von Lossow, a nephew of the Reichswehr general, in: HStA Munich, Dept. IV, HS 3388; as well as Joachim Fest, *Hitler. Eine Biographie* (Munich, 2000), 326.

127. Privately owned by the Hausleitner family in Zell. I am grateful to the family for kindly giving me copies of parts of these papers.

128. Jochmann (ed.), *Monologe,* 204f. With regard to Hitler's need for anonymity, see also Ulrich Chaussy, *Nachbar Hitler. Führerkult und Heimatzerstörung am Obersalzberg* (Berlin, 2001), 30ff.

129. For the biography of this former Freikorps fighter, see Günter Rinke, *Sozialer Radikalismus und bündische Utopie. Der Fall Peter Martin Lampel* (Frankfurt a.M., 2000). Lampel's unpublished memoirs are located in: Staats- und Universitätsbibliothek Hamburg, NL Lampel, NK 432.

130. Lampel, *Niemandes Knecht,* 416ff, in: ibid.

131. Hanfstaengl's unpublished reminiscences (1956), in: BSB, NL Hanfstaengl, Ana 405/47.

CHAPTER 4

1. For more detail, see now Barbara Zehnpfennig, *Hitlers "Mein Kampf"* (Munich, 2000); and the standard work: Eberhard Jäckel, *Hitlers Weltanschauung* (Stuttgart, 1991, 4th ed.).

2. For the political reorientation, for the creation of the Führer myth and for Hitler's rise to become the unchallenged party chief, see the relevant chapters in Ian Kershaw, *Hitler,* Vol. 1: 1889–1936. Hubris. 1st American ed. (New York, 1999).

3. See the photographs in: Wulf Schwarzwäller, *»Der Stellvertreter des Führers.« Rudolf Heß. Der Mann in Spandau* (Vienna/Munich/Zurich, 1974).

4. Hanfstaengl's unpublished reminiscences (1956), in: BSB, NL Hanfstaengl, Ana 405/47.

5. Hess in a letter to his wife on June 18, 1945, in: Ilse Hess, *Ein Schicksal in Briefen. England – Nürnberg – Spandau. Gefangener des Friedens. Antwort aus Zelle Sieben* (Leoni, 1984), 102.

6. Albert Krebs, *Tendenzen und Gestalten der NSDAP. Erinnerungen an die Frühzeit der Partei* (Stuttgart, 1959), 171.

7. The above quotes were taken from: Otto Strasser, *Gangsters around Hitler* (London, 1942), 38; Ernst Hanfstaengl, 'Adolf Hitler' (1942), in: Franklin D. Roosevelt Library (New York), Henry Field's Papers, Box 44, p. 29; interview with Ernst Hanfstaengl on October 28, 1951, in: IfZ Munich, ZS 60; the two following quotes were taken from Peter Padfield, *Hess. Flight for the Führer* (London, 1991), Prologue; Erich Ebermayer, *Denn heute gehört uns Deutschland . . . Persönliches und politisches Tagebuch* (Hamburg/Vienna, 1959), 381. With regard to Hess' homosexuality, see also Bernd-Ulrich Hergemöller, *Mann für Mann. Biographisches Lexikon zur Geschichte von Freundesliebe und mannmännlicher Sexualität im deutschen Sprachraum* (Hamburg, 1998), 350ff., who has other titles in his bibliography.

8. *Die Deutsche Revolution,* No. 9 (July 8, 1934, 'Gilt der § 175 nur für Tote? Eine Frage an Adolf Hitler'); see also *Die Deutsche Revolution,* No. 10 (July 15, 1934, 'Liste homosexueller Großwürdenträger des Hitler-Regimes').

9. Kurt G. W. Lüdecke, *I knew Hitler. The Story of a Nazi Who Escaped The Blood Purge* (New York, 1937), 586f. (The quote reads, "I couldn't quite see the epithet of 'Fräulein,' for he was the virility itself.")

10. Hess in a letter to Ilse Pröhl on October 24, 1923, in: *Rudolf Hess,*

Briefe 1908–1933 (Wolf-Rüdiger Hess, ed. With an introduction and comments by Bavendamm, Munich/Vienna, 1987), 309. As a collection of authentic first-person testimonies of a person close to Hitler, this edition of letters edited by the son of Rudolf Hess is a rare fortune. It includes, however, only a chosen number of letters which in addition have been reproduced only in excerpts. Out of consideration for living family members, "letters of an excessively intimate nature" were excluded from the outset. (Introduction, p. 8).

11. Hess in a letter to his cousin Milly Kleinmann on April 11, 1921, in: Hess, *Briefe 1908–1933*, 267.

12. Hess in a letter to Ilse Pröhl on July 23, 1924, in: ibid., 346.

13. For the biography of Rudolf Hess, see especially Kurt Pätzold/Manfred Weißbecker, *Rudolf Heß. Der Mann an Hitlers Seite* (Leipzig, 1999), here 12–87.

14. Ilse Hess, *Schicksal in Briefen*, 48.

15. With regard to the nature of this friendship, see Hans-Adolf Jacobsen, *Karl Haushofer. Leben und Werk*, Vol. 1: *Lebensweg 1869–1946 und ausgewählte Texte zur Geopolitik* (Boppard, 1979), 225ff.

16. Hess in a letter to his parents on June 17, 1920, in: Hess, *Briefe 1908–1933*, 261.

17. Quoted from Jacobsen, *Karl Haushofer*, 231.

18. So Ilse Hess said to Hans-Adolf Jacobsen in 1972; quoted from ibid., 227f.

19. This is how it was referred to in the letters Hess wrote on August 31, 1946, and July 19, 1953, in: Ilse Hess, *Schicksal in Briefen*, 110 and 301.

20. Hess in a letter to his cousin Milly Kleinmann on April 11, 1921, in: Hess, *Briefe 1908–1933, 267*.

21. Party member Heinrich Dolle in a letter to Hitler in 1921, quoted from Schwarzwäller, *Stellvertreter*, 81.

22. *Völkischer Beobachter*, No. 63 (August 11, 1921, 'Zum Flugblatt gegen Hitler').

23. Hess in a letter to Gustav Ritter von Kahr on May 17, 1921, in: IfZ Munich, F 18, 5f.

24. Ilse Hess, *Schicksal in Briefen*, 43.

25. Anonymous (Karl Mayr), 'I was Hitler's Boss,' in, *Current History*, Vol. 1, No. 3 (November 1941), 198. (The entire quote reads: "Before every important speech Hitler was, sometimes for days, closeted with Hess who in some unknown way got Hitler into that frenetic state in which he came forth to address the public.") Hess later confirmed in the Spandau prison that he helped Hitler rehearse his speeches; see Eugene K. Bird,

Heß der "Stellvertreter des Führers." Englandflug und britische Gefangenschaft (Munich, 1974), 302, here quoted from Pätzold/Weißbecker, *Heß,* 474.

26. *Völkischer Beobachter,* No. 63 (August 11, 1921, 'Zum Flugblatt gegen Hitler').

27. See Raffael Scheck, "Swiss Funding for the Early Nazi Movement. Motivation, Context, and Continuities," in *The Journal for Modern History,* Vol. 71 (1999), 803.

28. See the letters to his girlfriend on August 31, 1922, November 11, 1922, September 13, 1922, or August 10, 1923, for example, in: Hess, *Briefe 1908–1933.*

29. Hess in a letter to his mother on May 16, 1924, in, ibid., 325.

30. See Hans Kallenbach, *Mit Adolf Hitler auf Festung Landsberg* (Munich, 1933), 55.

31. Note taken during a conversation of the prison warden with Hansjörg Maurer on December 4, 1924, quoted from Winfried Schmidt (ed.): *"war gegen den Führer äußerst frech." Der Chefredakteur und nachmalige Tierarzt Hansjörg Maurer und seine Würzburger politischen Tagebuchblätter aus den Jahren 1936 und 1937* (Karlstacht, 1999), 53. The "repeated requests to take walks in the prison garden without his shirt on" were not granted by the warden. Such was the report by prison guard Franz Hemmrich in his unpublished reminiscences: "Die Festung Landsberg am Lech" (manuscript dated 1970), in: IfZ Munich, ED 153.

32. Hess in a letter to Ilse Pröhl on May 28, 1924, in: Hess, *Briefe 1908–1933,* 326.

33. Kershaw, *Hitler,* Vol. 1, 240.

34. See Bruno Hipler, *Hitlers Lehrmeister. Karl Haushofer als Vater der NS-Ideologie* (St. Ottilien, 1996), 108f. and 121f.

35. So Hess called himself in a conversation with Albert Krebs, quoted from *Tendenzen und Gestalten,* 170.

36. Hess in a letter to his parents on April 24, 1925, in: Hess, *Briefe 1908–1933,* 367.

37. So Joseph Goebbels wrote in his diary on April 13, 1926, after his first meeting with Hess, in: Elke Fröhlich (ed.), *Die Tagebücher von Joseph Goebbels. Sämtliche Fragmente,* Vol. I/1 (Munich etc., 1987), 172.

38. For more detail, see now also Ulrich Chaussy, *Nachbar Hitler. Führerkult und Heimatzerstörung am Obersalzberg* (Berlin, 2001), 29ff.

39. Hess in a letter to his mother on January 14, 1928, in: Hess, *Briefe 1908–1933,* 390.

40. Hess in a letter to his parents on November 20, 1927, here quoted from Wolf-Rüdiger Hess, *Mord an Rudolf Heß?* (Leoni, 1989), 41f.
41. Quoted from Ernst Hanfstaengl, *Zwischen Weißem und Braunem Haus. Memoiren eines politischen Außenseiters* (Munich, 1970), 324.
42. Quoted from Schwarzwäller, *Stellvertreter*, 101.
43. Notes taken of a conversation with Hitler's personal physician Karl Brandt in the summer of 1945, in: Ulrich Schlie (ed.), *Albert Speer. "Alles, was ich weiß." Aus unbekannten Geheimdienstprotokollen vom Sommer 1945* (Munich, 1999), 237; as well as Hess in a letter to his wife on June 26, 1947, in: Ilse Hess, *Schicksal in Briefen*, 147.
44. *Goebbels Diaries* I/1 (1987), 144, 173, 389, and 172 (entries made on November 23, 1925, April 13, 1926, June 22, 1929, and April 13, 1926).
45. Hess in a letter to Ilse Pröhl on June 29, 1924, in: Hess, *Briefe 1908–1933*, 342.
46. *Goebbels Diaries* I/1 (1987), 175 (entry made on April 19, 1926).
47. Ilse Hess, *Schicksal in Briefen*, 23.
48. For more information regarding the "Fall Wyneken" [Wyneken Case], see the relevant passages in Ulfried Geuter, *Homosexualität in der deutschen Jugendbewegung. Jungenfreundschaft und Sexualität im Diskurs von Jugendbewegung, Psychoanalyse und Jugendpsychologie am Beginn des 20. Jahrhunderts* (Frankfurt am Main, 1994), 195ff. Also, Thijs Maasen, *Pädagogischer Eros. Gustav Wyneken und die Freie Schulgemeinde Wickersdorf* (Berlin, 1995).
49. Gustav Wyneken, *Eros* (Lauenburg, 1921), 48f.
50. Hans Blüher, *Die Rolle der Erotik in der männlichen Gesellschaft* (Jena, 1917), 243 and 248.
51. Hess in a letter to Ilse Pröhl on October 24, 1923, in: Hess, *Briefe 1908–1933*, 309.
52. Hess in a letter to his wife on June 4, 1950, in: Ilse Hess, *Schicksal in Briefen*, 215.
53. Ilse Hess in a letter to Hess on October 11, 1954, in: ibid., 256 (stresses made in the original).
54. Hess in a letter to his wife on January 31, 1933, in: Hess, *Briefe 1908–1933*, 425f.
55. Radio talk given on June 25, 1934, quoted from the transcript published in the *Völkischer Beobachter*, No. 177 (June 26, 1934).
56. So Hitler said in a speech at the NSDAP convention on January 30, 1922, in: Eberhard Jäckel/Axel Kuhn (eds.), *Hitler. Sämtliche Aufzeichnungen* (Stuttgart, 1980), 559.

57. See the reference Hitler wrote for Maurice on August 1, 1928, regarding his work, in: IfZ Munich, ZS 270. See also Maurice's curriculum vitae dated February 23, 1948, in: StA Munich, Spruchkammer, Box 1131.

58. So Schaub said during his questioning on July 26, 1951, in: IfZ Munich, ZS 137.

59. With regard to his curriculum vitea in general, see the Spruchkammer [German denazification court] files, in: StA Munich, Spruchkammer, Box 1131.

60. See Kallenbach, *Mit Adolf Hitler* (Munich, 1933), 55f.

61. Henriette von Schirach, *Frauen um Hitler. Nach Materialien von Henriette von Schirach* (Munich, 1983), 55.

62. *Goebbels Diaries* I/1 (1987), 192 (entry on July 12, 1926).

63. Maurice in a letter to Hitler on January 24, 1925, in: IfZ Munich, ZS 270. In 1933, Maurice proudly stressed on a questionnaire for the first members of the NSDAP that he was a "friend of the Führer permitted to use the fraternal *Du*" (October 8, 1933), in: BAB, BDC Emil Maurice. See also Hitler's birthday greeting for Maurice on January 19, 1925, reproduced in: Hans Kallenbach, *Mit Adolf Hitler auf Festung Landsberg* (Munich, 1943, revised edition), 150.

64. See Hitler's letter to Maurice on September 13, 1927, reproduced in: Henry Picker, *Hitlers Tischgespräche im Führerhauptquartier* (Wiesbaden, 1983), photographs.

65. This is confirmed by the documents in the Spruchkammer [German denazification court] files, in: StA Munich, Spruchkammer, Box 1131. The files the police headquarters Munich collected on Maurice could not be found anymore.

66. Adolf Hitler, *Mein Kampf* (Munich, 1930, 3rd ed.), 566.

67. Hess in a letter to his wife on September 19, 1954, in: Ilse Hess, *Schicksal in Briefen*, 254.

68. Schirach, *Frauen*, 58 and 62.

69. Kallenbach, *Mit Adolf Hitler* (Munich, 1933), 92. With respect to this event, see also Hemmrich, *Erinnerungen*, in: IfZ Munich, ED 153, p. 33.

70. Kallenbach, *Mit Adolf Hitler* (Munich, 1933), 93. See also *Mit Adolf Hitler* (1943), 102ff.

71. Heinrich Hoffmann, *Friend* (London, 1955), 145. (The entire quotes reads, "I shall never forget the look of astonishment and horror on Hitler's face! . . . Bewildered and helpless as a child, Hitler stood there, biting his lip in an effort to master his anger.")

72. Hemmrich, *Erinnerungen*, in: IfZ Munich, ED 153, p. 44.

73. Quoted from Nerin Erin Gun, *Eva Braun-Hitler. Leben und Schicksal* (Kiel, 1994, revised edition), 20.

74. Christa Schroeder, *Er war mein Chef. Aus dem Nachlaß der Sekretärin von Adolf Hitler*, edited by Anton Joachimsthaler (Munich, 1985), 153.

75. Quoted from Gun, *Eva Braun-Hitler*, 57.

76. See Schirach, *Frauen*, 244f.; Hanfstaengl's unpublished reminiscences (1956), in: BSB, NL Hanfstaengl, Ana 405/47; as well as *Außenseiter*, 184; *Goebbels Diaries* I/2 (1987), 253 (entry on October 5, 1932).

77. Schroeder, *Chef*, 157ff. Hitler corresponded with Ada Klein as late as 1934, see the reproduction of a letter by "Wolf" to this female friend on September 30, 1934, in: Anton Joachimsthaler, *Hitlers Weg begann in München 1913–1923* (Munich, 2000), 299.

78. For the following, see Günter Peis, "Hitlers unbekannte Geliebte," in: *Der Stern*, No. 24 (1959), 28–34 and 62–65; as well as Gun, *Eva Braun-Hitler*, 58ff.

79. Hitler in a letter to Maria Reiter on December 23, 1926, reproduced and reprinted in: Peis, "Unbekannte Geliebte."

80. Statement made by Rudolf Pfeiffer-Bechstein in the television documentary "Die Frauen und Hitler," Part I, Thomas Hausner (Director), Bayerischer Rundfunk, 2000.

81. The latest study regarding this relationship, unfortunately not differentiating the sources sufficiently critically, comes from Ronald Hayman, *Hitler & Geli* (New York/London, 1997).

82. See Anna Maria Sigmund, *Die Frauen der Nazis* (Vienna, 1998), 136 and 138; as well as Schroeder, *Chef*, 296 (here notes, edited by Anton Joachimsthaler); see also Alfred Maleta, *Bewältigte Vergangenheit. Österreich 1932–1945* (Graz, 1981), 48ff.

83. Hess in a letter to his family on September 17, 1927, in: Hess, *Briefe 1908–1933*, 384f.

84. This letter was reproduced and printed in the auction catalogue issued by the Munich auction house Hermann Historica of 1993. According to Emil Maurice's son, Dr. Klaus Maurice, it used to belong to his family; here quoted from Sigmund, *Frauen der Nazis*, 140f.

85. Minutes taken of the public meeting of the Spruchkammer [German denazification court] of the internment camp Regensburg on May 13, 1948, in: StA Munich, Spruchkammer, Box 1131.

86. See Maurice's curriculum vitae dated February 23, 1948, in: ibid.

87. Quoted from Gun, *Eva Braun-Hitler*, 20.

88. Hitler in a letter to Winifred Wagner on December 30, 1927, in: Bärbel

Dusik (ed.), *Hitler. Reden, Schriften, Anordnungen,* Vol. II/2 (Munich, 1992), 587.

89. See Schroeder, *Chef,* 364 (notes). For more detail on the dispute before the court, see also Hanfstaengl's unpublished reminiscences (1956), in: BSB, NL Hanfstaengl, Ana 405/47; as well as the statement Hans Kallenbach made under oath on May 7, 1947, in: StA Munich, Spruchkammer, Box 1131.

90. Otto Strasser, *Hitler und ich* (Konstanz, 1948), 97f.

91. Günter Peis, "Hitlers unbekannte Geliebte," in: *Der Stern,* No. 24 (1959).

92. Draft of a letter Walter Buch was to write to Hitler on October 1, 1928, in: Albrecht Tyrell, *Führer befiehl . . . Selbstzeugnisse aus der »Kampfzeit« der NSDAP. Dokumentation und Analyse* (Dusseldorf, 1969), 212.

93. *Goebbels Diaries* I/1 (1987), 246 (entry made on July 17, 1928).

94. Draft of a letter Walter Buch was to write to Hitler on October 1, 1928, in: Tyrell, *Führer befiehl,* 212f. The part in parentheses was deleted by Buch in the original.

95. *Goebbels Diaries* I/1 (1987), 280 (entry made on October 19, 1928).

96. See the reference Hitler wrote for Maurice on August 1, 1928, regarding his work; in: IfZ Munich, ZS 270: "Herr Emil Maurice was in my employ as a driver between July, 1921, and January, 1928. Herr Maurice has proven to be an excellent and extremely safe driver and his skills go far beyond those of the average driver."

97. Maurice's curriculum vitae dated February 23, 1948, in: StA Munich, Spruchkammer, Box 1131.

98. See Strasser, *Hitler und ich,* 98.

99. See the minutes taken of the public meeting of the Spruchkammer [German denazification court] of the internment camp Regensburg on May 13, 1948, in: StA Munich, Spruchkammer, Box 1131.

100. "Nachlaß Julius Schaub (Sammlung Irving)," Vol. 1, in: IfZ Munich, ED 100/202, p. 3.

101. So Emil Maurice told Nerin Erin Gun, quoted from *Eva Braun-Hitler,* 20.

102. Hanfstaengl's unpublished reminiscences (1956), in: BSB, NL Hanfstaengl, Ana 405/47.

103. Schroeder, *Chef,* 153.

104. Quoted from Hoffmann, *Friend,* 150.

105. Schroeder, *Chef,* 235.

106. Schirach, *Frauen,* 64.

107. See Maurice's letter to the Staatsministerium für Sonderaufgaben [roughly: State Ministry for Special Tasks] on September 12, 1949, in: StA Munich, Spruchkammer, Box 1131.

108. See the minutes taken of the public meeting of the Spruchkammer [German denazification court] of the internment camp Regensburg on May 13, 1948, in: ibid.

109. Decision made by the Appeals Court on July 17, 1949, in: StA Munich, Spruchkammer, Box 20.

110. The existence of such a letter written by Hitler on March 13, 1933, is evidenced by the statement the widow of Emil Maurice made under oath on August 3, 1993, private property of Dr. Klaus Maurice, whom I thank very much for kindly making a copy available to me.

111. See the Exhibition Catalogue, "München – Hauptstadt der Bewegung" (Munich, 1993), 234.

112. See Wolfram Selig, "Ermordet im Namen des Führers. Die Opfer des Röhm-Putsches in München," in: Winfried Becker/Werner Chrobak (eds.), *Staat, Kultur, Politik. Festschrift für Dieter Albrecht* (Kallmünz, 1992), 341–356, here 344.

113. *Berliner Illustrierte Nachtausgabe,* No. 154 (July 5, 1934).

114. See Julius Schaub, "Der Führer in der Festung Landsberg," in: *Adolf Hitler. Bilder aus dem Leben des Führers* (Altona/Bahrenfeld, 1936), 127f.; as well as the photograph, in: ibid., 118.

115. Investigative report on Maurice dated March 1, 1948, in: StA Munich, Spruchkammer, Box 1131.

116. Statement of defense dated April 22, 1948, in: ibid.

117. Affidavit submitted by his wife, Dr. Hedwig Maurice, on August 3, 1993, private property of Dr. Klaus Maurice.

118. See *Völkischer Beobachter,* No. 133 (May 13, 1935).

119. See affidavit submitted by his wife, Dr. Hedwig Maurice, on August 3, 1993, private property of Dr. Klaus Maurice.

120. Secret memorandum written by Heinrich Himmler on August 31, 1935, quoted from Peter Hoffmann, *Die Sicherheit des Diktators. Hitlers Leibwachen, Schutzmaßnahmen, Residenzen, Hauptquartiere* (Munich/Zurich, 1975), 66f.

121. Auguste Behrend, "Meine Tochter Magda Goebbels," in: *Schwäbische Illustrierte* (April 5, 1952).

122. See ibid., as well as the somewhat melodramatic reconstruction of the atmosphere in Otto Wagener, *Hitler aus nächster Nähe. Aufzeichnungen*

eines Vertrauten 1929–1932, edited by Henry A. Turner (Frankfurt a.M., 1978), 375ff.

123. Quoted from Leni Riefenstahl, *Memoiren* (Munich, 1987), 201.

124. Lüdecke, *I knew Hitler*, 418.

125. See Ralf Georg Reuth, *Goebbels. Eine Biographie* (Munich, 1990), 196ff.; as well as Anja Klabunde, *Magda Goebbels, Annäherung an ein Leben* (Munich, 1999), 144.

126. Wagener, *Hitler aus nächster Nähe*, 358.

127. Hess in a letter to Ilse Pröhl on June 8, 1924, in: Hess, *Briefe*, 332.

128. Anna Maria Sigmund, *Frauen der Nazis*, 154f., shows that Hitler's piety was very limited at the time.

129. Between May 22 and 26, 1932, Hitler was indeed campaigning in the county of Oldenburg, see Klaus Schaap, *Oldenburgs Weg ins Dritte Reich* (Oldenburg, 1983), 112ff.; as well as Edgar Grundig, *Chronik der Stadt Wilhelmshaven* (typescript of 1957), Vol. 2, 153, in: StA Oldenburg.

130. Riefenstahl, *Memoiren*, 159f.

131. For more information in this regard, see Rainer Rother, *Leni Riefenstahl. Die Verführung des Talents* (Berlin, 2000).

132. Lüdecke, *I knew Hitler*, 476f. (The entire quote reads, "In those days I was the happiest man in the world.")

133. *Goebbels Diaries* I/2 (1987), 253f. (entry made on October 5, 1932).

134. Quoted from Hoffmann, *Friend*, 141. (The entire quote reads, "You know my point of view, Hoffmann. It's perfectly true that I love flowers; but that's no reason why I should become a gardener!")

135. Lüdecke, *I knew Hitler*, 477. (The entire quote reads, "I said that it was better for you to have women than men.")

136. See Curzio Malaparte, *Der Staatsstreich*, Leipzig 1932, pp. 234, 236.

137. See *inter alia*, Robert Schirokauer's essay "Die Frau Hitler," published in *Das Freie Wort*, the Social Democrat periodical, no. 45, Nov. 6, 1932 (pp. 4–9): "If one were not acquainted with the homosexual misdemeanors of the Nazi leaders and their members, one would have to theoretically infer them from the character of their party." (p. 7)—Malaparte remarked on the politically explosive nature of his *Staatsstreich* in a foreword to the German edition of his celebrated novel *Kaputt* (Stuttgart 1951, p. 7f.).

138. Quoted from Riefenstahl, *Memoiren*, 214. In addition, see the reminiscences of the Gauleiter of Hannover: Hartmann Lauterbacher, *Erlebt und mitgestaltet. Kronzeuge einer Epoche 1923 bis 1945* (Preußisch Oldendorff, 1984), 166f.

139. Eugenio Dollmann, *Roma Nazista* (Milano, 1949), 41. (The original quote reads, "'Sempre la missione, la missione, la missione, il sacrificio e l'abnegazione: a questo modo', osservò con un sorriso, 'abbiamo felicimente realizzato l'autentico Reich maschile'. Naturalmente la gente crederà che la mia esistenza si svolga in ben altra maniera: se sapesse!")

140. Interrogation of Julius Schaub on March 12, 1947, in: StA Nürnberg, KV-Interrogations S-35.

141. Statement made by Herbert Döring in the television documentary "Die Frauen und Hitler," Part I (Thomas Hausner, Director, Bayerischer Rundfunk, 2000), where he adds, "Let me be completely honest with you. We did some spy work back then—no one knew about that—to see if we could find anything in the beds. And in all those years, that never happened. I am sure of that. But that's all I want to say about this private matter."

142. Article series "Heinrich Hoffmanns Erzählungen," in: *Münchener Illustrierte,* No. 47 (November 20, 1954).

143. Schroeder, *Chef,* 191.

144. Dollmann, *Roma Nazista,* 42. (The original quote reads, "'A pensarci bene', esclamò una volta Eva, 'questa mia situazione di amica ha dei lati buoni e dei vantaggi; immagini un po' quanto sia comodo per una donna non dovere mai essere gelosa di un 'altra'").

145. For general information on this phenomenon, see Marcel Proust, *Sodom und Gomorra (Auf der Suche nach der verlorenen Zeit 4)* (Frankfurt/Main, 1999), 73.

146. *Völkischer Beobachter,* No. 141 (May 20, 1936, 'Der Führer nahm Abschied von seinem treuen Begleiter').

147. See program for the "Beisetzung des Pg. Schreck" [Schreck's funeral], in: BAB, BDC Julius Schreck; as well as *Völkischer Beobachter*, No. 141 (May 20, 1936).

148. Quoted from Hans Kallenbach, *Mit Hitler auf der Festung Landsberg* (Munich, 1939, revised edition), 13.

149. Speech given by the Reichsführer SS at the grave of SS Brigadeführer Schreck on May 19, 1936, in: IfZ Munich, MA 311, Bl. 1823f.

150. The cause of his death is not entirely clear, some said it was maxillary sinusitis (*Völkischer Beobachter,* May 16, 1936), others, meningitis (*Völkischer Beobachter,* May 17, 1936).

151. For Schreck's biographical information, see the documents in: BAB, NS 26/1269.

152. See Hoffmann, *Sicherheit des Diktators,* 22.

153. See Heinz Höhne, *Der Orden unter dem Totenkopf. Die Geschichte der SS* (Gütersloh, 1967), 27f.

154. Member of the leadership Ernst Wagner in a letter to Hitler on May 20, 1926, quoted from ibid., 29.

155. See the Regional Council, Oberfranken, in a letter to police headquarters in Munich on December 16, 1925, for example. im: StA Munich, Polizeidirektion München, No. 10148, where it becomes evident that Schreck had accompanied Hitler even back then.

156. See Herbert Seehofer, *Mit dem Führer unterwegs. Kleine Stimmungsbilder einer großen Reise* (Munich, 1939), 103.

157. So Schaub said in the *Völkischer Beobachter,* No. 140 (May 19, 1936, 'Ich hatt' einen Kameraden').

158. "How I loved to drive out into the other parts of the Reich back then !" Hitler said with enthusiasm as late as January 16/17, 1942, at his headquarters; in: Werner Jochmann (ed.), *Adolf Hitler. Monologe im Führerhauptquartier 1941–1944* (Munich, 1980), 205.

159. See Lüdecke, *I knew Hitler,* 583, for example.

160. Quoted from Gitta Sereny, *Das Ringen mit der Wahrheit. Albert Speer und das deutsche Trauma* (Munich, 1995), 133.

161. See Klaus Behnken (ed.), *Deutschland-Berichte der Sozialdemokratischen Partei Deutschlands (Sopade). Dritter Jahrgang. 1936* (Salzhausen, 1980), 683.

162. "Nachlaß Julius Schaub (Sammlung Irving)," Vol. 2, in: IfZ Munich, ED 100/203, Bl. 242.

163. Julius Schreck, "Der Führer auf Reisen," in: *Adolf Hitler. Bilder aus dem Leben des Führers* (Altona/Bahrenfeld, 1936), 16.

164. See the interviews with Friedlinde Wagner, in: *Office of Strategic Services, Hitler Source Book,* 4f. (here quoted from the Nizkor Project: www.nizkor.org).

165. Oral statement made to the author by Frau Jobst, Bayreuth, on February 29, 2000.

166. Magda Schreck in a letter to Hitler on June 9, 1936, in: BAB, NS 10/121.

167. Maria Schreck in a letter to the Reich Chancellery on June 11, 1936, in: ibid.

168. Notes taken by Bouhler after a telephone conversation with Schaub on June 25, 1936, in: ibid. The fact that Schaub was the messenger suggests that Hitler personally made this decision.

169. So Albert Speer said to Joachim C. Fest, see *Hitler. Eine Biographie* (Munich, 2000), 716.

170. Hans Grimm, *Suchen und Hoffen. 1928–1934* (Lippoldsberg, 1972), 11.

171. See Hoffmann, *Sicherheit des Diktators,* 189.

172. See Horst Möller (ed.), *Die tödliche Utopie. Bilder, Texte, Dokumente, Daten zum Dritten Reich* (Munich, 1999), 15ff.

173. See Otto Dietrich, *12 Jahre mit Hitler* (Munich, 1955), 162; with regard to Hitler's stays in Hamburg, see Werner Johe, *Hitler in Hamburg. Dokumente zu einem besonderen Verhältnis* (Hamburg, 1996), 238f.

174. This term was coined by Ernst Hanfstaengl; *Außenseiter,* 310.

175. *Goebbels Diaries* I/1 (1987), 551 (entry made on May 24, 1930).

176. See the interrogation of Julius Schaub on March 12, 1947, in: StA Nürnberg, KV-Interrogations S-35.

177. Schroeder, *Chef,* 42.

178. Greetings telegram Speer sent to Schaub on August 21, 1942, in: BAB, NS 51/39, Bl. 55.

179. Quoted from Hans-Otto Meissner, "Der letzte Befehl" (unpublished manuscript), in: IfZ Munich, MS 291, S. 4.

180. Hanfstaengl, *Außenseiter,* 103.

181. Interrogation of Schaub in Nuremberg on December 7, 1946, in: StA Nürnberg, KV-Interrogations S-35.

182. The fact that Schaub knew many people there is evidenced by the many letters of congratulations he received on the occasion of his forty-fourth birthday in August 1942, in: BAB, NS 51/39.

183. Schroeder, *Chef,* 44.

184. Hanfstaengl, *Außenseiter,* 227.

185. Letter written by "several inhabitants and residents of Ickstatt" on April 5, 1923, in: StA Munich, Polizeidirektion München, No. 10142.

186. Kallenbach, *Mit Adolf Hitler* (1943), 79.

187. See *Nachlaß Julius Schaub (Sammlung Irving),* Vol. 1, in: IfZ Munich, ED 100/202, Bl. 8.

188. According to Christa Schroeder, Schaub even brought "his girlfriend" with him to the Obersalzberg, where he went in great haste in April 1945, to destroy Hitler's private papers. She was "a dancer with the 'Metropol' in Berlin" (Schroeder, *Chef,* 214).

189. Schroeder, *Chef,* 43.

190. *Goebbels Diaries* I/3 (1987), 380 (entry made on December 23, 1937).

191. Reprinted in Werner Maser, *Hitlers Briefe und Notizen. Sein Weltbild in handschriftlichen Dokumenten* (Dusseldorf, 1973).

192. See the list of checks Hitler wrote through the Reichsbank, in: StA Nuremberg, Nürnberger Dokumente, NG-5346.

193. See Hans-Otto Meissner, "Der letzte Befehl" (unpublished manuscript), in: IfZ Munich, MS 291, S. 1. – With regard to this event, see also Schroeder, *Chef*, 213.

194. Quoted from Meissner, "Befehl," in: IfZ Munich, MS 291, S. 1.

CHAPTER 5

1. See Ernst Röhm, *Die Geschichte eines Hochverräters* (Munich, 1934, 6th ed.), 350.

2. See Heinrich Bennecke, "Die Memoiren des Ernst Röhm. Ein Vergleich der verschiedenen Ausgaben und Auflagen," in: *Politische Studien*, Vol. 14 (1963), 186–188.

3. See Röhm, *Hochverräter*, 357ff.

4. See Ian Kershaw, *Hitler*, Vol. 1: 1889–1936. Hubris. 1st American ed. (New York, 1999), 309ff.

5. See Peter Longerich, *Die braunen Bataillone. Geschichte der SA* (Munich, 1989), 93ff.

6. See Adolf Hitler's proclamation "An die gesamte SA und SS" [To the entire SA and SS] on September 2, 1930, published in Heinrich Bennecke, *Hitler und die SA* (Munich/Vienna, 1962), 252.

7. With regard to the Stennes crisis and its repercussions, see Kershaw, *Hitler*, Vol. 1, 346ff.; as well as Susanne Meinl, *Nationalsozialisten gegen Hitler* (Berlin, 2000), 167ff.

8. See the advertisements for books in the board newspaper of the ocean vessels belonging to Norddeutscher Lloyd, *Lloyd-Zeitung*, No. 1 (January 1934).

9. See Otto Wagener, *Hitler aus nächster Nähe. Aufzeichnungen eines Vertrauten 1929–1932*, edited by Henry A. Turner (Frankfurt a.M., 1978), 195ff.

10. Quoted from Bennecke, *Hitler und die SA*, 253.

11. Entry made on February 27, 1931, in: Elke Fröhlich (ed.), *Die Tagebücher von Joseph Goebbels. Sämtliche Fragmente*, Vol. I/2 (Munich, etc., 1987), 27. Goebbels had made an entry in his diary as early as June 2, 1929, where he said, "This vice goes around like the plague"; "I hate it with all my soul so that I cannot even bring myself to be as tolerant as I would be with any robber and murderer" (ibid., 381).

12. Ibid., 125 (entry made on February 9, 1932).

13. See Peter Martin Lampel, "Niemandes Knecht" (unpublished memoirs), in: Staats- und Universitätsbibliothek Hamburg, NL Lampel, NK 432, 418.

14. With regard hereto, see Edmund Heines: *Gerhard Rossbach, Mein Weg durch die Zeit. Erinnerungen und Bekenntnisse* (Weilburg, 1950), 137ff. and 234; as well as Kurt G. W. Lüdecke, *I knew Hitler. The Story of a Nazi Who Escaped The Blood Purge* (New York, 1937), 246, 351, 619, and especially 777; see also Bernd-Ulrich Hergemöller, *Mann für Mann. Biographisches Lexikon zur Geschichte von Freundesliebe und mann-männlicher Sexualität im deutschen Sprachraum* (Hamburg, 1998), 332f.; and Hermann Weiß (ed.), *Biographisches Lexikon zum Dritten Reich* (Frankfurt a.M., 1999), 191f.

15. See Konrad Heiden, *Der Führer. Hitler's Rise to Power* (Boston, 1944), 294; as well as Hergemöller, *Mann für Mann,* 341f. with further proof.

16. This is how Arno Schickedanz, Alfred Rosenberg's substitute in Berlin and great connoisseur of the local Nazi scene, called it in his letter to Rosenberg on June 4, 1932, in: BAB, NS 8/116, Bl. 41. – With regard to Helldorff's NS career, see also Ted Harrison, "'Alter Kämpfer' im Wider-stand. Graf Helldorff, die NS-Bewegung und die Opposition gegen Hitler," in: VfZ, Bd. 45 (1997), 385–423.

17. With regard to Karl Ernst's beginnings, see the statement contemporary witness Christian Adolf Isermeyer made to Andreas Sternweiler (ed.), in: *Liebe, Forschung, Lehre. Der Kunsthistoriker Christian Adolf Isermeyer* (Berlin, 1998), 36; also Lampel, "Niemandes Knecht," in: Staats- und Universitätsbibliothek Hamburg, NL Lampel, NK 432, S. 532ff.; as well as Hergemöller, *Mann für Mann,* 206f. and 591 with additional sources.

18. *Goebbels Diaries* I/2 (1987), 98 (entry made on August 6, 1931).

19. Statement Isermeyer made to Sternweiler, quoted from *Liebe, Forschung, Lehre,* 36.

20. Eugenio Dollmann, *Roma Nazista* (Milano, 1949), 34. (The original quote reads, "Dopo il 30 giugno del 1934, trovandomi a Monaco, Los-sow mi assicurò che Hitler sapeva da tempo minutamente quanto accadeva nelle case di Roehm e dei suoi aiutanti, appunto perché i Michael, Joseph e Maxl erano ormai membri delle SA.") Many pieces of evidence herefore can further be found in: StA München, Polizeidirektion München, No. 15540; as well as in: BAB, R 22/5005.

21. With regard to this matter, see also the many references in: Andreas Dornheim, *Röhms Mann fürs Ausland. Politik und Ermordung des SA-Agenten Georg Bell* (Münster, 1998), 53ff.

22. Ministerial conference on July 3, 1934, in: *Akten der Reichskanzlei. Die Regierung Hitler. Teil I: 1933/34, Bd. 2* (edited by Karl-Heinz Minuth, Boppard a.Rh., 1983), 1355.

23. See Meinl, *Nationalsozialisten,* 168f.

24. See the fragments of a secret report for the party leadership with handwritten date of December 21, 1931, in: BAB, NS 26/87.

25. *Goebbels Diaries* I/2 (1987), 65 (entry made on May 17, 1931).
Goebbels had wondered as early as April 29 if "he and Göring are playing dishonest games with me" (ibid., 57).

26. *Rote Fahne,* No. 53 (March 11, 1932).

27. See *Münchener Post* dated April 14, 1931, where an article entitled "Stammtisch 175" [Table Reserved for 175ers] accuses the SA of being ruled by a "175ers" clique. Röhm and Heines are mentioned by name. In the April 23, 1931, edition, the *Münchener Post* widened its accusations by accusing Röhm of amusing himself with male prostitutes.

28. Fragments of a secret report for the party leadership with handwritten date of December 21, 1931, in: BAB, NS 26/87.

29. For more details regarding Schulz, see Dornheim, *Röhms Mann fürs Ausland,* 107ff.

30. *Goebbels Diaries* I/2 (1987), 45 (entry made on April 9, 1931). See also the entry made on April 21, 1931: "I am in total agreement with Schulz. He understands the problem regarding Prussia. The way Munich sees it, will not work. . . . Schulz sees it clearly and unerringly" (ibid., 53).

31. Ibid., 67 (entry made on May 20, 1931).

32. Ibid., 72 (entry made on June 2, 1931).

33. Fragments of an undated secret report to the party leadership (probably August 1931), in: BAB, NS 26/87.

34. *Münchener Post,* No. 142 dated June 24, 1931 ("Das Braune Haus der Homosexuellen" [The Braunes Haus Filled With Homosexuals]).

35. *Goebbels Diaries* I/2 (1987), 83 (entry made on June 24, 1931).

36. Quoted from the facsimile of the letter Röhm wrote to an unidentified "comrade" on July 17, 1931, in: *Rote Fahne,* No. 53 (March 11, 1932).

37. *Münchener Post,* March 23, 1932.

38. For more details regarding this event, see the documentation put together by Herbert Heinersdorf (pen name for Richard Linsert), "Akten zum Falle Röhm," in: *Mitteilungen des Wissenschaftlich-humanitären Komitees,* No. 32 (January/March 1932), 349–363, No. 33 (April/August 1932), 387–396, and No. 34 (September 1932/February 1933), 419–428.

39. See also the files in the brochure published by Wilhelm Hillebrand, *Herunter mit der Maske! Erlebnisse hinter den Kulissen der N.S.D.A.P.* (Berlin-Lichterfelde, undated, but published in 1929), especially 50f. In Goebbels' diaries we read that the Berlin Gauleiter, a man of extremely antihomosexual sentiments who initially was greatly afraid of the Göt-

ting affair, was irritated by Hitler's "easy way out" of not getting involved, but he then gave in: Götting "really is a nice guy. I don't really think that he is a practicing 175er" (*Goebbels Diaries* I/1 (1987), 331, entry made on February 13, 1929; see also ibid., 285f. and 295).

40. See Nos. 140 and 141 of the *Münchener Post* of June 22 and 23, 1931 ("Warme Brüderschaft im Braunen Haus" [A Warm Brotherhood in the Braunes Haus]). Here, too, Otto Strasser is supposed to have been involved. See the undated secret report to the party leadership (most likely August 1931), in: BAB, NS 26/87.

41. So Ernst Röhm's attorney Dr. Walter Luetgebrune wrote in a letter dated March 7, 1932, published in the *Völkischer Beobachter* of March 9, 1932, here quoted from Heinersdorf, *Akten zum Fall Röhm,* Part III, 419–428, especially 419f.

42. Quoted from "Heinrich Hoffmanns Erzählungen," in: *Münchener Illustrierte,* No. 50 (1954).

43. See Kershaw, *Hitler,* Vol. 1, 360ff.

44. See Erwin Barth, *Joseph Goebbels und die Formierung des Führer-Mythos 1917–1934* (Erlangen, 1999), 110ff.

45. *Münchener Post,* No. 57 (March 9, 1932).

46. See the *Hamburger Echo,* No. 63 (March 9, 1932), for example, where "the love letters of Chief of Staff Röhm" are discussed in detail. The SPD [Social Democratic Party of Germany] central organ, *Vorwärts,* had published paraphrases from the letters under the heading "The Röhm System. Revelations about Chief Mercenary Hitler" in its No. 113 (March 7, 1932). In later numbers, the paper exploited these revelations like a good scandal.

47. See *Münchener Post,* No. 140 (June 22, 1931: "Warme Brüderschaft im Braunen Haus" [Warm Brotherhood in the Braunes Haus]).

48. Helmuth Klotz, *Euer Hochwohlgeboren* (Berlin-Tempelhof, 1932); the second printing was entitled *Der Fall Röhm* (Berlin-Tempelhof, 1932).

49. See minutes taken during Röhm's questioning in 1931, printed in the *Vorwärts,* No. 117 (March 10, 1932: "Röhm bestätigt!" [Röhm Confirms!"). See also *Vorwärts,* No. 157 (April 4, 1932: "Die Röhm-Briefe echt!" [Röhm Letters Authentic!]).

50. For the biography of Klotz, see Herbert Linder, *Von der NSDAP zur SPD. Der politische Lebensweg des Dr. Helmuth Klotz (1894–1943)* (Konstanz, 1998).

51. Helmuth Klotz, *Wir gestalten durch unser Führerkorps die Zukunft* (Berlin, 1932, 2nd ed.).

52. See Linder, *Von der NSDAP zur SPD,* 171. For an interpretation of the

campaign, see also Harry Oosterhuis, "The 'Jew' of the Antifascist Left. Homosexuality and Socialist Resistance to Nazism," in: Gert Hekma u.a. (eds.), *Gay Men and the Sexual History of the Political Left* (New York, 1995), 227–257.

53. For a sexohistorical interpretation of this self-description, see Eleanor Hancock, "'Only the Real, the True, the Masculine Held Its Value.' Ernst Röhm, Masculinity, and Male Homosexuality," in: *Journal of the History of Sexuality,* Vol. 8 (1997/98), 628ff.

54. Quoted from Klotz, *Der Fall Röhm,* 7.

55. Quoted from ibid., 8f.

56. Quoted from ibid., 16f.

57. See Appendix to the minutes taken during the questioning performed by the Sicherheitspolizei and the SD in January 1941, in: BAB-DH, NJ 2993, Vol. 2, here taken from Linder, *Von der NSDAP zur SPD,* 168f., where the following quotes come from was well. See also the article Klotz wrote entitled "Doktor Diehls schlechtes Gewissen" in the periodical *Volkswille* (February 7, 1934), in: BAB-DH, ZR 881, Vol. 6, Bl. 124.

58. This event caused some National Socialists to brutally mistreat Klotz in the Reichtstag lobby on May 12, 1932, among them Röhm's close friend Edmund Heines. About ten years later, the Peoples Court sentenced Klotz to death. He was executed in Plötzensee in February 1943; see Linder, *Von der NSDAP zur SPD,* 174ff. and 318ff.

59. Klotz, *Der Fall Röhm,* 4.

60. Appendix to the minutes taken during the questioning by the Sicherheitspolizei and the SD in January 1941, in: BAB-DH, NJ 2993, Vol. 2, here quoted from Linder, *Von der NSDAP zur SPD,* 169.

61. See Carl Severing, *Mein Lebensweg.* Vol. 2: *Im Auf und Ab der Republik* (Cologne, 1950), 332.

62. Appendix to the minutes taken during the questioning by the Sicherheitspolizei and the SD in January 1941, in: BAB-DH, NJ 2993, Vol. 2, here quoted from Linder, *Von der NSDAP zur SPD,* 169.

63. That was the day when the Prussian government with SPD majority was removed from office by a coup led by Reich Chancellor Franz von Papen.

64. BAB, BDC Rudolf Diels, printed in Christoph Graf, *Politische Polizei zwischen Demokratie und Diktatur. Die Entwicklung der preußischen Politischen Polizei vom Staatsschutzorgan der Weimarer Republik zum Geheimen Staatspolizeiamt des Dritten Reiches* (Berlin, 1983), 411; the following information were taken from ibid., 322.

65. See Rudolf Diels, *Lucifer ante portas . . . es spricht der erste Chef der Gestapo . . .* (Stuttgart, 1950), especially 253ff. and 376ff.

66. See Spruchgerichtsakte [German denazification court files] Rudolf Diels, in: BAK, Z 42 IV/1960, Bl. 273ff.

67. So the then Diels colleague Walther Korrodi wrote in his brochure published anonymously, *Ich kann nicht schweigen* (Zurich, 1936), 167. See also Graf, *Politische Polizei*, 322.

68. The meticulous study performed by Alexander Bahar/Wilfried Kugel, *Der Reichstagsbrand* (Berlin, 2001) comes to very similar conclusions in its biographical research regarding Diels. See 717ff.

69. Hans Bernd Gisevius, *Bis zum bitteren Ende. Vom Reichstagsbrand bis zum 20. Juli 1944* (Zurich, 1961), 100.

70. Anonymous (Walther Korrodi), *Ich kann nicht schweigen*, 162ff.

71. Speech given on the occasion of the eleventh anniversary of the NSDAP in the Munich Hofbräuhaus on February 24, 1931, in: Klaus A. Lankheit (ed.), *Hitler. Reden, Schriften, Anordnungen*, Vol. V/1 (Munich, 1996), 224.

72. For more details, see the documents in: Landesarchiv Berlin, Rep. 58, Zug 399, No. 517, Vols. I–III.

73. For this event and the one described below, see the detailed reconstruction of the investigation against Röhm on the basis of primary sources in: Burkhard Jellonnek, *Homosexuelle unter dem Hakenkreuz* (Paderborn, 1990), 62ff.

74. Reprint of the Munich police report dated April 7, 1931, quoted from: Heinersdorf, *Akten zum Fall Röhm* (Part III), 425. See also Jellonnek, *Homosexuelle*, 62.

75. "Official Statement" made by Staatsanwaltschaftsrat [District Attorney] Dr. Kreismann on August 4, 1932, in: GStA PK Berlin, I. HA Rep. 84 a, No. 52606.

76. See statement made by Albert Grzesinski to the American Secret Service on May 8, 1943, in: *Office of Strategic Services, Hitler Source Book* (here quoted from the Nizkor Project: www.nizkor.org).

77. Undated secret report to the party leadership (probably from August 1931), in: BAB, NS 26/87. See also BAK, NL Rheindorf No. 427, Bl. 20ff.

78. Braun in a letter to Brüning ("by his own hand") dated March 4, 1932, in: BAK, R 43 I/2683, Bl. 27.

79. Röhm's attorney Walter Luetgebrune presented it as a "fact that the Reich Chancellor—a man who did not have the slightest relationship

with any kind of prosecuting activities in Prussia or Bavaria—had nothing more important to do than to request and gain insight into the files on Röhm." *Ein Kampf um Röhm* (Diessen, 1933), 10.

80. For more information on the tactics used by Brüning, see Herbert Hömig, *Kanzler in der Krise der Republik. Eine Weimarer Biographie* (Paderborn, 2000), 486ff., who does not say anything about the attempt made by the Prussian prime minister.

81. So Röhm's attorney Luetgebrune wrote in a letter to the Bavarian Minister of Justice Gürtner on March 1, 1932, in: BAB, R 22/5005 with the additional information that the Reichswehr Minister had declared "he would not tolerate such a manner of fighting."

82. Memorandum of a discussion with Franz Pfeffer von Salomon on February 20, 1953, in: IfZ Munich, ZS 177.

83. Lüdecke, *I knew Hitler,* 493f. (The entire quote reads, "It's also true, and I admit it to my shame, that the vulnerability you mentioned has delivered me into his hands. It's a terrible thing. . . . I've lost my independence for always. . . . You know as well as I do how Hitler can wear you down. . . . And we, *we ourselves*, have made him what he is. . . . My position is so precarious. . . . I stick to my job, following him blindly, loyal to the utmost—there's nothing else left me" (stresses made by the original author).

84. See Hierl's letter to Hitler dated March 24, 1932, in: BAK, NL Epp No. 73, Bl. 1ff.

85. For more details, see Hans-Günther Richardi/Klaus Schumann, *Geheimakte Gerlich/Bell. Röhms Pläne für ein Reich ohne Hitler* (Munich, 1993), 72ff.; as well as Dornheim, *Röhms Mann fürs Ausland,* 53ff., who has detailed source information.

86. So Hitler declared on April 6, 1932; in: Klaus A. Lankheit (ed.), *Hitler. Reden, Schriften, Anordnungen,* Vol. V/1 (Munich, 1996), 32. See also the relevant commentary in the *Vossische Zeitung,* No. 168 (April 7, 1932); the *Vorwärts,* No. 163 (April 7, 1932) as well as the *Münchener Neueste Nachrichten* (April 8, 1932).

87. See the relevant passage in the confidential letter Martin Bormann wrote to Hess on October 5, 1932, in: IfZ Munich, Fa 36.

88. *Völkischer Beobachter,* March 9, 1932.

89. See Harry Oosterhuis, *The "Jew,"* 228ff.; as well as Hancock, *Male Homosexuality,* 228ff.

90. *Vorwärts,* No. 163 (April 7, 1932).

91. Klaus Mann, "Die Linke und das Laster," in: *Europäische Hefte/Aufruf*

(1934), 675–678, here 676. For more context, see Manfred Herzer, "Communists, Social Democrats, and the Homosexual Movement in the Weimar Republic," in: Hekma (ed.), *Gay Men*, 197–226.

92. So Goebbels said in an article entitled "Adolf Hitler als Mensch" [Adolf Hitler as a Human Being], in: *Der Angriff*, No. 64 (April 4, 1932).

93. For more detail, see the reminiscences of Hitler's then attorney: Hans Frank, *Im Angesicht des Galgens. Deutung Hitlers und seiner Zeit auf Grund eigener Erlebnisse und Erkenntnisse* (Munich-Gräfelfing, 1953), 87ff.

94. So Klotz wrote in the second edition of his brochure "Der Fall Röhm" in September 1932, 2.

95. *Frankfurter Zeitung*, November 14, 1932.

96. See the conclusion Paul Schulz came to in his 1951 "Memorandum" on these events, printed in a brochure published by his son Alexander Paul Schulz entitled "Rettungen und Hilfeleistungen an Verfolgte 1933–1945 durch Oberleutnant a.D. Paul Schulz" (Laichingen, 1967), 8. I would like to thank Dr. A. P. Schulz for his kind permission to gain insight into this document.

97. See Dollmann, *Roma Nazista*, 35.

98. In a detailed letter to Rudolf Hess in early October 1932, Martin Bormann voiced the shock over Hitler's behavior felt in the membership of the NSDAP. It says there, Röhm is the "weakest link of our front" and he puts the movement through one endurance test after the next; to keep him would be "extremely dangerous" with regard to elections. "From this point of view, I cannot understand the boss's [Hitler's – LM] attitude." (Bormann in a letter to Hess on October 5, 1932, in: IfZ Munich, Fa 36). Hitler's adjutant Schaub is alleged to have "instigated an underhanded plot against Röhm—apparently to make him appear unacceptable" (*Goebbels Diaries* I/2 (1987), 253, entry made on October 5, 1932). In October 1932, the publisher and later associate of Goebbels, Ernst Lehmann, tried to convince Hitler by providing him with the expert report of a respected German psychiatrist who stated that homosexuality was still seen as one of the "most serious signs of degeneration" among experts and that therefore Röhm was not suitable for any executive duties. All of this made the "Führer" angry. (Oswald Bumke, *Erinnerungen und Betrachtungen. Der Weg eines deutschen Psychiaters* [Munich, 1952], 163ff.).

99. The fact that homosexuality must have played a large role there is evident from a comment Goebbels made to Leni Riefenstahl on the eve of this meeting. See Riefenstahl, *Memoiren* (Munich, 1987), 183f.

100. Quoted from Bumke, *Betrachtungen,* 163. According to the *Münchener Post* dated October 15/16, 1932, Hitler is supposed to have said this as early as in the middle of October 1932.

101. Undated minutes of the interrogation of Walter Luetgebrune's longtime employee Edith Gehse (Appendix to a letter Heydrich wrote to party judge Buch on October 26, 1934), in: BAB, BDC Walter Luetgebrune.

102. This has become evident from the letter Röhm wrote to Luetgebrune on September 5, 1932, where he assures the "dear, most esteemed Gentleman" that he had already "talked with the Führer regarding the not very pleasant manner about which you were justifiably upset in the Kaiserhof last time" (BAK, NL 150/115). Luetgebrune himself mentions this "single conversation with the Führer regarding this matter" in his letter to councilor of state von Strauss on September 16, 1936, in: BAB, BDC Walter Luetgebrune.

103. Walter Luetgebrune, *Ein Kampf um Röhm* (Diessen, 1933), 4; the following quotes are ibid., 6ff. (stresses made by the original author).

104. Walter Buch in a letter to detective chief inspector Obermüller at the Munich Police Headquarters (most likely in the summer of 1949, shortly before Buch committed suicide), in: StA Munich, Staatsamwaltschaften, No. 28791/1.

105. *Völkischer Beobachter,* No. 270, September 27, 1933 ("Gegen das Muckertum" [Against Cant]).

106. Diary entry made by Hermann Pünder on August 18, 1932, after a conversation with Undersecretary in the Reich Chancellery Planck, quoted from Pünder, *Politik in der Reichskanzlei. Aufzeichnungen aus den Jahren 1929–1932,* edited by Thilo Vogelsang (Stuttgart, 1961), 141.

107. See *Völkischer Beobachter,* No. 1/2 (January 2, 1934).

108. As Heinrich Böll writes in his memoires, even after 1933 people wrote on the walls of buildings, "Wash Your SA Ass! Röhm Is On The Way!" (Böll, *Was soll aus dem Jungen bloß werden? Oder: Irgendwas mit Büchern* [Bornheim, 1981], 37f.).

109. Anonymous (Walther Korrodi), *Ich kann nicht schweigen,* 107 and 110. More information on the political functions and activities of Karl Ernst can be found in Bahar/Kugel, *Reichstagsbrand,* 559ff.

110. See the drastic depiction in Bella Fromm, *Als Hitler mir die Hand küßte* (Berlin, 1993), 154f., which refers to a gala reception in the embassy of Turkey on October 30, 1933.

111. Hermann Rauschning, *Gespräche mit Hitler* (Zurich, 1940), 94f. (stresses made by the original author).

112. Lüdecke, *I knew Hitler,* 673. (the entire quote reads, "that Damocles sword isn't going to hang over me any longer.")

113. Quoted from Fromm, *Hitler,* 122.

114. Hanfstaengl's unpublished reminiscences of 1956, in: BSB, NL Hanfstaengl, Ana 405/47.

115. In October 1932, Bell had written a confidential report for his attorney regarding the work he did for Röhm. That report was discovered and published a few years ago. See Richardi/Schumann, *Geheimakte,* 214–221.

116. Alfred Rosenberg, *Das politische Tagebuch Alfred Rosenbergs. Aus den Jahren 1934/35 und 1939/40,* edited by Hans-Günther Seraphim (Göttingen, 1956), 35 (entry made on July 7, 1934), where he even says, Strasser "called these kinds of people free masons where one man helps another against all of mankind without any kind of inhibitions."

117. Bell later bragged that he would be able to prove "under oath" as well as "with documents and witnesses" that "Röhm did not just look to the SPD for support against the political leadership of the NSDAP" (registered letter Bell sent to the Reich leadership of the NSDAP on October 8, 1932, in: BAB, BDC Georg Bell).

118. With regard to Bell's conspirative activities, see now also Dornheim, *Röhms Mann fürs Ausland,* who has information regarding other sources as well; and Bahar/Kugel, *Reichstagsbrand,* 653ff.; with regard to Mayr's shady career, see Karl Rohe, *Das Reichsbanner Schwarz Rot Gold* (Dusseldorf, 1966), 169ff.; as well as Dornheim, *Röhms Mann fürs Ausland,* 101ff.

119. Röhm in a letter to Mayr on September 28, 1932, printed in the *Münchener Post,* No. 240 (October 15/16, 1932). In an affidavit, Mayr even spoke of his "honorable responsibility," *Vorwärts,* No. 471 (October 6, 1932, "Röhm wird widerlegt" [Röhm is proven wrong]).

120. *Völkischer Beobachter,* October 6, 1932.

121. That was the title of the brochure published by the KPD in October 1932.

122. Goebbels, too, understood immediately that these secret negotiations had to do with homosexuality when he learned about them, see *Goebbels Diaries* I/2 (1987), 253 (entry made on October 5, 1932). In addition, see the statements made by Mayr in the so-called Tscheka trial in the summer of 1932, in: BAB, NS 26/600.

123. *Vorwärts,* No. 471 (October 6, 1932, "Röhm wird widerlegt").

124. This statement has been reported by Charles Drage, a longtime war comrade of Stennes: *Als Hitler nach Canossa ging. Biografie des Walther Stennes* (Berlin, 1982), 126.

125. Röhm hinted at that in his secret negotiations with Mayr. See *Vorwärts,* No. 471 (October 6, 1932, "Röhm wird widerlegt").

126. Severing, *Mein Lebensweg.* Vol. 2., 322; as well as the photograph before 321.

127. Bredow, *Hitler rast,* 20f.

128. For more information regarding the cooperation between Schleicher and the NS leadership during the summer of 1932, see Kershaw, *Hitler,* Vol. 1, 365ff.

129. Quoted from a report by Wolfgang Abée on the negotiations of the Hochkapitel des Jungdeutschen Ordens on July 3/4,1932, in Berlin, which had been sent to von Bredow, the head of the office of the Reichswehr Ministry, in: BAB, R 43 I, Nr. 1238, Bl. 107. Otto Strasser is mentioned there as the informant. This information is credible because of the fact that Schleicher decided not to fight this rumor with a complaint against Strasser. See the letter of the undersecretary in the Reich Chancellery to the head of the ministry office dated August 29, 1932, in: ibid., Bl. 124. – See also the suggestive statement of the head of the Freikorps Gerhard Rossbach: Schleicher "did without wine and women but loved song and horses" (*Mein Weg,* 115).

130. Levetzow in a letter to Göring on May 5 or 6, 1932, quoted from Gerhard Granier, *Magnus von Levetzow. Seeoffizier, Monarchist und Wegbereiter Hitlers* (Boppard a.Rh., 1982), 175.

131. The latter has been especially stressed by Fritz Günther von Tschirschky, *Erinnerungen eines Hochverräters* (Stuttgart, 1972), 80; the former by Rudolf Olden, *Hitler* (Amsterdam, 1935), here quoted from the new printing (Frankfurt a.M., 1984), 52f.

132. Bredow, *Hitler rast,* 21.

133. Bell, who served several masters at one, was killed by a special SS unit in April 1933, and Röhrbein was sent to Dachau shortly thereafter. For more details, see Richardi/Schumann, *Geheimakte,* 129ff.; Dornheim, *Röhms Mann fürs Ausland;* as well as Bahar/Kugel, *Reichstagsbrand,* 634ff. and 653ff.

134. Undated secret report to the party leadership (probably August 1931), in: BAB, NS 26/87.

135. Quoted from Ernst von Salomon, *Der Fragebogen* (Hamburg, 1951), 446f.

136. Tschirschky, *Erinnerungen eines Hochverräters,* 115f.

137. See Kershaw, *Hitler,* Vol. 1, 500ff.

138. It was therefore an open secret among those members of the Party who had access to the inner circle: "The Führer couldn't just get rid of the Chief

of Staff, because the latter knew too much about 1923" (statement made by Danzeisen on August 1, 1932, quoted from Richardi/Schumann, *Geheimakte,* 194). In this context, "1923" is synonymous for Hitler's beginnings.

139. Report of the German news office regarding an interview Hitler supposedly gave the American professor Pearson on July 6, 1934, and which was published by the Paris edition of the *New York Herald,* in: *Akten der Reichskanzlei. Die Regierung Hitler I/2,* 1375ff., here 1377.

140. Anonymous (Walter Korrodi), *Ich kann nicht schweigen,* here and the following quotes: 113.

141. This is also the argument of the nonidentifiable "Klaus Bredow" in the brochure *Hitler rast,* which had been published right after the so-called Röhm putsch in Saarland, an area of Germany that had not yet been brought "home into the Reich": "Hitler could not dare to not support Heines because the latter was threatening a scandal, which would have caused the downfall of the entire party leadership, including the Führer" (16).

142. So Hitler said in his speech before the Reichstag on July 13, 1934, in: *Stenographische Berichte der Verhandlungen des Deutschen Reichstages,* Vol. 458. IX. Wahlperiode, 21.

143. See Diels, *Lucifer ante portas,* 379ff.

144. See Immo von Fallois, *Kalkül und Illusion. Der Machtkampf zwischen Reichswehr und SA während der Röhm-Krise 1934* (Berlin, 1994), 125 and 131.

145. See Kershaw, *Hitler,* Vol. 1, 506.

146. Vgl. Longerich, *Bataillone,* 205.

147. BAB, NS 23/1.

148. Ernst in a letter to Heines on June 5, 1934, reprinted in the *Weißbuch über die Erschießungen des 30. Juni 1934. Authentische Darstellung der deutschen Bartholomäusnacht* (Paris, 1934), 108–111, here 110. The authenticity of this document has been questioned but may be less improbable than Hans Mommsen suggests. See "Nichts Neues in der Reichstagsbrandkontroverse. Anmerkungen zu einer Donquichotterie," in: *Zeitschrift für Geschichtswissenschaft,* Vol. 49 (2001), 352–357. If this was indeed forged by Willi Münzenberg, then he must have done it extremely well. Something like this cannot be simply invented, but at most "tweaked."

149. Martin H. Sommerfeldt, *Ich war dabei. Die Verschwörung der Dämonen 1933–1939. Ein Augenzeugenbericht* (Darmstadt, 1949), 61.

150. This is how Himmler's Adjutant Karl Wolff tells it; quoted from Jochen

von Lang, *Der Adjutant. Karl Wolff. Der Mann zwischen Hitler und Himmler* (Frankfurt a.M., 1989), 34.

151. Quoted from Longerich, *Bataillone,* 210.

152. Ernst Hanfstaengl, *Zwischen Weißem und Braunem Haus. Memoiren eines politischen Außenseiters* (Munich, 1970), 340f.

153. See Heydrich passing on the order to "all officers and employees of the Geheime Staatspolizei [Gestapo]" on June 25, 1934, in: BAB, R 58/241, Bl. 24. See also Jens Banach, *Heydrichs Elite. Das Führerkorps der Sicherheitspolizei und des SD. 1936–1945* (Paderborn etc., 1998), 95.

154. See Kershaw, *Hitler,* Vol. 1, 510f.

155. See Longerich, *Bataillone,* 215.

156. Quoted from *Völkischer Beobachter,* No. 177 (June 26, 1934).

157. Quoted from Michael Schramm, *Der Gleichschaltungsprozeß der deutschen Armee 1933–1938* (Munich, 1990), 135.

158. For the number of the victims, see Kershaw, *Hitler,* Vol. 1, 517; for the identity of the victims, see Otto Gritschneder, *"Der Führer hat Sie zum Tode verurteilt . . .". Hitlers "Röhm-Putsch"-Morde vor Gericht* (Munich, 1993), 60ff. and 121–149.

159. Ministerial conference on July 3, 1934, in: *Akten der Reichskanzlei. Die Regierung Hitler I/2,* 1358.

160. Reprinted in *Der Angriff,* No. 152 (July 2, 1934); the following quotes ibid. (stresses made by the original author).

161. Quoted from the special edition of the *Völkischer Beobachter* (July 1, 1934).

162. Ministerial conference on July 3, 1934, in: *Akten der Reichskanzlei. Die Regierung Hitler I/2,* 1355ff.

163. So Gregor Strasser's brother Otto wrote in his exile publication *Die Deutsche Revolution,* No. 16 (August 26, 1934).

164. Klausener was in possession of "embarrassing material" on the NSDAP leadership. "The other of these lines has seen part [!] of these materials himself" (Bredow, *Hitler rast,* 52f.). See also Luetgebrune, *Kampf um Röhm,* 12, where he also repeats that Klausener had collected "compelling material fit to fight the despised National Socialism."

165. With regard to Lossow and his secret dossiers, see chapter 2.

166. With regard to Zehnter, see: Gritschneder, *"Röhm-Putsch"-Morde,* 148; Otto Strasser, *Die deutsche Bartholomäusnacht* (Zurich, 1935, 3rd ed.), 88f.; Wolfram Selig, "Ermordet im Namen des Führers. Die Opfer des Röhm-Putsches in München," in: Winfried Becker/Werner Chrobak (eds.), *Staat, Kultur, Politik. Festschrift für Dieter Albrecht* (Kallmünz, 1992), 341–356, here 355.

167. With regard to Schätzl, see: Gritschneder, *"Röhm-Putsch"-Morde*, 143; Selig, *Opfer des Röhm-Putsches in München*, 347; BAB, BDC Martin Schätzl. See also the informative documents with regard to the relationship Schätzl-Röhm, in: StA Munich, Staatsanwaltschaften, No. 28791/41.

168. See Friedrich-Karl von Plehwe, *Reichskanzler Kurt von Schleicher* (Frankfurt a.M., 1989), 222 and 229.

169. This is a nationalistic organization whose structure closely resembled the traditions of the medieval Deutscher Orden.

170. Quoted from the copy of a report by Wolfgang Abée regarding the negotiations of the Hochkapitel [leadership] of the Jungdeutscher Orden dated July 3/4, 1932, in Berlin, in: BAB, R 43 I, No. 1238, Bl. 107. The fact that Mahraun was indeed involved in very personal disputes with Schleicher can be seen even in the hagiographic sketch Johann Hilley presents in his book *Mahraun, der Pionier des Arbeitsdienstes* (Leipzig, 1933), 44ff. and 50.

171. Olden, *Hitler*, 53; also Bredow, *Hitler rast*, 21f.

172. For details with compelling evidence, see Bahar/Kugel, *Reichstagsbrand*, 678ff. and 708f.

173. See Diels, *Lucifer ante portas*, 203.

174. Salomon, *Fragebogen*, 444ff. With respect to the persecution and expulsion from the Party and the SA, see the informative BDC documents compiled by Luetgebrune, especially the six-page-long letter Heydrich wrote to Buch on October 26, 1934, with excerpts from the Gestapo documents, in: BAB.

175. See Strasser, *Bartholomäusnacht*, 39.

176. Quoted from Friedelind Wagner, *Nacht über Bayreuth. Die Geschichte der Enkelin Richard Wagners* (Berlin, 1999), 150f.

177. See the testimonies presented in Bahar/Kugel, *Reichstagsbrand*, 725ff.; as well as with respect to Hanns Heinz Ewers (as one of the many examples): Wilfried Kugel, *Der Unverantwortliche. Das Leben des Hanns Heinz Ewers* (Düsseldorf, 1992), 356f.

178. See Jellonnek, *Homosexuelle*, 103.

179. Speech before the Reichstag on July 13, 1934, in: *Stenographische Berichte der Verhandlungen des Deutschen Reichstages*, Vol. 458. IX. Wahlperiode, 24.

180. See Hitler's explanations to this end during the ministerial conference on July 3, 1934, in: *Akten der Reichskanzlei. Die Regierung Hitler I/2*, 1358.

181. The stenographic reports include this rather often, see *Stenographische*

Berichte über die Verhandlungen des Deutschen Reichstages, Vol. 458. IX. Wahlperiode, 27ff.

182. Ibid., 33, as well as the following quote.

183. Quoted from Alexander Zinn, *Die soziale Konstruktion des homosexuellen Nationalsozialisten. Zu Genese und Etablierung eines Stereotyps* (Frankfurt am Main, 1997), 114. Zinn, who otherwise presents a very good reconstruction and analysis of the discussion of this question by those living in exile, himself falls prey to a clichéd pattern of interpreting the political subject homosexuality constituted during National Socialism, and this often led him to draw hasty conclusions. It may be that the designers of the "homosexual nationalist" were not always as wrongly homophobic as his research would make us believe.

184. *Die Deutsche Revolution,* No. 9 (July 8, 1934).

185. *Die Deutsche Revolution,* No. 10 (July 15, 1934). See also *Neuer Vorwärts* (July 8, 1934), which listed the same names except for Wilhelm Brückner. Six months later, Strasser added the names of the Reich press chief Otto Dietrich, of Reich Minister Hans Frank and of SA Obergruppenführer Dietrich von Jagow to the list, who, too had been "counted as members of the 'warm party' for a long time" (*Die Deutsche Revolution,* No. 1, January 6, 1935).

186. Report of the German news office regarding an interview Hitler supposedly gave the American professor Pearson on July 6, 1934, and which was published by the Paris edition of the *New York Herald,* in: *Akten der Reichskanzlei. Die Regierung Hitler I/2,* 1377.

187. It was an open secret among the Berlin diplomats that many men in Hitler's inner circle were homosexuals; it was only speculation whether Hitler himself was one as well. See Martha Dodd, *Through Embassy Eyes* (New York, 1939), 214.

188. With regard to this and the following matter, see Bernward Dörner, *"Heimtücke". Das Gesetz als Waffe. Kontrolle, Abschreckung und Verfolgung in Deutschland 1933–1945* (Paderborn, 1998), 9ff. and 20ff.

189. See ibid., 67ff. with numerous examples. Statistically, "statements about national socialist leaders" were sanctioned almost only with regard to Hitler, but these comprised by far the largest percentage of all the legal proceedings tried under the Malicious Practices Act (see ibid., 69).

190. Taken from the file in the StA Bamberg, Sondergericht Bamberg, No. 389.

191. With regard to this matter, see the case studies compiled by Dörner, *"Heimtücke,"* 189ff., who did not exhaust the subject but nevertheless did pioneer work in this respect.

192. For more information, see the documents in: StA Bamberg, Sondergericht Bamberg, No. 847.
193. For more information, see the documents in: BAB, Sondergerichtsakte, 30.01, IV g 5 774/42.
194. See Dörner, *"Heimtücke,"* 191f.
195. Quoted from Günter Grau, *Homosexualität in der NS-Zeit. Dokumente einer Diskriminierung und Verfolgung* (Frankfurt a.M., 1993), 74. See also Hans Günter Hockerts, *Die Sittlichkeitsprozesse gegen katholische Ordensangehörige und Priester 1936/1937. Eine Studie zur national-sozialistischen Herrschaftstechnik und zum Kirchenkampf* (Mainz, 1971), 11f.
196. See Jellonnek, *Homosexuelle,* 110ff.; as well as Kai Sommer, *Die Strafbarkeit der Homosexualität von der Kaiserzeit bis zum Nationalsozialismus* (Frankfurt a.M., 1998), 310ff.
197. With regard to this matter, and with examples and numerous reference to the current research, see Joachim Müller/Andreas Sternweiler, *Homosexuelle Männer im KZ Sachsenhausen* (Berlin, 2000); as well as Stephan R. Heiß, "Ein Schandfleck für das Dritte Reich. Homosexuelle als Opfer von Verfolgung und Vernichtung während der Diktatur des Nationalsozialismus in Bayern," in: Michael Farin (ed.), *Polizeireport München* (Exhibition Catalogue), Munich, 1999. In addition Till Bastian, *Homosexuelle im Dritten Reich. Geschichte einer Verfolgung* (Munich, 2000).
198. Lastly, see Till Bastian, *Homosexuelle im dritten Reich. Geschichte einer Verfolgung* (Munich, 2000).
199. With regard to the Brückner affair, see the sources named in Jellonnek, *Homosexuelle,* 96.
200. With regard to this as well as the following matter, see the relevant files in: BAB, BDC Helmut Brückner; as well as BAK, NS 19/1270.
201. See Brückner's letter to Darré dated October 10, 1934, in: BAB, BDC Helmut Brückner. Woyrsch himself was rumored to be a homosexual, see Hergemöller, *Mann für Mann,* 155f. According to Heinz Höhne, *Mordsache Röhm* (Reinbek, 1984), 299f. and 343, one copy of this memorandum is supposed to be in the "private Tobias archives."
202. Brückner in a letter to Himmler on December 14, 1934, in: BAK, NS 19/1270.
203. Quoted from a report written for Hitler by an associate of Heinrich Himmler on November 1, 1935, regarding the Brückner affair, in: ibid., the following quotes come from the same source.

204. See the entry in the letter diary of Reich Minister of Justice Gürtner on
      October 22, 1935, for example; in: BAB, R 22/1080.

205. Reichsführer-SS in a letter to the Geheimes Staatspolizeiamt [Gestapo] on
      November 6, 1935, in: BAK, NS 19/1270.

206. See BAB, BDC Helmut Brückner; as well as the entry Gürtner made in
      his letter diary of on May 20, 1936, in: BAB, R 22/929.

207. See Telford Taylor, *The Anatomy of the Nuremberg Trials* (New York,
      1992), 547f. See also Jellonnek, *Homosexuelle*, 87ff. The *Weissbuch
      über die Erschiessungen des 30. Juni 1934* also mentioned that Dr. Heim-
      soth was in possession of letters written by Schirach and Frank, "which
      made obvious their homosexual tendencies" (125). See also Bredow,
      Hitler rast, 17. Within party circles, people even spoke of "illicit relations
      between the Führer and Schirach" in 1935 (entry Gürtner made in his
      letter diary on September 10, 1935, in: BAB, R 22/1088).

208. I received this information from Frank Bajohr at the Hamburger
      Forschungsstelle für Zeitgeschichte [Hamburg Research Institute for
      Contemporary History].

209. See Dollmann, *Roma Nazista*, 35.

210. With regard to this matter, see the impressive evidence compiled by Ian
      Kershaw in *Der Hitler-Mythos* (Stuttgart, 1999), 109ff.

211. Hitler in a letter to Ada Klein on September 30, 1934. A facsimile is
      included in: Anton Joachimsthaler, *Hitlers Weg begann in München*
      (Munich, 2000), 299.

212. Speech given at the so-called Saar Loyalty Rally on the Ehrenbreitstein
      near Koblenz on August 26, 1934, here quoted from the reprint in the
      Völkischer Beobachter, No. 240 (August 28, 1934).

CHAPTER 6

1. Erich Ebermayer, *Denn heute gehört uns Deutschland . . . Persönliches
    und Politisches Tagebuch* (Hamburg/Vienna, 1959).

2. See ibid., 327ff.

3. Ibid., 331f. (entry made on June 30, 1934, stresses made by the original
    author).

4. Ibid., 67, 294, and 202 (entries made on April 20 and 24, 1934, and
    November 12, 1933).

5. See Ludwig Ebermayer, *Fünfzig Jahre Dienst am Recht. Erinnerungen
    eines Juristen* (Leipzig, 1930).

6. Undated autobiographical summary written by Ebermayer (probably
    from 1937), in: BAB, BDC Erich Ebermayer.

7. See Kai Sommer, *Die Strafbarkeit der Homosexualität von der Kaiserzeit bis zum Nationalsozialismus. Eine Analyse der Straftatbestände im Strafgesetzbuch und in den Reformentwürfen (1871–1945)* (Frankfurt a.M., 1998), 156f. and 236.

8. See Klaus-Detlev Godau-Schüttke, *Rechtsverwalter des Reiches. Staatssekretär Dr. Curt Joel* (Frankfurt a.M., 1981), 141f. bzw. 191f.; with regard to the political influence, see also Herbert Hömig, *Kanzler in der Krise der Republik. Eine Weimarer Biographie* (Paderborn, 2000), 180f., 394f., 438, and 529ff.

9. For more information regarding this matter, see Martin Sabrow, *Der Rathenau-Mord. Rekonstruktion einer Verschwörung gegen die Republik von Weimar* (Munich, 1994), 103ff. and 212ff., for example.

10. Ebermayer in a letter to Rosenberg on June 3, 1939, in: BAB, BDC Erich Ebermayer.

11. See Ekkehard Reiter, *Franz Gürtner. Politische Biographie eines deutschen Juristen 1881–1941* (Berlin, 1976).

12. See Ebermayer, *Tagebuch*, 81 and 129f. (entries made on May 13 and July 3, 1933). See also Helmut Külz to the editors of the *NS-Schulungs- briefe* on June 2, 1939, in: BAB, BDC Erich Ebermayer.

13. With regard to Wilhelm Külz's biography, see the not nearly exhaustive research done by Armin Behrendt, *Wilhelm Külz. Aus dem Leben eines Suchenden* (Berlin [Ost], 1968); as well as Hergard Robel (ed.), *Ein Lib- eraler zwischen Ost und West. Aufzeichnungen 1947–1948* (Munich, 1989).

14. See Killinger's letter to Külz dated March 26, 1933, here quoted from Behrend, *Wilhelm Külz,* 280f.

15. See the autobiographical manuscript entitled "Aus dem Leben des Dr. Wilhelm Külz," Vol. II/6, 41, here quoted from Behrend, *Wilhelm Külz,* 268.

16. For more information regarding this matter, see also the description of the well-informed contemporary journalist and Hitler biographer Rudolf Olden, *Hitler* (Amsterdam, 1935), here quoted from the new edition (Frankfurt a.M., 1984), 52ff.

17. See "Persönliche Akten des Ministers Külz," in: BAB, R 1501, No. 13098.

18. As a key document, see the (undated) letter Helmut Külz wrote to Erich Ebermayer on the occasion of the latter's sixtieth birthday. Published in: Peer Baedeker/Karl Lemke (eds.), *Erich Ebermayer. Buch der Freunde* (Lohhof near Munich, 1960), 28.

19. Letter written by the Gestapo Berlin to the Reich Minister of Justice

dated April 9, 1937, here quoted from the entry Gürtner made into his letter diary on April 12, 1937, in: BAB, R 22/721.

20. See *Die Briefe Thomas Manns. Regesten und Register*, vol. 1, edited by Hans Bürgin (Frankfurt a.M., 1976), No. 1921/76 and 105.

21. With regard to this matter, see Joachim S. Hohmann, *Der heimliche Sexus. Homosexuelle Belletristik in Deutschland der Jahre 1920–1970* (Frankfurt a.M., 1979), 296ff.; as well as Marita Keilsoyn-Lauritz, *Die eigene Geschichte. Literatur und Literaturkritik in den Anfängen der Schwulenbewegung am Beispiel des Jahrbuchs für sexuelle Zwischenstufen und der Zeitschrift Der Eigene* (Berlin, 1997), 202ff.

22. Thomas Mann in a letter to Ebermayer dated November 2, 1924, in: Baedeker/Lemke (eds.), *Buch der Freunde*, 41.

23. See Andreas Sternweiler (ed.), *Liebe, Forschung, Lehre. Der Kunsthistoriker Christian Adolf Isermeyer* (Berlin, 1998), 22f.

24. Wyneken had been convicted of sexual assault on his pupils in a spectacular trial in 1921/22; for more details, see Ulfried Geuter, *Homosexualität in der deutschen Jugendbewegung. Jungenfreundschaft und Sexualität im Diskurs von Jugendbewegung, Psychoanalyse und Jugendpsychologie am Beginn des 20. Jahrhunderts* (Frankfurt a.M., 1994), 195ff.; as well as Thijs Maasen, *Pädagogischer Eros. Gustav Wyneken und die Freie Schulgemeinde Wickersdorf* (Berlin, 1995), 140ff.

25. See the slightly enhanced retrospective regarding this story of their relationship in Erich Ebermayer, *Gustav Wyneken. Chronik einer großen Freundschaft* (Frankfurt a.M., 1969).

26. So Ebermayer stated in his undated curriculum vitae (probably from 1947), in: DLA Marbach, NL Ebermayer.

27. See Ebermayer, *Tagebuch*, 257 (entry made on February 7, 1934).

28. Erich Ebermayer, "Jugend und Eros," in: *Junge Menschen. Monatsheft für Politik, Kunst, Literatur und Leben aus dem Geist der jungen Generation*, No. 3 (March, 1926), 61; the following quote was taken from there as well.

29. See Ebermayer, *Kampf um Odilienburg* (Vienna, 1929), 257f. He goes on to say: "This new eros would be a fire, a glowing ember, a being-touched-by-God when confronted by youthful beauty, enlightenment, grace, bliss, asexual, suprasexual, an ever new product of beauty and spirit, life-creating as only the act of begetting can be, lending the man strength for his work, happiness, pride, devotion, bestowing an obligation on the boy whom the Leader has chosen to be his companion. Dark and dangerous territory."

30. Hans Blüher, *Die Rede des Aristophanes. Prolegomena zu einer Soziologie des Menschengeschlechtes* (Hamburg, 1966), 64ff. (stresses made in the original).

31. See Jeremy Noakes, "Philipp Bouhler und die Kanzlei des Führers der NSDAP," in: Dieter Rebentisch/Karl Teppe (eds.), *Verwaltung contra Menschenführung im Staat Hitlers* (Göttingen, 1986), 208–236; see also the letters Bouhler wrote to Ebermayer, in: DLA Marbach, NL Ebermayer.

32. Ebermayer in a letter to Costa dated October 19, 1933. I would like to thank the Zsolnay Verlag in Vienna for kindly letting me have a copy of this letter from the publishing house's archives.

33. See Elke Nicolai, *"Wohin es uns treibt . . ." Die literarische Generationsgruppe Klaus Manns 1924–1933* (Frankfurt a.M., 1998), 51ff.; furthermore, see Nicole Schaenzler, *Klaus Mann. Eine Biographie* (Frankfurt a.M., 1999); as well as Uwe Naumann (ed.), *"Ruhe gibt es nicht, bis zum Schluß." Klaus Mann (1906–1949). Bilder und Dokumente* (Reinbek, 1999).

34. See Fredric Kroll (ed.), *Klaus-Mann-Schriftenreihe,* Vol. 3 (Wiesbaden, 1979), 208ff.; as well as Nicolai, *Literarische Generationsgruppe,* 56.

35. Klaus Mann in a letter to Ebermayer dated February 4, 1933, in: StaBi [Staatsbibliothek] Berlin, NL Ebermayer.

36. Similar information was also spread in Reichswehr circles, as can be seen from the second, unpublished part of the "Tagebuch eines Reichswehrgenerals" [A Reichswehr General's Diary] which fell into the hands of Himmler's Sicherheitsdienst when they arrested Helmuth Klotz in France in 1940. The entry made on February 6, 1933, makes express reference to Hitler's "intimate friendships à la Röhm" and speculates how much money the Reich Chancellor may be spending on such enjoyments, in: BAB, Zentrales Parteiarchiv der SED, St 3/467, 42. With regard to Klotz and the publication of his "Tagebuch," see also chapter 3, Footnote 32.

37. Quoted from Kroll (ed.), *Klaus-Mann-Schriftenreihe,* Vol. 3, 222.

38. Klaus Mann in a letter to Ebermayer dated April 17, 1933, in: StaBi Berlin, NL Ebermayer.

39. Ebermayer, *Tagebuch,* 28f. (entry made on February 21, 1933).

40. Ibid., 90ff. (entry made on May 21, 1933).

41. In a letter to Ebermayer dated January 13, 1935, Ziegler even spoke of "good comrades," published in: ibid., 465, which was more than unusual when speaking to a non-Party member.

42. Ibid., 92f. (entry made on May 21, 1933).

43. With regard to this matter, see Peter Michalzik, *Gustaf Gründgens. Der Schauspieler und die Macht* (Berlin, 1999), 134ff.

44. Ebermayer, *Tagebuch*, 315 (entry made on June 3, 1934), the following quotes: ibid., 315ff.

45. Blüher, *Aristophanes*, 69f.

46. See Murray G. Hall, *Der Paul Zsolnay Verlag. Von der Gründung bis zur Rückkehr aus dem Exil* (Tübingen, 1994), 258f.

47. Ebermayer in a letter to Costas dated October 19, 1933, in: Archives of the Paul Zsolnay Verlag, Vienna.

48. Ebermayer, *Tagebuch*, 190 (entry made on October 22, 1933). In 1933 the Fritz Todt mentioned here, a cousin of Ebermayer by marriage and Hitler's "inspector general of the German road system," was only at the beginning of his brilliant career.

49. Ebermayer in a letter to Klaus Mann ("Herr Reisinger") dated October 23, 1933, in: Stadtbibliothek Munich, Monacensia, Literaturarchiv, NL Klaus Mann.

50. In December 1934, Klaus Mann was worried about his old friend: "I am afraid that the latest raids in the Reich must have been devastating for him." In a letter to Franz Goldstein dated December 30, 1934, in: Klaus Mann, *Briefe*, edited by Friedrich Albrecht (Berlin (Ost)/Weimar, 1988), 200. For general information regarding this matter, see the exemplary research done by Andreas Pretzel/Gabriele Roßbach, *Wegen der zu erwartenden hohen Strafen. Homosexuellenverfolgung in Berlin 1933–1945* (Berlin, 2000).

51. *Das Schwarze Korps*, No. 9 (May 1, 1935: "Ein sonderbarer Vertreter des deutschen Schrifttums" [A Strange Representative of German Literature]).

52. Addendum to a letter the SD sent to the personnel representative of the Reich film director general dated November 17, 1942, in: BAB, BDC Erich Ebermayer.

53. Ebermayer in a letter to Costas dated October 6, 1935, quoted from Hall, *Zsolnay Verlag*, 610.

54. Copy of a letter written by the Amt für Schrifttumspflege [Office of the Preservation of Literature] to the NSDAP's Central Training Office dated June 19, 1939, in: BAB, BDC Erich Ebermayer.

55. See Hall, *Zsolnay Verlag*, 599f.; as well as Boguslaw Drewniak, *Der deutsche Film 1938–1945* (Dusseldorf, 1987), 140ff. and 511f.

56. The Sicherheitspolizei and SD Chief in a letter to the personnel representative of the Reich film director general dated October 16, 1942, in: BAB, BDC Erich Ebermayer.

57. Hans Severus Ziegler, *Adolf Hitler. Aus dem Erleben dargestellt* (Göttingen, 1964).

58. For more information on this matter, see ibid., 291ff.; also, Ziegler's denazification file, in: HStA Düsseldorf, NW 1005 – Ge 35/105.

59. From 1925 until 1933, there is evidence that Hitler went to Weimar more than thirty times, not counting the numerous visits he paid incognito. For these visits, there are clues, but no precise proof. See Holm Kirsten, "Hitlers Besuche in Weimar" (Master's Thesis, Jena, 1999), 72ff. as well as the addendum "Chronologie der Hitler-Besuche" (this thesis will most likely be published in the fall of 2001, entitled: *Weimar im Banne des Führers. Die Besuche Adolf Hitlers 1925–1940* [Köln, etc., 2001]).

60. Ziegler, *Erleben*, 87 and 156f.

61. Hans Severus Ziegler, "Der Führer im alten 'Elephanten'. Erinnerungen," in: Fritz Sauckel (ed.), *Der Führer in Weimar 1925–1938* (Weimar, 1938), 34.

62. *Thüringer Staatszeitung* (October 3, 1934), quoted from Kirsten, "Hitlers Besuche," 75.

63. Ziegler, *Erleben*, 68.

64. Ibid., 62.

65. For more information regarding this matter, see now Fritz Redlich, *Hitler. Diagnosis of a Destructive Prophet* (New York/Oxford, 1999), 290, who utilized all available sources, most of which date back to the war years, however.

66. Ziegler, *Erleben*, 80, 113f., 52, 119, and 121.

67. Carl B. N. von Schirach in a letter to Werner Detjen dated April 17, 1933, in: Goethe- und Schiller-Archiv Weimar, 132/740.

68. See Thüringisches HStA Weimar, Generalintendanz des DNT, No. 128/1.

69. Ziegler, *Erleben*, 52f. See also the letter Ziegler wrote to Hitler on February 25, 1936, in: Thüringisches HStA Weimar, Volksbildungsministerium, No. 34848 (Personnel File Ziegler).

70. Ziegler, *Erleben*, 72.

71. Guest book Hanfstaengl (entry made on August 18, 1932), privately owned by Egon Hanfstaengl, Munich, whom I thank for kindly letting me read it.

72. Ziegler, *Erleben*, 64, ibid.; the following quotes are on pages 64ff.

73. See Kirsten, "Hitlers Besuche," Appendix.

74. Declaration of the Interior Minister of Thuringia on July 3, 1934, in: Thüringisches HStA Weimar, Volksbildungsministerium, No. 34848 (personnel file Ziegler).

75. See Ziegler, *Der Führer im alten "Elephanten,"* 33.
76. Ziegler in a letter to Ebermayer dated January 13, 1935, published in: Ebermayer, *Tagebuch,* 465 (stresses made by the original author); the following quotes: ibid.
77. Press release by the Education Minister of Thuringia dated March 18, 1935. This was preceded on March 7, 1935, by the declaration "that Dr. Ziegler committed *no* acts punishable under criminal law," in: Thüringisches HStA Weimar, Volksbildungsministerium, No. 34848 (personnel file Ziegler).
78. Ziegler in a letter to Ebermayer dated June 2, 1935, published in: Ebermayer, *Tagebuch,* 535.
79. Ziegler in a letter to Hitler (via Brückner) dated October 19, 1935, in: Thüringisches HStA Weimar, Reichsstatthalter in Thüringen, No. 395.
80. See Ziegler, *Erleben,* 13.
81. Ibid., 110.
82. See Michalzik, *Gründgens,* 130ff.; as well as Burkhard Jellonnek, *Homosexuelle unter dem Hakenkreuz* (Paderborn, 1990), 87ff. Schirach is alleged to have projected an expressly homophobic picture of himself in the HJ Hitlerjugend [Hitler Youth] even after "June 30."
83. Ziegler, *Erleben,* 157f. and 156.
84. Joachim Fest, *Speer. Eine Biographie* (Berlin, 1999), 71 and 487.
85. I am also grateful to Brigitte Hamann for the interesting discussion I was able to have with her in Munich in November 2000 regarding her new book.
86. See also Peter P. Pachel, Siegfried Wagner, *Genie im Schatten* (Munich, 1988), 236 and 360, as well as Renate Schoslack, *Hinter Wahnfrieds Mauern* (Hamburg, 1998), 51ff.
87. Quoted from Zdenko von Kraft, *Der Sohn* (Graz, 1969), 247, as well as Ziegler, *Erleben,* 157.
88. Hans-Jürgen Syberberg, *Syberbergs Filmbuch* (Munich, 1976), 165
89. *Goebbels Diaries* II/4 (1995), 408 (entry made on May 30, 1942); see also the entry Gürtner made into his letter diary on May 14, 1937, in: BAB, R 22/721.
90. Quoted from Syberberg, *Filmbuch,* 271; the following quote: ibid.
91. So Hitler said on January 24/25, 1942, in: Werner Jochmann (ed.), *Adolf Hitler. Monologe im Führerhauptquartier 1941–1944* (Munich, 1980), 225.
92. With regard to Siegfried Wagner's apolitical position, see Ziegler, *Erleben,* 157; see also Jochmann (ed.), *Monologe,* 224 (January 24/25,

1942) and 308 (February 28/March 1, 1942): "personally, he was a friend of mine; he was passive politically."

93. Quoted from the wording in Syberberg's documentary, "Winifred Wagner und die Geschichte des Hauses Wahnfried" [Winifred Wagner and the history of Wahnfried], 1975.

94. Magnus Hirschfeld, *Die Homosexualität des Mannes und des Weibes* (Berlin, 1920, second, unchanged printing), 689.

95. For more information regarding these events, see the entries Gürtner made in his letter diary on May 27 and November 20, 1937, in: BAB, R 22/721.

96. Henry Picker (ed.), *Hitlers Tischgespräche im Führerhauptquartier* (Wiesbaden, 1983), 116 (February 28/March 1, 1942) and Jochmann (ed.), *Monologe*, 259 (February 3/4, 1942); the following quote, ibid., 308.

97. Interview the author conducted with Frau Jobst in Bayreuth on February 29, 2000.

98. Quoted from Gerald McKnight, *The Strange Loves of Adolf Hitler* (London, 1978), 140.

99. Quoted from Baedeker/Lemke (eds.), *Buch der Freunde*, 37.

100. As I learned from Frau Verena Lafferenz-Wagner in a letter July 22, 2000, Ebermayer "wanted to represent my mother during the denazification proceedings as her attorney (this did not occur), so he probably has great knowledge of details—but only until 1945. Later both Ebermayer and Ziegler had social contacts with the Siegfried Wagner household; since my mother was very free and open in her remarks, both gentlemen may have 'harvested'."

101. See Bouhler's letter to "dear Erich" dated October 15, 1930, where he "unfortunately" has to turn down his "request to publish an interview with Herr Hitler in a literary newspaper" because "Hitler only gives general, political interviews," in: DLA Marbach, NL Ebermayer.

102. For more information regarding this matter, see the statement made by the mother of the bride to the general prosecutor in the Staatsministerium für Sonderaufgaben [roughly: State Ministry for Special Tasks] on December 19, 1949, which spoke of a "hasty wedding," in: StA Munich, Spruchkammerakten, Box 179. NS-agricultural politician Richard Darré spoke in his memoirs about the "not very good" reputation of this great beauty from the film industry: "Frau Bouhler was a 'fast' lady in character and nature," in: Darré, "Aufzeichnungen von Walter Darré von 1945–1948," Vol. 3, in: IfZ Munich, Ed 110.

103. With regard to Bouhler's political career, see Bernd Diroll, *Personen-*

Lexikon der NSDAP, Vol. 1. *SS-Führer A-B* (Norderstedt, 1998), 322ff.

104. So Ebermayer's editorial preface to his published diary.

105. See Emmy Göring, *An der Seite meines Mannes. Begebenheiten und Bekenntnisse* (Göttingen, 1967), 322f., where she writes that Ebermayer himself offered to represent her and do so free of charge. His motive may therefore has been his need for information.

106. I would like to thank the Zsolnay Verlag in Vienna for kindly letting me have copies of the press releases from its archives.

107. Klaus Mann, *Tagebücher 1931 bis 1933,* edited by Joachim Heimannsberg, Peter Laemmle, and Wilfried F. Schoeller (Munich, 1989), 64.

108. Klaus Mann, "Zwilling der Sexualpathologie," in: *Das Tagebuch,* No. 53 (December 31, 1932).

109. The following was quoted from the reprint of Klaus Mann/Kurt Tucholsky, *Homosexualität und Faschismus* (Hamburg, 1990, 3rd ed.), 5–13.

110. See the interesting essay by Michael Maar, *Das Blaubartzimmer. Thomas Mann und die Schuld* (Frankfurt a.M., 2000).

111. Klaus Harpprecht, *Thomas Mann. Eine Biographie* (Reinbek, 1995), 1020.

112. Thomas Mann, "Bruder Hitler," in: Mann, *Politische Reden und Schriften.* Vol. 3 (Frankfurt a.M., 1968), 58; the following quotes: ibid., 53f.

113. Thomas Mann, *Tagebücher 1937–1939,* edited by Peter de Mendelssohn (Frankfurt a.M., 1980), 115 (entry made on October 13, 1937).

114. With regard to its genesis, see Klaus Mann, *Der Wendepunkt. Ein Lebensbericht* (Reinbek, 1984), 590ff. and 709ff.

115. Ibid., 352–356.

116. See Theodor Lessing, *Haarmann. Geschichte eines Werwolfs* (Berlin, 1925). Many well-known writers of the Weimar Republic, such as Döblin, ran wild in this vivid psychoanalytical character and background study; for more information, see the introduction of Rainer Marwedel to the new edition of Lessing's works (Frankfurt a.M., 1989), esp. S. 21ff. Lessing published parts of his work on Haarmann in the magazine *Das Tagebuch,* for which Klaus Mann wrote as well.

117. Here the author makes reference to the name change revealed in the spring of 1932, that Hitler's father, Alois Schicklgruber, who was born out of wedlock, had taken his foster-father's name in 1876. See Brigitte Hamann, *Hitlers Wien. Lehrjahre eines Diktators* (Munich/Zurich, 1997), 64ff.

118. See Maar, *Blaubartzimmer,* 11.

119. Heinrich Mann, *Der Hass. Deutsche Zeitgeschichte* (Amsterdam, 1933), here quoted from the new printing (Berlin [Ost]/Weimar, 1983), 66f. and 68.

120. Ebermayer, *Tagebuch*, 551f. (entry made on July 3, 1935, stresses made by the original author).

CHAPTER 7

1. So Hanfstaengl said about himself in his article "Wie ich Adolf Hitler kennenlernte" (originally published in English as "My Leader"), here quoted from *Der Freiheitskampf*, No. 293 (October 21, 1934).

2. From the memorandum "Adolf Hitler," which Hanfstaengl furnished for the American Secret Service in the summer of 1942, in: Franklin D. Roosevelt Library (New York), Henry Field's Papers, Box 44, 30f.

3. Notarized copy of Hitler's questioning on January 17, 1923, in: HStA Munich, Mju/16312.

4. So Hitler said on October 30, 1941, in: Werner Jochmann (ed.), *Adolf Hitler. Monologe im Führerhauptquartier 1941–1944* (Munich, 1980), 117.

5. Hanfstaengl in a letter to Julius Streicher dated December 19, 1937 (copy), in: BAK, NS 10/149.

6. Rudolf Diels, *Lucifer Ante Portas. . . . es spricht der erste Chef der Gestapo . . .* (Stuttgart, 1950), 124 and 382.

7. See Kurt G. W. Lüdecke, *I knew Hitler. The Story of a Nazi Who Escaped The Blood Purge* (New York, 1937), 20f.

8. "Abschrift Blattsammlung der Staatsanwaltschaft bei dem Königlichen Landgericht II Berlin Strafsache gegen Lüdecke wegen Erpressung" [Copies of the Pages Collected by the Prosecutor's Office at the Königliches Landgericht II Berlin Regarding the Trial of Lüdecke for Blackmail] (from 1911), in: PAA Berlin, R 100097.

9. Undated investigation report of the police headquarters Munich (probably from January 1923), in: HStA Munich, MA. 1943. D.R., No. 473; another copy can be found in: BAB, BDC Kurt Lüdecke.

10. Quoted from ibid.

11. See Keith Sward, *The Legend of Henry Ford* (New York, 1948), here quoted from the new edition (New York, 1968), 106ff.; the following information was taken from there as well.

12. Henry Ford (ed.), *Der internationale Jude. Ein Weltproblem; das erste amerikanische Buch über die Judenfrage. Ins Deutsche übertragen von Paul Lehmann* (Leipzig, 1921). This publication was distributed through

the Hammer-Verlag, a publisher specializing in *völkisch* and antisemitic literature.

13. This becomes evident from the files the Munich police compiled on Lüdecke during the winter of 1922/23. They are largely preserved as copies in: HStA Munich, Mju/16312.

14. Notarized copy of the questioning of Hitler on January 17, 1923, in: ibid.

15. Notarized copy of a memorandum furnished by Max Amann dated August 29, 1922, in: ibid.

16. Notarized copy of the police questioning of Dietrich Eckart on March 3, 1923, in: ibid.

17. See Lüdecke, *I knew Hitler,* 1f. and 13.

18. Notarized copy of the questioning of Hitler on January 17, 1923, in: HStA Munich, Mju/16312.

19. This was reported by a correspondent from *The New York Times,* who also made reference to the many translations of Ford's *International Jew* that were lying around at party headquarters of the NSDAP, see *The New York Times,* No. 23.706 (December 20, 1922 "Berlin hears Ford is backing Hitler. Bavarian Anti-Semitic Chief has American's Portrait and Book in his Office. Spends Money Lavishly").

20. Lüdecke, *I knew Hitler,* 105.

21. Minutes taken during the questioning of Hermann Esser on February 15, 1923, in: HStA Munich, MJu/16312.

22. Minutes taken during the questioning of Lüdecke on March 23, 1923, in: ibid.

23. Notarized copy of the questioning of Hitler on January 17, 1923, in: ibid.

24. See the statement published by the People's Court Munich I on March 7, 1923, for example. In: ibid.

25. Minutes taken during the questioning of Lüdecke on March 23, 1923, in: ibid.

26. See Hanfstaengl's unpublished reminiscences (1956), in: BSB, NL Hanfstaengl, Ana 405/47.

27. *Völkischer Beobachter,* No. 59 (April 5, 1923, "Zum Fall Lüdecke" [More on the Ludecke Case]).

28. *Münchener Zeitung,* No. 86 (March 29, 1923).

29. This visit to Linz is confirmed in a letter Hitler wrote to his childhood friend Fritz Seidl dated October 16, 1923, in: BAB, NS 26/14.

30. Lüdecke, *I knew Hitler,* 234. (The entire quote reads, "our intimate meeting on the Poestlingberg," "Gladly I eschewed the subject as too delicate.")

31. The following quotes were taken from ibid., 135–139. (The quotes read, "When his words came close to poetry" [136]; or, "in private speech he often is gifted with beauty of language" [136]; or, "poetic mood" [138]; "Next afternoon, Hitler revealed still another side of his character" [136]; "Hitler gazed over the vast landscape with love in his eyes" [137]; "The selfless grandeur of his vision held me spellbound" [138]; "Also, Hitler was plainly embarrassed, as I was, by the memory of our intimate meeting on the Poestlingberg, when we had *mutually vowed* so many things which never came to pass. Gladly I eschewed the subject as too delicate" [234]).

32. See the sources found in Ernst Deuerlein (ed.), *Der Hitler-Putsch. Bayerische Dokumente zum 8./9. November 1923* (Stuttgart, 1962), 452 and 543ff.

33. For more detail in this regard, see Joachim Köhler, *Wagners Hitler. Der Prophet und sein Vollstrecker* (Munich, 1997), 231ff.

34. For more information, see the somewhat condensed depiction by Zdenko von Kraft, *Der Sohn. Siegfried Wagners Leben und Umwelt* (Graz/Stuttgart, 1969), 234ff.; as well as the rather richly embellished description by James Pool, *Who Financed Hitler. The Secret Funding of Hitler's Rise to Power, 1919–1933* (New York, 1997, 2nd ed.), 89ff.

35. A facsimile of this letter dated January 4, 1924 was included in Lüdecke, *I knew Hitler,* after page 190.

36. Ibid., 234. (The entire quote reads, "Also, Hitler was plainly embarrassed, as I was, by the memory of our intimate meeting on the Poestlingberg, when we had mutually vowed so many things which never came to pass. Gladly I eschewed the subject as too delicate.")

37. See the questioning of Lüdecke by the Munich police on January 2, 1925, in: HStA Munich, Mju/16312.

38. Notarized copy of a police interview held in Landshut on May 22, 1925, in: ibid.

39. *Völkischer Kurier* (February 28/March 3, 1925, "Hitler gegen Pittinger" [Hitler Vs. Pittinger]), here quoted from Clemens Vollnhals (ed.), *Hitler. Reden, Schriften, Anordnungen,* Vol. I (Munich, 1992), 12.

40. See Lüdecke, *I knew Hitler,* 271ff.

41. Ibid., 271.

42. Ibid., 276f.

43. Ibid., 273. (The entire quote reads, "This time I meant to satisfy my burning curiosity.")

44. See the facsimilated document, for instance. In: ibid., 799.

45. Hanfstaengl's unpublished reminiscences (1956), in: BSB, NL Hanfstaengl, Ana 405/47.

46. Hanfstaengl referred to this conspiracy even fifteen years later; see his two letters to Esser dated January 31 and February 23, 1939, here quoted from David George Marwell, *Unwanted Exile. A Biography of Ernst "Putzi" Hanfstaengl, Ph.D.* (New York, 1988), 379 and 389.

47. See Lüdecke, *I knew Hitler,* 230ff. For more context, see Ian Kershaw, *Hitler,* Vol. 1: 1889–1936. Hubris. 1st American ed. (New York, 1999), 224ff.

48. See Hitler's letter to Rosenberg dated April 2, 1925, in: Archives du Centre de Documentation Juive Contemporaine Paris, document LXII – 1.

49. Hanfstaengl's unpublished reminiscences (1956), in: BSB, NL Hanfstaengl, Ana 405/47.

50. Ernst Hanfstaengl, *Zwischen Weißem und Braunem Haus. Memoiren eines politischen Außenseiters* (Munich, 1970), 163ff. and 170.

51. Hitler in a letter to Rosenberg dated April 2, 1925, in: BAB, NS 8/143, Bl. 13.

52. Hanfstaengl in a letter to Reich Treasury Minister Schwarz dated March 9, 1936, in: BAB, BDC Ernst Hanfstaengl.

53. Hanfstaengl's unpublished reminiscences (1956), in: BSB, NL Hanfstaengl, Ana 405/47.

54. *Völkischer Beobachter* (March 5, 1925, "Erklärung" [Declaration]).

55. *Völkischer Beobachter* (October 15, 1925, "Hitlers 'Verlobung'" [Hitler's 'Engagement']).

56. Hanfstaengl's unpublished reminiscences (1956), in: BSB, NL Hanfstaengl, Ana 405/47.

57. Hanfstaengl, *Außenseiter,* 189.

58. For more details regarding this activity for the Secret Service, see the research rich in material in Steven Casey, "Franklin D. Roosevelt, Ernst 'Putzi' Hanfstaengl and the 'S-Project', June 1942–June 1944," in: *Journal of Contemporary History,* Vol. 35 (2000), 339–359. See furthermore Christof Mauch, *Schattenkrieg gegen Hitler. Das Dritte Reich im Visier der amerikanischen Geheimdienste 1941–1945* (Stuttgart, 1999), 74ff.

59. A copy of this dossier compiled since the late summer of 1942 dated December 3, 1942, can be found in: Franklin D. Roosevelt Library (New York), Henry Field's Papers, Box 44.

60. Hanfstaengl's unpublished reminiscences (1956), in: BSB, NL Hanfstaengl, Ana 405/47.

61. Interview with Ernst Hanfstaengl on October 28, 1951, in: IfZ Munich, ZS 60.

62. Hanfstaengl's unpublished reminiscences (1956), in: BSB, NL Hanfstaengl, Ana 405/47.

63. Ernst Hanfstaengl, *Hitler. The Missing Years* (London, 1957), 169.

64. Hanfstaengl's unpublished reminiscences (1956), in: BSB, NL Hanfstaengl, Ana 405/47.

65. See also the comment made by Theo Schwarzmüller, *Zwischen Kaiser
und "Führer." Generalfeldmarschall August von Mackensen* (Paderborn,
1995), 78, 176, and 196. Schwarzmüller is in possession of the private
correspondence between the field marshall and his son Georg, the former
adjutant of the prince. Based on his insight into the sources, he considers
this inclination unmistakable. I would like to thank Theo Schwarzmüller
for the information he kindly shared with me.

66. Hanfstaengl's unpublished reminiscences (1956), in: BSB, NL Hanfstaengl, Ana 405/47, where the following quote was taken from as well.

67. See "Certified Copy of Marriage Record," in: PAA Berlin, R 1000097.

68. See Ralf Georg Reuth, *Goebbels. Eine Biographie* (Munich, 1995), 350
(which includes references to unpublished parts of Goebbels' diaries).

69. See Lüdecke, *I knew Hitler,* 317.

70. See the evidence provided by Sappo Kuusisto, *Alfred Rosenberg in der
nationalsozialistischen Außenpolitik 1933–1939* (Helsinki, 1984), 46.

71. Letter written by the NSDAP Treasurer on November 19, 1931, in: BAB,
BDC Kurt Lüdecke.

72. The following was taken from Lüdecke, *I knew Hitler,* 414–537.

73. Quoted from ibid., 477f.

74. See BAB, BDC Kurt Lüdecke.

75. See the facsimile in: Lüdecke, *I knew Hitler,* opposite of p. 531.

76. See Lüdecke's letter to Hitler dated April 10, 1934, in: Archives du Centre de Documentation Juive Contemporaine Paris, CXXIXa-120. See also
the photographs in Lüdecke, *I knew Hitler,* 530ff.

77. Hanfstaengl's unpublished reminiscences (1956), in: BSB, NL Hanfstaengl, Ana 405/47.

78. So Goebbels wrote in his diary on November 22, 1929, in: Elke Fröhlich
(ed.), *Die Tagebücher von Joseph Goebbels. Sämtliche Fragmente,* Vol.
I/1 (Munich, etc., 1987), 459.

79. See Hanfstaengl, *Außenseiter,* 217.

80. See Hanfstaengl's letter to his associate Voigt dated October 31, 1937
(draft), here quoted from Marwell, *Unwanted Exile,* 251f.

81. See BAB, BDC Ernst Hanfstaengl.

82. Hanfstaengl, *Außenseiter,* 314.

83. Ibid., 283. See also *Goebbels Diaries* I/2 (1987), 126 (entry made on February 11, 1932).
84. Hanfstaengl, *Außenseiter,* 301.
85. Ibid., 106 and 302.
86. See Bella Fromm, *Als Hitler mir die Hand küßte* (Berlin, 1993), 106 (entry in her diary made on March 17, 1933); Martha Dodd, *Through Embassy Eyes* (New York, 1939), 25f.; Philip Metcalfe, *1933.* (Sag Harbor/New York, 1988), 167f.; Karlheinz Schädlich, *Die Mitford Sisters* (Düsseldorf, 1993), 111ff.
87. See Kuusisto, *Außenpolitik,* 44ff.; as well as Andreas Molau, *Alfred Rosenberg* (Koblenz, 1993), 101ff.
88. For the following, see Lüdecke, *I knew Hitler,* 573ff. (The original quote reads, "Although he has learned to exercise marvellous self-control, he is by nature too impulsive entirely to control his eyes and mouth. Whenever something really touches him and he passes over it without a word, one who has known him from the early days can read a lot in the expression of his mobile face." 575; "'And the whispering-campaign branding you as a homosexual is common talk now. It . . .' 'Tstse . . . tstse . . .' Hitler interrupted me, looking annoyed. 'Incredible!' He clearly wanted to hear no more of that." 575)
89. See the excerpts from sources in: Kuusisto, *Außenpolitik,* 48f.
90. Hanfstaengl in a letter to Hitler dated February 4, 1938, in: BAB, BDC Ernst Hanfstaengl.
91. *New Yorker Staatszeitung*, No. 113 (May 12, 1933, "Große Säuberungsaktion der Nazis im eigenen Lager" [Nazis Go Through Great Purge in Their Own Ranks]).
92. See Lüdecke, *I knew Hitler,* 686.
93. Lüdecke in a letter to Buch dated September 16, 1933, in: BAB, NS 43/157.
94. Lüdecke, *I knew Hitler,* 705. The original of this letter was not preserved. (The original quote reads, "acted contrary to the tact and rhythm of the movement.")
95. Ibid., 735. (The original quote reads, "An unpleasant business, this Ludecke affair. A strange bird, a good head, but a dangerous brother!")
96. Lüdecke in a letter to Amann dated February 28, 1934, in: Hoover Institution Archives Stanford, Ludecke Papers, TS Germany P 214a.
97. See the reminiscences of his cellmate Kurt Hiller, *Leben gegen die Zeit* (Hamburg, 1969), 276.
98. For more information, see the letter Rosenberg wrote to Brückner dated April 17, 1934, in: BAB, NS 8/175, Bl. 172; as well as Lüdecke's letter to

Hitler dated April 10, 1934, in: Archives du Centre de Documentation Juive Contemporaine Paris, document CXXIXa-120.

99. Lüdecke in a letter to Hitler dated April 10, 1934, in: ibid. The following quotes were taken from there as well (stresses made by the original author).

100. *Evening Star* (May 5, 1934, "Kurt Ludecke Believed Headed for U.S. After Escape in Germany").

101. So Hanfstaengl wrote in his letter to Julius Streicher dated December 19, 1937, in: BAK, NS 10/149, Bl. 198.

102. The Gestapo in a letter to the Auswärtiges Amt [German State Department] dated October 3, 1934, in: PAA Berlin, R 100097.

103. See Himmler's letter to Rosenberg dated August 28, 1934, in: Archives du Centre de Documentation Juive Contemporaine Paris, document CXXIXa-120.

104. "Mend-Protokoll," in: HStA Munich, Dept. IV, HS 3231.

105. As one example, see *Münchener Post,* No. 30 (February 6, 1923).

106. *Goebbels Diaries* I/2 (1987), 457 (entry made on August 13, 1933).

107. Quoted from Hanfstaengl, *Außenseiter,* 319.

108. Quoted from Franz Langoth, *Kampf um Österreich. Erinnerungen eines Politikers* (Wels, 1951), 146; See also *Akten zur deutschen auswärtigen Politik, Serie C,* Vol. II,1 (Göttingen, 1973), Nos. 35 and 71. Hanfstaengl included a depiction of his first diplomatic intervention in Italy in the first printed version of his memoirs "Ich habe gewarnt," in: *Badische Illustrierte Woche,* No. 1 (January 5., 1952); for background information, see: *Akten zur deutschen auswärtigen Politik, Serie C,* Vol. III,1, No. 26.

109. Quoted from Hanfstaengl, *Außenseiter,* 360.

110. See *Hamburger Fremdenblatt,* No. 355 (December 24, 1933, "Dr. Ernst Hanfstaengl").

111. Quoted from *Deutsche Allgemeine Zeitung,* No. 410/411 (September 21, 1933, "Internationale und regionale Kunst. Ein Gespräch mit Dr. Ernst Hanfstaengl" [International and Regional Art. A Conversation with Dr. Ernst Hanfstaengl]).

112. See Fromm, *Hitler,* 185f.

113. Quoted from *Völkischer Beobachter,* No. 105 (April 15, 1934, "Dr. Hanfstaengl über die Aufgaben der Auslandsberichterstattung" [Dr. Hanfstaegl Regarding the Responsibilities of Foreign Correspondents]).

114. Lüdecke in a letter to Hitler dated April 10, 1934, in: Archives du Centre de Documentation Juive Contemporaine Paris, document CXXIXa-120.

115. See *Time,* Nos. 15 and 16 (April 9 and 16, 1934); as well as *The New York Times* (April 25, 1934).

116. See Lüdecke, *I knew Hitler,* 755, where he also mentions a letter sent to Goebbels. Neither document has been preserved and Lüdecke does not paraphrase them.

117. See ibid., 756.

118. See the sources in: Metcalfe, *1933,* 242f.

119. Hanfstaengl, *Außenseiter,* 339 and 341.

120. See *Weser-Zeitung,* No. 163 (July 15, 1934, "Schiffsverkehr in bremischen Häfen" [Maritime Traffic in the Bremen Harbors]).

121. Information kindly provided by Dr. Elke Fröhlich, the editor of the *Goebbels Diaries,* in anticipation of the volume containing the entries for 1934, which has not yet been published.

122. Hanfstaengl, *Außenseiter,* 346.

123. See Luther's letter to the Auswärtiges Amt [German State Department] dated September 27, 1934, in: PAA Berlin, R 1000097.

124. See *Hamburger Nachrichten,* No. 411 (September 4, 1934).

125. *Völkischer Beobachter,* No. 236 (August 24, 1934).

126. Metcalfe, *1933,* 279f.; as well as Fromm, *Hitler,* 210 (diary entry made on November 14, 1934).

127. *Daily Express,* No. 10720 (September 19, 1934).

128. Quoted from *Badische Illustrierte Woche,* No. 5 (February 2, 1952). See also Jody Skinner, *Bezeichnungen für das Homosexuelle im Deutschen,* Vol. II: *Ein Wörterbuch* (Essen, 1999), 259.

129. See *Daily Express,* No. 10721 (September 20, 1934, "The Herr Doktor has a busy day").

130. See *Daily Express,* No. 10723 (September 22, 1934, "Dr. Ernst Hanfstaengl").

131. For more information regarding the result of the trial, see *Völkischer Beobachter,* No. 339 (December 5, 1935, "Gütliche Vereinbarung" [Amicable Agreement]); as well as the report on the trial in *The Times,* No. 47237 (December 3, 1935, "High Court of Justice").

132. Auswärtiges Amt [German State Department] in a letter to the Gestapo dated September 28, 1934, in: PAA Berlin, R 100097.

133. Daluege in a letter to Diels dated May 16, 1934, in: BAB, BDC Kurt Lüdecke.

134. Helfferich in a letter to SS-Gruppenführer Scholz with the NSDAP's liaison staff dated December 2, 1934, in: BAB, BDC Ernst Hanfstaengl.

135. See *Deutsche Zeitung* (New York), No. 42 (October 20, 1934,

"Abschluß der Dickstein-Komödie" [The End of the Dickstein Comedy]).

136. Hanfstaengl in a letter to Brückner dated December 31, 1937, in: BAK, NS 10/144.

137. Quoted from Hanfstaengl, *Außenseiter,* 356.

138. The report furnished by the Gestapo and included as a copy was dated as early as October 26, 1934, in: PAA Berlin, R 100097. The following quotes were taken from there as well.

139. See HStA Munich, Mju/16312.

140. See Hanfstaengl's letter to Bülow-Schwante dated November 14, 1934, in: PAA Berlin, R 100097.

141. Hanfstaengl in a letter to Doebig dated November 13, 1934, in: HStA Munich, Mju/16312.

142. See Hanfstaengl, *Außenseiter,* 153.

143. For more details, see the documents in: PAA Berlin, R 100097.

144. Döbig in a letter to Schaub dated November 29, 1934, in: HStA Munich, Mju/16312.

145. See Schaub's letter to Döbig dated December 7, as well as Döbig's letter to Frank dated December 11, 1934, in: ibid.

146. This bundle of documents is now being kept in: Hoover Institution Archives, Collection Kurt Ludecke, Ts Germany, P 214a.

147. "Bericht für den Reichsführer Herrn Adolf Hitler und die Reichsleitung der N.S.D.A.P." [Report for the Reich Führer Adolf Hitler and N.S.D.A.P. National Executive], dated December 15, 1934, in: ibid.

148. See *Philadelphia Deutscher Weckruf* (January 19, 1935, extra edition).

149. Bouhler in a letter to Glaser dated January 12, 1935 (making reference to the letters Glaser wrote on December 15 and 21, 1934), as facsimile reprinted in Lüdecke, *I knew Hitler,* 801.

150. Quoted from the *Philadelphia Deutscher Weckruf* (January 19, 1935).

151. According to the information provided by the Princeton University Library which received large parts of the publishing house's archives, their documents do not contain the publisher's correspondence with Lüdecke.

152. Lüdecke, *I knew Hitler,* 731f.

153. See ibid., 417ff.

154. Ibid., 673. (The original quote reads, "Such a more or less 'natural' abnormity is nobody's business. I do as I please within my own four walls, like any one else.")

155. See Hanfstaengl's letter to Voigt dated November 26, 1937, here quoted from Marwell, *Unwanted Exile,* 255.

156. For more information regarding this matter, see the research done by Rudolf Stoiber and Boris Celovsky on Wiedemann's then lover and Hitler's secret agent Stephanie von Hohenlohe; in: *Stephanie von Hohenlohe* (Munich, 1988), 144ff.

157. Dieckhoff in a letter to the Auswärtiges Amt [German State Department] dated November 1, 1938; and Thomsen in a letter to the Auswärtiges Amt dated January 1, 1939, in: PAA Berlin, R 100097.

158. Hanfstaengl received this notice directly from the owner of the paper, Victor F. Ridder; see Hanfstaengl's letter to Hitler dated February 4, 1938 (via Deutsche Botschaft [German Embassy] London), in: BAK, NS 10/149, Bl. 201.

159. In April 1938, Hitler's adjutant Wiedemann had ordered a collection of book reviews published in the English press from the Auswärtiges Amt [German State Department] and received it soon thereafter; see BAK, NS 10/35, Bl. 64ff.

160. See the book review "Close-up," in: *Calvacade. The British News Magazine*, No. 10 (March 5, 1938), 37f., for example.

161. See *The New York Times Book Review* (November 28, 1937, "An Inside View of the Nazis by a Former Party Member"); and *The Saturday Review* (December 4, 1937, "The Nazi Mind").

162. Deutsche Botschaft [German Embassy] Washington in a letter to the Auswärtiges Amt dated January 1, 1939, in: PAA Berlin, R 100097.

163. Lammers in a letter to the Auswärtiges Amt dated February 6, 1939, in: ibid.

164. Memorandum dated June 29, 1938, in: ibid.

165. Alfred Rosenberg, Das *politische Tagebuch Alfred Rosenbergs. Aus den Jahren 1934/35 und 1939/40*, edited by Hans-Günther Seraphim (Göttingen, 1956), 59 (entry made on March 12, 1935).

166. See the two letters Hanfstaengl wrote to Schwarz dated December 12, 1935, in: BAB, BDC Ernst Hanfstaengl.

167. See Schwarz's letter to Hanfstaengl dated December 20, 1935, in: ibid.

168. Hanfstaengl in a letter to Schwarz dated March 9, 1936, in: ibid.

169. Schwarz in a letter to Hanfstaengl dated March 23, 1936, in: ibid.

170. Marwell alludes to the fact that Unity Mitford was involved in this; see *Unwanted Exile*, 156.

171. See the draft of a letter Hanfstaengl wrote to Göring in early July of 1938, here quoted from ibid., 334. See also Hanfstaengl in a letter to Schaub dated June 25, 1939, in: BAK, NS 10/340, Bl. 216f.

172. Hertha Oldenbourg (née Frey) in a letter to Fritz Wiedemann dated July 6, 1936 (via certified mail), in: BAK, NS 10/231, Bl. 222f.

173. Wiedemann in a letter to Oldenbourg dated July 9, 1936, in: ibid., Bl. 221.
174. *Goebbels Diaries* I/2 (1987), 652f. (entries made on August 1 and 2, 1936).
175. Oldenbourg in a letter to Wiedemann dated July 11, 1936, in: BAK, NS 10/231, Bl. 220.
176. Ernst Hanfstaengl, *Tat gegen Tinte. Hitler in der Karikatur der Welt* (Berlin, 1934), 57.
177. *Goebbels Diaries* I/2 (1987), 662 and 665 (entries made on August 16 and 21, 1936).
178. So Helene Niemeyer told the American Hitler biographer John Toland, quoted from Toland, *Adolf Hitler* (New York, 1976), 395.
179. Hanfstaengl later described this attack in detail; see *Außenseiter,* 362ff. In addition, see Albert Speer, *Erinnerungen* (Frankfurt a.M., 1969), 140f.; Reinhard Spitzy, *So haben wir das Reich verspielt. Bekenntnisse eines Illegalen* (Munich, 1986), 201ff.; as well as *Goebbels Diaries* I/3 (1987), 40f. It would appear as if Hitler was not completely honest even with his closest confidants, thereby giving rise to many different stories.
180. *Goebbels Diaries* I/3 (1987), 76 (entry made on March 12, 1937) and 80 (entry made on March 16, 1937).
181. See Göring's letter to Hanfstaengl dated March 19, 1937, facsimilated in Hanfstaengl, *Außenseiter,* 372.
182. See Marwell, *Unwanted Exile,* 178f.
183. *Goebbels Diaries* I/3 (1987), 85 (entry made on March 20, 1937).
184. Ibid., 109 and 113 (entry made on April 13 and 16, 1937).
185. See Marwell, *Unwanted Exile,* XVf.
186. See BAB, BDC Ernst Hanfstaengl.
187. Memorandum of a conversation Hanfstaengl had on May 14, 1937, quoted from Marwell, *Unwanted Exile,* 199. (The original quote reads, "Don't become a schwein"; "the people [at the RK] are not clean, not even A.H." "A queer and a blackmailer accounts for more at the highest level than I do!! That shows what kind of spirit lives in the higher regions where comradeship and cleanliness is the talk .")
188. Hanfstaengl in a letter to Julius Streicher dated December 19, 1937, in: BAK, NS 10/149, Bl. 194.
189. Hanfstaengl in a letter to Voigt dated November 30, 1937, quoted from Marwell, *Unwanted Exile,* 256. (The original quote reads, "Not only have I, as the only one, risked my position to exclude this . . . ambisexual [sic] schwein from the movement and the Führer's circle, . . .")
190. Hanfstaengl in a letter to Streicher dated December 19, 1937, in: BAK, NS 10/149, Bl. 199f. Hanfstaengl's letter to Brückner dated December 31, 1937, is similary provoking; in: ibid., Bl. 190f.

191. *Goebbels Diaries* I/5 (2000), 105 (entry made on January 19, 1938).

192. Marginalia by Himmler dated February 27, 1938, on the enclosure to Hanfstaengl's handwritten letter dated February 5, 1938, in: BAB, BDC Ernst Hanfstaengl.

193. Weizsäcker per order of Ribbentrop in a letter to Woermann, the German consul in London, dated March 29, 1938, in: PAA Berlin, F 11/504–503. Ribbentrop had made similar comments to Woermann on March 21, 1938, after he had "discussed the Hanfstaengl case with the 'Führer'," in: ibid.

194. *The New Republic,* No. 1221 (April 27, 1938, "Undesirable Refugees").

195. Draft of a letter Hanfstaengl wrote to Dirksen on May 30, 1938, quoted from Marwell, *Unwanted Exile,* 302f. (the original quote reads, "a shocking defamation of the character of the Führer").

196. Hanfstaengl in a letter to his mother dated July 5, 1938, quoted from ibid., 313f. (The original quote reads, "because we first damage the prospect in the Washington trial and then the reputation of A.H. as a man. . . . Homosexuality in connection with A.H. in the court room! My hair stands on end when I think of the press. What can I do then?")

197. Hanfstaengl's mother in a letter to her son dated August 20, 1938, quoted from ibid., 327f.

198. Göring in a letter to Hanfstaengl dated August 22, 1938, quoted from ibid., 331f. (The original translation reads, "Tintenkuli," "I believe that I don't need to remind you that you have made notes in a not very pretty fashion about the Führer so that the Führer withdrew at first from you. . . . Above all give up your crazy persecution mania.")

199. See Hanfstaengl's letter to Göring dated September 9, 1938, here quoted from ibid., 338ff.

200. Hanfstaengl in a letter to Göring and Ribbentrop dated November 18, 1938, quoted from ibid., 356. (The original translation reads, "I therefore inquire whether any particular wishes are under discussion for handling of both cases which involve the honor and private life of the Führer.")

201. Draft of a letter Hanfstaengl wrote to Hitler dated November 23, 1938, quoted from ibid., 356f. (The original quote reads, "as I have learned the opposition intends to use the trial for an evil attack on you," "to protect you and the reputation of Germany from defilement.")

202. Hanfstaengl in a letter to Göring dated December 14, 1938, quoted from ibid., 364f. (The original quote reads, "The court then will merely have to decide whether the opposition can produce real proof of the slander that the Führer and I had punishable relations in the sense of

paragraph 175 or not." "that the Führer is guilty of the crime of homosexuality.")

203. See entry Hanfstaengl made in his diary on January 28, 1939, here
quoted from ibid., 377.

204. See Winifred Wagner's letter to Hanfstaengl dated December 28, 1938,
here quoted from ibid., 368.

205. Hanfstaengl in a letter to Hitler dated February 12, 1939, in: BAK, NS
10/149, Bl. 186f.

206. See Martin Bormann's letters to Himmler dated March 6, 1939, and to
Hanfstaengl dated August 15, 1939, in: BAB, BDC Ernst Hanfstaengl; as
well as the letter Bodenschatz wrote to Hanfstaengl dated February 13,
1939; here quoted from Marwell, *Unwanted Exile,* 387.

207. Hanfstaengl in a letter to Winifred Wagner dated July 26, 1939, in: BAK,
NS 10/149, Bl. 189.

208. See the report of the trial published in *The Times,* No. 48.310 (May 20,
1939, "German's Libel Action against Selfridge and Co. fails").

209. Hanfstaengl in a letter to Hitler dated July 2, 1939, quoted from Marwell, *Unwanted Exile,* 417. (The original quote reads, "Schwein," "You
know me, Herr Hitler, and you know as well as I do what led me to you
in 1922–1923: It was you and you alone to whom I subordinated myself
as to the chosen one. No one else has the right to advance a claim to my
loyalty and obedience. As long as you are there, I will react to your voice
and not to another. You alone can call me back. I wrote from my heart;
you do the same. That, I ask for you.")

210. Bormann in a letter to Wolff dated August 4, 1939, in: BAB, BDC Ernst
Hanfstaengl.

211. Memo written by Walter Hewels dated September 5, 1939, in: PAA
Berlin, F 11/498.

EPILOGUE

1. For more information, see Joachim Fest, *Speer. Eine Biographie* (Berlin,
1999), especially 59ff. – The quote comes from Speer's head of office
Karl Maria Hettlage, quoted from ibid., 153.

2. Günther Weisenborn, *Memorial* (Berlin, 1948), 205.

3. So Fest said in an interview with the German TV station ZDF, quoted
from the feature, "Hitlers unglückliche Liebe Albert Speer" broadcast in
October 1999.

4. Interview in *Der Spiegel,* No. 19/2001.

5. For more information, see now the latest research results published by Heinrich Schwendemann in the *Frankfurter Allgemeine Zeitung* (April 26, 2000, "Lebensläufer über verbrannter Erde" [Lifelong Runner Across Scorched Earth]).

6. For more details, see Fest, *Speer,* 360ff.

7. See Christa Schroeder, *Er war mein Chef. Aus dem Nachlaß der Sekretärin von Adolf Hitler,* edited by Anton Joachimsthaler (Munich, 1985), 156; Nerin Erin Gun, *Eva Braun-Hitler. Leben und Schicksal* (Kiel, 1994, new edition), 203; John Mendelsohn (ed.), *Covert Warfare,* Vol. 14: *A Man Called A.H.* (New York/London, 1989), 688.

8. Hans Severus Ziegler, *Adolf Hitler aus dem Erleben dargestellt* (Göttingen, 1964), 265f.

9. See Gun, *Eva Braun-Hitler,* 32f. and 46.

10. Hans Blüher, *Die Rede des Aristophanes. Prolegomena zu einer Soziologie des Menschengeschlechtes* (Hamburg, 1966), 65.

11. Adolf Hitler, *Mein Kampf* (Munich, 1930, 3rd ed.), 6 and 93f.

POSTSCRIPT

1. Eugenio Dollmann, *Roma Nazista (Traduzione Dal Tedesco Di Italo Zingarelli)* (Milano, 1949).

2. *Corriere della Sera* May 21, 1950). The review was published under the title "Dollmann Reports on His Italian Experience. In Serving Hitler, He Was Mightier Than Him."

3. See Dollmann, *Roma Nazista,* 30ff.

4. Ibid., 9f.

5. See Blüher, *Rolle der Erotik* (new edition, 1962), 26ff. (Preface to the 1949 edition). Blüher enlarged and extended these reflections in the posthumously published manuscript 'Die Rede des Aristophanes' (Hamburg, 1966).

6. See the first critical edition of this work published in different versions: Jean Genet, *Werke in Einzelbänden,* Vol. III: *Das Totenfest* (Pompes funèbres) (Gifkendorf, 2000). See ibid., 368ff. for the postscipt regarding the history of the work as well as the interpretation.

7. See Nicolaus Sombart, *Pariser Lehrjahre 1951–1954* (Hamburg, 1994), 279ff.

8. This novel, finished in the United States in 1944, was first published in New York in 1947 entitled *The End is Not Yet.* In 1948, the Hallwag-Verlag published it in Berne. The most important passages regarding

Hitler's homosexuality can be found on pp. 434ff. and 446ff. of the German edition.

9. See Karola Schulz, *Fast ein Revolutionär. Fritz von Unruh zwischen Exil und Remigration (1932–1962)* (Munich, 1994), 23ff. and 64ff.

10. See Ulrich Rudolf Fröhlich, *Fritz von Unruhs Spätwerk, Der nie verlor* (Ann Arbor, 1980).

11. Erich Ebermayer, *Denn heute gehört und Deutschland . . . Persönliches und politisches Tagebuch. Von der Machtergreifung bis zum 31. Dezember 1935* (Hamburg/Vienna, 1959), here especially 331f.

Bibliography

Adolf Hitler: Bilder aus dem Leben des Führers. Edited by Cigaretten-Bilderdienst [Choice and Artistic Editing of the Pictures by Heinrich Hoffmann]. Altona/Bahrenfeld: Cigaretten-Bilderdienst, 1936.

Baedeker, Peer / Lemke, Karl (eds.). *Erich Ebermayer. Buch der Freunde.* Lohhof near Munich: Lemke, 1960.

Banach, Jens. *Heydrichs Elite. Das Führerkorps der Sicherheitspolizei und des SD. 1936–1945.* Paderborn/Munich/Vienna: Schöningh, 1998.

Bartsch, Rudolf Hans. *Schwammerl. Ein Schubertroman.* Leipzig: Staakmann, 1912.

Bastian, Till. *Homosexuelle im Dritten Reich: Geschichte einer Verfolgung.* Munich: Beck, 2000.

Behnken, Klaus (ed.). *Deutschland-Berichte der Sozialdemokratischen Partei Deutschlands.* Deutschland–Berichte der Sopade. Third Year, 1936. Salzhausen: Nettelbeck, 1980.

Behrendt, Armin. *Wilhelm Külz: Aus dem Leben eines Suchenden.* Berlin (Ost): Verlag der Morgen, 1968.

Bennecke, Heinrich. *Hitler und die SA.* Munich/Vienna: Olzog, 1962.

Blazek, Helmut. *Rosa Zeiten für Rosa Liebe. Geschichte der Homosexualität.* Frankfurt a.M.: Fischer Taschenbuch Verlag, 1996.

Blüher, Hans. *Die Rede des Aristophanes. Prolegomena zur einer Soziologie des Menschengeschlechtes.* Hamburg: Kala-Verlag, 1966.

———. *Die Rolle der Erotik in der männlichen Gesellschaft: eine Theorie der menschlichen Staatsbildung nach Wesen und Wert*. Jena: Dietrichs, 1917. New Edition, Stuttgart: Klett, 1962.

———. *Werke und Tage: Geschichte eines Denkers*. Munich: List, 1953.

Böhm, Karl Werner. *Zwischen Selbstzucht und Verlangen. Thomas Mann und das Stigma der Homosexualität*. Untersuchung zu Frühwerk und Jugend. Würzburg: Königshausen und Neumann, 1991.

Boehringer, Robert. *Mein Bild von Stefan George* (Text). Munich/Düsseldorf: Küppler, 1951.

Böll, Heinrich. *Was soll aus dem Jungen bloß werden? Oder: Irgendwas mit Büchern*. Bornheim: Lamuv-Verlag, 1981.

Brandmayer, Balthasar. *Meldegänger Hitler: erlebt und erzählt von Balthasar Brandmayer*. 2nd extended ed., edited by Heinz Bayer. Munich: Walter, 1933.

Bredow, Klaus. *Hitler rast: Der 30. Juni. Ablauf, Vorgeschichte und Hintergründe*. Saarbrücken: Volksstimme, 1934.

Broche, François. *Assassinat du Chancellier Dollfuss*. Paris: Balland, 1977.

Bürgin, Hans (ed.). *Die Briefe Thomas Manns*. Regesten und Register, Vol. 1. Edited by Hans Büring and Hans-Otto Mayer. Frankfurt a.M.: Fischer, 1976.

Bullock, Alan. *Hitler and Stalin. Parallel Lives*. New York: Knopf, 1952.

Bullock, Alan. *Hitler. A Study in Tyranny*. London: Odhams Pr., 1991.

Bumke, Oswald. *Erinnerungen und Betrachtungen. Der Weg eines deutschen Psychiaters*. Munich: Pflaum, 1952.

Chauncey, George. *Gay New York: Gender, Urban Culture, and the Making of the Gay Male World, 1890–1914*. New York: Basic Books, 1994.

Chaussy, Ulrich. *Nachbar Hitler: Führerkult und Heimatzerstörung am Obersalzberg*: Berlin. Links, 2001.

Clemens, Detlev. *Herr Hitler in Germany. Wahrnehmung und Deutung des Nationalsozialismus in Großbritannien, 1920 bis 1939*. Göttingen: Vandenhoeck & Ruprecht, 1996.

Demmel, Fritz. *Geschichte und G'schichten aus der Gemeinde Garching a. d. Alz*. Garching an der Alz: Gemeinde Graching an der Alz, 1999.

Deuerlein, Ernst (ed.). *Der Hitler-Putsch: Bayerische Dokumente zum 8./9. November 1923*. Stuttgart: Deutsche Verlagsanstalt, 1962.

Diels, Rudolf. *Lucifer ante portas. ... es spricht der erste Chef der Gestapo. . . .* Stuttgart: Deutsche Verlags-Anstalt, 1950.

Dietrich, Otto. *12 Jahre mit Hitler*. Munich: Isar-Verlag, 1955.

Diroll, Bernd. *Personen-Lexikon der NSDAP*, Bd. 1, SS-Führer A-B. Norderstedt: Patzwall, 1998.

Dodd, Martha. *Through Embassy Eyes*. New York: Harcourt, Brace, 1939.

Dollmann, Eugenio. *Roma Nazista*. Milano: Longanesi, 1949.

Domarus, Max (ed.). *Hitler. Reden und Proklamationen 1932–1945*: kommentiert von einem deutschen Zeitgenossen, Vol. II/2. Wiesbaden: Löwith, 1973.

Dörner, Bernward. *"Heimtücke": Das Gesetz als Waffe. Kontrolle, Abschreckung und Verfolgung in Deutschland 1933 bis 1945*. Paderborn: Schöningh, 1998.

Dornheim, Andreas. *Röhms Mann fürs Ausland. Politik und Ermordung des SA-Agenten Georg Bell*. Münster: Lit, 1998.

Drage, Charles. *Als Hitler nach Canossa ging*. Berlin: ikoo-Buchverlag, 1982.

Ebermayer, Erich. *Denn heute gehört uns Deutschland . . . : Persönliches und politisches Tagebuch, von der Machtergreifung bis zum 31. Dezember 1935*. Hamburg/Vienna: Zsolnay, 1959.

———. *Gustav Wyneken: Chronik einer großen Freundschaft*. Frankfurt a.M.: dipa-Verlag, 1969.

———. *Kampf um Odilienburg*. Berlin/Vienna: Zsolnay, 1929.

———. *Magisches Bayreuth: Legende und Wirklichkeit*. Stuttgart: Steingrüber-Verlag, 1951.

Ebermayer, Ludwig. *Fünfzig Jahre Dienst am Recht. Erinnerungen eines Juristen*. Leipzig: Grethlein & Co., 1930.

Fallois, Immo von. *Kalkül und Illusion. Der Machtkampf zwischen Reichswehr und SA während der Röhm-Krise 1934*. Berlin: Dunker & Humblot, 1994.

Fest, Joachim. *Hitler: Eine Biographie*. 5th ed. Frankfurt a.M./Berlin: Propyläen Verlag, 1973. Unabridged, with a preface by the author. Berlin: Propyläen verlag, 1995. Munich: Econ, 2000.

———. *Speer. Eine Biographie*. Berlin: Fest[SvE2], 1999.

Fischer, H. C./ Dubois, E. X. *Sexual Life during the World War*. London: Alder, 1937.

Ford, Henry (ed.). *Der internationale Jude: Ein Weltproblem*. Translated into German by Paul Lehmann. Leipzig: Hammer-Verlag, 1921.

Frank, Hans. *Im Angesicht des Galgens: Deutung Hitlers und seiner Zeit auf Grund eigener Erlebnisse und Erkenntnisse*. Written in the Nürnberger Prison of Justice. Munich-Gräfelfing: Beck, 1953.

Frank, Leonhard. *Links wo das Herz ist*. Berlin: Aufbau Verlag, 1955.

Franz-Willing, Georg. *Ursprung der Hitlerbewegung 1919–1922*. Preußisch Oldendorf: Schütz, 1974.

Fröhlich, Ulrich Rudolf. *Fritz von Unruhs Spätwerk, Der nie verlor*. Ann Arbor, Mich.: University Microfilms International, 1980.

Fromm, Bella. *Als Hitler mir die Hand küßte*. Berlin: Rowohlt, 1993.

Genet, Jean. *Werke in Einzelbänden*, Bd. III: *Das Totenfest. Pompes Funèbres*. Gifkendorf: Merlin Verlag, 2000.

Geuter, Ulfried. *Homosexualität in der deutschen Jugendbewegung. Jungenfreundschaft und Sexualität im Diskurs von Jugendbewegung, Psychoanalyse und Jugendpsychologie am Beginn des 20. Jahrhunderts*. Frankfurt a.M.: Suhrkamp, 1994.

Gisevius, Hans Bernd. *Bis zum bitteren Ende. Vom Reichstagsbrand bis zum 20. Juli 1944*. Zurich: Fretz & Wassmuth, 1946. New edition Gütersloh: Bertelsmann, 1961.

Godau-Schüttke, Klaus-Detlev. *Rechtsverwalter des Reiches. Staatssekretär Dr. Curt Joel*. Frankfurt a.M./Bern: Lang, 1981.

Goebbels, Joseph. *Die Tagebücher von Joseph Goebbels*. 9 vols., edited by Elke Fröhlich, Jana Richter (et al.). Munich: Saur, 1987–2001.

Göring, Emmy. *An der Seite meines Manne: Begebenheiten und Bekenntnisse*. Göttingen: Schütz, 1967.

Graf, Christoph. *Politische Polizei zwischen Demokratie und Diktatur. Die Entwicklung der preußischen Politischen Polizei vom Staatsschutzorgan der Weimarer Republik zum Geheimen Staatspolizeiamt des Dritten Reiches*. Berlin: Coloquium Verlag, 1983.

Granier, Gerhard. *Magnus von Levetzow: Seeoffizier, Monarchist und Wegbereiter Hitlers*. Lebensweg und ausgewählte Dokumente. Boppard a.Rh.: Boldt, 1982.

Grau, Günter. *Homosexualität in der NS-Zeit: Dokumente einer Diskriminierung und Verfolgung*. Frankfurt a.M.: Fischer-Taschenbuch-Verlag, 1993.

Grimm, Hans. *Suchen und Hoffen: 1928–1934*. 2. Aufl. Lippoldsberg: Klosterhaus-Verlag, 1972.

Gritschneder, Otto. *"Der Führer hat Sie zum Tode verurteilt . . .": Hitlers "Röhm-Putsch"-Morde vor Gericht*. Munich: Beck, 1993.

Grunberg, Bela/ Dessuant, Pierre. *Narzismus, Christentum und Antisemitismus: eine psychoanalytische Untersuchung*. Stuttgart: Klett-Cotta, 2000.

Gugenberger, Eduard. *Hitlers Visionäre. Die okkulten Wegbereiter des Dritten Reiche*. Vienna: Ueberreuter, 2001.

Gun, Nerin Erin. *Eva Braun-Hitler: Leben und Schicksal*. Kiel: Arndt-Verlag, 1994.

Hall, Murray G. *Der Paul Zsolnay Verlag. Von der Gründung bis zur Rückkehr aus dem Exil*. Tübingen: Niemeyer, 1994.

Hamann, Brigitte. *Hitlers Wien: Lehrjahre eines Diktators*. Munich/Zurich: Piper, 1997.

Hanfstaengl, Ernst. *Hitler: The Missing Years*. London: Eyre & Spottiswood, 1957.

———. *Tat gegen Tinte. Hitler in der Karikatur der Welt*. Ein Bildsammelwerk von Ernst Hanfstaengl. Series: Braune Bücher. Berlin: Rentsch, 1934.

———. *Tat gegen Tinte: Hitler in der Karikatur der Welt*. Neue Folge. Ein

Bildsammelwerk von Ernst Hanfstaengl. Series: Braune Bücher. Berlin: Rentsch, 1934.

———. *Zwischen Weißem und Braunem Haus: Memoiren eines politischen Außenseiters*. Munich: Piper Verlag, 1970.

Harpprecht, Klaus. *Thomas Mann: Eine Biographie*. Reinbek near Hamburg: Rowohlt, 1995.

Hartmann, Christian. *Halder: Generalstabschef Hitlers 1938–1942*. Paderborn: Schöning, 1991.

Hayman, Ronald. *Hitler & Geli*. New York/London: Bloomsbury, 1997.

Heiber, Beatrice / Heiber, Helmut (ed.) *Die Rückseite des Hakenkreuzes: Absonderliches aus den Akten des Dritten Reiches*. Munich: Deutscher Taschenbuch-Verlag, 1993.

Heiden, Konrad. *Adolf Hitler: das Zeitalter der Verantwortungslosigkeit*. A Biography. Zurich: Europa-Verlag, 1936.

———. *Der Führer. Hitler's Rise to Power*. Boston: Houghton Mifflin, 1944.

Heinz, Heinz A. *Germany's Hitler*. London: Hurst & Blackett, 1934.

Heiß, Stephan R. *Ein Schandfleck für das dritte Reich: Homosexuelle als Opfer von Verfolgung und Vernichtung während der Diktatur des Nationalsozialismus in Bayern*. In: Michael Farin (ed.). *Polizeireport München: 1799–1999* [Catalogue for the exhibit under the same title in the Munich Stadtmuseum, April 23 until August 22]. Munich: Belleville, 1999.

Hekma, Gert (ed.). *Gay Men and the Sexual History of the Political Left*. New York: Haworth, 1995.

Herbst, Ludolf. *Der Fall Hitler: Inszenierungskunst und Charismapolitik*. In: Wilfried Nippen (ed.). *Virtuosen der Macht: Herrschaft und Charisma von Perikles bis Mao*. Munich: Beck, 2000.

Hergemöller, Bernd-Ulrich. *Mann für Mann: Biographisches Lexikon zur Geschichte von Freundesliebe und mannmännlicher Sexualität im deutschen Sprachraum*. Hamburg: MännerschwarmSkript-Verlag, 1998.

Hess, Ilse. *Ein Schicksal in Briefen. England – Nürnberg – Spandau. Gefangener des Friedens. Antwort aus Zelle Sieben*. Leoni am Starnberger See: Druffel Verlag, 1984.

Hess, Rudolf. *Briefe 1908–1933*. Edited by Wolf Rüdiger Hess, with an introduction and commentary by Dirk Bavendamm. Munich/Vienna: Langen Müller, 1987.

Hess, Wolf Rüdiger. *Mord an Rudolf Heß*. Leoni am Starnberger See: Druffel-Verlag, 1989.

Hille, Johann. *Mahraun, der Pionier des Arbeitsdienstes*. Leipzig: Kittler, 1933.

———. *Leben gegen die Zeit*. Reinbek near Hamburg: Rowohlt, 1969.

Hinkel, Hans. *Einer unter Hunderttausend*. Munich: Knorr & Hirth, 1938.

Hipler, Bruno. *Hitlers Lehrmeister: Karl Haushofer als Vater der NS-Ideologie.* St. Ottilien: EOS-Verlag, 1996.

Hirschfeld, Gerhard / Kettenacker, Lothar. *Der "Führerstaat": Mythos und Realität: Studien zur Struktur und Politik des Dritten Reiches*. Stuttgart: Klett-Cotta, 1981.

Hirschfeld, Magnus. *Die Homosexualität des Mannes und des Weibes*. 2. Aufl. Berlin: Marcus, 1920.

———. (ed.). *Sittengeschichte des Ersten Weltkriegs*. Hanau a. Main: Schustek, 1929.

Hirsinger, Hauke. *Hitler im Ersten Weltkrieg. Fakten und Legenden*. Master's Thesis, Bremen University, 2001.

Hitler, Adolf. *Mein Kampf*. 3rd ed. Munich: Eher, 1930.

Hitler: Reden, Schriften, Anordnungen, February 1925–January 1933, Vol. I. Published by the Institut für Zeitgeschichte. Associate: Clemens Vollnhals. Munich: Saur, 1992.

Hitler: Reden, Schriften, Anordnungen, February 1925–January 1933, Vol. II/2. Edited by Bärbel Dusik. Munich: Saur, 1992.

Hitler: Reden, Schriften, Anordnungen, February 1925–January 1933, Vol. IV/1. Edited by Constantin Goschler and Christian Hartmann. Munich: Saur, 1994.

Hitler: Reden, Schriften, Anordnungen, Vol. V/1. Edited by Klaus A. Lankheit et al. Munich/New York: Saur, 1996.

Hitler-Liederbuch 1924. Munich: Eher, 1924.

Hockerts, Hans-Günther. *Die Sittlichkeitsprozesse gegen katholische Ordensangehörige und Priester: 1936/37*. Eine Studie zur nationalsozialistischen Herrschaftstechnik und zum Kirschenkampf. Mainz: Mathias-Grünewald-Verlag, 1971.

Hoffmann, Heinrich. *Hitler Was My Friend*. London: Burke, 1955.

Hoffmann, Peter. *Die Sicherheit des Diktators: Hitlers Leibwachen, Schutzmaßnahmen, Residenzen, Hauptquartiere*. Munich/Zurich: Piper, 1975.

Höhne, Heinz. *Canaris: Patriot im Zwielicht*. Munich: Bertelsmann, 1976.

———. *Der Orden unter dem Totenkopf: Die Geschichte der SS*. Gütersloh: Mohn, 1967.

———. *Mordsache Röhm: Hitlers Durchbruch zur Alleinherrschaft 1933–1934*. Reinbek near Hamburg: Rowohlt, 1984.

Hömig, Herbert. Brüning: *Kanzler in der Krise der Republik: eine Weimarer Biographie*. Paderborn/Munich/Vienna: Schöningh, 2000.

Hohmann, Joachim S. *Der heimliche Sexus. Homosexuelle Belletristik im Deutschland der Jahre 1920–1970*. Erzählungen, Skizzen und Kurzgeschichten von Alfred Arnold. Frankfurt a.M.: Foersters, 1979.

Igra, Samuel. *Germany's National Vice*. London: Quality Press, 1945.

Jacobsen, Hans-Adolf (ed.). *Karl Haushofer: Leben und Werk*, Vol. 1: *Lebensweg 1869–1946 und ausgewählte Texte zur Geopolitik*. Published by the Bundesarchiv Koblenz. Boppard am Reihn: Boldt, 1979.

Jäckel, Eberhard /Kuhn, Axel (eds.). *Hitler: Sämtliche Aufzeichnungen 1905–1924*. Stuttgart: Deutsche Verlags-Anstalt, 1980.

———. *Hitlers Weltanschauung: Entwurf einer Herrschaft*. Enlarged and newly edited, 4th ed. Stuttgart: Deutsche Verlags-Anstalt, 1991.

Janßen, Karl-Heinz /Tobias, Fritz. *Der Sturz der Generäle: Hitler und die Blomberg-Fritsch-Krise 1938*. Munich: Beck 1994.

Jellonnek, Burkhard. *Homosexuelle unter dem Hakenkreuz: die Verfolgung der Homosexuellen im Dritten Reich*. Paderborn: Schöningh, 1990.

Jenks, William A. *Vienna and the Young Hitler*. New York: Columbia University Press, 1960.

Jetzinger, Franz. *Hitlers Jugend: Phantasien, Lügen und die Wahrheit*. Vienna: Europa-Verlag, 1956.

Joachimsthaler, Anton. *Hitlers Weg begann in München 1913–1923*. Munich: Herbig, 2000.

Jochmann, Werner (ed.). *Adolf Hitler: Monologe im Führerhauptquartier 1941–1944*. Hamburg: Knaus, 1980. New edition. Munich: Orbis-Verlag, 2000.

Johe, Werner. *Hitler in Hamburg: Dokumente zu einem besonderen Verhältnis*. Hamburg: Ergebnis-Verlag, 1996.

Kallenbach, Hans. *Mit Adolf Hitler auf Festung Landsberg*. Edited by Ulf Uweson. Munich: Parcus, 1933. Edited by Hans Kallenbach. Munich: Kreß & Hornung, 1939. Newly edited, 4th ed. Munich: Kreß & Hornung, 1943.

Kaltenborn, Hans von. *Fifty Fabulous Years 1900–1950: A Personal Review*. 6th Impr. New York: Putnam, 1950.

Keilson-Lauritz, Marita. *Die eigene Geschichte: Literatur und Literaturkritik in den Anfängen der Schwulenbewegung am Beispiel des Jahrbuchs für sexuelle Zwischenstufen und der Zeitschrift Der Eigene*. Berlin: Verlag Rosa Winkel, 1997.

Kelley, Douglas M. *Twenty-Two Cells in Nuremberg. A Psychiatrist Examines the Nazi-Criminals*. New York: Greenberg, 1947.

Kershaw, Ian. *Der Hitler-Mythos: Führerkult und Volkmeinung*. Stuttgart: Deutsche Verlags-Anstalt, 1999.

———. *Hitler*, Vol. 1: 1889–1936. Hubris. 1st American ed. New York: W.W. Norton, 1999.

———. *Hitler*, Vol. 2: 1936–1945. Nemesis. 1st American ed. New York: W.W. Norton, 2000.

Kirsten, Holm. *Hitlers Besuche in Weimar*. Master's Thesis, Jena, 1999. (The book will most likely be published in the fall of 2001 entitled *"Weimar im Banne des Führers": die Besuche Adolf Hitlers 1925–1940* [Cologne: Böhlau, 2001].)

Kisch, Egon Erwin. *Gesammelte Werke*, vol. 7, 4th ed. Berlin: Aufbau-Verlag, 1992.

———. *Gesammelte Werke*, vol. 10. Berlin: Aufbau-Verlag, 1993.

Klabunde, Anja. *Magda Goebbels, Annäherung an ein Leben*. 3rd ed. Munich: Bertelsmann, 1999.

Kläger, Emil. *Durch die Quartiere der Not und des Verbrechens*: Wien um die Jahrhundertwende. Vienna: Hannibal-Verlag, 1908.

Kleemann, Elisabeth. *Zwischen symbolischer Rebellion und politischer Revolution: Studien zur deutschen Boheme zwischen Kaiserreich und Weimarer Republik*. Frankfurt a.M.: Lang, 1985.

Klotz, Helmuth. *Euer Hochwohlgeboren*. Berlin-Tempelhof 1932; the 2nd ed. was printed under the title *Der Fall Röhm*. Berlin-Tempelhof: APK-Dr.Klotz, 1932.

———. *Wir gestalten durch unser Führerkorps die Zukunft*. 2nd ed. Berlin-Tempelhof: APK-Dr.Klotz, 1932.

Knopp, Guido. *Hitler: eine Bilanz*. Munich: Goldmann, 1997.

Köhler, Joachim. *Wagners Hitler: Der Prophet und sein Vollstrecker*. Munich: Blessing, 1997.

Koch-Hillebrecht, Manfred. *Homo Hitler: Psychogramm des deutschen Diktators*. Munich: Siedler, 1999.

Kraft, Zdenko von. *Der Sohn. Siegfried Wagners Leben und Umwelt*. With an Appendix: The Succession Bayreuth 1913–1944. Graz/Stuttgart: Stocker, 1969.

Krebs, Albert. *Tendenzen und Gestalten der NSDAP. Erinnerungen an die Frühzeit der Partei*. Stuttgart: Deutsche Veralgs-Anstalt, 1959.

Kroll, Fredric (ed.). *Klaus-Mann-Schriftenreihe*. Vol. 3. Wiesbaden: Blahak, 1979.

Kruck, Alfred. *Geschichte des Alldeutschen Verbandes 1890–1939*. Wiesbaden: Steiner, 1954.

Kubizek, Alfred. *Adolf Hitler: Mein Jugendfreund*. 2nd ed. Graz/Göttingen: Stocker, 1953.

Külz, Wilhelm. *Ein Liberaler zwischen Ost und West: Aufzeichnungen 1947–1948*. Edited by Hergard. Robel. Munich: Oldenbourg, 1989.

Kugel, Wilfried. *Der Unverantwortliche. Das Leben des Hanns Heinz Ewers*. Düsseldorf: Grupello-Verlag, 1992.

Kutter, Paul. *Das materielle Elend der jungen Münchener Maler*. Munich: Foth Nachf, 1911.

Kuusisto, Sappo. *Alfred Rosenberg in der nationalsozialistischen Außenpolitik 1933–1939*. Helsinki: SHS, 1984.

Lang, Jochen von. *Der Adjutant: Karl Wolff: Der Mann zwischen Hitler und Himmler*. Frankfurt a.M.: Ullstein, 1989.

Langer, Walter C. *The Mind of Adolf Hitler*. London: Secker & Warburg, 1973.

Langoth, Franz. *Kampf um Österreich: Erinnerungen eines Politikers*. Wels: Verlag Welsermuehl, 1951.

Large, David Clay. *Where Ghosts walked. Munich's Road to the Third Reich*. New York: W.W. Norton, 1997.

Lauterbacher, Hartmann. *Erlebt und mitgestaltet: Kronzeuge einer Epoche 1923 bis 1945*. Preußisch Oldendorff: Schütz, 1984.

Lessing, Theodor. *Haarmann: Geschichte eines Werwolfs*. Berlin: Verlag Die Schmiede, 1925.

Lewis, David. *The Secret Life of Adolf Hitler*. London: Hanau, 1977.

Linder, Herbert. *Von der NSDAP zur SPD: Der politische Lebensweg des Dr. Helmuth Klotz (1894–1943)*. Konstanz: UVK, Universitäts-Verlag, 1998.

Linsert, Richard. *Kabale und Liebe: über Politik und Geschlechtsleben*. Berlin: Man Verlag, 1931.

Longerich, Peter. *Die braunen Bataillone: Geschichte der SA*. Munich: Beck, 1989.

Luetgebrune, Walter. *Ein Kampf um Röhm*. Diessen near Munich: Huber, 1933.

Lüdecke, Kurt G. W. *I knew Hitler. The Story of a Nazi Who Escaped the Blood Purge*. New York: AMS Press, 1937.

Lukacs, John. *The Hitler of History*. New York: Knopf, 1997.

Maar, Michael. *Das Blaubartzimmer: Thomas Mann und die Schuld*. Frankfurt a.M: Suhrkamp, 2000.

Maasen, Thijs. *Pädagogischer Eros: Gustav Wyneken und die Freie Schulgemeinde Wickersdorf*. Berlin: Verlag Rosa Winkel, 1995.

Maleta, Alfred. *Bewältigte Vergangenheit: Österreich 1932–1945*. Graz: Verlag Styria, 1981.

Mann, Heinrich. *Der Hass: Deutsche Zeitgeschichte*. Amsterdam: Querido-Verlag 1933, New Edition. Berlin (Ost)/Weimar: Aufbau-Verlag, 1983.

Mann, Klaus. *Briefe*. Edited by Friedrich Albrecht. Berlin (Ost)/Weimar: Aufbau-Verlag, 1988.

———. *Tagebücher 1931 bis 1933*. Edited by Joachim Heimannsberg, Peter Laemmle and Wilfried F. Schoeller. Munich: Spangenberg, 1989.

———. *Der Wendepunkt. Ein Lebensbericht*. Reinbek bei Hamburg: Rowohlt, 1984.

Mann, Klaus / Tucholsky, Kurt. *Homosexualität und Faschismus*. Hamburg: Libertäre Assoz., 1981. New Edition Kiel: Verlag Frühlings Erwachen, 1990.

Mann, Thomas. *Politische Reden und Schriften*, Bd. 3. Frankfurt a.M.: Fischer, 1968.

———. *Tagebücher 1937–1939*. Edited by Peter de Mendelssohn. Frankfurt a.M.: Fischer, 1980.

Marchand, W. *Die Knabenliebe in München! Münchens Homosexuelle. Sittenbild aus der Großstadt.* Munich: Verlag der Münchner Stadt-Telegramme, 1904.

Marwell, David George. *Unwanted Exile. A Biography of Ernst "Putzi" Hanfstaengl.* Ph.D., New York, Ann Arbor, Mich.: University Microfilms International, 1988.

Maser, Werner. *Adolf Hitler: Legende, Mythos, Wirklichkeit.* Munich: Bechtle, 1971.

—— (ed.). *Hitlers Briefe und Notizen: sein Weltbild in handschriftlichen Dokumenten.* Düsseldorf: Econ-Verlag, 1973.

Matussek, Paul /Matussek, Peter /Marbach, Jan. *Hitler: Karriere eines Wahns.* Munich: Herbig, 2000.

Mauch, Christof. *Schattenkrieg gegen Hitler: Das Dritte Reich im Visier der amerikanischen Geheimdienste 1941–1945.* Stuttgart: Deutsche Verlags-Anstalt, 1999.

McKnight, Gerald. *The Strange Loves of Adolf Hitler.* London: Sphere, 1978.

Meinl, Susanne. *Nationalsozialisten gegen Hitler: die nationalrevolutionäre Opposition um Friedrich Wilhelm Heinz.* Berlin: Siedler, 2000.

Mend, Hans. *Adolf Hitler im Felde: 1914–18.* Diessen near Munich: Huber, 1931.

Mendelsohn, John (ed.). *Covert Warfare: Intelligence, Counterintelligence, and Military Deception during the World War II era,* vol. 14: *A Man Called A. H.* New York/London: Garland, 1989.

Metcalfe, Philip. *1933.* Sag Harbor/New York: Permanent Pr., 1988.

Michalzik, Peter. *Gustaf Gründgens: Der Schauspieler und die Macht.* Berlin: Quadriga, 1999.

Molau, Andreas. *Alfred Rosenberg: der Ideologie des Nationalsozialismus; eine politische Biographie.* Koblenz: Bublies, 1993.

Möller, Horst (ed.). *Die tödliche Utopie. Bilder, Texte, Dokumente, Daten zum Dritten Reich.* Munich: Institut für Zeitgeschichte, 1999.

Moll, Martin (ed.). *Führer-Erlasse 1939–1945: Edition sämtlicher überlieferter, nicht im Reichsgesetzblatt abgedruckter, von Hitler während des 2. Weltkriegs schriftlich erteilten Direktionen aus dem Bereich Staat, Partei, Wirtschaft, Besatzungspolitik und Militärverwaltung.* Summarized by and introduced by Martin Moll. Stuttgart: Steiner, 1997.

Mommsen, Hans. "Hitlers Stellung im nationalsozialistischen Herrschaftssystem." In: Hans Mommsen. *Von Weimar nach Auschwitz: zur Geschichte in der Weltkriegsepoche.* Stuttgart: Deutsche Verlags-Anstalt, 1999.

Mork, Andrea. *Richard Wagner als politischer Schriftsteller: Weltanschauung und Wirkungsgeschichte.* Frankfurt a.M./New York: Campus, 1990.

Mühsam, Erich. *Namen und Menschen: Unpolitische Erinnerungen.* Berlin: Guhl, 1977.

Müller, Joachim/ Sternweiler, Andreas. *Homosexuelle Männer im KZ Sachsenhausen.* [Published in conjuction with the Exhibition "Verfolgung Homosexueller Männer in Berlin 1933–45" (Persecution of Homosexual Men in Berlin in 1933–1945) by the Schwulen Museum in cooperation with the Sachsenhausen Memorial. Edited by the Schwulen Museum Berlin. Berlin: Verlag Rosa Winkel, 2000.

München—Hauptstadt der Bewegung. [Exhibition in the Munich Stadtmuseum October 22, 1993–March 27, 1994. Editor: Ulrike Haerendel.] Munich: Münchener Stadtmuseum, 1993.

Naumann, Uwe (ed.). *"Ruhe gibt es nicht, bis zum Schluß." Klaus Mann (1906–1949). Bilder und Dokumente.* Reinbek near Hamburg: Rowohlt, 1999.

Nicolai, Elke. *"Wohin es uns treibt ...": die literarische Generationsgruppe Klaus Manns 1924–1933. Ihre Essayistik und Erzählprosa.* Frankfurt a.M./Berlin: Lang, 1998.

Noakes, Jeremy. "Philipp Bouhler und die Kanzlei des Führers der NSDAP." In: Dieter Rebentisch/Karl Teppe (eds.), *Verwaltung contra Menschenführung im Staat Hitlers.* Göttingen: Vandenhoeck & Ruprecht, 1986.

Olden, Rudolf. *Hitler.* Amsterdam: Querido-Verlag, 1935. Unabridged New Edition: Frankfurt a.M.: Fischer, 1984.

Pachl, Peter P. *Siegfried Wagner. Genie im Schatten.* Mit Opernführer, Werkverzeichnis, Diskographie. Munich: Nymphenburger, 1988.

Padfield, Peter. *Hess: Flight for the Führer.* London: Weidenfeld & Nicolson, 1991.

Pätzold, Kurt / Weißbecker, Manfred. *Rudolf Heß: der Mann an Hitlers Seite.* Leipzig: Militzke Verlag, 1999.

Pechel, Rudolf. *Deutscher Widerstand.* Erlenbach-Zurich: Rentsch, 1947.

Petersen, Jens. *Hitler–Mussolini. Die Entstehung der Achse Berlin–Rom. 1933–1936.* Tübingen: Niemeyer, 1973.

Picker, Henry. *Hitlers Tischgespräche im Führerhauptquartier.* Mit bisher unbekannten Selbstzeugnissen Adolf Hitlers, Abbildungen, Augenzeugenberichten und Erläuterungen des Autors. Wiesbaden: VMA-Verlag, 1983.

Plehwe, Friedrich-Karl von. *Reichskanzler Kurt von Schleicher: Weimars letzte Chance gegen Hitler.* Frankfurt a.M./Berlin: Ullstein, 1989.

Plewnia, Margarete. *Auf dem Weg zu Hitler: der "völkische" Publizist Dietrich Eckart.* Bremen: Schünemann, 1970.

Pool, James. *Who Financed Hitler: The Secret Funding of Hitler's Rise to Power, 1919–1933.* New York: Pocket Books, 1997.

Pretzel, Andreas / Roßbach, Gabriele (eds.). *Wegen der zu erwartenden hohen*

Strafen. Homosexuellenverfolgung in Berlin 1933–1945. Berlin: Verlag Rosa Winkel, 2000.

Proust, Marcel. *Sodom und Gomorra*. Vol. 4: Marcel Proust. *Auf der Suche nach der verlorenen Zeit*. Frankfurt a.M.: Suhrkamp, 1999.

Pünders, Hermann. *Politik in der Reichskanzlei: Aufzeichnungen aus den Jahren 1929–1932*. Edited by Thilo Vogelsang. Stuttgart: Deutsche Verlags-Anstalt, 1961.

Rauschning, Hermann. *Gespräche mit Hitler*. Unchanged new Printing. Zurich: Europa Verlag, 1940.

Reck-Malleczewen, Friedrich Percyval. *Tagebuch eines Verzweifelten*. Stuttgart: Bürger Verlag, 1947.

Redlich, Frederik C. *Diagnosis of a Destruktive Prophet*. New York/Oxford: Oxford University Press, 1999.

Reichel, Hans-Günther. *Das Königliche Schauspielhaus unter Georg Graf von Hülsen-Häseler 1903 – 1918*. Mit Berücksichtigung der zeitgenössischen Tagespresse. Phil. Diss. Berlin (West) FU, 1962.

Reiter, Ekkehard. *Franz Guertner: politische Biographie eines deutschen Juristen 1881–1941*. Berlin: Duncker und Humlot, 1976.

Reuth, Ralf Georg. *Goebbels: eine Biographie*. Munich: Piper, 1990.

Richardi, Hans-Günther / Schumann, Klaus. *Geheimakte Gerlich/Bell: Röhms Pläne für ein Reich ohne Hitler*. Munich: Ludwig, 1993.

Riefenstahl, Leni. *Memoiren*. Munich: Knaus, 1987.

Rinke, Günter. *Sozialer Radikalismus und bündische Utopie. Der Fall Peter Martin Lampel*. Frankfurt a.M.: Lang, 2000.

Röhm, Ernst. *Die Geschichte eines Hochverräters*. 7. Aufl.. Munich: Eher, 1934.

Rohe, Karl. *Das Reichsbanner Schwarz Rot Gold: Beiträge zur Geschichte und Struktur der politischen Kapfverbände zur Zeit der Weimarer Republik*. Düsseldorf: Droste, 1966.

Rosenbaum, Ron. *Explaining Hitler. The Search for the Origins of his Evil*. New York: Random House, 1998.

Rosenberg, Alfred. *Das politische Tagebuch Alfred Rosenbergs. Aus den Jahren 1934/35 und 1939/40*. Nach der photographischen Wiedergabe der Handschriften aus den Nürnberger Akten. Edited by Hans-Günther Seraphim. Göttingen: Musterschmidt, 1956.

———. (ed.). *Dietrich Eckart: Ein Vermächtnis*. Munich: Eher, 1928.

Rossbach, Gerhard. *Mein Weg durch die Zeit: Erinnerungen und Bekenntnisse*. Weilburg (Lahn): Vereinigte Weilburger Buchdruckereien, 1950.

Rother, Rainer. *Leni Riefenstahl: die Verführung des Talents*. Berlin: Henschel, 2000.

Sabrow, Martin. *Der Rathenau-Mord. Rekonstruktion einer Verschwörung gegen die Republik von Weimar.* Munich: Oldenbourg, 1994.

Salomon, Ernst von. *Der Fragebogen.* Hamburg: Rowohlt, 1951.

Schaap, Klaus. *Oldenburgs Weg ins "Dritte Reich."* Oldenburg: Holzberg, 1983.

Schädlich, Karlheinz. *Die Mitford sisters.* Düsseldorf: Claasen, 1993.

Schaenzler, Nicole. *Klaus Mann: Eine Biographie.* Frankfurt a.M.: Campus-Verlag, 1999.

Schaub, Julius. *Der Führer in der Festung Landsberg.* In: *Adolf Hitler. Bilder aus dem Leben des Führers.* Edited by the Cigaretten-Bilderdienst. Altona/Bahrenfeld: Cigaretten-Bilderdienst, 1936.

Schaumburg-Lippe, Friedrich Christian zu. *. . . Verdammte Pflicht und Schuldigkeit...: Weg und Erlebnis 1914–1933.* Leoni am Starnberger See: Druffel-Verlag, 1966.

Schirach, Henriette von. *Frauen um Hitler.* Nach Materialien von Henriette von Schirach Munich: Herbig, 1983.

Schlie, Ulrich (ed.). *Albert Speer: "Alles, was ich weiß": aus unbekannten Geheimdienstprotokollen vom Sommer 1945.* Munich: Herbig, 1999.

Schmidt, Winfried (ed.). *". . . war gegen den Führer äußerst frech . . .": Der Chefredakteur und nachmalige Tierarzt Hansjörg Maurer. Würzburger politischen Tagebuchblätter aus den Jahren 1936 und 1937.* Karlstadt: Kralik, 1999.

Schoslack, Renate. *Hinter Wahnfrieds Mauern: Gertrud Wagner—ein Leben.* Hamburg: Hoffmann und Campe, 1998.

Schramm, Michael. *Der Gleichschaltungsprozeß der deutschen Armee 1933–1938: Kulminationspunkte und Linien.* Munich: Univ. Diss., 1990.

Schreck, Julius. *Der Führer auf Reisen.* In: *Adolf Hitler: Bilder aus dem Leben des Führers.* Edited by the Cigaretten-Bilderdienst [Choice and Artistic Editing of the Pictures by Heinrich Hoffmann]. Altona/Bahrenfeld: Cigaretten-Bilderdienst, 1936.

Schroeder, Christa. *Er war mein Chef: aus dem Nachlaß der Sekretärin von Adolf Hitler.* Edited by Anton Joachimsthaler, Munich: Langen Müller, 1985.

Schuler, Alfred. *Cosmogonische Augen: gesammelte Schriften.* Edited, commented and introduced by Baal Müller. Paderborn: Igel-Verlag, 1997.

Schulz, Alexander Paul (ed.). *Rettungen und Hilfeleistungen an Verfolgte 1933–1945 durch Oberleutnant a.D. Paul Schulz.* Laichingen: Published by the Author, 1967.

Schwarzmüller, Theo. *Zwischen Kaiser und "Führer": Generalfeldmarschall August von Mackensen.* Paderborn: Schöningh, 1995.

Schwarzwäller, Wulf. *Der Stellvertreter des Führers: Rudolf Heß: der Mann in Spandau.* Vienna/Munich/Zurich: Molden, 1974.

Schulz, Karola. *Fast ein Revolutionär: Fritz von Unruh zwischen Exil und Remigration (1932–1962).* Munich: Iudicium-Verlag, 1994.

Seehofer, Herbert. *Mit dem Führer unterwegs: kleine Stimmungsbilder einer großen Reise.* Munich : Eher, 1939.

Selig, Wolfram. "Ermordet im Namen des Führers: Die Opfer des Röhm-Putsches in München." In: Winfried Becker / Werner Chrobak (eds.). *Staat, Kultur, Politik: Festschrift zum 65. Geburtstag von Dieter Albrecht.* Beiträge zur Geschichte Bayerns und des Katholizismus. Kallmünz: Laßleben, 1992.

Sereny, Gitta. *Das Ringen mit der Wahrheit. Albert Speer und das deutsche Trauma.* Munich: Kindler, 1995.

Severing, Carl. *Mein Lebensweg,* vol. 2: *Im Auf und Ab der Republik.* Köln: Greven, 1950.

Sigmund, Anna Maria. *Die Frauen der Nazis.* Vienna: Ueberreuter, 1998.

Skinner, Jody. *Bezeichnungen für das Homosexuelle im Deutschen.* Essen: Verlag die Blaue Eule, 1999.

Slapnicka, Harry. *Hitler und Oberösterreich: Mythos, Propaganda und Wirklichkeit um den "Heimatgau des Führers."* Grünbach: Steinmaßl, 1998.

———. *Oberösterreich: die politische Führungsschicht 1918–1938.* Linz: Oberösterreichischer Landesverband, 1976.

Smith, Bradley F. *Adolf Hitler: His Family, Childhood and Youth.* Stanford, Calif.: Hoover Inst. on War, Revolution and Peace, 1967.

Sombart, Nicolaus. *Pariser Lehrjahre: 1951–1954.* Hamburg: Hoffmann und Campe, 1994.

Sommer, Kai. *Die Strafbarkeit der Homosexualität von der Kaiserzeit bis zum Nationalsozialismus: eine Analyse der Straftatbestände im Strafgesetzbuch und in den Reformentwürfen (1871–1945).* Frankfurt a.M./Berlin/Bern/New York/Paris/Vienna: Lang, 1998.

Sommerfeldt, Martin H. *Ich war dabei: die Verschwörung der Dämonen 1933–1939: ein Augenzeugenbericht.* Darmstadt: Drei Quellen-Verlag, 1949.

Speer, Albert. *"Alles, was ich weiß": aus unbekannten Geheimdienstprotokollen vom Sommer 1945.* Edited by Ulrich Schlie. Munich: Herbig, 1999.

———. *Erinnerungen.* Frankfurt a.M.: Ullstein, 1969.

Spitzy, Reinhard. *So haben wir das Reich verspielt: Bekenntnisse eines Illegalen.* Munich: Langen, 1986.

Spotts, Frederic. *Bayreuth. A History of the Wagner Festival.* New Haven/London: Yale University Press, 1994.

Stern-Rubarth, Edgar. *. . . Aus zuverlässiger Quelle verlautet . . .: ein Leben für Presse und Politik.* Stuttgart: Kohlhammer, 1964.

Sternweiler, Andreas (ed.). *Liebe, Forschung, Lehre: der Kunsthistoriker Christian Adolf Isermeyer.* Berlin: Verlag Rosa Winkel, 1998.

Stoiber, Rudolf/Celovsky, Boris. *Stephanie von Hohenlohe: sie liebt die Mächtigen der Welt*. Munich: Herbig, 1988.

Strasser, Otto. *Gangsters around Hitler* With a Topical Postscript: *"Nazi gangsters in South America."* London: Allen, 1942.

———. *Hitler und ich*. Konstanz: Asmus, 1948.

———. *Die deutsche Bartholomäusnacht*. Zurich: Reso-Verlag, 1935.

———. *Ich kann nicht schweigen*. Edited by Walther Korrodi, with an Expert Report by District Attorney Staatsanwalt Dr. E. Zürcher and a Preface by the Publisher. Zurich: Europa-Verlag, 1936.

Sward, Keith. *The Legend of Henry Ford*. New York: Russell & Russell, 1948. Unchanged New Edition New York: Russell & Russell, 1968.

Syberberg, Hans-Jürgen. *Syberbergs Filmbuch*. Munich: Nymphenburger Verlags-Buchhandlung, 1976.

Taylor, Telford. *The Anatomy of the Nuremburg Trials. A Personal Memoir*. New York: Knopf, 1992.

Thyssen, Fritz. *I paid Hitler*. London: Hodder Stoughton, 1941.

Toland, John. *Adolf Hitler*. New York: Doubleday, 1976.

Tresckow, Hans von. *Von Fürsten und anderen Sterblichen: Erinnerungen eines Kriminalkommissars*. Berlin: Fontane, 1922.

Tschirschky, Fritz Günther von. *Erinnerungen eines Hochverräters*. Stuttgart: Deutsche Verlags-Anstalt, 1972.

Tyrell, Albrecht (ed.). *Führer befiehl . . : Selbstzeugnisse aus der "Kampfzeit" der NSDAP. Dokumentation und Analyse*. Düsseldorf: Droste, 1969.

Ueberschär, Gerd R. /Vogel, Winfried. *Dienen und Verdienen. Hitlers Geschenke an seine Eliten*. Frankfurt a.M.: Fischer, 1999.

Unruh, Fritz von. *Der nie verlor*. Bern: Hallwag-Verlag, 1948.

Wächter, Katja-Maria. *Die Macht der Ohnmacht: Leben und Politik des Franz Xaver Ritter von Epp (1868–1946)*. Frankfurt a.M.: Lang, 1999.

Wagener, Otto. *Hitler aus nächster Nähe. Aufzeichnungen eines Vertrauten 1929–1932*. Edited by Henry A. Turner. Frankfurt a.M.: Ullstein, 1978.

Wagner, Friedelind. *Nacht über Bayreuth: die Geschichte der Enkelin Richard Wagners*. Berlin: Ullstein, 1999.

Wagner, Nike. *Wagner Theater*. 2nd ed. Frankfurt a.M.: Insel Verlag, 1998.

Weisenborn, Günther. *Memorial*. Berlin: Aufbau-Verlag, 1948.

Weiß, Hermann (ed.). *Biographisches Lexikon zum Dritten Reich*. Frankfurt a.M.: Fischer-Taschenbuch-Verlag, 1999.

Weiss, John. *Ideology of Death. Why the Holocaust happened in Germany*. Chicago: I.R. Dee, 1996.

Weißbuch über die Erschießungen des 30. Juni 1934: authentische Darstellung der deutschen Bartholomäusnacht. Paris: Ed. Du Carrefour, 1934.

Weyrauch, Wolfgang (ed.). *Ausnahmezustand: eine Anthologie aus "Weltbühne" und "Tagebuch"*. Munich: Desch, 1966.

Wiedemann, Friedrich. *Der Mann, der Feldherr werden wollte: Erlebnisse und Erfahrungen des Vorgesetzten Hitlers im I. Weltkrieg und seines späteren Persönlichen Adjutanten*. Velbert: Blick und Bild Verlag für Politische Bildung, 1964.

Wilhelm, Hermann. *Dichter, Denker, Fememörder: Rechtsradikalismus und Antisemitismus in München von der Jahrhundertwende bis 1921*. Berlin: Transit, 1989.

———. *Die Münchener Bohème: von der Jahrhundertwende bis zum Ersten Weltkrieg*. Munich: Buchendorfer, 1993.

Wyneken, Gustav. *Eros*. Lauenburg: Saal, 1921.

Zehnpfennig, Barbara. *Hitlers Mein Kampf: eine Interpretation*. Munich: Fink, 2000.

Ziegler, Hans Severus. *Adolf Hitler: aus dem Erleben dargestellt*. Göttingen: Schütz, 1964.

———. *Der Führer im alten "Elephanter": Erinnerungen*. In: Fritz Sauckel (ed.). *Der Führer in Weimar 1925–1938*. Weimar: NSDAP, Gauleitung Thüringen, 1938.

Zinn, Alexander. *Die soziale Konstruktion des homosexuellen Nationalsozialisten: zu Genese und Etablierung eines Stereotyps*. Frankfurt a.M.: Lang, 1997.

Zweig, Stefan. *Die Welt von gestern: Erinnerungen eines Europäers*. Frankfurt a.M.: Suhrkamp, 1947.

Index

Abwehr opposition group, 66, 210
Academy of Fine Arts, 28
Adolf Hitler im Felde 1914–1918
    (Mend), 35, 82
    as counterpropaganda, 74–77
    destroyed, 84
Adolf Hitler. Mein Jugendfreund
    (Kubizek), 35
Amann, Max, 77, 163
    in entourage, 176
    impression of Lüdecke, 268
    and Rosenberg, 285
    and Schmidt, 97
    as wartime comrade, 90, 91
Antisemitism, 62–63
    Eulenburg scandal, 49
    of Hanfstaengl, 289
    of Henry Ford/Lüdecke, 267, 268
    international congress, 272
    radicalized under Eckart, 121
    sexually based, 50–51
    in Vienna, 50
Arnold, Ida, 159
Artists in Munich, 60–62

Assault Squad, 152
Auf gut deutsch (Eckart), 119
Aust, Hans Walter, 225
Austrian army, 52, 67
Austrian National Socialist party, 52

Bachelor, Hitler as, 162
Bartsch, Rudolf Hans, 35, 36
Bavarian army. *See also* Military
    service.
    attempts to join, 62
    homosexuality in, 68
    Schmidt joins, 89
Bayreuth, Germany
    as homosexual rendezvous, 39
    Hitler's visits to, 254
    visited by Eckart and Hitler, 121
    visited by Kubizek and Hitler, 34
    visited by Röhm and Hitler, 110
Bechstein, Lotte, 156
Bell, Georg, 208
    with inside information about
        Hitler, 210

Berlin Telegraph, 256
Binion, Rudolph, 10
Biography, 9, 15
    as historiography, 6
Bisexuality
    of Helmut Brückner, 227
    of Emil Maurice, 154, 155
Blackmail, 73, 295–296
    against Kubizek, 33
    attempts by SA against Hitler, 212
    fear as motive for Röhm putsch,
        220–221
    by Hanfstaengl, 300–301,
        304–308, 309
    by Lüdecke, 267, 283, 298–299.
        See also Lüdecke blackmail case.
    by Maurice, 159–161
    by Mend, 79
    threats by Maria Schreck, 174–175
Bloodbath of 1934. *See* Röhm putsch.
Bluebeard, 262
Blüher, Hans, 108, 238, 316, 320
    analysis of Röhm putsch, 242–243
    and Ebermayer, 237
    and homoeroticism, 110
    and youth movement, 150
Bodenschatz, Karl, 303, 304, 309
Bomhard, Guido Karl, 119
Book burning, 244
Bormann, Martin, 21
    and Hanfstaengl's blackmail, 309
Bouhler, Philipp, 21, 296
    and Ebermayer, 239, 244, 255
Bourgeoisie (German), 7
Boyfriend, 306, 308
Brandenburg concentration camp, 285
Brandmayer, Balthasar, 90, 91
Braun, Eva, 169–170, 250
    asexual relationship with Hitler,
        170
    marriage *in extremis*, 316
    role in Hitler's life, 169, 314, 316

suicide and suicide attempts, 21,
    170, 315
Braun, Otto, 199
Bredow, Ferdinand von, Röhm putsch
    victim, 217, 218
Brownshirts, 96, 163
Brückner, Helmut, 222, 226
    trial against, 227–228
Brückner, Wilhelm, 22, 222
Buch, Walter, 159–160
    and Klotz, 192
    and Röhm affair, 206
Bullock, Alan, 4, 7, 9
    demythologization of Hitler, 5
    interpretation of Hitler's ideology, 6

Café Heck, 78, 161, 250
Camouflage, 20
    Eva Braun as, 170
    Geli Raubal as, 161–162
    marriage as, 24, 98, 128, 149
    need for, 317
    sexual, 166, 167
Car journeys, 155, 232
    with Schreck, 172, 173
Castration, 195
Character assassination, 201, 205,
    283–284
Charisma politics, 13, 14–15
Charles Scribner's Sons, 297
Chauffeurs, 142, 151, 152, 171
    role of, 153
Chauffeureska. *See* Entourage.
Childhood of Hitler, 27
Claß, Heinrich, 122–123
Combat, exemption from, 88
Combat League, 108–109, 114
Combat veteran myth, 74
Communists, 70–71, 196
Con man, 102
    Lüdecke as, 267, 268, 272

Conspiracy theory, 50
Corriere della Sera, 319
Counterfeiter, political, 12
Coup d'état, 105, 146. See also
    Munich putsch.
Critical analysis, 321
Cult figure, 146
Cultural scene, 122
Cumulative radicalization, 11, 12

Dachau concentration camp, 220
Daily Express, 291, 292
DAP, 105, 106. See also NSDAP.
Das Buch der Freunde, 255
Das Parlament, 257
Das Tagebuch, 258
Death in Venice (Thomas Mann), 236
Defamation suit by Rosenberg against
    Hanfstaengl, 274
Demythologization, 5
Denazification, 35, 98, 164
Der Angriff, 187
Der Gerade Weg, 78
Der Hass (Heinrich Mann), 262
Der nie verlor (Unruh), 320
Der Reichswart, 268
Der Stern, 155
Der Vampyr (Ewers), 127
Deutsche Artbeiter Partei. See DAP.
Deutscher Kampfbund. See Combat
    League.
Deutscher Rundschau, 123
Deutsche Volksblatt, 49
Deutsche Volks-Zeitung, 222
Dictatorship consolidated by Röhm
    putsch, 230
Die Alraune (Ewers), 127
Die Deutsche Revolution, Hitler's
    homosexuality, 222
Diels, Rudolf, 22, 197, 282
    as collaborator with NSDAP, 197

on death list, 220
and I Knew Hitler, 266
and Röhm, 194, 195, 196, 213
Die Meistersinger (Wagner), 110
Die Rolle der Erotik in der
    männlichen Gesellschaft
    (Blüher), 150
Dietrich, Otto, 82
Die Welt, 15, 256
Die Zukunft, 47
Discrimination against homosexuals,
    103
Dissimulation of Hitler, 103, 139, 317
Dissociation, 17
Documents
    confiscated during Röhm putsch,
        220–221
    destruction of, 179, 231, 317
    military, 235–236
    about Nazi elite, 303
Dollfuss, Engelbert, 56
Dollmann, Eugen, 20, 23, 169
    conversations with Eva Braun, 315
    on Hitler's homosexuality, 134, 320
    and homosexuality in SA, 186
    life of, 133–138
    memoirs published in Italy, 137,
        319–320
    reports of secret files, 133
Dollmann, Paula, 133
Döring, Herbert, 170
Double standards, Hitler's policy of,
    243, 252, 253
Dr. Angelo (Ebermayer), 236, 245
Drexler, Anton, 71

Ebermayer, Erich, 22
    adapting to post–Röhm conditions,
        246
    campaign against Paragraph 175,
        237

diary, 231–233, 256–257, 321
informants of, 255
information sources of, 255, 256
and Klaus Mann, 239
life of, 233–234, 236–237
literary work attacked by SS, 245
portrayal of Hitler's homosexual-
    ity, 257
and Winifred Wagner, 255
and Wyneken, 237
Eckart, Dietrich, 114–125
    career of, 115–117
    fugitive from justice, 124
    and Hess, 144
    and Lüdecke, 268
    as mentor/role model, 117,
        120–121
    as misogynist, 118
    relationship with Hitler, 116,
        119–124, 125, 139
Eckart, Du Moulin, 188, 220
Eckart, Rose, 119
Eher-Verlag publishing house, 285
Ein Schubertroman (Bartsch), 35–36
Elections, 182, 190–191, 199, 202
Elite, traditional German, 182, 230
Embezzlement, 29, 33
Employer-employee relationships, 142
Enterbt (Ewers), 127
Entourage
    and concealment of private life, 22
    described, 175
    loyalty of, 179
    male environment of, 24
    members of, 176, 281
Epochal nostalgia, 9
Epp, Ritter von, 106, 107
Ernst, Karl
    attacked by Schulz and Goebbels,
        188
    hiding important evidence, 213
    on Hitler's homosexuality, 208

as Röhm putsch victim, 217
in SA, 185, 207
Eros (Wyneken), 150
Esser, Hermann, 176, 274
Eulenburg scandal, 47, 48, 49
Evening Star, 287
Ewers, Hanns Heinz
    relationship with Hanfstaengl,
        126–128, 277–278
Ewers, Josephine, 126–127
Exhibitionism, 124
Extortion, 266

Fascism, identified with homosexual-
    ity, 259
Fest, Joachim, 6–9
    speculations about Winifred Wag-
        ner, 254
    on Speer and Hitler, 313–314
Film, Nazi propaganda, 288
Finances in Vienna and Munich, 55,
    60–62
Fischer, Paula von. See Dollmann,
    Paula.
Ford, Henry
    antisemitic campaign of, 267, 268
    and Lüdecke, 267, 269, 272
Foreign policy for NSDAP, 280
Foreign press office, 280, 283, 299
Frank, Hans, 21, 112
    and Hanfstaengl/Lüdecke case,
        294
    after Röhm putsch, 229
Frankfurter Allgemeine Zeitung, 257
Frankfurter Rundschau, 15
Frankfurter Zeitung, 115, 116, 159
Fraternity, 238. See also Male commu-
    nity; Entourage.
Freikorps Epp, 94
    Hitler's participation in, 71, 71,
        94, 106

homosexuality in, 138
and Schreck, 171
Frey, Hertha, 300–301, 302
Friendship
cultural role of, 108
with Hitler, 23, 99, 313
Fromm, Erich, 10
Functionalism, 11–12

Gehrlich, Fritz, 21
Genet, Jean, 320
Geneva, Switzerland, 286, 289
George, Stefan, 60
Gerade Weg, 163
Gerlich, Fritz, 78, 163, 217
German constitution, 66
German National Theater, 249
Geschichte eines Hochverräters
(Röhm), 181, 183, 192
Gesellschaft, Kaiser Wilhem, 134
Gestapo
arrests Mend, 83
confiscates Hanfstaengl's belong-
ings, 304
Diels as head of, 196
and Helmut Brückner's confession,
226
and Lüdecke, 287, 294
and Röhm putsch, 213, 221
Ghost Rider. See Hans Mend.
Gigolo, Lüdecke, 267
Glaser, Alexander, 217
Goebbels, Joseph, 12, 142, 168, 191
destruction of Röhm, 186, 188,
214, 215
problems with Hanfstaengl, 303,
304, 305
homophobic, 184
intervenes for Ebermayer,
245–246
and Lüdecke, 301–302

on Raubal/Maurice/Hitler triangle,
160
speeches, 215, 232
Goebbels, Magda (Quandt), 166
familiarity with Lüdecke, 279, 297,
301–302
relationship with Goebbels and
Hitler, 165–166, 168
Göring, Hermann
arrested Lüdecke, 283
elimination of communists, 196
problems with Hanfstaengl, 303,
304, 306–307, 309
and Röhm putsch, 214, 215
suicide of, 21
Gossip, 168, 224
Graf, Ulrich, 176
Grimm, Hans, 175
Groscurth, Helmuth, 66
Gründgens, Gustaf, 241
Grzesinski, Albert, 199
Gürtner, Franz, 234
Gutmann, Sigmund, 92

Haarmann, Fritz, 261
Hamann, Brigitte, 57, 58
Hanfstaengl art gallery in New York,
126
Hanfstaengl, Egon, 128, 130
Hanfstaengl, Ernst, 19–20, 22, 56,
113, 125–133, 178, 299, 304
blackmail against Hitler, 300–301,
302–303, 304, 309–310
demands apology from Hitler, 305,
307
deported to Canada by British, 311
and Eckart, 124
in entourage, 281
efforts to destroy Lüdecke, 266,
282, 283, 287, 293, 294, 295,
304, 305

efforts to eliminate Rosenberg,
274, 282, 288
on Ernst, 208
escape to Switzerland, 303
on Geli Raubal, 161–162
impressions of Hitler's sexual identity, 277–278, 306
investigates Hitler's past, 274
jealousy of Hess, 275–276
libel actions, 291–292, 306–307
military service, 126
rapprochement, 280–281
relationship with Ewers, 126–128
relationship with Hitler, 129–133,
276, 306
in U.S., 126, 289–290
Hanfstaengl, Helene, 128, 130, 303
Hanisch, Reinhold, 47, 55
at Brigittenau hostel, 29
friendship with Hitler, 51–54
Hanitante. See Pölzl, Johanna.
Harden, Maximilian, 49, 50
and Eulenburg scandal, 47
Harpprecht, Klaus, 259
Harvard University, 126, 289–290
Haushofer, Karl, 144–145
Häusler, Rudolf, 29, 56–57, 95
with Hitler in Munich, 58, 59
Hearst, William Randolph, 291
Heiden, Konrad, 52
Heimsoth, Karl-Günther
in Freikorps, 108
relationship with/letters from
Röhm, 191–196, 198
Röhm putsch victim, 217
Heines, Edmund
and Hitler, 138, 212
Röhm putsch victim, 217
as Röhm's sweetheart, 111
in SA, 185
Helldorf, Wolf Heinrich von, 21, 185
Henchmen, 177–178
Hentig, Werner Otto von, 65

Hepp, Ernst, 62
Hepp, Martha, 62
Herbst, Ludolf, 14
Hess, Rudolf, 32, 144, 146
active in NSDAP, 145
advised to marry, 148–149
as close associate, 142
homosexuality disclosed by
Strasser, 222
on Geli Raubal, 157
in Landsberg, 146, 232
as mentor/advisor, 146, 148
relationship with Haushofer,
144–145
relationship with Hitler, 142, 145,
232, 275
rewarded for services, 151
after Röhm putsch, 229
on Schreck, 171
Hess, Ilse, 143, 144, 146, 150, 151
complaints about marriage, 149
and Geli Raubal, 158
on Hess and Hitler, 145
Hessen, Philipp von, 22, 184
Heterosexualizing, 43
Hewel, Walter, 21
Heydrich, Reinhard, 304
blacklists, 229
and elimination of Röhm, 213,
214
galvanized by Hanfstaengl's blackmail, 309
Hildebrand, Klaus, 14
Hillebrand, Wilhem, 189
Himmler, Heinrich, 171, 309
and Brückner trial, 228
destruction of Röhm, 214
and Ebermayer, 245, 246
homosexual registry and persecution, 226, 337
and Lüdecke blackmail case, 272,
287
and Maurice, 163

spying on Röhm, 213
suicide, 21
Hindenburg, Paul von, 3
    presidential election, 190–191, 203
    and Röhm letters, 204
Hirschfeld, Hans, 194
Hirschfeld, Magnus, 39, 42, 49, 54,
    87, 109
    Eckart's campaign against, 118
    on homosexual activities in hostels,
        51
    transcripts of young men, 138
Historicocritical analysis, 17
Hitler, Klara, 27, 28, 42
Hitler, Paula, 27
Hitler and Stalin (Bullock), 5, 9
Hitler documents, 179. *See also* Docu-
    ments.
    confiscated by Gestapo, 83–84
    of Hentig, 65
    of Kubizek, 31, 32
Hitler rast (Bredow), 210
Hitler Song Book (Hanfstaengl),
    131–132
Hitler: A Study in Tyranny (Bullock), 4
Hoffmann, Heinrich, 22, 154, 190
    in entourage, 176
    on Geli Raubal and Hitler, 162
Hoffmann, Henriette, 154
Hofweber, Max, 144
Homelessness, 47, 93
Homoeroticism, 21, 23–24
    as force for National Socialist
        movement, 232
    of Hess and Hitler, 150
    orientation of SA, 186
    political tribute to, 109–110
    of Speer and Hitler, 313
Homophobia, 228, 245
Homosexual community/subculture,
    betrayed by Hitler, 239
    systematic persecution of, 226
    in Vienna, 48

Homosexual emancipation movement,
    48, 236
Homosexuality, 19, 23, 39, 60, 228,
    242
    advances to young men by Hitler,
        136–137, 138
    in army, 68, 91
    blacklists, 229
    decriminalizing, 234
    denial/concealment/secrecy, 19–20,
        21, 42, 44, 50, 87
    and fascism/politics, 17–25, 186,
        259
    of Hitler, 86, 87, 189, 199, 201,
        212, 222, 232, 257, 278,
        297–299, 306, 319–321
    laws against, 337
    and Malicious Practices Act, 224
    at men's hostels, 29, 51, 54–56
    and Prince Philipp Eulenburg, 47
    as privilege for Hitler and chosen
        associates, 230
    racially charged, 109
    reports of investigations, 229
    of Röhm, 102, 208, 298
    in SA, 185, 204
    simultaneously proscribed and pro-
        tected, 244
    stigma of, 19, 321
    tolerated, 91, 242
Homosocial orientation, 102
Honisch, Karl, 55
Hostels for homeless men. *See* Men's
    hostels.
Hülsen-Haeseler, Georg von, 116, 119
Humiliation, 103
Hush money, 161, 287, 297
Hypocrisy, 70, 222, 256

I Knew Hitler (Lüdecke), 266,
    297–299, 305
Idealism, of Hess, 151

Illustrierter Beobachter, 97
Inexplicability of Hitler, 3, 16
Informer, Hitler as, 94
Inkofer, Josef, 90
Institute of Contemporary History, 65
Intellectuals, distrust of, 4
Intentionalism, 11
International Jewry conspiracy theory, 50
Interpretations of Hitler and his origins, 10
Intimidation, 182, 208
Iron Cross, 68, 69, 71, 92, 236
Iron Fist right-wing conspirators, 106
Irving, David, 10
Isermayer, Christian, 185–186

Jealousy, 37–38, 54, 170, 275–276
Jetzinger, Franz. 35, 36, 42, 46
Jewish press, 307
Jews. *See also* Antisemitism.
    Ford's smear campaign against, 267, 268
    sexually based hatred against, 50
Joël, Curt, 234
Jungdeutscher Orden, 218, 219
Jürgen Ried, (Ebermayer), 245

Kahr, Gustaf Ritter von, Röhm putsch victim, 137, 217
Kallenbach, Hans, 147, 154
Kaufmann, Karl, 222, 229
Kempka, Erich, chauffeur, 151
Kershaw, Ian, 2, 9, 13–15
Kessel, Eugen von, 217
Louis II of Bavaria (King Ludwig), 67
Kisch, Egon Erwin, 75, 91
Klausener, Erich, 217
Klein, Ada, 155
Klotz, Helmuth

campaign against Röhm, 192, 203, 204
    publication of Röhm letters, 193, 194–195
Knudsen, Helge, 65
König, Eva, 86, 87
Koppler, Marianne, 57, 58
Korrodi, Walter, 212
Kriebel, Hermann, 146
Kriminalzeitungen, 48
Kubizek, August, 22, 55, 99
    contact with Hitler, 28, 32, 34
    conversation with Hess, 32
    denial of homosexuality, 42–44
    early life, 31
    and Hitler documents, 31, 32, 34
    memoirs, 30, 35, 36–37
    military service, 46
    relationship with Hitler, 36–37, 39–41, 46–47
Külz, Wilhem, 232
    and Erich Ebermayer, 235
    viewing Hitler's military records, 235–236

Lammers, Hans, 100, 299
Lampel, Peter Martin, 138
Lance corporal, unpromoted, 69, 91–92
Landsberg prison, 142, 146, 152
    amenities to detainees, 147
    changes in Hitler during detainment, 141, 274–275
Lauboeck, Fritz, 73
Laux, Karl, 86
Left-wing groups, rejected from, 70, 71
Leidenroth, Karl, 53
Leonding, family home in, 27
Levetzow, Magnus von, 210

Libel action
  by Hanfstaengl against Beaver-
    brook/*Daily Express*, 292
  by Hanfstaengl against *The New
    Republic*, 306, 307, 310
  by Lüdecke against Hanfstaengl,
    284
  by Lüdecke against *New Yorker
    Staatszeitung*, 298
Libertinism, 126
Linge, Heinz, 22
Linz, Austria, 27, 38, 42
Lippert, Karl, 68, 90
List Regiment, Bavarian army, 67, 89,
    91
London, England, 304
Loneliness, 8
Loquacity, 4
Lossow, Otto von, 20, 137
  and Dollmann, 134
  and incriminating police file,
    135–137
  and Röhm, 106
  secret papers/documents, 133, 138
Loyalty
  to Röhm, 201
  of Speer to Hitler, 314
  purchased from Schaub, 178
Lüdecke blackmail case, 286,
    298–299
  changed to Hanfstaengl blackmail
    case, 289, 293–294
  Hitler's responses, 296–297
Lüdecke, Kurt, 22, 168, 266–268,
    286, 294. *See also* Lüdecke
    blackmail case.
  arrested, 283, 285
  blackmailer in Europe and U.S.,
    267, 282
  criminal record broadcast, 291, 296
  familiarity with Magda Goebbels,
    279

flight to Geneva, 286, 289
  and foreign policy/press in U.S.,
    280, 283
  and Hanfstaengl, 128, 288, 293,
    295
  I Knew Hitler, 266, 297–299, 305
  on Quandt/Goebbels/Hitler trian-
    gle, 166
  relationship with Hitler, 265,
    270–271, 273, 284
  and Röhm, 112, 200
  on Rudolf Hess, 143
  as spy for Hitler, 268, 273
  treason case, 269–270
Luetgebrune, Walter, 205, 217, 219
Lukacs, John, 2
Lying, 102

Machiavellia, 4
Male community, 91, 108
  of military service, 90
Male eros, 238
Male prostitution, 48, 51, 54–56,
    111, 294
Malicious Practices Act, 223–225
Manliness reconciled with homosexu-
    ality, 113
Mann, Heinrich, 244, 262
Mann, Klaus, 19, 239
  in exile, 240, 245
  and Hitler, 258, 259, 260
  and ineffectiveness of Röhm letters,
    202
Mann, Thomas, 19, 236, 259, 263
Marginalization, 15
Marriage
  as camouflage, 24, 98, 128, 149
  in extremis to Eva Braun, 316
Martial stylization of homosexuality,
    109
Marx, Rose. *See* Eckart, Rose.

Maser, Werner, 10, 65, 93
Maurice, Emil, 22, 142, 153, 164
    as bisexual, 154, 155
    blackmail threats, 159–161
    as chauffeur, 152, 155
    with Jewish forebear, 164
    and Geli Raubal, 157–158
    as henchman/SS officer, 163, 164
    hush money paid to, 161
    in Landsberg, 146–147, 153
    marriage, 164
    reentered service after Geli's death,
        163
Maurice, Hedwig, 164
Mayr, Karl, 146
    employed Hitler as informer,
        94–95
    and Hess, 144
    ordered killed, 21
    secret negotiations with Röhm,
        209
Media manipulation during Röhm
    case, 202
Megalomania, 123, 124, 317
Mein Kampf (Hitler), 5, 49, 74, 141,
        183, 191
    description of Munich, 59
    Hess's role in ideology, 147–148
    and Maurice, 152
Memoirs
    Dollmann, 137
    Hanisch, 53–54
    Kubizek, 30
    Lampel, 138
    Lüdecke, 270, 299
    Mend, 74–75
    Speer, 22
Mend, Hans, 66. See also Mend Pro-
    tocol.
    arrested by Gestapo, 83
    blackmail by, 79
    denunciation by, 78–79, 85

imprisonment and death, 21, 80,
        84–85, 86
    interrogated by Schmid Noerr, 66,
        67–71
    ostracized, 81–82
    persecuted by Nazi legal system, 86
    as propagandist, 75
    receipt of money, 73
    Schmidt and Hitler information,
        98–99
    WWI accounts, 66–67, 72, 74–75,
        82
Mend Protocol
    credibility of, 296
    and Lüdecke hush money, 287
    role in German resistance move-
        ment, 65–66
Men's hostels, 58
    in Briggittenau district, 29
    as hubs of homosexual activity, 51
    in Meidling, 29
    in Munich, 69
    in Vienna, 51, 56
    prostitution in, 54–56
Meyer, Dr., 188, 189, 192
Military service, 29, 87, 90
    effort to evade, 59
    homosexuality in, 68, 91
    records, 235–236
    rejected from Austrian, 29
    unpromoted, 91–92
Miller, Alice, 10
Misogyny, 118
Mistress role, 170, 315
Mistrust, 102–103
Mitteldeutsches Jahrbuch, 257
Modernization, 8
Mommsen, Hans, 12
Moral integrity, 44
Morality, 112
Mother. See Hitler, Klara.
Movement, the. See NSDAP.

Movies, 177, 288
Mühsam, Erich, 59–60
Münchener Post, 74, 129, 187, 189, 191
Münchener Zeitung, 270
Münchner Illustrierte, 31
Mund, Max, 90
Munich, Germany, 60–62, 69, 70
    Häusler and Hitler in, 29, 58–63
    Hitler as young man in, 59–63
    homosexuality, 138
Munich clique, 175–179
Munich putsch, 142, 146, 152, 163, 172, 192
Mussolini, Benito, 56, 269, 288
Myth
    created by Hess, 147
    threatened, 223
    unsuitability of, 229
Mythos des 20. Jahrhunderts, 183

Narcissism, 277, 278
Nationalism, 104
    homoerotic aspects of, 95
National Socialism, 9, 11, 86, 132
National Socialist German Workers' Party. *See* NSDAP.
National Socialist party. *See* NSDAP.
Nationalsozialistische Deutsche Arbeiterpartei. See NSDAP.
Nazi leadership, 204
    behavioral strategy, 200
    homosexuals remaining after Röhm putsch, 229
    reactions to Hanfstaengl's blackmail, 304, 305, 308
    and Röhm, 204, 205
Nazi Party. *See* NSDAP.
Nero Order, 314
Neue Revue, 57
Neumann, Josef, 29, 53

Newburger, Franz, 31–34
New Republic, The, 52–53, 306, 307
Newspapers (Viennese), 48, 49
Niemandes Knecht, 138
Niemeyer, Helene. *See* Hanfstaengl, Helene.
Night of the long knives. *See* Röhm putsch.
NSDAP
    anti-Röhm front, 181, 187
    assumption of power, 202
    change of image, 141
    Dollmann's membership in, 134
    Eckart's leadership, 120
    as fraternity, 232
    Häusler as member, 57
    Hitler's first political speech, 106
    and Lüdecke, 270, 279, 280
    and Mend, 74
    media machine, 75
    Schmidt as head of, 98
    and Ziegler, Ebermayer, Baedeker, 241
Nuremberg Trials, 4

Oberbuchner, Philipp, 98
Obermüller, Elisabeth. *See* Schmidt, Elisabeth, 98
Oesterreichische Kriminal-Zeitung, 47
Olden, Rudolf, 52
Oncken, Herman, 134
Operatic music, 93–94
Oranienburg concentration camp, 286
Orphan's pension, 28, 29

Pacelli, Eugenio, 133
Paintings, 52, 55, 60–62, 82
Paragraph 175, 185, 187, 222, 237
    Hanfstaengl and Hitler, 308
    and Röhm, 192, 198

reform discussed, 234
strengthening, 226
time to abolish, 238
Paramilitary organizations, 71, 94, 106
Pariser Kabarett, 50
Party, the. *See* NSDAP.
Paulus, Herbert, 86
Pechel, Rudolf, 123
Persecution mania, 316–317
Personality cult, 12
Philosophy, personal, 53
Photographs, 83
Physical appearance, 173, 260–261
Physical contact, 315
Pictures, 52, 55, 61, 93
Platonic cohabitation with Eva Braun, 169, 315
Playacting, 7, 102
Plewnia, Margarete, 121
Police records on Julius Schaub, 178
Political agitation, 123, 146
Political career, 24–25
Political speeches, 68, 69, 106
Political strategy, 141, 230
Politics, 18, 46, 101, 321
Polycratic system, 11
Pölzl, Johanna, 27, 28, 46
Pompes funèbres (Genet), 320
Pope Pius XII, 133
Popp, Anna, 30, 57, 60
Power, mystique of, 13
Press, 222, 223
Private life, 8
concealment of, 22, 317
divergence of Hess and Hitler, 151
efforts to destroy all evidence of, 20–21
of Hitler in Ebermayer's diary, 321
importance of, 110
incriminated by Lossow, 135–137
linked to political life, 18

scrutinized during election campaign, 191
Professor Unrat (Heinrich Mann), 244
Pröhl, Ilse. *See* Hess, Ilse.
Propaganda, 92, 97
and Iron Cross award, 92
Nazi film, 288
during Röhm case, 202
in U.S., 292
völkisch, 131
of wartime memoirs, 75–76
Property owners, 71
Prostitution, 48, 51, 54–56
Protégé, 120
Prussian ministry of interior, 194, 195, 198
Pseudobohemian, 27, 116
Psychoanalytical approach, 10–11
Publications/books on Hitler, 3, 6, 9, 15
Purge of 1934. *See* Röhm putsch.
Putsch of November 1923. *See* Munich putsch.

Quandt, Magda. *See* Goebbels, Magda.

Raubal, Angela. *See* Raubal, Geli.
Raubal, Geli, 8
as camouflage, 161–162
death, 21, 162–163, 166, 167
dispute over Maurice, 158
in love with Maurice, 157–158
relationship with Hitler, 156–162
Rauschning, Hermann, 100
Red Terror, 8
Regimental runners, Bavarian army, 67, 68
closeness of, 89–90

Registry of homosexuals, 337
Reichswehr, 211, 213
Reiebel, Karl, 65–66
Reiter, Maria, 155–156, 159
Resistance movement (German),
    65–66
Reventlow, Ernst von, 268
Rhetoric as means to success, 101
Riefenstahl, Leni, memoirs, 166, 167
Right-wing extremists, 71, 72, 73,
    268
Röhm, Ernst, 21, 44, 106, 139, 181,
    188, 206, 213
    appointed because of his proclivity,
        200
    assigned SA positions to homosex-
        uals, 185
    as bait to promote Hitler, 202–203
    campaign against. See Röhm
        putsch.
    conflict with Hitler, 209, 210–213
    employed Hitler as informer, 94
    homoeroticism and National
        Socialism, 109, 110
    homosexual clique centered on,
        208
    homosexuality of, 95, 102, 111,
        184, 187, 189, 298
    letters. See Röhm letters.
    and Lüdecke, 272, 284, 287
    massacre. See Röhm putsch.
    and Maurice's reward, 163
    NSDAP plans to murder, 201
    as patron of Hitler, 105–114
    re-acceptance/rehabilitation,
        204–205, 206–207, 233
    reasons for success, 112, 113
    relationship with Epp, 107
    relationship with Ernst, 207
    relationship with Hitler, 102, 113,
        114, 208
    as SA commander, 114, 181, 183

Röhm letters, 191–196
    Diels and Klotz, 198–199
    and election campaign, 202
Röhm murders. See Röhm putsch.
Röhm putsch, 212, 215–221, 292
    according to Ebermayer, 231
    political policy, 230
    procedure, 218
    repercussions on Nazi attitudes,
        242–243
    victims, 217
Röhrbein, Paul, 188
    with inside information about
        Hitler, 210
    as Röhm putsch victim, 217
    in SA, 185
Roma Nazista (Dollmann), 319
Rosenbaum, Ron, 3, 6
Rosenberg, Alfred, 118, 275
    Hanfstaengl's efforts to destroy,
        132, 274, 288
    Jewish mistress of, 282, 283
    and Lüdecke, 272, 301
    and Röhm, 193
Rossbach, Gerhard, 107
Rote Fahne, 187
Rual Rhede concentration camp, 85

SA, 196, 204
    disputes with NSDAP, 182–183
    as electoral strong-arm, 182
    homosexuals in top ranks, 185
    intelligence service, 208, 214
    leadership massacre, 215, 216–221
    mistrust of Hitler, 212
    Röhm as head, 114, 181, 213, 214
Sack, Alfons, 217, 219, 284
Saint-Exupéry, Antoine de, 239
Salomon, Franz Pfeffer von, 200
Scandal, 159
Schacht, Hjalmaar, 208, 295

Schätzl, Martin, 110, 218
Schaub, Julius, 22, 224–225, 300
   burning of secret documents, 179
   and Eva Braun, 169
   important role of, 176–177
   marriage, 178
   police records, 178
Schirach, Baldur von, 22, 82, 222
   remaining in Nazi leadership after
     Röhm putsch, 229
Schirach, Carl B. N. von, 249
Schirach, Henriette von, 153, 162
Schirmer, Fritz, 193
Schirmer, Hans, 61
Schleicher, Kurt von, 210, 217, 219
Schmid Noerr, Friedrich Alfred, 66,
   72, 85
Schmidt, Elisabeth, 98
Schmidt, Ernst, 22, 76–77, 90, 91, 96,
   99
   with Hitler in Munich, 71, 93
   intimacy with Hitler, 67, 68, 69,
     88, 89, 92
   joins SA, 96
   life of, 89–100
   mayor of Garching, 98
   regimental runner, 76
   visits to Reich Chancellery, 97
Schneidhuber, August, 21, 217
Schopenhauer, Arthur, 125, 149
Schreck, Julius, 82, 173
   chauffeur, 142, 171, 172
   death, 171
   with Hitler, 173, 254
   marriage, 173–174
Schreck, Maria, 174
Schröder, Christa, 23, 155
   on Eva Braun, 170
   on Schaub, 177
Schubert, Franz, 36
Schuler, Alfred, 62–63
Schulz, Paul, 187, 188, 189

Schutzstaffel. *See* SS.
Schwabing, Germany, 59–60, 63
Schwammerl, 35, 36
Schwarz, Franz Xaver, 299–300
Schwind, Moritz von, 36
Secret files, 133–139
Secret police. *See* SS.
Seeds, William, 123
Self-delusion, 6
Sentimentality, 149, 271
Severing, Carl, 195, 210
Sexual abstinence, 43
Sexual camouflage, 166, 167
Sexual denunciation, 47, 79, 199
Sexual frustration, 8
Sexual orientation, 23, 276–278, 321
Sexuality, 5, 18
Siedler, Fritz von, 277
Siegfried (Wagner), 110
Sister. *See* Hitler, Paula.
Slander, 86
Social Democratic Party of Germany.
   See SPD.
Soliloquist, 37
Solitary confinement, 80–81
Source material, 231
SPD, 192
Speer, Albert, 22, 24
   political pay-off, 314
   relationship with Hitler, 312–313
   on Schreck, 172
Spiritual dichotomy, 144
Spying, 213, 268, 273
SS, 172, 214, 245
Stadelheim Prison, 111
Stennes, Walter, 186, 209
Sterneckerbräu, 96
Stigmatization of homosexuality, 19
Storm troopers. *See* SA.
Stosstrupp Hitler. *See* Assault Squad.
Strasser, Otto, 161, 198, 219
   accused Hess, 143

and Hitler's homosexuality, 222
  Röhm putsch victim, 217
Streicher, Julius, 21
Sturmabteilung. See SA.
Süddeutscher Rundfunk, 257
Suits (legal), 274, 284, 291–292, 298,
  306–307, 310. *See also* Defamation suit; Libel actions.
Switzerland, 286, 303

Taboo of Hitler's homosexuality,
  319
Tanhäuser, Eugen, 92
Theater, 177
Three-cornered relationships,
  158–159, 166
Thule Association, 144
Toland, John, 10
Treason (to Hitler), 269–270, 290,
  304
Tschirschky, Fritz Günther von, 211
Turning Point, The (Klaus Mann), 260

U.S. intelligence, 311
Unruh, Fritz von, 320
Utopians, racist, 63

Vienna, Austria, 28, 43, 47
  homosexual subculture, 48
  Kubizek and Hitler in, 38–41,
    45–46
  Neumann and Hitler, 54
  women in, 42
Vienna Boys' Choir, 39
Vol de nuit (Saint-Exupéry), 239
Völkisch movement, 105, 141
  Hess joins, 144
  and homosexuality, 108–109
  leadership of, 129

and Lüdecke, 272
  right wing, 192, 247
Völkischer Beobachter, 78, 145, 155,
    171, 202, 291
  edited by Eckart, 120
  Hitler's letter to Röhm, 206–207
  Lüdecke as representative, 270,
    273
Völkischer Kurier, 273
Voss, Gerd, 217, 219
Vulgarity, 177

Wagener, Otto, 166
Wagner Festival, 250
Wagner, Richard, 131
  passion for, 37, 39, 58
Wagner, Siegfried, 271
Wagner, Winifred, 220, 255
  destroyed secret documents, 22
  intervenes for Hanfstaengl, 309
  speculations about, 254
  in U.S. with Lüdecke, 271–272
Waite, Robert G. L., 10
Wandervogel movement, 108, 150
Wanivenhaus, Hugo, 33
War records and counterpropaganda,
    74, 235–236
Wartime comrades, 87, 99–100
Weber, Christian, 176
Weber, Friedrich, 146
Weimar, 106, 192, 203, 234, 247, 248
Weisenborn, Günther, 312
Weiss, Jacob, 70, 90
Welt am Montag, 191
Welt am Sonntag, 15
Westenkirchner, Ignaz, 93
Wiedemann, Fritz, 22, 90
  disclosures about Hanfstaengl, 301
  secret mission on Lüdecke blackmail, 298
Wilde, Oscar, 60

Wilhelm, August, 184, 280, 320
Wimmer, Franz, 68, 90
Wolfskehl, Karl, 63
Woman problem, 159, 165
Women
    attitude/beharior toward, 142,
        154, 155–156, 165
    aversion to physical contact with,
        168, 315
    indifference toward, 41–42
    platonic cohabitation with, 169,
        315
World War I, 63, 87
Wyneken, Gustav, 150, 237

Young man in Vienna, 38–41, 47–51,
    53–54, 55
Youth, 37–38

Youth movement and homoeroticism,
    150

Zaeper, Max, 94
Zehnter, Karl, 218
Ziegler, Hans Severus, 23
    devotee of Hitler, 246–249
    on Eva Braun's relationship with
        Hitler, 316
    homosexual, 249
    and NSDAP, 241
    persecution of, 251
    under political protection,
        252–253
    vacationing with Hitler, 250
Zsolnay-Verlag, 231
Zweig, Stefan, 48
Zwickau Penitentiary, 86